"一带一路"
国家投资并购指南

冯斌 李洪亮 Gvantsa Dzneladze（格） Tamar Menteshashvili（格）/ 编著

图书在版编目（CIP）数据

"一带一路"国家投资并购指南／冯斌等著. —北京：中国海关出版社有限公司，2020.3
ISBN 978-7-5175-0422-1

Ⅰ.①一… Ⅱ.①冯… Ⅲ.①"一带一路"—企业兼并—跨国兼并—指南—汉、英 Ⅳ.①F271.4-62

中国版本图书馆 CIP 数据核字（2020）第 022625 号

"一带一路"国家投资并购指南
"YIDAIYILU" GUOJIA TOUZI BINGGOU ZHINAN

作　　者：	冯　斌　李洪亮　Gvantsa Dzneladze（格）　Tamar Menteshashvili（格）
策划编辑：	马　超
责任编辑：	吴琳旖　郭　坤　叶　芳
责任监制：	赵　宇

出版发行：中国海关出版社有限公司

社　　址：	北京市朝阳区东四环南路甲1号	邮政编码：	100023
网　　址：	www.hgcbs.com.cn；www.customskb.com/book.com		
编 辑 部：	01065194242-7554（电话）	01065194234（传真）	
发 行 部：	01065194221/4238/4246/4227（电话）	01065194233（传真）	
印　　刷：	北京鑫益晖印刷有限公司	经　销：	新华书店
开　　本：	710mm×1000mm　1/16		
印　　张：	32.75	字　数：	661 千字
版　　次：	2020 年 3 月第 1 版		
印　　次：	2020 年 3 月第 1 次印刷		
书　　号：	ISBN 978-7-5175-0422-1		
定　　价：	98.00 元		

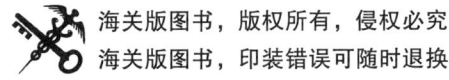

海关版图书，版权所有，侵权必究
海关版图书，印装错误可随时退换

序言

中国崛起，改变世界！

1978年，中国开始实行改革开放的时候，我还是一个生活在中国东部小城寻常百姓家的9岁孩子。在那个年代，过年吃上大鱼大肉是最快活的事。2018年是改革开放40周年，而我也年近半百。中国已经是世界第二大经济体，驱动全球经济增长的发动机。在中国马路上风驰电掣的汽车的档次与欧美国家的相比已经没有多大差距，甚至还更高。

2004年，我有幸被当时的空调业领军人物——春兰（集团）公司CEO陶建幸选派，担任江苏春兰进出口有限公司总经理，从此与海外市场结缘6年。海外业务这个"万花筒"，主要围绕着订单、客户、提单、信用证等展开，在我的职业生涯上画上了浓重的一笔。在广交会、科隆展、米兰展熙熙攘攘的人群中，在西西里岛低调巨富的震撼下，在从希腊雅典到该国北部港口城市塞洛尼基的一路狂奔中，我也算提前理解了"一带一路"投资并购的内涵。

外贸只是中国企业走向世界的开始。随着全球产业链的重构，中国企业在经济全球化过程中扮演的角色也在不断变化，从过去主要从事"三来一补"和低成本加工，到国际企业高增值产品制造，再到如今通过协同创新引领全球新兴产业的全产业链运营。

2014年，我有幸入职中国著名的贸工技企业江苏苏美达集团有限公司（以下简称苏美达集团），开始接触跨境并购业务，从此对这种更高层次的全球化商业活动一见倾心。起初，我接触的是美国上市公司并购中国资产标的，后来是苏美达集团并购德国和美国的实体企业标的。2015年，江苏苏美达资本控股有限公司（简称苏美达资本）成立时，恰逢中资出海浪潮涌动，苏美达资本一度将海外并购作为公司的核心业务来开拓，美国硅谷的金融科技（Fintech）公司也进入了我们的投资视野。苏美达资本的股东和董事会领导与团队一起去探访圣弗朗西斯科的初创金融科技企业,美方对中国动力带来的创新与嫁接的渴望至今令我记忆犹新。

如今的国际经济竞争,不仅是企业产品间的竞争,而且是整个价值链条各环节的竞争,企业必须优化价值链的各个环节,才能取得成功。面对全球价值链重构的机遇和挑战,中国企业能够采取的有效应对策略之一,就是在"一带一路"国家和地区建设全球产业链,改写早期以中国市场为主的商业版图。有先见之明的企业,如有"非洲手机之王"称号的深圳传音控股有限公司,其成功具有典型性,其2018年的营业收入高达226亿元人民币,已于科创板上市。

在苏美达资本,我有幸与国内外不少一流投资并购专家切磋、交流。我逐步认识到,海外并购的过程其实是科学和艺术的结合体,既离不开科学严谨的法律尽职调查和财务尽职调查,也少不了基于估值报告的谈判艺术,最关键的是企业家的拍案决断能力。并购交易完成后,其实又是一个从零开始的过程,投后整合事关交易成败。

在投资并购的工作学习中,我有幸与出身名门的资本运作高手李洪亮博士相识。李洪亮博士长期在东软集团工作。东软集团作为国内软件行业的标杆企业,其创始人刘积仁博士在追求产品和技术创新的同时,也非常善于利用资本的力量助力企业的发展。在东软集团工作期间,李洪亮博士作为东软集团企业发展部的负责人,负责整个东软集团的资本运作工作。他负责完成十几家国内外标的公司的并购,并完成东软医疗、东软熙康、东软望海、东软睿驰和东软控股的架构搭建和融资工作,总融资金额超过50亿元人民币。李博士具有非常丰富的企业资本运作的经验。在本书写作过程中,他也特别愿意分享自己多年的实战心得。

后来,我有幸与欧洲的两位法律金融背景的"一带一路"专业人士Tamar和Gvansta结识,她们也欣然加入了写作团队,写作团队也已经"一带一路"化。Tamar兼具欧洲与中国的金融和法律背景,还是一位活跃于欧洲、美国、中国三大经济体金融科技领域的专家。Gvansta兼具欧洲与中国的名校法律和经济专业背景,可用4种语言流利交流。我们4位作者一拍即合,决定共同创作本书。具体分工是,我负责设计本书的框架,撰写第二章、第六章和

第七章；李博士负责本书的统筹，撰写第一章、第四章和第八章；Tamar 和 Gvansta 分别撰写了第三章和第五章。她们还联合收集、整理了附录"'一带一路'国家投资并购案例集"，为本书增色不少。

特别感谢中国海关出版社有限公司的马超编辑，没有她的悉心指导，本书难以问世。本书有幸在 2019 年 2 月通过了国家出版基金资助项目申报的评审，这是业内专家对本书的高度认可。特别感谢东软控股有限公司首席执行官荣新节，葛洲坝集团国际工程有限公司董事长吕泽翔，欧洲研究区和创新委员会理事会成员、格鲁吉亚肖塔·鲁斯塔维利国家科学基金会总干事兹瓦德·加布森尼亚博士、教授为本书撰写了推荐语。

"一带一路"国家和地区投资并购领域高手如云，这本书是 4 位作者抛砖引玉的作品，恳请行业专家"拍砖"。

编者

2019 年 12 月

Prologue

China rises, the world changes!

When China began to implement reform and opening up in 1978, I was still a 9-year-old child living in an ordinary family in a small town of eastern China. In that era, the happiest thing is to eat abundant fish and meat during the Spring Festival. 2018 is the 40th anniversary of reform and opening up, and I am going into my years of 50s. China is already the second largest economy in the world and the engine of global economic growth. Compared with those of America and European countries, the cars galloping on China's roads are no worse, but with even more excellent performances.

In 2004, I was fortunate to be selected by Tao Jianxing, a leader in the air-conditioning industry at that time, CEO of Chunlan (Group) Company, as General Manager of Jiangsu Chunlan Import and Export Co., Ltd., and has since been attached to overseas markets for 6 years. The "kaleidoscope" of overseas business mainly revolves around orders, customers, bills of lading, letters of credit, etc., and it's a big part of my career. Among the bustling crowds of the Canton Fair, Cologne and Milan, and shocked by the low-key wealth of Sicily, I also really understood the connotation of "Belt and Road" investment and M&A in advance during the rush from Athens to the northern port city Thessaloniki. Foreign trade is just the beginning of Chinese companies going global. With the restructuring of the global industry chain, the role of Chinese companies in the process of economic globalization is also constantly changing: from the past mainly engaged in the "Three-plus-one" trading-mix and low-cost processing, to the manufacture of high value-added products of international enterprises, by now, leadingthe whole industry chain operation of the global emerging industries by collaborative innovation.

In 2014, I was fortunate to join SUMEC Group Corporation (SUMEC), a well-known trade industry and technology company in China, and began to engage in cross-border M&A. From then on, I became obsessed with such high-level global business activities. At first, I was in contact with a US listed company's acquisition of Chinese assets, and later, SUMEC's acquisitions of entities in Germany and the United States. In 2015, when SUMEC Capital Holding Co., Ltd (SUMEC Capital) was established, it coincided with the wave of Chinese investment. SUMEC Capital once explored overseas M&A as the company's core business. Fintech companies in Silicon Valley of the United States also entered our investment horizon. SUMEC Capital's shareholders, board leaders and team members went to visit San Francisco's start-up Fintech companies. The US desire for innovation and graft brought by China's dynamics is still very much alive in my memory.

Today's international economic competition lies not only among enterprise products, but also in all links of the entire value chain. Enterprises must optimize all links in the value chain to succeed. Facing opportunities and challenges of global value chain restructuring, one of the effective countermeasures that Chinese companies can adopt is to build a global industrial chain in the "Belt and Road" countries and regions, and rewrite the early business landscape that is mainly based on the Chinese market. Foresight-savvy companies, such as Shenzhen TRANSSION Holdings Co., Ltd., the "King of Africa's Mobile Phone", have typical success stories. In 2018, its operating income is as high as RMB 22.6 billion. It is planning to be listed on the Sci-Tech innovation board.

In SUMEC Capital, I am fortunate to have a place at the tablealong with many top-ranking investment and M&A experts from domestic and overseas. I gradually realized that the process of overseas M&A is actually a combination of science and art. It cannot be separated from scientific and rigorous legal due diligence and financial due diligence reports, and the art of negotiation based on valuation reports. The most important thing is the enterprise's ability of decision making. After the completion of the M&A transaction, it is actually a process from scratch. Post-investment integration is critical to the success of the transaction.

In the work and study of investment and M&A, I had the honor to meet Dr. Li Hongliang, a well-known capital operation expert of gentle birth. Dr. Li Hongliang has worked for Neusoft Group for a long time. Neusoft Group is benchmarking company in the domestic software industry, the founder Dr. Liu Jiren, pursues product and technological innovation, while is good at using the power of capital to help the development of enterprises. As the head of the Neusoft Group's Enterprise Development Department, Dr. Li Hongliang was in charge of the capital operation of the entire Neusoft Group. He is responsible for completing the M&A of dozens of domestic and overseas target companies, and completing the construction and financing of Neusoft Medical Systems, Neusoft Xi Kang, ViewHigh, Neusoft Reach and Neusoft Holdings, with a total financing amount of more than RMB 5 billion. Dr. Li has very rich experience in corporate capital operations. In the process of writing this book, he is particularly willing to share his many years of practical experience.

Later, I was fortunate to meet with two European "Belt and Road" professionals Tamar and Gvansta who have legal and financial backgrounds. They also happily joined the writing team, making it a "Belt and Road" team. Tamar has both European and Chinese financial and legal backgrounds. She is also an active expert in the Fintech field in the three major economies of Europe, the United States and China. Gvansta has a background in law and economics from prestigious European and Chinese schools and works fluently in 4 languages. Our four authors hit it off and decided to co-author this book. The specific division of labor is that I am responsible for designing the framework of this book, writing Chapter 2, 6 and 7; Dr. Li is responsible for coordinating this book, writing Chapter 1, 4, and 8; Tamar and Gvansta wrote Chapter 3 and 5, respectively. They also collected and sorted out appendix "Belt and Road" investment and M&A cases, which greatly enhanced this book.

I would like to show my special thanks to Ma Chao, editor of China Customs

Press. Without her careful guidance, this book would be difficult to come into being. With her strong recommendation, this book was fortunate to pass the review of projects funded by the National Publication Fundation in February 2019. Thanks Mr. Rong Xinjie, CEO of Neusoft holdings, Mr. Lv Zexiang, Chairman of CGGC International engineering Co., LTD., Prof. Dr. Zviad Gabisonia, director general at Shota Rustaveli National Science Foundation of Georgia, Governing Board Member at European Research Area and Innovation Committee (ERCA) for writing the preface and the recommendations for this book.

There are so many master-hands in the field of "Belt and Road" countries' investment and M&A. This book is only to throw out a brick to attract a jade. We sincerely look forward to critics from experts of this field.

Author

April, 2019

目 录

第一章 中国对"一带一路"国家开展投资并购的现状和新特点 ··········001

    第一节 "一带一路"概述 ············ 003
    第二节 中国对"一带一路"国家的投资和并购情况回顾 ········ 005
    第三节 "一带一路"倡议背景下的全球化投资和并购发展特点 ··· 013

第二章 在"一带一路"国家进行投资并购的目标 ············017

    第一节 海外投资并购成败五要素 ············ 019
    第二节 投资并购"一带一路"国家企业的目标 ············ 022

第三章 在"一带一路"国家进行投资并购的模式和融资安排 ··········027

    第一节 "一带一路"国家投资并购的合理交易架构 ············ 029
    第二节 资产收购和股权收购的模式 ············ 030

第三节 "一带一路"沿线国家的投资风险和融资趋势 …………… 036

第四章 "一带一路"国家投资并购的团队组建 ……………045

第一节 "一带一路"国家投资并购团队的组建 …………… 048
第二节 "一带一路"国家投资并购的公司内部团队 …………… 051
第三节 "一带一路"国家投资并购外部团队(第三方中介机构) 057
第四节 如何处理好内部投资并购团队和外部第三方顾问团队的关系 …………………………………………………………… 066

第五章 交易架构、投资估值与"一带一路"国家投资并购 ……………………………………………………………069

第一节 海外交易架构:税收、便利和费用 …………… 073
第二节 并购交易中的便利性评价和成本评估 …………… 081
第三节 估值:科学还是艺术 …………………………… 084

第六章 "一带一路"国家投资并购的交易文件 ……………091

第一节 交易文件代价不菲 ……………………………… 093
第二节 交割文件靠法律和财务尽职调查 ………………… 095
第三节 前期交易文件 …………………………………… 105
第四节 正式交易文件 …………………………………… 113

第七章 "一带一路"国家投资并购境内外监管与合规 …… 119

第一节 监管环境变化 …… 121
第二节 境内监管：发展改革管理部门、商务部门、外汇管理部门 123
第三节 境外监管：反垄断审查和政府审批 …… 132
第四节 境内上市公司信息披露及合规 …… 153

第八章 "一带一路"国家投资并购的投后管理 …… 163

第一节 并购整合后面临的挑战 …… 165
第二节 并购整合的内容和方法论 …… 167
第三节 并购整合的评估与管理 …… 175
第四节 投后管理经典案例分享 …… 180

附录 "一带一路"国家投资并购案例集 …… 189

案例一 华信收购俄罗斯石油公司 14.16% 的股权（失败）…… 191
案例二 中石油收购阿拉伯联合酋长国阿布扎比陆上石油公司 8% 的股权 …… 193
案例三 海航实业收购新加坡 CWT …… 195
案例四 阿里巴巴再投 20 亿美元双倍下注来赞达 …… 198
案例五 KS ORKA 收购印度尼西亚地热能源 95% 的股权 …… 200
案例六 中国欢聚时代参与新加坡视频社交平台 Bigo D 轮融资 …… 202
案例七 上汽集团对通用汽车印度哈洛尔工厂的收购 …… 205

案例八　长电科技并购星科金朋 …………………………………… 207

案例九　京新药业向以色列 Mapi 公司投资 1 000 万美元 ……… 209

案例十　京新药业以 500 万美元收购 P2B 的股权 ………………… 211

案例十一　吉利收购马来西亚的宝腾和莲花汽车 ………………… 212

案例十二　复星集团以 2.9 亿新谢克尔收购阿哈瓦的全部股权 … 215

案例十三　水晶光电战略投资以色列 Lumus …………………… 217

案例十四　安踏以 3.32 亿元人民币收购 FILA 在中国地区的商标
　　　　　使用权和经营权 ……………………………………… 218

案例十五　光大国际以 1.23 亿欧元收购 NOVAGO ……………… 220

CONTENTS

Chapter 1　The Current Situation and Trend of China's Investment and M&A along the "Belt and Road" Countries ·················· 223

　　Section 1　Overview of the "Belt and Road Initiative" ······ 225
　　Section 2　Review of China's Investment and M&A in the "Belt and Road" Countries ································ 228
　　Section 3　Characteristics of Global Investment and M&A Development under the "Belt and Road Initiative" 239

Chapter 2　Investment and M&A Objectives in the "Belt and Road" Countries ································ 243

　　Section 1　Five Determining Factors of Overseas Investment and M&A ·· 245
　　Section 2　Objectives of Investment and M&A in the "Belt and Road" Countries ································ 249

Chapter 3 Models and Financing Arrangements of Investment and M&A along the "Belt and Road" Countries …… 257

  Section 1 The Transaction Structure of Investment and M&A along the "Belt and Road" Countries ………… 260

  Section 2 Model of Asset Acquisition and Equity Acquisition ……………………………………………… 261

  Section 3 Investment Risks and Financing Trends along the "Belt and Road" Countries ……………………… 269

Chapter 4 Team Building for Investment and M&A along the "Belt and Road" Countries …………………… 279

  Section 1 The Formation of Investment and M&A Team along the "Belt and Road" Countries………………… 283

  Section 2 The In-house Team for the "Belt and Road" Countries' Investment and M&A Projects……… 287

  Section 3 The External Team for the "Belt and Road" Countries' Investment and M&A Projects (Third-party Intermediaries) ……………………… 295

  Section 4 How to Deal with the Relationship between the Internal M&A Team and the External Third-party Agencies ………………………………………… 307

Chapter 5 Deal Structure, Investment Valuation and the "Belt and Road" Countries' Investment and M&A 311

Section 1 Overseas Trading Structure: Taxes, Convenience and Fees 316
Section 2 Convenience Evaluation and Cost Evaluation in M&A Transactions 326
Section 3 Valuation: Science or Art 330

Chapter 6 The "Belt and Road" Countries' Transaction Documents 339

Section 1 High Costs of Transaction Documents 341
Section 2 Transaction Documents Depend on Legal and Financial Due Diligence 343
Section 3 Preliminary Transaction Documents 355
Section 4 Share Purchase Agreement (SPA) 364

Chapter 7 The "Belt and Road" Countries' Domestic and Overseas Supervision and Compliance 371

Section 1 Changes of Supervision Environment 373
Section 2 Domestic Supervision: Development and Reform

               Departments, Commerce and State Administration
               of Foreign Exchange Departments ·············· 376
Section 3   Overseas Supervision: Anti-monopoly Review and
            Governmental Approval ································ 390
Section 4   Information Disclosure and Compliance of
            Domestically-listed Companies ···················· 416

Chapter 8   Post-merger Integration of Investment and M&A along the "Belt and Road" Countries ············ 425

Section 1   Challenges after Post-merger Integration ·········· 428
Section 2   M&A Integration Content and Methodology ······ 430
Section 3   Assessment and Management of M&A
            Integration ·· 441
Section 4   Classic Cases of Post-merger Integration ······ 448

Appendix   Cases of Investment and M&A along the "Belt and Road" Countries ·· 459

Case 1   CEFC Acquired 14,16% Stake in Rosneft
         Oil (Failure) ·· 461
Case 2   PetroChina Acquired an 8% Stake in ADCO Petroleum
         Company ·· 463
Case 3   HNA Holding Acquired CWT Singapore ·············· 466

Case 4	Alibaba Doubled the Bet with a New USD 2 Billion Investment	468
Case 5	KS ORKA Acquired 95% of Indonesia SGI Ahares	470
Case 6	YY Participates in the Singapore Video Social Platform Bigo's D Round Financing	473
Case 7	SAIC's Acquisition of GM's Halol Plant in India	476
Case 8	Changdian Technology Co., Ltd Acquired STATS ChipPAC	477
Case 9	Jingxin Pharmaceutical Invested USD 10 Million in Israel Mapi	480
Case 10	Jingxin Pharmaceutical Acquired P2B Shares for USD 5 Million	482
Case 11	Geely Acquired Proton and Lotus in Malaysia	483
Case 12	Fosun Group Acquired the Entire Share Capital of AHAVA for 290 Million New Shekel	485
Case 13	Crystal Optoelectronics Strategically Invested Israel Lumus	487
Case 14	Anta Acquired the Trademark Use Rights and Management Rights of FILA in China for RMB 332 Million	489
Case 15	Everbright International Acquired NOVAGO for EUR 123 Million	491

参考文献 494

第一章

中国对"一带一路"国家开展投资并购的现状和新特点

第一节 "一带一路"概述

2013年9月7日，习近平主席在出访中亚国家期间，首次提出共建"丝绸之路经济带"。同年10月，他又提出共同建设"21世纪海上丝绸之路"，二者共同构成"一带一路"倡议。

"一带一路"倡议由两部分构成。一个是"丝绸之路经济带"，包括三大走向，分别是从中国西北、东北经中亚、俄罗斯至欧洲、波罗的海；从中国西北经中亚、西亚至波斯湾、地中海；从中国西南经中南半岛至印度洋。另一个是"21世纪海上丝绸之路"，包括两大走向，分别是从中国沿海港口过南海，经马六甲海峡到印度洋，延伸至欧洲；从中国沿海港口过南海，向南太平洋延伸。

"一带一路"包含以下六条国际经济合作走廊：新亚欧大陆桥，中国—蒙古国—俄罗斯，中国—中亚—西亚，中国—中南半岛，中国—巴基斯坦、孟加拉国，中国—印度—缅甸。

"一带一路"建设对中国具有重要意义，有助于促进中国的经济增长。预计"一带一路"建设将为中国商品创造新的市场，中国的优质产能可以被有效地引导到"一带一路"区域。中国宣布通过向参与国提供低成本贷款为其提供资金。

自2013年中国向世界发出共同建设"丝绸之路经济带"和"21世纪海上丝绸之路"倡议以来，"一带一路"建设在探索中前进、在发展中完善、在合作中成长，建设的进度和成果都远远超出预期。随着"一带一路"的"朋友圈"越来越大，"一带一路"建设已成为化理念为行动、变梦想为现实的重大国际合作倡议。

以下是"一带一路"倡议的重大事件：

2013年9月，中国国家主席习近平在哈萨克斯坦纳扎尔巴耶夫大学演讲时首次提出共同建设"丝绸之路经济带"的设想。

2013年10月，习近平提出建立一个紧密结合的中国—东盟社区，并为建设"21世纪海上丝绸之路"提供指导，以促进海上合作。

习近平在印度尼西亚国会发表演讲时提议建立亚洲基础设施投资银行（AIIB），为基础设施建设提供资金，促进区域互联互通和经济一体化。

2014年2月，习近平与俄罗斯总统普京关于"一带一路"建设和与俄罗斯欧亚铁路连接达成共识。

2014年10月，21个首批意向创始成员国签署《筹建亚投行备忘录》，共同决定成立亚洲基础设施投资银行。

2014年11月，在北京APEC峰会期间，习近平宣布中国将出资40亿美元成立丝绸之路基金，为"一带一路"沿线国家的基础设施建设、资源开发、产业合作和金融合作等提供投融资支持。

2015年3月28日，国家发展和改革委员会（简称国家发展改革委）、外交部、商务部共同发布了《推动共建丝绸之路经济带和21世纪海上丝绸之路的愿景与行动》。

2015年5月，《推进国际产能和装备制造与合作的指导意见》出台。

2015年12月，亚洲基础设施投资银行正式成立。

2017年5月，第一届"一带一路"国际合作高峰论坛在北京举行。

2017年6月，《"一带一路"建设海上合作设想》发布。

2017年10月，将推进"一带一路"建设等内容写入《中国共产党章程》。

2018年1月22日，中国—拉美和加勒比国家共同体论坛第二届部长级会议在智利开幕。会议通过了《圣地亚哥宣言》《中国与拉美和加勒比国家合作（优先领域）共同行动计划（2019-2021）》和《"一带一路"特别声明》。

2018年5月16日，"一带一路"税收合作会议在哈萨克斯坦首都阿斯塔纳闭幕，与会者讨论并联合发布了《阿斯塔纳"一带一路"税收合作倡议》。

2018年5月,"一带一路"中欧对话会在欧盟总部所在地布鲁塞尔举行。

2018年7月,中国—阿拉伯国家合作论坛第八届部长级会议在北京举行。

2018年7月,国家外汇管理局"一带一路"国家外汇管理政策研究小组发布《"一带一路"国家外汇管理政策概览》。

2018年11月,首届中国国际进口博览会在上海举办。

2018年12月,"一带一路"国际合作高峰论坛咨询委员会第一次会议在北京举行。

2019年4月,第二届"一带一路"国际合作高峰论坛在北京召开。

第二节 中国对"一带一路"国家的投资和并购情况回顾

2018年3月11日,商务部部长钟山提到中国对"一带一路"相关国家累计直接投资已经超过了600亿美元,涉及农业、制造业、基础设施等诸多领域。一批铁路、公路、港口等基础设施相继建成,一批能源、资源合作项目顺利推进,一批制造业项目竣工投产。中国在"一带一路"相关国家已经建设了75个境外经贸合作区,累计投资270多亿美元。

一、情况回顾

图1-1对比了2013年至2017年中国外贸增长率和中国与"一带一路"国家外贸增长率。中国对"一带一路"国家的贸易和投资总体保持增长态势。2013年至2018年,中国与"一带一路"沿线国家的货物贸易总额超过6万亿美元,年均增长4%。根据数据分析,韩国、越南、马来西亚、印度、俄罗斯等国是中国最主要的"一带一路"贸易伙伴。

图 1-1　中国外贸增长率与中国和"一带一路"国家外贸增长率对比

在直接投资方面，2013 年到 2018 年中国对"一带一路"沿线国家的直接投资超过 900 亿美元，年均增长超过 5%。同期，中国新签对外承包工程合同额超过 6 000 亿美元，年均增长 11.9%。一批重点项目，包括亚吉铁路、中老铁路、斯里兰卡科伦坡港口城等有序推进，起到很好的示范作用。

从投资行业上看，国家外汇管理局、商务部、财政部颁布一系列限制非理性对外投资的政策，中国对外投资的结构也发生了变化，化工、电力、制造、能源等产业并购增多，1 亿美元以上的并购项目超过 60 个，推动实体经济、高新技术等走向世界舞台。未来 5 年，中国企业在"一带一路"国家的投资会继续保持快速增长，投资领域会从大型基础设施、能源、资源等项目拓展到旅游、电子商务、人文教育与交流等领域。

"一带一路"项目投资的参与者呈现多元化的态势。在"一带一路"倡议提出的初期，国有企业领衔"一带一路"建设，目前，民营企业、外资企业的参与程度在不断加大。国企和民企在"一带一路"沿线国家投资中的特点主要表现为：国企相对于民企投资金额较大，而民企在投资数量上要超过国企。

并购是中国企业海外投资的主要形式，在 2016 年高峰时期，中国企业差不多每天有 2 起以上的海外并购行为。通过海外并购，中国企业获得了优质的品牌、技术、市场、资源，降低了成本，提升了全球影响力。相比国内的资产价格，海外的资产价格较低，中国企业可以通过海外并购在国际上配置优质资源。据统计，2018年中国企业发起的海外并购达到125起，并购金额达到288亿美元，主要集中在科技、制造、医疗健康、TMT（科技、媒体和通信3个英文单词的首字母缩写）、金融、消费等领域。原来占比较大的能源、电力、原材料等领域的并购比例开始下降，上市公司已经成为并购的主力军。上市公司并购的主要优势在于其有融资平台，同时国内外市场存在着估值的差异。在参与海外并购的企业中，民营企业占比进一步提升。未来，我国企业在"一带一路"沿线国家的投资并购数量会保持较快的增长，原因是：一方面，中国企业实力不断增强，希望在全球范围配置资源；另一方面，"一带一路"沿线国家对中国的经济发展充满信心。

"一带一路"沿线国家投资并购的区域，主要集中在南亚、东南亚和西亚，印度、新加坡和以色列位居前三。同时，我们也可以看到，越来越多的中国企业正在考虑在中、东欧国家进行投资并购。

二、"一带一路"国家投资并购高速增长和变化的原因

（一）中国经济的高速增长

自改革开放以来，中国经济长期保持8%以上的增长。中国成为全球第二大经济体。2018年，位列世界500强的中国企业有120家，该数字非常接近美国的126家。中国企业实力增强，也为中国企业海外并购的成功打下了基础。企业规模的扩大，也意味着传统的内生增长已经不能持续拉升企业的价值，海外投资并购成为常用的、有效的业绩增长手段。

（二）中国庞大的国内市场需求

中国有着14亿人口，也是全球最大的市场。中国企业通过在"一带一路"沿线国家投资并购，获取海外优质的资源、技术、市场和人才，然后将其嫁接到中国市场以获得加速发展。"全球并购，中国整合"已经成为很多公司的海外并购指导思想。之后，他们在通过中国市场获得成功后进一步加大

海外并购的力度。很多大家耳熟能详的中国企业，例如海尔集团、美的集团、吉利控股集团、复星集团、鹏欣集团等的发展史也是中国企业走向全球的并购史。

（三）中国资本市场的高估值和优质资产的缺乏

相比于美国、欧洲等成熟资本市场，中国资本市场的整体估值更高。通过海外投资并购，中国公司可以以较低市盈率收购海外资产，再将其溢价整合进上市公司。收购后带来的股价上涨（市盈率水涨船高）意味着企业可以用更高的估值收购更多的海外优质公司，从而形成一个良性循环。然而，很多公司溢价收购的行为推高了公司的商业信誉，一旦没有实现收购业绩目标，商业信誉减值就会带来盈利锐减和股价暴跌的情况。

（四）中国经济转型和发展的需要

中国国内很多行业（基建、房地产、制造业等）的产能处于饱和状态。最初，企业从沿海地区向中部、西部转移，经济发展梯度为产业转移提供了可能。下一步，企业的转移方向可能就是"一带一路"沿线国家，中国在东南亚、南亚、西亚投资并购的快速增长也印证了这个推测。

同时，中国企业需要向价值链上游转移，通过投资并购获取海外技术、人才和市场变得更加迫切。新加坡、以色列和欧洲的一些国家有着良好的产业基础和创新能力，很多标的企业可以满足中国企业产业升级的需要。我们也看到，这些国家一直是"一带一路"建设的投资并购热点区域。另外，传统的资源型投资并购项目依旧保持在一定的比例，这和中国经济发展需要是分不开的。

三、中资企业在"一带一路"国家和地区的投资情况

过去几年，中资企业在"一带一路"国家和地区的重要投资并购案例

很多。万科等公司以116亿美元并购普洛斯；上海复星医药（集团）股份有限公司（简称复星医药）以10.9亿美元收购印度制药公司Gland Pharma Limited（简称GLand Pharma）74%股份；阿里巴巴集团以10亿美元增持东南亚电商来赞达（Lazada）至83%股权；上汽集团收购通用汽车公司印度哈洛尔（Halol）工厂……此外，阿里巴巴、复星医药、腾讯、三胞集团、中国石油化工集团有限公司、中国广核集团等企业在"一带一路"国家和地区的投资并购交易远不止一宗。这些显示出民企、国企对"一带一路"倡议的信心。晨哨集团[①]监测数据显示，2017年中资海外并购交易宗数下降23%、披露金额下降13.54%，而"一带一路"沿线并购交易宗数同比增长21.82%，披露交易金额增长47.40%。自2013年以来，"一带一路"建设不断取得进展。表1-1总结了中国企业进行海外投资并购的成绩突出的50家企业。

表1-1 中国企业进行"一带一路"投资并购成绩突出的50家企业

买方	时间	标的	交易金额（百万美元）	标的国家
阿里巴巴及蚂蚁金服	2016/4/12 2017/6/28	印度尼西亚来赞达	2 000.00	新加坡
	2014/5/28	新加坡邮政	248.94	新加坡
	2017/3/3	Paytm	177.00	印度
	2015/10/7	One97 40%股权	680.00	印度
	2016/6/18	Ascend Money	—	泰国
	合计	5	3 105.94	
中国华信	2017/9/8	俄罗斯石油公司	9 100.00	俄罗斯
	2015/12/14	哈萨克斯坦国家石油公司国际公司	—	哈萨克斯坦
	2015/9/7	Travel Service	—	捷克
	2017/2/19	阿布扎比陆上石油公司	900.00	阿拉伯联合酋长国
	合计	4	10 000.00	

---

① 晨哨集团：一家中国资本跨境并购服务提供商。

续表

买方	时间	标的	交易金额（百万美元）	标的国家
复星集团及复星医药	2016/4/10	AHAVA	76.38	以色列
	2017/5/24	Delhivery	30.00	印度
	2017/10/27	Bond IT	14.25	以色列
	2017/10/3	Gland Pharma	1 091.00	印度
	合计	4	1 211.63	
腾讯控股	2016/12/21	Sanook.com	—	泰国
	2016/8/17	Hike Messenger	175.00	印度
	2017/10/9	OLA	400.00	印度
	合计	3	575.00	
三胞集团及南京新百	2016/7/1	康盛人生集团	64.30	新加坡
	2017/7/12	Lotan Nursing Service	18.51	以色列
	2014/12/9	Natali Seculife Holdings Ltd	70.00	以色列
	合计	3	152.81	
中石化	2015/12/17	西布尔	1 338.00	俄罗斯
	2017/2/19	阿布扎比陆上石油公司8%股权	1 800.00	阿拉伯联合酋长国
	合计	2	3 138.00	
中国广核集团	2016/11/3	Malicounda 太阳能电站	—	塞内加尔
	2016/3/23	马来西亚电力资产	2 300.00	马来西亚
	合计	2	2 300.00	
招商局集团	2017/7/29	汉班托塔港的运营权	1 120.00	斯里兰卡
	2016/12/9	科伦坡港	1 100.00	斯里兰卡
	合计	2	2 220.00	
中国移动	2014/6/9	Ture Corporation PCL	877.10	泰国
	2014/4/23	巴基斯坦 3G、4G 牌照	516.00	巴基斯坦
	合计	2	1 393.10	

续表

买方	时间	标的	交易金额（百万美元）	标的国家
中国海运(集团)总公司	2016/9/29	阿布扎比哈里发港口二期集装箱码头	738.00	阿拉伯联合酋长国
	2017/5/15	KTZE-Khorgos Gateway	38.00	哈萨克斯坦
	合计	2	776.00	
洲际油气	2014/4/8	North Caspian Petroleum JSC	37.50	哈萨克斯坦
	2014/8/8	马腾石油	525.00	哈萨克斯坦
	合计	2	562.50	
光大国际	2016/9/1	NOVAGO	135.62	波兰
	2016/10/7	地拉那国际机场	—	阿尔巴尼亚
	合计	2	135.62	
浙江开山压缩机股份有限公司	2016/8/16	OTP Geothermal	60.00	新加坡
	2016/8/8	PT Sokoria Geothermal Indonesia	—	印度尼西亚
	合计	2	60.00	
万科、厚朴投资、高瓴资本、中银集团	2017/12/1	普洛斯	11 718.95	新加坡
巨人网络等财团	2016/9/23	Playtika	4 400.00	以色列
沙隆达股份	2016/9/14	安道麦	2 775.54	以色列
光明乳业	2015/3/31	Tnuva	2 167.20	以色列
海洋石油工程股份有限公司	2014/7/10	亚马尔	1 600.00	俄罗斯
上海电力、协鑫集团	2016/11/1	K-Electrical	1 600.00	巴基斯坦
丝路基金	2016/3/16	亚马尔液化石油天然气项目	1 400.00	俄罗斯
北京控股	2016/11/9	公众股份	1 100.00	俄罗斯
中信产业投资基金	2016/4/19	柏盛国际	1 050.00	新加坡

续表

买方	时间	标的	交易金额（百万美元）	标的国家
光汇石油	2014/2/18	美国阿纳达科石油公司旗下渤海湾油田项目	1 046.00	中国
海航集团	2016/12/11	CWT	1 000.00	新加坡
中远太平洋有限公司	2015/12/10	Kumport 集装箱码头	940.18	土耳其
长电科技	2014/11/6	STATS ChipPAC Ltd.	780.00	新加坡
中粮集团	2016/3/3	来宝产业	750.00	新加坡
上海医药	2017/10/19	康德乐的中国业务	557.00	中国
联立铜业	2016/1/5	哈萨克斯坦铜矿资源	480.00	哈萨克斯坦
工商银行	2015/5/22	土耳其银行	316.00	土耳其
中国熔盛重工	2014/8/21	Central Point Worldwide Inc.	281.74	吉尔吉斯斯坦
广东农垦集团	2016/9/21	泰华树胶	269.71	泰国
中国进出口银行	2017/1/17	Invitel 集团	214.37	匈牙利
中化国际	2016/3/28	Halcyon Agri Corporation	174.75	新加坡
华为	2016/12/8	Toga Net works、Hexa Tier	150.00	以色列
云南水务	2017/3/17	Galaxy New Spring	136.50	新加坡
恒源石油化工	2016/1/12	壳牌马来西亚炼油公司	130.00	马来西亚
中兴通讯	2016/12/6	NETAŞ TELEKOMÜNIKAS-YONAŞ	130.00	土耳其
华夏幸福	2017/6/5	AMI 公司两块地块	102.16	印度尼西亚
京东世纪贸易	2017/8/27	Go-jek	100.00	印度尼西亚
四川和邦生物科技	2015/10/16	S.T.K Stockton Group	90.00	以色列
南极电商	2016/6/15	Cartelo Crocodile	89.96	新加坡
上证所、深证所、中国金融期货交易所、中巴投资公司	2016/12/27	巴基斯坦交易所 40% 股权	85.00	巴基斯坦

续表

买方	时间	标的	交易金额（百万美元）	标的国家
中山达华智能科技	2017/4/18	Topbest Coast Limited	73.00	塞浦路斯
陕鼓动力	2015/7/11	EKOL	51.90	捷克
成都康弘药业	2017/10/20	IOPtima Ltd. 100% 股权	46.72	以色列
山东如意	2017/11/23	Bagir	16.50	以色列
上汽集团	2017/7/9	Halol 工厂	—	印度
万洲国际	2017/6/1	Hamburger Pini、Pini Polska、Royal Chicken	—	波兰
中国建设银行	2016/9/29	PT Bank Windu Kentjana International Tbk		印度尼西亚

第三节 "一带一路"倡议背景下的全球化投资和并购发展特点

自2013年"一带一路"倡议提出以来，中国企业在"一带一路"沿线国家的投资和并购活动越来越多。"一带一路"倡议背景下的全球化投资和并购展现出了以下五个方面的新特点。

一、中国企业国际化是大势所趋

随着中国加入全球经济的竞争，中国企业需要在全球范围内来配置资源，将供应链系统延伸到全世界。中国企业可以将采购、生产、销售等环节转移到世界各地，打造贯穿产业链的生态圈。中国企业的海外并购重心由欧美发达国家，逐渐向"一带一路"沿线国家转移，中亚和东南亚等新兴经济体成为"一带一路"并购的新热点。在全球范围内融资对于企业投资并购非常关键，已经有多家银行在国内外发行债券。在资金来源方面，越来越多的当地低成本资金积极参与到并购项目中来。

二、"国企搭台，民企唱戏"新格局

"一带一路"项目投资的参与者正在呈现多元化态势。初期，国有企业领衔"一带一路"建设和投资，目前民营企业、外资企业的参与程度也在不断增大。国有企业更加关注布局。国企以大型投资并购项目为先导开展工作，民营企业随后跟进。相比于国企，民营企业在"一带一路"沿线国家的投资并购的专业性有待提高，需要借助中介机构来把控风险。此外，为了降低海外投资风险，确保在当地持续发展，各类企业寻找合适的当地合作伙伴、成立合资公司等将成为常见的投资形式。

三、投资模式，跨国并购，迅速发展

中国企业在铁路、电力、基础设施等方面具有优势，这正好与"一带一路"沿线国家的资源优势和市场需求互补，未来在这些方面的投资有望进一步提升。跨国并购近年来正在迅速发展，成为企业投资的主要方式。与其他投资模式相比，跨国并购并不需要很长的建设期，因此，成为许多想要加快市场规模扩大速度，在短时间内进入目标市场的跨国公司的首选方式。本书提到的投资模式主要指跨国并购。

四、促进实体经济的发展成为海外投资重点

国家外汇管理局、商务部、财政部出台一系列加强对外投资的真实性和合规性审核要求后，从2017年开始，房地产、酒店、娱乐业等领域的非理性投资得到遏制，而医药、先进制造、高科技等国家鼓励的行业成为新的投资热点。

五、国际人才将成为未来"一带一路"国家投资并购增长的关键

中国企业参与海外并购不但需要具有行业背景良好、金融知识和专业知识厚实的人才,而且需要能够用外语交流、熟悉国际通行规则和跨文化沟通的国际人才。很多"一带一路"国家并购案例的失败,主要是由于跨文化沟通和交流的不顺畅,相关人员不了解国际规则,标的公司与中国企业无法真正融合。中国企业只有提前做好国际化投资并购人才的储备,并根据企业的并购目标来调整人才政策,才能保证并购的成功,实现投资收益的最大化。

第二章

在"一带一路"国家
进行投资并购的目标

第一节 海外投资并购成败五要素

海外并购对企业发展来说是牵一发而动全身的事,据统计,半数以上的海外并购案都失败了。下面以几家知名中国企业海外并购案例的媒体公开信息,来说明事关海外投资并购成败的五个方面的要素。

一、企业战略引领

"企业'走出去'是基于战略需要,不能为了'走出去'而'走出去',要量力而行",山东重工集团有限公司[①](以下简称山东重工集团)总经理江奎在总结近年实施海外并购的成功经验时表示。山东重工集团的海外并购过程:2009年1月,法国经济陷入低谷,潍柴动力股份有限公司(以下简称潍柴动力)以299万欧元收购法国博杜安国际发动机有限公司;2012年1月,意大利经济步履维艰,潍柴动力收购了法拉帝集团;2012年9月,德国受困于欧债危机,潍柴动力收购了德国凯傲集团25%的股份及其旗下的德国林德液压有限公司70%的股份。

2016年,苏美达集团下属的江苏苏美达机电有限公司成功并购了德国ISH公司,ISH公司成立于1992年,主要生产铰链等汽车零部件,是戴姆勒、宝马和大众等德国主要车企的供应商。苏美达集团"大汽配"业务板块战略

---

① 山东重工集团有限公司是由潍柴控股集团有限公司、山东工程机械集团有限公司和山东省汽车工业集团有限公司等企业全部国有产权组建的国有独资公司。潍柴动力股份有限公司是潍柴控股集团有限公司的子公司。

目标在海外拓展和布局中起到了积极作用，为其在更高层次、更高平台上的产业协同运作奠定了良好基础。公司在并购一个企业之前，必须制定明确的公司战略，在此基础上对目标企业所从事的业务、资源状况进行调查。只有当公司收购目标企业后，目标企业能够很好地与本公司的战略相配合，从而通过对目标企业的收购，增强本公司的实力，最终达到增强本公司的竞争优势的目的时，才可以考虑对目标企业进行收购。

二、顺应行业发展的趋势

从国外车企进入中国，再到中国汽车走向全球，这是汽车行业的宏观大势，也是中国车企由大到强的必经之路。"国际化"作为中国汽车行业响应国家扩大开放政策、提升企业国际市场话语权的重要方式，是助推升级体系能力、整合优化资源、提升企业竞争力的关键驱动力。

苏美达集团抓住了全球汽车产业和市场的机遇期，明确定位和发展模式，融入大平台，充分发挥"贸工技金"能力优势，在"大汽配"产业布局和海外并购两个方向上持续发力，进一步做优、做强、做大"大汽配"产业版图。苏美达集团并购的德国 ISH 公司的自动化程度、精益管理水平以及员工专业技能，都为苏美达集团"大汽配"业务板块的制造业转型升级和全球布局提供了国际一流的标杆。

三、对目标企业进行彻底尽职调查

海外并购有很多机遇，但是也有很多风险。跨境并购过程中最大的问题就是风险管理，要对此进行全面尽职调查（简称尽调）。尽职调查一般分为财务、法律、商业调查三个方面，有时还需要进行技术知识产权调查。尽职调查是保护买方利益和获得重要谈判筹码的基础，一定要重视，否则中国公司会丧失主动权。许多企业并购失败的原因是事先没有很好地对目标企业进行详细的调查。在并购过程中，由于信息不对称，买方很难像卖方一样对目标企业进行充分的了解，但是许多收购方在事前都想当然地以为自己很了解目标企业，相信自己可以通过对目标企业的良好运营使其体现价值。然而，很多买方在交割后，才发现事实并非想象中的那样，目标企业中可能存在着买方没有注意的重大问题，最终导致并购失败。

四、并购交易的投后整合靠团队

苏美达集团于 2016 年成功并购德国 ISH 公司后，迅速选聘行业资深职业经理人担任首席执行官（CEO），组建了资深的管理团队。山东重工集团总经理江奎曾表示，虽同在欧洲，但山东重工收购的德国凯傲集团和意大利法拉帝集团的治理架构有很大不同，主要表现为以下几个方面：一是文化不同；二是企业发展背景不同，法拉帝集团一直是家族企业，而凯傲集团经历了产业、财务、股东轮动，公众化水平更高；三是潍柴动力在这两个公司中的股权不同，潍柴动力对法拉帝集团是绝对控股，对于决策机构具有控制权，而对凯傲集团，潍柴动力是单一第一大股东，处于相对控制地位。所以，管理这两家公司的方式是不同的。

五、并购后迅速有效地整合

实施并购以来，苏美达集团严格执行德国当地法律法规，充分尊重 ISH 公司的管理模式、文化和价值观，采取了一系列有利于长期经营、业务整合、员工发展的举措，开展必要的资产优化，推进组织、流程、人员及文化层面的系统建设等，有力保障了 ISH 公司的平稳高效运行，并于 2016 财年一举实现扭亏为盈，受到当地政府、企业员工的认可和赞扬。

2017 年 6 月 9 日，中国驻德国商务参赞处王卫东公参赴萨克森州海尼兴市（Hainichen）出席 ISH 公司成立 25 周年庆典并致辞时表示，"25 年来，ISH 逐步发展成为行业领军企业，我们为公司取得的成功感到自豪。与 25 年前相比，今天的 ISH 已经发生了巨大的变化，尤其是去年和苏美达成为战略合作伙伴，迎来新的历史起点。借此机会我用三句话表达对公司未来发展前景的良好祝愿。一是直面与中国企业合作后发生的各种变化，在变化中寻找新的发展机会；二是建立互信，务实合作，共同面对激烈的竞争；三是锐意创新，成为创新合作的'黄金搭档'。"

第二节 投资并购"一带一路"国家企业的目标

中国企业在"一带一路"沿线国家进行投资并购之前，一定要想清楚并购的目标是什么，也就是为什么要做投资并购。我们认为"获得资源、获得技术和占领市场"是最为常见的海外并购目标。

在分解目标之前，需要特别注意国别风险。一般来说，国别风险关注政治、经济金融、营商环境（行政效率、税收体系、法律体系、投资环境）这三个方面。中国的大型涉外金融机构内部会给目的国做国别风险评级，国际三大评级机构——穆迪公司、标准普尔和惠誉国际也会对主权风险进行评级。

一、目标之一：获得资源

中国是全球锂电池的制造和领导者，市场份额超过全球的50%。目前中国锂电池应用最广的领域是新能源汽车，随着新能源汽车市场的快速发展，全球对上游材料——锂的需求大增。世界一流的锂资源主要集中在南美洲和澳大利亚。锂正处于行业鼎盛时期，金属锂价格2017年涨幅约100%~150%。据晨哨集团统计，仅2017年，中资企业在海外布局锂矿资源项目近20起，收购方式分为收购股权和签署承购协议两种，以前者为主，其中15笔披露了金额，涉及约37.48亿元人民币。

受益于国内新能源动力电池市场对锂产品需求的大幅增长，天齐锂业股份有限公司（简称天齐锂业）成长为国内锂电池核心材料的行业巨头。2018年5月18日，天齐锂业发布公告，披露了拟收购智利矿业化工（Sociedad Qulmicay Minerade Chile S.A.，简称SQM）23.77%股权的事项，耗资约259亿元人民币。2016年9月，天齐锂业斥资2.09亿美元收购了智利的锂盐生产企业 SailingStone Capital Partners（SCP）。2014 年 5 月，天齐锂业斥资 5 亿美元，完成了对澳大利亚泰利森锂业 Sailing Stone Capital Partners（SCP）有限公司（Talison）母公司文菲尔德（Windfield）51% 权益的收购，间接控股泰利森锂业。

二、目标之二：获取技术

下面，我们来看看一家制造健康防护手套的行业龙头企业，如何借助资本市场的力量和产业资本的杠杆，介入高端医疗器械制造市场，一举拿下国际领先的心脏支架行业稀缺标的，迈入三类医疗器械制高点——心脏支架领域，并成为国内该领域的龙头企业。

在清科研究中心公布的"2017 年中国股权投资年度排名"中，中信产业投资基金管理有限公司（简称中信产业基金）位列"2017 年中国私募股权投资机构 100 强"前 10。2016 年 4 月 19 日，中国银行为中信产业基金私有化柏盛国际集团有限公司（简称柏盛国际）发放总金额 5.8 亿美元的并购贷款，并协助中信产业基金完成投资人与并购贷款资金归集与私有化对价支付，推动该项目成功完成交割。中信产业基金收购柏盛国际，是中资私募基金在资本市场上私有化大型海外上市企业、获取国际高端医疗器械制造技术的经典案例。中信产业基金通过旗下所管理的基金成功对柏盛国际实施私有化收购，交易总对价折合 10.5 亿美元。

柏盛国际是世界排名第四的心脏支架等相关医疗设备的研发制造及销售商，排名仅次于雅培、波士顿科学及美敦力公司，拥有全球领先的心脏支架研发技术，拥有全球首个可降解聚合物药物洗脱支架（DES）爱克塞尔（EXCEL）药物洗脱支架、全球首个将双重抗血小板治疗（DAPT）时间缩短至 1 个月的无聚合物药物洗脱支架（DCS）BioFreedom 支架的生产技术，公司总部位于新加坡，于 2005 年在新加坡证券交易所主板上市，市值约为 13 亿新元。中信产业基金通过收购柏盛国际进入心脏支架市场，这是其打造心血管产业链生态圈的第一步。老龄化进程加快和心血管疾病发病率升高等原因，推动冠状动脉介入手术（PCI）需求的持续增长，根据西南证券有限公司的数据，这一需求的全球增速约为 5%~10%、中国约为 15%。柏盛国际凭借强大的研发实力和销售能力，心脏支架销量在全球排名第四、中国排名第三。随着其新产品上市放量，市场占有率有望进一步提升。

2018年5月，蓝帆医疗发布《发行股份及支付现金购买资产并募集配套资金暨关联交易之标的资产过户完成的公告》（简称《公告》），收购CBCH II公司62.61%股份，并发行股份购买CBCH V 100%股份。其中CBCH V 100%的原股东为北京中信投资中心（有限合伙），简称北京中信，北京中信是中信产业基金旗下基金。这次交易完成后，北京中信持有蓝帆医疗19%的股份，成为其第二大股东。根据《公告》，这次交易蓝帆医疗分别与淄博蓝帆投资有限公司（简称蓝帆投资）、北京中信及管理层签署业绩对赌协议，承诺2018年度、2019年度、2020年度实现的净利润分别不低于38 000万元、45 000万元、54 000万元。

三、目标之三：占领市场

全球四大会计师事务所之一的德勤有限公司（简称德勤）发布的"2017全球奢侈品百强"，山东如意科技集团（简称如意集团）控股的法国SMCP服装品牌集团、日本主板上市公司瑞纳（RENOWN）分别排名第51位和第58位。2016年，如意集团控股2家企业合并营业额13.4亿美元，如意集团也是中国唯一通过控股进入服饰类奢侈品百强的公司。如意集团2016年用13亿欧元收购法国时尚集团SMCP 84%的股份，是目前中国时尚领域金额最大的并购交易。

表2-1 如意集团并购情况

时间	标的	国家/地区	金额
2010	RENOWN公司	日本	40亿日元
2012	YeonSeung	韩国	—
2012	GWA毛纺公司	印度	—
2013	Carloway	苏格兰	—
2014	PeineGruppe	德国	—
2016	SMCP	法国	13亿欧元

续表

时间	标的	国家/地区	金额
2017	雅格狮丹（Aquascutum）	英国	1.17亿美元
2017	英威达（Invista）	美国	20亿美元（估）
2017	利邦控股	中国香港	2.84亿美元
2018	巴丽	瑞士	7亿美元（估）

如意集团众多海外并购并不以上市公司（证券代码：002193，证券简称：如意集团）为收购主体，因为上市公司的海外并购，在信息披露、会计审计、审批备案、对价支付以及税收监管等方面均具有特殊性，但目前针对海外并购的专门监管缺少针对性的要求及豁免规则。如意集团的股东除了山东如意国际时尚产业投资控股有限公司外，还包括银川市金融控股有限公司、伊藤忠商事株式会社、澳大利亚麦德国际贸易有限公司和伊藤忠（中国）集团有限公司，分别持有如意科技26%、11.72%、6.59%和2.20%的股权。

以上三个目标，在不少案例中会同时出现两个，上市公司南京奥特佳新能源科技有限公司（简称奥特佳）并购空调国际就是其中的典型。

案例2-1　奥特佳并购世界第八大汽车空调企业空调国际

交易金额：1.35亿美元

目标国家：澳大利亚

行业：汽车

案例背景：奥特佳是中国汽车空调压缩机龙头企业，是全球最大的涡旋式汽车空调压缩机生产企业。其实施了收购空调国际的相关事宜，在香港成立全资子公司作为此次收购的主体，最终于2015年10月1日，与空调国际热能系统公司AITS L.P.完成了本次交易股权交割的相关手续。空调国际是全球领先的暖通空调系统生产商之一，主要为整车企业提供暖通空调系统（HVAC）和动力总成冷却系统（PTC）

等产品，是通用汽车公司、大众汽车、克莱斯勒等国际知名整车企业的供应商。截至2015年，空调国际旗下共有15家下属公司，其中包括位于中国和印度的两家合资公司，分别为南方英特空调有限公司与空调国际热能系统公司，空调国际持有合资公司50%股权。同时，经过不断的内生式增长与外延式发展，空调国际业绩取得了长足进步，最近五年营业收入复合增长率高达17%，实现了高于全球市场平均水平的增长。

案例分析：本笔收购兼具占领市场和获取技术两个目标。汽车电动空调压缩机是汽车空调的"心脏"，收购空调国际后，奥特佳的空调压缩机业务与空调国际的汽车空调系统业务形成互补，奥特佳仍专注于空调压缩机业务，在产品上与空调国际进行合作。空调国际的产品能够帮助奥特佳在汽车空调领域形成完整的产品组合，使其有能力向国内外整车企业提供质量优异的汽车空调压缩机与汽车暖通空调系统。同时，在客户渠道上，奥特佳与空调国际可以实现共享，奥特佳可利用空调国际国际化的客户和渠道网络寻求海外业务拓展机会，并在空调国际的协助下打入中高端市场，跻身国际一流整车企业的全球供应商行列。

空调国际热能系统公司首席执行官Todd Sheppelman称："我对能够与奥特佳形成新的合作关系感到十分高兴。这次收购将进一步提升我们的投资能力，在进一步成长的同时，我们的能力与技术也得到提升，从而能更好地支持日益增长的客户群和全球业务。"

目前在汽车暖通空调系统方面，全球已形成日本株式会社电装（DENSO）、法雷奥集团（Valeo）、韩国汉拿伟世通空调株式会社（HVCC）、德国马勒集团（Mahle）、美国德尔福派克电气公司（Delphi）五大巨头。空调国际正在通过改进技术、开拓市场、优化全球布局持续扩大全球市场份额。在中国汽车空调市场，除五大巨头外，空调国际占据了较大的市场份额。

第三章

在"一带一路"国家进行投资并购的模式和融资安排

投资和并购是"一带一路"建设的核心环节之一。据统计，从 2000 年到 2016 年，在"一带一路"国家中总计完成超过 13 100 次、总价值高达 1.31 万亿美元的跨国并购交易。有兴趣参与"一带一路"投资并购的中国企业非常有必要了解"一带一路"建设不同的投资并购模式，了解其优缺点，并依据项目情况采用最为合理的交易模式。很多中国企业的投资并购并非完全依靠自有资金，需要从第三方进行融资，所以，融资安排也是中国企业在"一带一路"投资并购过程中需要解决的一个关键问题。

本章介绍"一带一路"国家投资并购模式和融资安排，分为三节。第一节主要介绍投资"一带一路"国家的合理交易架构；第二节将介绍资产收购和股权收购两种常见的并购模式；第三节介绍"一带一路"国家的投资风险和融资趋势。

第一节 "一带一路"国家投资并购的合理交易架构

合理的交易架构设计对于"一带一路"国家投资并购项目的成功至关重要。交易架构的关键因素包括交易主体、税收安排、支付类型和收购形式。交易架构的设计需要根据双方的商业目的、税收安排和所在国的法律法规要求进行调整，每个项目的交易架构都有所不同，没有通行的法则。一个设计不当的交易架构会给卖方、买方和贷款人带来灾难性的影响。同时，"一带一路"投资并购交易需要大量资金在多个国家间有效部署，中国企业除了运用自有资金外，还需要向国际投资者、金融机构、投资机构进行融资来获取足够的资金完成交易，合理的交易架构和融资模式对投资并购的成功至关重要。因此，对于中国企业来说，寻求能最有效促进并购交易的、安全的、创新的交易架构和融资模式始终具有挑战性。我们在附录中总结了19个"一带一路"经典并购案例，准备进行"一带一路"投资并购的中国企业，可以参考这些案例，合理设计交易架构和有效安排资金，有兴趣的读者可以进一步了解。

第二节　资产收购和股权收购的模式

资产收购和股权收购是投资并购的两种主要形式，本节介绍了这两种收购方式的优缺点，并通过具体的案例来进一步描述。

在任何并购交易中，交易各方的首要问题之一是使用何种所有权转移机制——收购形式。资产收购和股权收购是两种主要的投资并购形式。这两种收购形式有其各自的优缺点，需要基于每个项目的具体特点来进行合理的安排。有时，最佳交易架构是显而易见的，各方能够迅速达成协议，完成投资并购交易。然而，在大多数情况下，各方需要花费大量的时间和资源，努力就收购形式达成一致。

下面是两种将资产或股权和相关负债从目标公司向收购公司转移的方法，也就是我们通常所说的"资产收购"和"股权收购"。

（1）购买资产：卖方将目标资产的全部或一部分出售给买方，以换取买方股票、现金或者股票和现金的组合。买方可以选择承担全部、部分或者不承担卖方的负债。通常，买方不承担卖方目标资产的负债。

（2）购买股票：目标公司的股东向买方出售目标公司的股票。目标公司的股东可接受买方的股票、现金或者股票和现金的组合。通常，由买方承担目标公司的负债。

资产收购和股权收购是中国企业在"一带一路"沿线国家投资的两种主要并购形式，以此获取符合条件的海外目标，并接管目标公司或者目标资产的所有权或控制权。资产和股权收购方法广泛应用于物流、房地产、博彩、基础设施、食品、能源、医疗保健和金融等行业。

一、资产收购

资产收购交易通常涉及卖方公司向买方出售其在商业运作过程中使用的资产。购买的资产一般包含公司的所有资产，在某些特定情况下转让的资产只包括某些选定的资产。在以下三种情况下，收购资产可能是完成此类交易最实用的方法：(1) 买方只对特定的产品线感兴趣；(2) 买方只对母公司一个部门的多个产品线感兴趣；(3) 买方对卖方不作为独立的法律主体的部门的产品线感兴趣。

在资产交易中，当卖方保留对该公司股票的所有权时，买方通常会在购买协议中明确仅有部分负债作为确定的资产和负债被销售给买方。因此，买方通常要求在资产购买协议中明确买方不承担除标明负债以外的任何义务。资产收购对买方和卖方都有明显的好处。表 3-1 总结了资产收购给交易双方带来的好处。

表 3-1 资产出售给交易双方带来的好处

优势	买方	卖方
交易具有很大的灵活性，可以明确在交易中包含的资产与负债的种类	√	√
降低买方承担未知负债的风险	√	
无须购买不必要的资产	√	
可以仅处置资产包中的部分资产		√
处置不良业务相关资产的理想解决方案		√
仅出售与特定业务部门有关的资产	√	√
在买方对目标公司的负债存在很大疑虑情况下的理想解决方案	√	√
不存在少数股东	√	
在出售资产所有权的同时，继续保有公司的法律实体		√
允许在会计准则的截止日内对获得资产的市场价值进行重新评估	√	
有豁免需要股东批准的可能性	√	

尽管资产收购有表 3-1 提到的优点，然而，从买方和卖方的角度来看，购买资产仍然有几个缺点。从买方的角度来看，缺点包括以下几点。

（1）卖方经营净损失和税收抵免的损失；
（2）无法将许可证、特许经营权、专利权等资产的权利转让给买方；
（3）如果出售的资产被用作贷款抵押品，需要获得贷款人的同意才能进行转让。

在资产交易中，卖方的主要问题是与双重征税制度相关的税务问题。此外，卖方通常需要向政府提交将资产和负债的所有权转让给买方的相关法律文件，这些法律文件可能会产生额外的费用。

在资产收购的框架下，我们进一步讨论以下两种子交易类型：以现金收购资产、以股票购买资产。

（一）以现金收购资产

在以现金收购资产的过程中，买方通过支付现金来收购卖方的资产，并可选择接受卖方资产的部分或全部债务。只要卖方董事会投票出售全部或"大致上全部的"公司资产，卖方股东就必须批准交易。卖方在收到买方的现金后，可以将现金：

（1）全部重新投资到运营中；
（2）部分重新投资，并将其余部分作为付给股东的股息；
（3）对公司进行清算，将现金全部分配给股东。

当卖方公司的资产已全部被收购时，如果卖方股东批准公司清算，那么卖方的公司主体将不复存在。卖方在完成资产出售的同时，通过清算，将从买方获得的现金转移给卖方的股东。

（二）以股票收购资产

以现金换资产的替代形式是以股票换资产，即两个独立公司的股东将其所有者权益集中在买方公司中，买方持有两家公司的合并资产和负债。在这种情况下，当卖方董事会和股东批准时，卖方的股东会收到买方的股票以换取卖方的资产和负债。在以股票购买资产的过程中，卖方需在获得股东批准后解散公司，交易完成后，卖方公司将不再存续。

二、股权收购

股权（股份）收购交易是指购买目标公司的股票。在股权交易中，买方不是选择购买特定的资产和负债，而是购买整个公司的股权。交易完成后，买方代替卖方成为公司的所有者，公司业务可以继续进行；卖方对原公司业务的资产、负债或经营没有持续的权利或义务。因为所有已知的和未知的负债都将转移给买方，而卖方可以避免持续地承担责任，所以此类型的销售往往受到卖方股东的青睐。在股权收购之前，买方需要确保该公司具有干净的经营历史，或者在完成资产出售方面没有重大困难，例如：（1）限制从卖方向买方转移某些资产；（2）需要第三方的同意才可以转让资产。

在现金换股票或股票换股票交易中，买方直接从卖方的股东那里购买股票。如果目标是私人实体，收购则由收购方和目标股东之间达成股权购买协议完成。对于上市公司来说，由于上市公司股东人数众多，收购公司需向目标公司的股东提出收购要约。根据收购要约是否得到目标公司董事会和目标公司管理层的支持，来决定该收购被视为友好还是敌对的收购。购买股票是恶意收购中最常用的方法。如果买方不能说服所有卖方的股东出售他们的股份，少数卖方股东将继续持有卖方公司的股份，目标公司将成为买方非全资拥有的子公司。由于卖方的股权转让将通过公开的竞标来完成，因此在交易中不需要卖方股东批准。表 3-2 总结了股权收购给交易双方带来的好处。

表 3-2　股权收购给交易各方带来的好处

优势	买方	卖方
所有资产都可以与目标公司的股权一起转移，从而减少完成交易的文件数量	√	
保留使用目标公司的名称、许可证、特许经营权、专利权等权利	√	
可以保持合同的持续性与企业品牌的认可度	√	
卖方对原公司业务的资产、负债或经营没有持续的权利或义务		√
推迟纳税的能力		√
不存在卖方不希望保留但未被买方购买的资产处置的相关复杂情况		√

尽管有上述优点，股权交易也存在以下缺点。股票收购将为买方带来的

缺点包括：（1）未知或未公开的负债；（2）没有终止的工会协议或雇员福利计划；（3）在实施战略调整时，少数股东的存在可能会产生巨大的行政成本和执行障碍。卖方将面临的缺点主要包括：（1）没有选择保留哪些资产的能力；（2）所有潜在的税收减免的损失。

案例 3-1 和案例 3-2 分别是复星医药收购印度药企 Gland Pharma 的股权和招商局集团收购汉班托塔港 99 年运营权的案例。

案例 3-1　复星医药收购印度药企 Gland Pharma

交易金额：10.9 亿美元

目标国家：印度

行业：医疗

案例背景：2017 年，复星医药宣布计划以不超过 12.61 亿美元的价格收购 Gland Pharma 86.08% 的股权。然而，这笔交易引起了印度政府的担忧。印度允许外国资本对本国制药业投资的份额高达 100%，但高于 74% 需要获得政府批准。因为印度内阁经济事务委员会（CCEA）对该提案提出异议，所以复星医药决定将收购股权比例降低到 74%，估值不超过 10.9 亿美元。根据新条款，Gland Pharma 的创始股东有权在股份购买协议（SPA）截止日期届满后一年内行使认沽期权，以 3.55 亿美元的价格出售剩余股权。Gland Pharma 还成立了一个由 9 名成员组成的新董事会，复星医药有权任命其中大部分成员。

案例分析：复星医药对 Gland Pharma 的收购是一种现金换股票交易，买方直接购买卖方股东的股票。由于目标是私人实体，购买是通过收购方与目标公司股东之间的股票购买协议完成的，因此，收购公司没有必要向标的公司的股东发出收购要约。虽然收购过程有些曲折，但此次收购对复星医药和印度 Gland Pharma 的重要性显而易见。复星医药与 Gland Pharma 之间的这项合作协议为复星医药在现有的市场中销售 Gland Pharma 的产品创造了新的渠道。另外，此次交易是复星医药全球布局的关键点。

案例 3-2　招商局港口收购汉班托塔港 99 年运营权

交易金额：11.2 亿美元

目标国家：斯里兰卡

行业：基础设施

案例背景：汉班托塔港是一个深水港，位于斯里兰卡南部海岸。其三期港口开发项目涉及建设一个附属工业区的主要工业和服务。汉班托塔港的一期于 2011 年 12 月完工，并于 2012 年 6 月开始运作；二期建设工程于 2015 年 4 月完成，该港口有 10 个泊位，码头长度达 3 487 米，能够处理集装箱、散装、通用、滚装和大型船舶的液体散货。

2017 年 7 月，中国港口运营商招商局港口控股有限公司（简称招商局港口）宣布以 9.74 亿美元收购斯里兰卡汉班托塔港 85％股权。根据协议，招商局港口须在汉班托塔港口投资 11.2 亿美元，其中 9.74 亿美元直接支付给斯里兰卡港口管理局以收购 85％的汉班托塔国际港口集团（私人）有限公司股份，而汉班托塔国际港口集团（私人）有限公司收购港口服务公司 58％的股份。汉班托塔国际港口集团（私人）有限公司获得开发、运营和管理汉班托塔港口的独家权利，港口服务公司获得港口运营的权利。协议有效期为 99 年，协议中约定斯里兰卡政府和港口管理局在最初的 15 年内确保不会在 100 公里范围内直接开发与汉班托塔港的服务和业务竞争的任何港口或码头。

案例分析：汉班托塔港交易是以现金获得资产使用权和开发权的案例。随着中国经济快速发展，"一带一路"沿线国家的基础设施的连接和互通已经成为"一带一路"建设的基础。汉班托塔港拥有优越的地理位置和巨大的扩张潜力。斯里兰卡缺乏资金和技术，中国企业的投资会改善港口基础设施的条件和港口的服务能力，带动其经济的发展，实现双赢的局面。

第三节 "一带一路"沿线国家的投资风险和融资趋势

根据2018年10月国务院国有资产监督管理委员会发布的信息,在"一带一路"倡议提出后的5年中,中央企业已投资或参与了"一带一路"国家超过3 100个投资项目和工程。然而,对于"一带一路"倡议来说,这仅仅是一个开始。更为重要的是,中国企业将学会在国际市场上竞争,进行国际贸易与投资最佳实践,获取国际先进技术并在国际市场中实现规模化发展。当然,对于那些有志于和从事"一带一路"国家投资的中国企业来说,这并不是没有风险的。因此,创建新的投融资模式、鼓励政府与民间资本加强合作、建立多元化的融资体系和多层次的资本市场是非常重要的。

一、国有企业和私营企业参与

截至目前,中国政策性银行(中国国家开发银行和中国进出口银行)和丝路基金都是中国企业的出资方,而亚洲基础设施投资银行和金砖国家新开发银行则多是"一带一路"项目所在国家的出资方。至2030年时,中国将不再资助全部"一带一路"项目,预计超过一半的"一带一路"投资项目将由私人资本、多国银行和外国政府提供资金。引入多元化股东和合作伙伴是投资并购成功的关键因素之一。虽然中国国有企业在"一带一路"项目前期的开发和投资中处于主导地位,但越来越多的私营企业和外资企业开始主动参与。此外,为了在目的地国家减少风险和实现可持续发展,企业很可能会与当地合作伙伴建立合资企业或其他形式的合作关系。随着中国经济增速放缓,中国私营企业正在寻找新的机会,而其销售的产品和价格也适合"一带一路"沿线国家的消费者。目前,东南亚、西亚、非洲和南亚的国家是"一带一路"沿线国家中最受国有企业青睐的投资目的地。在"一带一路"

倡议的指导下，国有企业现在并将继续担任"集团负责人"的角色。然而，与国有企业不同的是，由于风险相对较低、市场经济成熟以及法律制度健全，因此私营和外资企业向美国和欧洲等发达地区投入更多资金。中国民营企业将在未来占有越来越多的出境活动市场份额，尤其是以投资并购的形式。"一带一路"沿线国家对中国民营企业来说无疑非常具有吸引力，而适当的融资安排则成为"一带一路"国家项目交易成功的重要组成部分。令人欣慰的是，现在大部分的融资安排来自私人资本，地方公私伙伴关系（PPP）也将发挥重要作用。

地方公私伙伴关系作为一种新型的融资机制，可以帮助"一带一路"沿线国家吸引私营投资者为其基础设施项目提供资金。它们还可以成为确保风险分担、识别潜在的成功项目和建立有效的项目监测系统的便利工具。因此，目前需要在中国和许多"一带一路"沿线国家推进公私伙伴关系框架。同时，项目的公开招标也是必要的。目前，对许多东盟国家来说，基础设施项目的融资已被视为一项挑战。本国的基础设施项目缺乏资金仍然是许多东盟国家的主要问题。中国共产党第十九次全国代表大会之后，"一带一路"建设和"粤港澳大湾区"的发展受到重视，未来投资并购活动和私募股权的增长是可以预见的。《亚洲私人股本洞察2018》（*Asia Private Equity Insights* 2018）报告指出，自2017年8月中国政府开始遏制资本外流以来，中国企业的并购活动同比减少40%。在2017年前9个月，私募股权基金支持的收购规模同比增长129%，达到480亿美元。私募股权基金主要关注于电信、可再生能源、教育和先进制造业等新兴产业，这些产业未来有着巨大的增长潜力。随着中国科技初创企业的崛起和快速发展，预计风投和私募股权基金行业也将迎来快速的增长。此外，在国内市场合格投资标的供需不平衡的现状下，"粤港澳大湾区"的发展为中国私募股权公司的发展开辟了新的路径，并将促进中国私募股权公司的发展。在这种情况下，市场面临的两个主要挑战将是交易定价和退出环境。由于市场的前景乐观，交易定价是最大的挑战之一，这使得卖方没有理由进行资本处置。由于基金一直关注具有潜力的行业（包括医药和技术），其中一些甚至已经设立了专项投资基金，因此探索高质量的交易也很困难。市场正在见证越来越多的新一代投资者进入市场。与上一代投资者不同的是，新一代投资者更倾向于将资本置于其控制之下。这些投资者更加开放，并且愿意承担更多风险。他们必须确保其融资和担保结构符合相关地方法律的规定，并可以得到良好的保护。

案例 3-3　内斯塔收购普洛斯控股权

交易金额：160 亿新加坡元

目标国家：新加坡

行业：物流资产

案例背景：2017 年，由万科集团、高瓴资本、厚朴投资、中银集团投资有限公司（简称中银投）组成的财团赢得了管理层收购，接管了新加坡物流巨头普洛斯。财团创立的内斯塔投资控股公司（Nesta Investment Holdings, L.P.，简称内斯塔）出价 160 亿新加坡元用于收购新加坡上市公司普洛斯的控股权，目的是将该公司从新加坡证交所摘牌，并将其私有化。万科集团成为普洛斯的最大股东，占股比例 21.4%，其余成员代表着普洛斯内部人士之间的利益平衡，分别是厚朴投资（21.3%）、高瓴资本（21.2%）、中银投（15%）、普洛斯管理层（21.1%）。此次收购由普洛斯最大股东——新加坡政府投资公司（GIC）提起，新加坡政府投资公司是新加坡的主权财富基金，持有普洛斯 36.93% 的股份。2010 年 10 月普洛斯在新加坡上市，2017 年年初新加坡政府投资公司要求普洛斯开展战略运营以提高股东价值，公司股价上涨约 12%。此后，普洛斯因为重组提高了人们的预期，所以其股价飙升，成为新加坡表现最好的股票。在收购交易达成后，普洛斯股票上涨了 21.9%，创下 3.29 新元的新纪录；万科集团在深圳的股价上涨了 0.6% 至 24.59 元人民币，在香港股市上涨了 2.4% 至 23.29 港元。

案例分析：该案例属于私募股权收购，被认为是亚洲有史以来最大的私募股权收购案。通过收购，万科集团成为普洛斯的主要股东，

> 万科集团与普洛斯预计会产生显著的协同作用。这笔交易帮助万科集团改善了其在物流地产领域的布局,并增强了其在该地区的影响力。因为价格确定、有限的先决条件限制、确定的完成时间框架,所以,普洛斯的管理层显然会支持该收购方案。

二、与投资并购有关的风险

到目前为止,中国政策性银行承担了在"一带一路"沿线国家投资的金融风险,而运营风险则落在中国国有企业身上。随着其他公司的参与,需要仔细评估与投资交易结构相关的风险和机遇。主要风险包括以下几点。

(一)并购交易的尽职调查风险

中国企业将越来越多地寻求并购"一带一路"沿线国家的公司,以加速进入当地市场。并购的过程充满挑战。首先,很多"一带一路"沿线国家的公司的盈利依靠其强大的政府关系,并购完成后,这些公司的业务能否保持稳定和盈利有着很大的不确定性;其次,境外的私人控股公司可以轻易地夸大他们的经营活动,导致中国买家支付较高的溢价;最后,由于"一带一路"沿线国家的公司通常具有强势的地方文化,并购后的文化整合也可能十分艰难。

(二)法律和监管风险

"一带一路"沿线国家的法律制度存在很大差异,这使得在各国之间复制项目具有挑战性。不同的法律制度可能会给投资带来障碍,尤其是在出现法律纠纷的时候。

（三）财务风险

中国的银行评估"一带一路"沿线国家信用风险的经验有限，这是政府担保和信用保险需求高涨的部分原因。中国的银行需要发展内部能力或找到与当地银行、全球银行合作的方式，这些银行在评估"一带一路"沿线国家的信用问题方面更具洞察力或拥有更丰富的经验。

（四）当地合作伙伴关系的重要性

中国领先的承包商已在"一带一路"沿线国家有几十年的业务开发经验，但其他很多企业没有类似的优势。大多数中国企业需要依靠与当地的知名合作伙伴合作才能取得投资的成功。

（五）有关自主知识产权（IPR）的风险

此类风险是指海外并购交易中涉及的知识产权纠纷。一些常见的防范措施包括：知识产权的尽职调查；分析侵犯第三方知识产权的风险；股权或资产收购协议中的知识产权保护条款以及交易完成后对知识产权的有效管理。

（六）税务风险、外汇风险

税务风险、外汇风险指目标公司未履行相关的税务义务以及货币汇率和利率变化导致投资价值发生变化的风险。收购海外目标公司可能会出现无法预测的税收风险和外汇风险。为了应对该风险可以采取的预防措施包括：税务尽职调查；考虑税收法规和收购资产的折旧方式；使用金融工具防止汇率和利率波动造成的损失；在并购过程中尽可能使用人民币作为结算货币。

（七）有关劳动法的风险

投资者在进行海外经营以及雇用当地劳动力时，应该注意有关劳动法的风险。主要包括与工资、补偿、调离、解雇有关的纠纷以及由于不同的就业规定而导致的处理劳资关系的不同方法。一些常用的预防措施包括：

（1）全面了解有关劳资关系和纠纷解决程序的当地法律法规；

（2）在充分掌握法律的基础上，深入了解有关劳动关系的文化背景，对并购交易涉及的相关劳动风险进行全面评估和预测；

（3）在并购后的整合阶段，中国投资者应当根据地方法律和文化解除原有的劳资关系，并在发生争议后按照适用法律和争端解决机制解决劳动争议。

（八）有关的政治风险

政治风险是指投资者所在地和目标所在地的政治环境的变化、不稳定的政治状态、法律和政策的改变导致的投资方遭受经济损失的风险。政治风险的类型包括：征用、目标国家违约、外汇限制、罢工、战争、政治暴动以及保险理赔。

以上风险将对商业可行性和获得融资的能力产生不利影响，中国企业在参与"一带一路"项目之前需要仔细考虑这些不利因素。到目前为止，中国公司主要依赖债务融资，在某些情况下也会通过私募股权融资。参与"一带一路"项目的中国公司越来越希望降低与长期贷款相关的利率风险、汇率风险和融资利息。这对于那些在"一带一路"高风险国家运营的公司来说尤为重要，因为它们承担着更高的成本和面对更大的不确定性。因此，中资银行对资金申请的处理将更加谨慎，这将促使中国公司寻求其他的融资渠道。"一带一路"建设所需资金将通过私人资本、多边银行和外国政府的资金组合来获得。在不熟悉的"一带一路"市场、法律制度和融资渠道的情况下进行复杂运作，中国企业将越来越多地需要当地合作伙伴、技术和零部件供应商的帮助，以洞悉标的所在国的真实情况。当然，这也为"一带一路"沿线国家各种各样的本地公司提供了极好的机会。

三、融资趋势

随着中国经济结构的转型升级，民营投资在"一带一路"国家投资中所占的比例正在逐渐上升。中国政府在2016年大幅限制了房地产和娱乐业的海外投资，鼓励对"一带一路"国家的投资。考虑到"一带一路"国家巨大的资金需求，未来需要多样化的资金来源。以下几个趋势将确保降低中国金融机构所面临的风险。

（1）全球的资本通过西方国家的银行和融资公司参与"一带一路"项目的投资；

（2）更为均衡的融资组合，包括股权融资以及丝路基金、中国国家开发银行和私募股权基金；

（3）"一带一路"国家的地方银行将提供债务融资，这将最大限度地降低外汇风险，并促使"一带一路"项目的融资本地化。

总体来说，这些趋势将极大地促进基于"一带一路"沿线国家"共商、共建、共享"原则的协作生态系统的形成。此外，随着中国推出"一带一路"债券来为大规模投资项目提供资金，企业也有了一条新的融资渠道。2018年3月，中国证券监督管理委员会（简称中国证监会，CSRC）宣布中国允许国内外公司通过上海和深圳证券交易所发行债券，为"一带一路"项目提供资金，"一带一路"沿线国家的政府支持的机构也可以在中国发行类似债券。截至2018年3月，中国证监会已经批准了7家境内外企业的申请，拟发行总额为500亿元人民币的"一带一路"债券来为投资项目融资。为了满足"一带一路"国家的巨大融资需求，"一带一路"债券发行量必将不断增加。

很多中国公司已经积极利用这一新的渠道获得融资：

（1）2018年6月，恒逸石化股份有限公司在深圳证券交易所发行了5亿元人民币的3年期"一带一路"公司债券。发债所筹集的资金将用于该公司在文莱的石化项目。

（2）2018年1月，民营水泥生产商红狮控股集团有限公司（简称红狮集团）在上海证券交易所发行了3亿元人民币的3年期"一带一路"公司债券。所得款项将用于购买老挝的水泥生产设备，该水泥厂预计日生产量高达5 000吨。被中国诚信集团评为AAA的红狮集团将3年期债券的票面收益率定为6.34%，债券的认购倍数为2.67倍。根据债券招股说明书，红狮集团在老挝的项目已被国家发展改革委列为红狮集团所在地浙江省的"一带一路"重点项目。

（3）2017年3月，俄罗斯铝业联合公司（UC Rusal）在上海证券交易所发行了10亿元人民币的3年期非赎回债券。这是"一带一路"国家完成的首支人民币债券。

（4）2018年1月，普洛斯宣布获得中国证监会的批准，在深圳证券交易所发行至多120亿元人民币的"一带一路"公司债券。这笔资金将用于偿还普洛斯在欧洲收购物流资产产生的相关债务。

上述各种融资工具为"一带一路"项目提供了新的资金来源，确保未来可以充分满足"一带一路"项目的巨额融资需求。

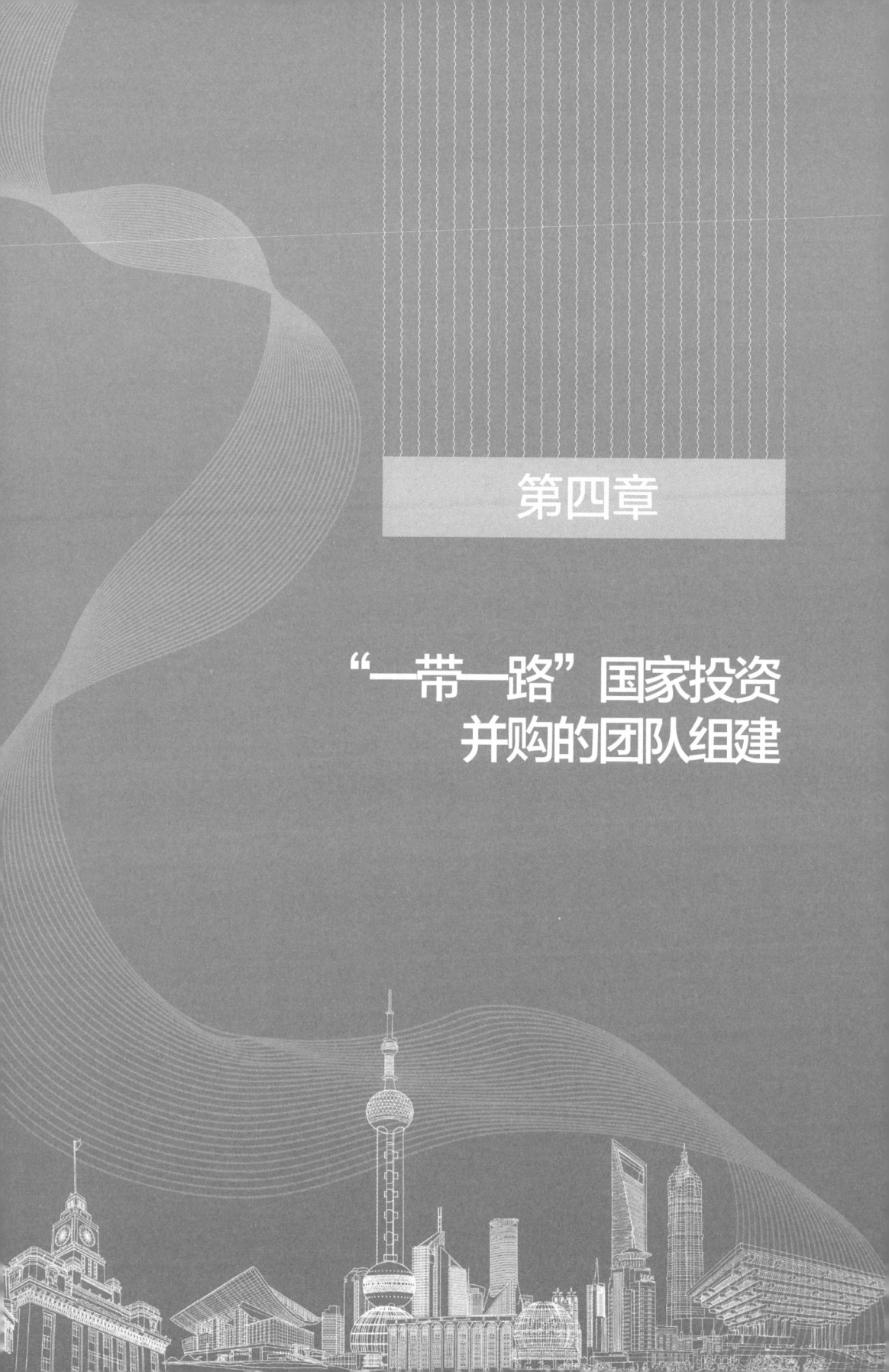

第四章

"一带一路"国家投资并购的团队组建

在如火如荼的海外并购中，中国买家仍然面临诸多问题，包括企业的并购思路不清晰，商业谈判能力不足，对市场和行业的理解不透彻，对被收购企业所在国家文化了解不足，尽职调查不够深入，风险控制能力弱，第三方资源整合和利用程度不够，投后整合能力不足等。因此，在海外并购过程中经常会出现诸如收购标的资产被高度溢价、收购后整合失败、企业商誉减值风险加剧、亏损加大等问题，导致整个并购交易失败并带来巨额的损失，甚至将中国母公司拖入泥潭，使企业一蹶不振。同时，由于海外并购市场存在不确定性高、交易流程复杂等特点，再加上中国企业海外并购经验尚浅等诸多因素，因此，中国企业海外并购频频碰壁、被否或被审查。

不可否认，海外并购失败有很多客观原因，但是笔者认为更多的还是中国企业主观上的问题，更准确地说是并购团队能力不足和经验欠缺。缺乏具有国际化并购经验的人才是中国企业海外并购成功最大的障碍。

案例 4-1　TCL 集团并购阿尔卡特公司手机业务

交易金额：5 500 万欧元

目标国家：法国

行业：手机行业

案例背景：2004 年 4 月 26 日，TCL 集团宣布收购法国阿尔卡特公司的手机业务。TCL 集团出资 5 500 万欧元，阿尔卡特公司出资 4 500 万欧元，阿尔卡特公司将向合资公司注入品牌、技术和渠道。当时，TCL 手机是中国第一品牌，阿尔卡特公司当年的手机销量达到 700 多万台。李东生希望通过收购阿尔卡特公司的手机业务，充分整合供应链，发挥协同效应以降低成本，同时利用阿尔卡特公司的技术推出创新产品。

然而，当合资公司开始运营后，双方在业务整合和文化整合方面都出现了问题。随着文化冲突的加剧，业务整合的失败，合资公司的经营状况迅速恶化，人才大量流失，当初双方投入的1亿欧元在第二年年初就所剩无几，公司亏损严重。2005年5月，TCL集团重组了合资公司，并和国内业务整合才逐渐摆脱困境。

案例分析：收购失败的原因主要有两个方面：（1）公司管理者没有形成清晰的并购策略，在收购前谨慎地选择收购对象，提前做好各项准备工作。TCL集团收购阿尔卡特公司的决定是在3个月内做出的，而当时TCL集团刚完成对汤姆逊彩电业务的收购。这笔收购缺乏对目标公司足够的研究，过于草率。（2）没有足够的人才储备。2004年正值中国企业参与全球投资并购大潮伊始，国际化人才严重不足。TCL集团在并购阿尔卡特公司之后才开始全球招聘，并购完成较长一段时间后，李东生仍然表示，他没找到一个合适的国际化助手，这为其并购失败埋下了伏笔。由此可见，"人"的因素对于投资并购最后的结果起着决定性的影响，很多中国海外并购项目失败的主要原因是没有选对"合作伙伴"，没有用好"人"。

第一节　"一带一路"国家投资并购团队的组建

"一带一路"国家投资并购是一项复杂的系统工程，需要由具备相关经验和能力的各类专业人士组建一个并购团队。团队各方参与者积极参与、分工协作、通力配合是确保并购交易成功的关键。中国企业普遍缺乏能够掌控大型海外并购项目的管理人才，包括项目管理、前期调研、商业谈判、整合规划及整合实施等各个方面，对第三方专业团队的依赖程度高。第三方专业团队需要参与并购过程中的各个环节，依据项目的进展情况给出专业意见。优秀的第三方团队对于并购成功至关重要。在项目推进过程中，中国企业需要依据最新的信息来不断调整谈判策略、甄别卖方企业的真实情况，通过协议条款的设置来规避"一带一路"投资并购交易过程中的潜在风险,以及通过合理的交易架构设计来降低并购的成本。

通常,"一带一路"投资并购团队包括公司内部团队和外部第三方专业团队。

一、公司内部团队

公司本身直接操作投资并购的团队,团队的构建要完整,包括投资团队、法律团队、人力资源团队、财务团队、运营团队、技术团队等。很多上市公司都设立了企业发展部或者战略投资部,以承担公司投资并购的组织、协调工作。投资项目立项后,企业发展部会依据项目的情况,迅速和其他部门组建公司投资并购的虚拟项目团队。企业内部团队中的项目投资负责人非常重要,他不但要进行前期并购机会的判断,之后还要做主导项目的尽职调查、商业谈判、交割和投后整合等各项工作。企业内部团队在并购过程中的"一头一尾"两项工作需要独立完成。"头"指的是"企业战略"制定,企业内部员工对企业的真实情况要有相对准确的把握,企业战略制定必须符合企业的真实情况。"尾"指的是"投后整合",企业签署股权转让协议之后,进入投后管理阶段,涉及两个公司的融合,这部分的工作基本上由企业内部的相关团队完成。外部第三方专业团队更多的是在交易过程中发挥作用。

在这里,我们重点讲并购后整合的重要性。并购失败的原因有很多种,并购后的整合失败是其中很重要的原因。组建一个有经验的并购整合团队对于并购来讲具有重要的作用。大多数情况下,公司在准备并购时,已经开始设计并购整合的方案,并组建相关的并购整合团队。在签署交易协议后,被并购方与并购方尽快构建一个团队,从公司战略、财务、销售、采购、文化、人力资源、技术等方方面面做好规划和安排。在被并购团队管理过程中,人力的匹配、文化价值的匹配、行为方式的匹配都需要公司内部团队提前做好功课,下很大的功夫。通常来讲,由于侧重点不同,并购团队和整合团队不是同一个团队,在签署股权转让协议之后,工作重心就从并购团队转移至整合团队,考虑到并购后整合的重要程度,整合团队越早参与到并购项目中来,对于项目了解越深入，并购后整合成功的可能性越大。

二、外部第三方专业团队

外部团队通常包括财务顾问、律师、审计和评估顾问、战略咨询顾问、公关公司在内的第三方并购中介机构和相关行业专家。好的外部第三方并购团队需要能够集合方方面面的力量和各种一流的人才，只有这样才能有效处理并购过程中的各种棘手问题。

据德勤有限公司（Deloitle）统计，中国企业海外并购最需要第三方机构在尽职调查执行，并购方案制订及并购标的搜寻、筛选、估值、交易谈判，并购整合这四个方面提供帮助和服务。

第三方团队由于参与不同企业的多个并购案例，因此经验更为丰富，能为企业的投资并购提供很多有价值的建议。很多项目交易结构相当复杂，涉及多个国家的不同法律实体，没有第三方专业团队的参与，光靠企业内部团队是不可能完成的。另外，很多企业做跨行业投资并购，由于企业内部没有相关的业务团队，因此外部专家团队非常重要。只有充分听取行业专家对于行业和目标公司的分析后，公司才能做出准确的判断和正确的决定。

外部顾问团队的选择非常重要，很多经常做海外并购的中国企业都有专家资源库、外部机构的筛选和评估流程，能够依据项目的具体情况和外部合作伙伴的"档期"来组建外部顾问团队。外部第三方团队的费用对于企业来说是"刚性成本"，也就是说无论并购是否完成，外部顾问团队的费用都要支付，这对于企业来讲是一笔不小的支出。在中国企业"走出去"初期，很多企业不愿意花大价钱聘用一流的第三方团队。由于交易过程中缺乏强有力的专业支撑，导致其在海外并购中处于被动的地位，在并购中付出较高的代价，遭遇所谓的"中国溢价"。

好的第三方团队一定要从专业、客观的第三方角度给企业提出有针对性的建议，而不是简单迎合企业的想法，或者仅仅为了快速完成交易拿到中介费用。企业在选择第三方团队时一定要慎重，不能仅仅依据服务费用或者"人情至上"的原则来选择服务机构，更要看中介机构合伙人的专业性、对于项目的重视程度、相关的行业经验等。外部团队的合伙人非常重要，很多中介机构的工作基本上是由项目经理完成的，如果合伙人对于项目的参与度不够，对于项目潜在的风险点就会把握不足。对于企业来讲，这不仅是费用的损失，有时还会令企业在交易过程中"骑虎难下"，导致交易失败，或者在交易过程中支付额外的成本。

在本章的第三节和第四节，我们将进一步讨论不同的第三方团队在投资并购项目中的角色和如何处理公司内部团队和外部第三方团队的关系。

第二节 "一带一路"国家投资并购的公司内部团队

公司内部并购团队的价值与地位毋庸赘言，他们的工作包括项目获取、商业谈判、尽职调查、交割和投后管理等。很多上市公司或者有些非上市公司设立了企业发展部、投资部等专门从事投资并购和资本运作的内部部门。投资部门的成员需要具有良好的行业背景、出色的内外部组织协调能力、全面的财务和法律知识、良好的外语能力。投资团队是整个公司并购的关键团队，并购团队的负责人是整个海外并购的核心，对于并购成功与否起着极其关键的作用。公司内部的财务、法律、风控和业务部门也需要积极参与"一带一路"并购项目，从不同的角度来评估风险和收益。财务团队的主要职责是针对被收购公司的财务和税务问题进行调查，发现潜在的财务风险，并给出公司的估值范围、税务筹划建议；法律团队的主要工作包括法律尽职调查、政府审批、交易协议的起草和评审等工作；业务团队需要对并购协同性、核心技术、并购整合等问题给出专业的意见；风控团队的工作主要是识别项目中的潜在风险点，并做好防范和应对措施。

投资并购是公司"一把手工程"，公司的并购活动取决于公司的发展战略。公司的"一把手"通常是"一带一路"投资并购项目的"最高统帅"，他们会关注"一带一路"投资并购活动的最新进展和买卖双方的主要分歧点，并快速做出决定。实际上，没有完美的公司，只有完美的交易。被收购公司一定会有这样那样的问题。随着尽职调查的深入，标的公司会揭开神秘的面纱，很多时候会出现如同川剧中的"大变脸"的情况。这就更需要公司的"一把手"依据公司的发展战略来权衡利弊，并做出是否投资并购的决定。

不同公司的"一把手"对于并购标的的选择会有很大的不同。有的"一把手"喜欢并购规模较大的公司，有的"一把手"喜欢并购"小而美"的公司。事实上，并购标的的选择没有绝对的标准，关键还要看公司自身的情况和投资并购后整合的效果，能否产生协同效应，提升企业的价值。例如，海尔集团董事局主席、CEO张瑞敏提出"休克鱼"的观点。海尔集团曾并购十多家企业，采用吃"休克鱼"的做法，取得很好的效果。"海尔文化激活休克鱼"的案例正式进入美国哈佛大学课堂，张瑞敏成为第一个登上哈佛讲坛的中国企业家。

案例 4-2　海尔集团并购历程

交易金额：几十亿美元

目标国家：美国、日本、泰国、新西兰、意大利

行业：家电行业

案例背景：海尔集团创立于1984年，从一个资不抵债的小企业，发展成为全球化的家电巨头。2018年，海尔集团的销售收入达到2 661亿元人民币，在全球拥有10个研发中心、25个工业园、122个制造中心、106个营销中心。海尔集团拥有海尔、卡萨帝、GEA、斐雪派克、Candy、AQUA、Leader等家电品牌。海尔集团的发展战略随着时代变化不断调整，先后提出了名牌战略、多元化战略、国际化战略、全球化品牌战略和网络化战略。在发展过程中，并购一直是海尔集团最重要的发展途径。在30余年的发展过程中，海尔集团先后并购多个全球知名品牌，2011年收购日本三洋株式会社的洗衣机和冰箱业务，2012年收购新西兰斐雪派克90%以上股份，2016年收购全球家电巨头美国通用家电，2018年收购意大利家电制造商Candy公司。海尔集团的发展史也是一部并购史。

案例分析：海尔集团的并购战略有以下4个特点。

（1）具有明确的发展战略。海尔集团的并购服务于公司的长期发展战略，收购完成后迅速将目标公司纳入其发展轨道。按照海尔人的话说，海尔吃的是"休克鱼"，这种企业的技术、设备、人才均不错，一旦注入新的管理思想和文化，企业很快就会被激活。

（2）独特文化融合。海尔并购后，非常重视文化的融合，海尔提倡的是"融合"而不是"统治"。海尔集团收购斐雪派克后，在7人的董事会中占有2个董事席位，其余5人仍是原有的管理人员。

（3）"跃进式并购"和"渐进式并购"相结合。对于已有合作基础，相对比较了解的目标企业，海尔集团会采用一次性收购的方式，也就是"跃进式并购"；对于体量较大、没有合作基础、业务比较复杂的目标公司，海尔集团采用"渐进式并购"的方式，分几个阶段来完成整体的收购。这样既可以达到快速整合的目的，又降低了并购的风险。

（4）充分发挥协同效应。海尔集团作为全球化的企业，并购后的协同效应对其至关重要。并购完成后，海尔集团能够在销售网络、采购成本、研发资源等核心要素上与被收购企业充分协同，切实发挥出"1+1>2"的效果，实现双赢。

整个公司内部团队是并购的执行者、并购交易的主导者，需要不断深入地理解收购公司与被收购公司的关联性，把握谈判的节奏和尺度，不断优化交易前期所制定的整合规划，并形成交易完成之后完善的文化、人力资源、财务的整合方案。这对团队有着很高的要求，需要团队成员对行业、经营管理、文化、资本市场规则有着深刻的理解，并拥有清晰的决策路线，以确保能够快速处理影响交易的偶发因素及在不同时点做出科学性的决定。"一带一路"海外并购通常会有明确的完成时间要求，整个并购流程时间短，需要在短时间内出决定，快速推进，特别是上市公司，还涉及证监会审批的流程，对团队的执行力和专业性有着极高的要求。

很多企业缺乏对海外并购能力的自测，主要体现在以下方面：

（1）战略层面分析不足，导致并购企业和被并购企业在公司战略上出现较大的分歧，无疑加大了整合的难度；

（2）文化层面认识不足，未能对标的所在国家、标的企业文化进行研究，导致收购方无法与被收购方实现充分融合，被收购企业难以产生认同感；

（3）财务层面准备不够，未能从自身的投资能力、融资能力、风险控制能力等维度做好分析和准备，难以未雨绸缪，出现问题时手足无措；

（4）在实际操作中，过于关注交易价格而对交易结构设计与税务筹划缺乏重视，花了很多冤枉钱，在并购完成后还要不断调整组织架构；

（5）认同财务尽职调查，对业务尽职调查的重要性缺乏认识，往往通过高管有限的实地探访，感性估计市场规模及目标市场的大致格局，缺乏专业的判断，忽略对潜在风险的充分认识和评估，缺乏有效的风险规避方案和应对措施；

（6）不重视对知识产权的调查，导致收购后还要支付高额的品牌费用，面临侵权和诉讼的风险；忽视中外方管理理念和实践的差异，文化、价值观的不同及被收购企业管理层的抵触情绪等因素；

（7）"一把手"对于并购团队授权不足，内部决策体系难以适应海外并购各阶段的快速反应要求；

（8）并未意识到主要瓶颈在于人才缺乏，而以为是团队的海外并购经验不足。

公司内部并购团队的构建不是一蹴而就的，需要在实践过程中不断打磨，使其成为一个具有战斗力的内部并购团队。中石油、中国化工集团有限公司（简称中国化工）等中国国有企业在进行海外并购之前，很重视人才培养。他们很早就选拔英语好的员工并将其派往欧美学习企业管理和业务。通过一段时间的学习和工作，他们对海外的思维方式和商业文化有了直接的了解。在操作具体的海外并购项目时，能够有针对性地调整谈判思路，绕开各种财务和法律的并购陷阱，有效整合海外并购企业。现在中国三大油企（中石油、中石化、中海油）主持海外并购的人，基本上都是在海外留学并实习过的，通过内生及外生型发展，三大油企旗下的上游旗舰企业均已进入国际超大石油公司行列。

从笔者多年上市公司的工作经验看，打造一个成熟的海外并购团队，团队成员需要具备以下六方面的能力。

一、极强的学习能力

笔者在东软集团股份有限公司（简称东软集团）工作多年，切身感受到TMT领域技术更新换代的速度之快。行内的人经常开玩笑说，计算机行业过的是"狗年"，即计算机行业的1年相当于其他传统行业的7年，只有为数不多的企业能像东软集团一样活过20年。投资并购团队的成员需要时刻关注最新的技术发展，保持对B（Blockchain，区块链）、A（AI，人工智能）、S（Security，安全技术）、I（IoT，物联网）、C（Cloud Computing，云计算）等先进技术的敏感性，并挖掘潜在的投资并购机会，同时密切关注资本市场环境的变化。例如，新浪等一大批中国互联网企业因为无法满足A股资本市场对于上市公司盈利的要求，而采用VIE架构（可变利益实体）到海外资本市场上市。同时，又有很多在海外上市的中国企业看重A股市场的高市盈率选择"拆红筹"的方式回归A股市场，国家对于"一带一路"投资并购在不断出台新的政策法规。在东软集团的海外并购中，涉及大量诸如此类的问题，相关行业和资本市场知识的学习和更新都是并购团队的必修课。

二、对于文化和人性的理解

所有问题归根到底都是人的问题，企业并购也是如此。笔者在东软集团时，有幸能够经常和东软集团董事长兼CEO刘积仁博士一起参与多起投资并购工作。作为中国软件行业的标杆性人物，刘积仁博士对于细节的重视程度令人惊讶。对于很多海外并购交易，刘积仁博士都会密切关注每次谈判的进展和双方分歧点，并及时做好应对。我们不太注意的很多细节往往会成为并购能否成功的关键。这就是为什么很多投资人说"投资是人生最后的一份职业"的原因，团队中有较多人生阅历的核心成员是公司内部团队的中流砥柱，会帮助投资并购团队规避很多难以察觉的风险。

三、国际化的思维模式

只有国际化的视野、国际化的思维方式、符合市场规则的操作才足以使并购团队获得平等参与"市场规则统治下的游戏"的机会，思维模式不在一个频道上，很容易出现"鸡同鸭讲"的情况，使并购陷入僵局。英文是海外并购的基础工作语言，并购团队需要有良好的英文沟通能力，能自如地与谈判对手、海外第三方中介机构进行沟通。很多中国企业的并购负责人英语能力差，需要用翻译完成谈判，这无疑极大降低了谈判的效率。东软集团拥有一批有海外并购经验的员工，他们在商业谈判时以英语作为沟通语言与谈判对手交流，常常令对手惊讶于东软集团国际化的程度，这在提高谈判效率的同时，也赢得了谈判对手的尊重。

四、扎实的专业知识和行业知识

投资、财务、法律、人力资源和业务各专业团队的成员只有拥有各领域的相关专业知识，才能充分发挥在并购团队中的作用，不至于成为团队的短板，给并购工作埋下隐患。对于专业团队来讲，深厚的行业知识积累是非常关键的，需要对行业特点和关键问题给出专业的意见。笔者在参与东软集团收购飞利浦持有的东软医疗的股权交易中，深刻地感受到飞利浦知识产权团队的专业性和飞利浦对于知识产权的重视。在整个谈判过程中，我们也从谈判对手那里学到很多书本上学不到的东西，提升了团队整体的能力。

五、丰富的项目经验

海外并购的复杂性、高度不确定性的特点决定了开展海外并购需要建立专业化的并购团队。海外并购是一个高难度的实践性工作，投资并购团队在海外并购项目数量上的积累必不可少。从东软集团海外并购的情况来看，每年有几百个项目，其中20%左右的项目会继续推进，5%左右的项目可以进入尽职调查阶段，最后能够完成投资的项目只有1%左右。团队只有在参与足够数量的项目基础上，才能对并购的交易流程、潜在的风险点有更为清楚的把握，才能保证对每个关键环节的关注，并有条不紊地完成各项工作。当看过几百个乃至上千个项目之后，并购团队就能练就一双"火眼金睛"，实现从"量变"到"质变"的转变。在这方面，没有捷径，缺少经验的团队和富有经验的团队会有完全不同的表现。可以说，"经验"是投资并购团队最终成功的保障。

六、良好的沟通和组织协调能力

海外并购交易往往有明确的时间表，好的并购标的经常会有多个买家同时追逐。卖家经常会要求买方支付高额的交易保证金，提交报价并尽快完成交割。买方的压力是非常大的，如何与卖方有效地沟通，通过各种渠道争取对被并购企业做更为深入的了解，发现潜在的风险点，了解竞争对手的情况等，这些对于并购团队的组织和协调能力的要求非常高。投资并购团队内部要分工明确，积极配合，还要有效管理投行、律师事务所、税务、审计、人力资源顾问、公关顾问等多家第三方中介机构。很多"一带一路"投资并购项目可能会涉及多个国家、多个团队，这无疑增加了组织协调的难度。有效的沟通和组织协调技巧是海外并购团队非常重要的软实力。

第三节 "一带一路"国家投资并购外部团队（第三方中介机构）

对于"一带一路"投资并购项目，交易风险、财税风险和法律风险是三个主要的风险点，具体可包括商业策略风险、并购对象信用风险、融资风险、利润率风险、市场风险、外汇风险、通货膨胀风险、税务风险、政府审批及劳工风险等。由于投资并购公司所在国的法律、文化、财务和中国有很大的不同，仅依靠公司内部团队是远远不够的，需要聘请第三方中介机构参与到并购团队中来。"一带一路"投资并购是一场"多兵种"的"军团会战"。俗话说"不打无准备之仗"，只有事先做好各项风险防控工作，才能保证整个交易如期、顺利地完成。如何在"一带一路"投资并购中使用好第三方中介机构，是所有走向海外的中国公司必须考虑的一个大课题。下面我们主要讨论财务顾问团队、财务和税务专家团队以及法律专家团队在"一带一路"投资并购中的主要职能和需要注意的事项。

一、财务顾问团队

财务顾问团队在并购交易中扮演着非常重要的角色。在海外并购中，买方和卖方一般都会聘请投资银行作为财务顾问来负责整个并购交易。客观地说，财务顾问在国内资本行业中的口碑一般。这个周旋于投资者与目标企业之间的群体的天然使命应当是消除交易双方信息不对称。很多财务顾问没有为中国企业提供有效服务，企业却还要支付高昂的顾问费用。

在"一带一路"投资并购中，经验丰富的财务顾问能够起到哪些作用呢？

（1）基于企业的战略目标，帮助企业寻找并购标的。好的财务顾问需要真正深入企业实际业务中并理解其增长逻辑。

（2）做好企业的财务模型。财务顾问需要比较精确地测算每项业务收入增长所带来的所有的资产负债和费用项变化，相对精确地测算出业绩增长，通过管理者收购（MBO）、杠杆收购（LBO）的交易估值模型测算财务成本和最终收益。

（3）设计交易架构，逐条推敲和确认并购核心要素，包括时间安排、融资杠杆、交易主体、收购股比、支付对价形式、融资方案等。

（4）帮助企业评审各类交易文件并协助与政府和监管部门沟通。海外并购涉及大量的政府审批，包括国家发展改革委、商务部、国家外汇管理局等审批部门，还有目标公司所在国的审批工作。如果买方或者卖方是上市公司，还涉及证监会和监管机构的审批。需要和审批部门提前做好沟通，了解政府的具体审批要求。

（5）组织、协调其他第三方中介机构，负责与卖方财务顾问团队沟通，制定并购整体推进时间表。

在中国企业的海外并购中，越来越多的中国公司聘请一流财务顾问团队来负责与卖方的财务顾问进行沟通。双方的财务顾问作为沟通的通道、卖方和买方的缓冲地带，对整个交易的达成起着非常重要的作用。好的财务顾问具有非常丰富的海外并购经验，是企业"走出去"的护卫舰，能够帮助企业规避并购过程中的各种潜在风险。

案例4-3 联想集团收购IBM全球个人电脑业务交易的并购团队组建

交易金额：12.5亿美元

目标国家：美国

行业：个人消费电子

案例背景：联想集团成立于1984年，1994年在香港证券交易所上市。2002年，联想电脑在国内的市场份额达27.3%，市场占有率位居国内第一。随着国内电脑市场竞争加剧、利润降低，并购成为联想集团国际化的首选策略。IBM的个人电脑业务包括笔记本电脑、台式机和服务器的生产和销售，排在戴尔、惠普之后位居世界第三。IBM的个人电脑业务拥有独特核心技术、品牌、知识产权和销售渠道。2004年，IBM个人电脑业务持续亏损，IBM打算向IT服务等高技术、高附加值领域转型，准备出售其个人电脑业务。联想集团希望通过收购IBM个人电脑业务，获得品牌、技术、管理、产品、销售渠道等方面的协同，提升公司的竞争力。经过13个月的谈判，联想集团以12.5亿美元的价格收购IBM全球个人电脑业务，跻身世界500强行列。

案例分析：联想集团组建了强大的内外部团队参与到IBM个人电脑业务的并购中。联想集团首席财务官马雪征和高级副总裁乔松是核心成员，内部的财务、研发、供应链、人力资源、IT、专利、行政等部门都派出专门人员全程参与谈判，公司内部并购团队人数接近100人。

整个并购涉及方方面面的知识,仅靠联想集团内部团队是无法完成的,于是,联想集团同时组建了强大的外部并购团队。公司聘用麦肯锡公司作为顾问,全面了解并购的可行性;聘用国际知名投行高盛集团作为并购顾问,高盛集团不但全程为联想集团出谋划策,还帮助联想获得6亿美元的融资,协助联想引入得克萨斯太平洋集团(TPG)、泛大西洋资本集团(General Atlantic)、新桥资本投资集团三个战略投资伙伴。三个战略投资者在为联想提供资金支持的同时,还充分利用自身丰富的经验和能力,帮助联想集团顺利完成收购、平稳过渡和整合等工作。联想集团聘请安永会计师事务所、普华永道会计师事务所作为财务顾问,奥美集团作为公关顾问。

外部并购团队对于完成整个交易起到非常大的作用。

二、财务和税务专家团队

财务和税务团队是"一带一路"投资并购团队的重要成员。财务团队主要研究目标公司的收入和利润、成本结构、财务状况、资产和负债、应收和应付情况、关联方交易、会计制度、现金流状况,依据公司过往的财务状况对公司未来的收入、利润、现金流的情况做出预估,并依据预测的结果评估公司的价值。审计团队要评估公司财务数据的真实性。税务团队评估公司的税务情况,通常包括税费种类、税费率、税收优惠、关联交易的税收政策、税收的汇算清缴情况等,并依据税收情况来策划合理的交易架构以帮助节省税务成本,提高交易的确定性和灵活性。在交易协议中通过交易条款的约定,寻求合理的保护和补偿机制。财务尽职调查的结果有助于公司评估企业并购的财务风险和投资价值,确定收购价格和收购条件,设计合理交易架构来降低企业收购成本,确定未来的整合方案。

相较于国内的并购交易,"一带一路"国家的投资并购交易的财务尽职调查有以下几方面的特点:

(1)通常,"一带一路"国家的企业采用的会计准则与中国企业会计准则有较大的差异,需要财务尽职调查专业团队将各个企业的收入、利润和资产负债等财务数据的口径统一到同一准则下进行比较，以便于买方内部决策交易定价。大多数"一带一路"国家属于发展中国家，经济发展水平相对落后，会计制度不完善，企业的会计信息不全面，监管不够严格。

（2）"一带一路"投资并购的目标企业有时可能隐瞒很多一次性成本和费用，或者隐瞒、弱化潜在亏损、表外负债等不利消息，夸大无形资产价值，从而使收购方做出错误的估计。

买方也需要重点关注目标公司的营运资金和现金流状况。在很多情况下，卖方都存在营运资金压力和现金短缺的情况，收购完成后需要买方投入大量的资金来弥补潜在的资金缺口。所以，收购方不但要评估标的企业的财务状况，也需要对自身的现金流做出评估。在考虑未来的技术资金需求时，也需要考虑未来企业整合涉及的员工养老金、关厂成本等问题，如果标的企业未来的资金需求超过了收购方的现金流承受能力，收购方就需要谨慎地做出收购决定。

（3）"一带一路"投资并购在定价时经常以零现金、零负债为基础，并要求采用诸如运营资金调价机制、净资产调价机制、锁盒（Locked Box）等其他价格调整机制，这些机制在国内并购交易中较为少见。"一带一路"投资并购集中在资本密集的领域，被投资企业可能存在大量债务和对外担保问题，企业需要对目标公司的债务情况进行彻底的调查，并了解公司是否存在逾期未支付的罚款和利息，并在交易协议中约定卖方需要承担的相关成本，或者在交易对价中将这部分费用扣除。

（4）跨境并购重组中的税务筹划涉及税额动辄数亿元，这不仅关乎交易的成败，还关系到企业的存亡，需要以系统、严谨的方法来进行筹划。很多"一带一路"国家会对某些方面的投资给出一定的税收优惠，企业在投资并购时，需要仔细研究优惠申请前提、条件和流程，充分享受目标公司所在国的优惠政策。"一带一路"国家不同的法律主体可能使用不同的税收优惠和外汇管制政策，在设计交易架构时可以考虑运用税负成本较低、风险较小的方案。在交易结构中做好合理的税务筹划，可以帮助买方节省大量交易成本，比如利用卢森堡或荷兰的公司作为中间控股公司收购欧洲标的企业，借助中国与卢森堡和荷兰的双边税收协议，节省未来利润汇回的预提所得税，为未来可能处置公司权益带来税务便利。

三、法律专家团队

企业"一带一路"投资并购的法律风险贯穿于并购的准备阶段、交易阶段以及整合阶段。"一带一路"投资并购涉及大量法律相关工作，法律专家团队需要从并购开始就参与包括保密协议、招标文件和报价函、意向书、条款条件清单、股权/资产购买协议、账户托管协议等文件的起草和评审，引导企业通过相应的安排使交易顺利进行。并购活动是买卖双方不断博弈和谈判的过程，并购交易文件是双方谈判的最终成果，是权利和义务的最终载体，也是出现纠纷时双方维护自身利益的主要依据。聘请跨境并购经验丰富的律师团队，能够有效提高企业在"一带一路"并购中的沟通和谈判效率，并且避免风险。

对于海外并购法律团队的构建，通常要注意以下几点。

（一）选择合适的律师事务所

"一带一路"投资并购一般都需要适用外国的法律，对外国法律缺乏理解，极易导致并购失败或引发较大的法律纠纷。如果并购标的是境外上市公司，则要熟悉其所在国的证券法规和相关的交易规则。仅仅依靠国内律师提供的法律服务很难满足海外并购的要求，选择合适的外国律师事务所成了顺利实现收购目标的关键。

笔者所在的东软集团的每个项目都要邀请几个律师事务所参与竞标，在比对各个律师事务所的专业经验、沟通效率、响应速度、服务报价、服务范围等方面之后，确定并购项目的法律专家团队。如果并购标的在多个国家有业务，可能会涉及不同国家的法律事宜，则需要聘用合适的当地律师事务所以获取法律支持。在律师事务所的选择上，一方面，要看律师事务所的知名度和行业经验；另一方面，还要看负责该项目的合伙人的专业能力和投入的时间、精力。在某种程度上，合伙人的重要程度要超过律师事务所的重要程度。合伙人的选择标准包括专业度、沟通能力、响应速度、价格、专注程度等多个维度的指标。

（二）进行深入的法律尽职调查

尽职调查是进行并购交易的关键环节，其将为交易决策、交易结构设计、交易价格的确定以及交易谈判提供依据。尽职调查的范围包括目标公司的业务、资产、历史沿革、合法设立、资产权属、执照许可、劳动社保、环境、税务、法律诉讼、股权结构等多方面的内容。中国企业应尽量避免承担不合理的风险。海外并购一般有严格的时间表，律师专家团队需要将监管部门的审批流程与收购时间表匹配好，这也是确保收购最终成功的关键要素之一。

（三）防范交易协议中的风险

与交易协议相关的法律风险可能存在于协议的各主要部分，包括：收购协议的生效条件、交割条件是否满足交易安全的要求，协议条款的设计是否违反管辖国或地区的法律规定以及履行可能性，协议各条款之间的关系以及周延性，适用的准据法及争议解决方式等一系列问题。对于中国企业而言，并购境外公司适用的准据法往往是目标企业注册地的法律或主要资产所在地的法律，企业不了解这些法律，极易在协议谈判中陷入被动，即使通过谈判在协议中加上对己方有利的条款，也很容易因为该条款难以在所适用的准据法下执行而导致目标落空和利益受损。另外，忽视一些可能产生重大影响的条款，则很可能在日后引发法律纠纷。以中化国际（控股）股份有限公司（简称中化国际）收购韩国仁川炼油厂失败为例，在签署排他性谅解备忘录时，中方没有增加附加条款限制对方再提价。结果韩国方面突然变卦，要求将原来的收购价格抬高，最终价格超出了中化国际的承受能力，导致此次并购以失败告终。

（四）熟悉各国法律法规和外资准入政策

企业需要对目标公司所在国的法律中的一些特定法律概念深入理解。以通常作为收购目标的"控股权"为例,在不同国家和地区的证券法律法规中,"控股权"的定义各有不同。例如,在新加坡上市公司守则中,持有公司5%的股权即有可能形成对公司的控制,持有公司15%以上股权即可被认定为"控股股东",这与我们通常理解的持有51%的股权才能取得控制权不太一致。

在海外并购过程中,东道国通常会对跨国企业的并购行为提出国家安全审查的要求。例如,美国设立外国投资委员会(CFIUS)专门评估针对美国本土企业的并购活动。在德国、法国、意大利等国家推动下,欧盟委员会开始考虑效仿美国,在欧盟层面设立投资审查机构(CFIEU)。俄罗斯颁布《俄罗斯联邦有关外资进入对保障俄罗斯国防和国家安全具有战略意义的经营公司的程序法》(简称《国家安全审查程序法》)明确列出42个行业为俄罗斯战略性行业,这些领域的外国投资除需符合《国家安全审查程序法》有关规定外,还受行业相关法律法规限制。在澳大利亚,大型的外国投资通常需要取得澳大利亚外国投资审查委员会(FIRB)的批准,2017年1月23日,澳大利亚政府宣布成立一个名为"关键基础设施中心"的新机构,该机构负责对于构成关键基础设施的资产进行登记。国家安全审查风险主要表现在对于影响诸如矿产、能源、国防、金融等特殊领域的准入和对我国国有企业身份的认定。国有企业海外并购更容易产生国家安全审查风险,比如在中海油并购美国优尼科公司失败的个案中,企业身份的认定就在一定程度上影响了对收购行为的审查。在轰动一时的"三一集团诉奥巴马案",美国外国投资委员会颁布要求三一集团停止相关项目的禁令,是非常典型的政府在某些特殊领域对于外资进行限制的行为。中国企业在收购海外公司之前,需要评估通过这些审查的可能性。

我国"一带一路"投资并购多采取横向并购模式,相对监管比较严格,一般会受到反垄断审查。反垄断审查通常以整个集团为审查主体,而不仅仅限于交易主体本身。反垄断审查涉及三个层面的审批风险,包括东道国反垄断风险、非东道国的其他国家反垄断风险和中国的反垄断风险。中国企业在"一带一路"国家进行投资并购前,需要仔细研究东道国反垄断法律规定、反垄断申报涉及的国家及需要准备的申报材料和流程,避免因为违反反垄断审查而带来罚款。"一带一路"国家的并购交易可能涉及多个国家的反垄断审查，在这种情况下，企业要提早做好准备，并想好应对措施，减少反垄断审查对交易的不利影响。

（五）防范其他风险

企业"一带一路"投资并购的法律风险还包括知识产权风险、环境保护风险、劳动保障风险、管理层的控制与激励风险等。中国企业由于缺乏核心技术，因此需要向外国企业支付高额的专利费，同时东道国会设置各种障碍来限制产品的知识产权向中国转移，以及中国企业获得外国企业的核心技术。在并购时，中国企业需要判断目标企业是否真正拥有有价值的知识产权，所有权是否有瑕疵，是否有地域性风险、时间性风险，是否有转让限制和知识产权的价值。中国很多企业的环保意识不强，未将环保风险纳入企业风险评估体系。我国有很多海外并购分布在矿产、能源等资源性产业，应提前从环境保护角度充分论证收购的可行性，避免陷入环境保护倾向下的贸易保护陷阱。在劳工保护方面，中国企业在并购时应该仔细研究东道国的工会法、劳动合同法、雇佣法和薪酬福利法等法律法规。上汽集团收购韩国双龙汽车公司、TCL集团的欧洲并购重组都因为忽视当地的劳工法律，而付出了很大的代价。劳工保护标准不一、劳资纠纷、解雇员工成本过高、工会阻碍并购是并购过程中几种常见的劳工风险。特别是有些国家工会过于强势，结果导致并购后双方矛盾不断升级。中国企业应该避免陷入当地劳动法律的"泥潭"，以便成功完成并购。东软集团在德国收购哈曼集团（Harman）导航团队时花了很长时间去处理与当地工会的沟通事宜，借此逐渐了解了当地劳动法和相关政策。在收购后，中国企业对国外管理层的控制与激励也是一个新的挑战。

（六）约定分手费或者反向分手费条款

分手费（break fee）通常是指目标公司在某些条件触发时应当向买方支付的一定金额的补偿金。这些触发条件包括与更高报价的并购方达成协议要求终止目前正在进行的交易,目标公司股东拒绝批准该并购交易,目标公司或卖方违反并购交易文件中的陈述和保证等。反向分手费(reverse break fee)通常是要求买方如果无法获得足够收购资金或者政府批准,应当向卖方或目标公司支付一定金额的补偿金。反向分手费的比例往往高于分手费,而卖方向中国买方索取的分手费往往高于向其他国家买方索取的。对于中国企业而言,应当尽量避免支付反向分手费,即使不得不支付,也要对触发条件作详细约定。

第四节 如何处理好内部投资并购团队和外部第三方顾问团队的关系

公司内部投资并购团队和外部投资并购团队之间的关系,可以大体分为三类:

(1)完全依赖型。内部团队没有任何投资并购经验,没有独立的工作能力,投资并购中的任何事项,无论大小,从项目的估值到英文的翻译,甚至连内部汇报的PPT,都需要外部顾问准备。这样的内部团队来做海外并购风险非常大,交易成本也非常高。

(2)部分依赖型。内部团队有了一定的投资并购经验,但是还不足以把控并购过程中的风险。这样的内部团队对外部顾问有一定程度的依赖,很多文件需要外部团队协助准备。这样的内部团队对于风险有了一定的把控能力,需要更多的项目磨炼和提升团队的战斗力。

(3)能征善战型。内部团队有着丰富的海外并购经验,熟悉各类型海外并购项目的运作流程、风险控制点,善于使用和驾驭外部顾问,能在并购项目中合理地利用外部顾问的帮助,但又不盲从、不偏信、不偏听。从公司的角度看,这样的成熟并购团队,对并购项目的风险有较好的控制能力,可以运作复杂的、大型的"一带一路"投资并购项目。

根据笔者的经验,在海外并购中,正确地使用中介公司和做好风险控制,需要注意以下事项。

一、明确中介机构的服务范围和收费标准

"一带一路"投资并购聘用的通常是国际团队,费用一般都是按照美元以每小时来计算的。中介费用对于公司来说是刚性成本,即无论并购最终是否完成,相关的中介费用都必须支付。一个并购项目下来,支出几百万甚至上千万美元是司空见惯的。很多中介服务机构在报价时,企业感觉费用还在预算范围之内,但是随着项目的推进,企业会发现许多新的服务项目和收费标准冒了出来,导致最后的服务费用远超原来的报价。对于中国企业来讲,在并购的初始阶段,以协议的方式明确具体的中介服务范围和收费标准是非常必要的,这样可以避免未来出现纠纷,也能有效地进行成本控制。公司也不能一味强调成本控制,好的中介机构的收费标准就是要比二流机构高出很多,需要依据并购项目的难度和公司内部团队的能力来合理配置第三方外部并购团队资源。

二、约定争议解决方式、管辖法律仲裁地等条款

建议中国公司尽量采用中立国的法律并通过国际仲裁机构解决争议。采用被收购企业当地法律或者通过其当地法院、仲裁机构进行争议解决明显不是一个好办法。即使同意适用当地法律,也不要把仲裁放到当地去进行,否则很难控制风险。

三、不要轻易向中介公司许诺"独家"合作或者"独家"聘用

有些当地中介公司往往将自己的能力吹得天花乱坠,乱作不可信的保证。如果将某个项目交给当地中介"独家"代理,往往会给业务开发带来障碍。保持商业上的灵活性永远是值得"一带一路"投资并购人员关注的事项之一。

四、最好持有任意解约权

持有任意解约权，可以让企业在合规风险或者潜在合规风险出现的时候，随时解约，至少在有证据证明中介有非合规行为时，公司可以任意解约。在很多项目的推进过程中，笔者发现不同律师事务所的响应速度和专业度差别很大，特别是"一带一路"投资并购，有些律师事务所或者合伙人之前没有接触过。如果双方在配合上有问题，要及时"止损"，重新选聘中介机构，避免影响整个投资并购交易。

五、要有追责和保障机制

作为专业的第三方服务机构，他们需要对所有的调查结果和法律文件负责，遵守陈述与保证或承诺条款。例如，笔者接触过的某个上市公司在参与"一带一路"投资并购时，由于第三方财务尽职调查机构没有发现标的公司对外有担保问题，在交易结束后，原有股东实现退出，被担保公司出现了问题，目标公司需要承担连带责任，导致该上市公司损失几百万美元。类似问题在其他"一带一路"投资并购项目中时有发生，所以在聘用协议中要加入追责和保障机制，需要第三方公司对所做的工作准确性、全面性和真实性做出承诺，对因为工作的疏忽给买方造成的损失承担法律责任并做出损害赔偿。

第五章

交易架构、投资估值与"一带一路"国家投资并购

第五章　交易架构、投资估值与"一带一路"国家投资并购

在现代商业界，跨境并购交易受到法规和商业标准全球化的推动，呈现快速增长的趋势。在跨境并购交易中，财务报告标准或者国际法的问题相对容易解决，但是公司估值和利弊权衡对于企业来说更具挑战性。

确定正确的交易架构和估值是一个复杂的过程，需要考虑一系列标准。选择最佳的交易架构是投资成功并实现最大效益的关键一环。由于将传统的交易架构和估值方法应用到"一带一路"的投资并购交易中将会使其更为复杂，因此，在开展"一带一路"投资并购时，投资者更应了解国际规则、当地税收制度、政策法规、会计标准以及中国与投资标的所在国之间的关系等重要信息。

在选择合适的交易架构时，投资者需要着重了解中国的对外投资政策和东道国的当地政策。中国的境外投资经常被怀疑会对中国外汇储备产生负面影响，这使得有关政府会顾忌中国投资者的不确定性。尽管多数的管制发生在特定行业，但我国仍认为非理性的对外投资会带来很多不利的影响。政府鼓励企业在投资决策中寻求并购机会。中国企业需要以获取新的专业技术作为增长点，来实现从全球制造业和重工业中心向以高端经济活动为主的经济中心的转移，而投资并购是一种可行的手段。

很多国家可能会对来自国外的投资加以限制。譬如德国出于对国家安全的考虑，出台了新的限制措施：允许部长们调查取得控制权的并购交易和涉嫌危及关键产业（如基础设施和技术）的收购。目前，一些欧盟国家有正规的系统来评估外国的投资以及它们可能给国家安全带来的风险。总的来看，各国越来越意识到外国投资的威胁，并可能对特定的交易架构有所限制。投资者需要确保商业活动不受法规变化的影响，并在未来不确定的情况下战略性地选择交易架构。

选择最佳交易架构和估值方法的重要准则包括，针对不同交易类型的本地和国际税收制度以及针对不同交易类型的税收分类。从估值的角度来看，在交易决策之前，需要对买方的关键财务指标进行评测，并可将其作为检验

卖方提供的目标公司的市场价格是否合理的工具。在预测目标公司财务指标时，投资者应确认税收对给定的假设的影响。例如，目标国是否使用累进税，累计税或按比例税收政策将影响买方的预估收益。此外，税收豁免对项目的关键盈利表现也有直接和间接的影响。在这方面，在融资模型中使用正确的税收假设将具有重要的意义。深入了解投资国的地方税收环境以及与中国或其他国家间的双边税收协定，可以确保交易架构的潜在税收效益最大化。从结构化的角度来看，买方时常通过最小化税收成本来实现有利于节税的交易结构。投资者在设计交易架构时，需着重考虑最优化税收、转让定价法、目标的递延所得税资产、亏损结转以及未来退出时如何节税等问题。这些问题将在本章讨论。

除国际关系和税收制度外，其他因素也会影响投资并购交易结构的性质。本章将论述境外投资决策需要考虑的主要因素，法律尽职调查和其他法律要求也将被论述。

在并购交易中，不同交易架构的选择主要取决于每个方案的价值，因此选择合适的估值方法并考虑给定技术的所有限制和假设是一个需要花费很长时间和精力的过程。尽职调查可能需要几个月。并购估值通常需要两个步骤：评估目标公司和评估企业合并后的协同效应。估值有两种模型，即绝对估值模型和相对估值模型。绝对估值模型主要依赖数学和定量分析，包含贴现现金流模型。投资估值不仅是一门科学，而且是一门艺术。尽管有几种广泛地用于评估投资价值的公式，但没有一种提供了具体的估值数值。因此，专业人员需要使用各种方法来粗略估计投资价值。有时投资者需要进行基本面分析，进而找到交易的准确价值，但在真实的商业世界中，大多数投资者需要在交易过程中信任他们的直觉，而不仅仅基于估值模型来给出估值数据。

考虑到"一带一路"投资并购的全球性特点，它的交易架构和估值可能会更加复杂。参与"一带一路"倡议的一些国家可能没有遵循国际会计准则或没有正常运作的商业体系，从而无法使用财务分析和定量评估工具。此外，即便投资国在做出估值假设时变得更国际化，仍有大量的细微差别需要注意。这些细微差别存在于财务预测、折旧及增长率的使用，以及数据的真实性中。

估值的艺术在于理解不同方法的利弊，并选择最合适的估值方法，或以最有效的方式将他们组合起来，从而对投资价值做出最准确的假设。接下来我们将详细讨论"一带一路"投资的各种估值量化工具的局限性和如何基于特定交易选择最好估值方法。

第一节 海外交易架构：税收、便利和费用

一、交易中的税收

自"一带一路"倡议启动以来，中国启动了重大的税制改革以鼓励投资者投资。中国一直致力于与"一带一路"沿线国家建立公平、公正、包容、有序的新型国际税收关系。

2018年5月14日，"一带一路"税收合作会议在哈萨克斯坦首都阿斯塔纳召开，这是首次以"一带一路"税收合作为主题的国际会议。截至2018年，中国税务部门已经与25个国际组织和区域税收组织建立了合作关系，与117个国家和地区建立了双边税收合作机制，与54个"一带一路"沿线国家和地区签署了税收协定，发布了75份国别投资税收指南。2015年4月，国家税务总局国际税务司公布了10项与"一带一路"投资者利益相关的服务措施。这些措施在总体上确保了"一带一路"倡议的执行，促进了不同区域执法的一致性，减少了涉税纠纷的发生，并为跨境纳税人提供了舒适的税收环境。这些措施提到的另一个问题是改善与税务有关的服务。省级税务机关有义务对对口国家的税收信息进行收集、分析和研究，以形成各省分国别对接机制；"一带一路"税收服务网平台分国别发布"一带一路"沿线国家税收指南；对中国"走出去"企业进行分期分批的培训，让企业运用税收协定保护自身权益，防范税收风险；要求省税务机关编写本地区"走出去"企业税收分析年度报告，并提交到国家税务总局，进而探讨跨境税务风险管理机制，逐步建立税务风险预防措施，推动"走出去"企业降低税收风险，积累出境交易税收风险管理方法和经验。

在考虑对交易架构类型的税收影响之前，投资者应当评估中国与投资东道国之间的总体税收环境与税收关系。检查中国和东道国之间是否有外交和经济关系，两国是否签署了"经贸合作协定""谅解备忘录"一类的合作协定和税收协定。在增加对外投资的同时，中国企业也面临着越来越多的税收问题和挑战。从这个角度看，国际税收协定是引导国际业务和评估税收筹划的重要工具。为此，国家税务总局于2015年4月发布《税务条例》（第60条）要求，积极解释和推动签订税收协定，并支持中国企业走出国门。税收协定不仅是为了合理运用税收法规，也是避免因滥用条约而产生税收风险的重要文件。

（一）自由贸易协定（Free Trade Agreement，FTA）

自由贸易协定规定了贸易国之间无限制的商品和服务交换，并确定了进出口的关税政策。自由贸易协定通过管理货物原产地规则、海关程序、卫生和动植物检疫措施、技术性贸易壁垒（如确保缔约方的标准和技术要求，避免造成不必要的技术性贸易壁垒）和贸易救济措施，使商业运作更具活力并刺激经济增长。就服务方面来说，此协定管理市场准入、国内法规、支付、转移以及透明度等方面。

自由贸易协定是我国扩大对外开放和加快国内改革的新平台，是我国融入全球经济、加强与其他经济体的经济合作的有效途径，也是多边贸易体制的重要补充。

此外，自由贸易协定还规定了物流合作、环境保护、竞争（反垄断）、知识产权和争端解决等的规则。

（二）避免双重征税协定（Avoidance of Double Taxation Agreements）

贸易国之间的避免双重征税协定是投资者对外投资应研究的重要文件。

避免双重征税协定保证个人或商业实体在同一收入上不重复征税。它详细规定了哪些个人有资格享受该福利，哪些税以什么方式被覆盖和在哪些国家应该被免税。这一协定源于各国税收制度的多样性，每个避免双重征税协定各不相同。协定的条款包括常驻地、常设机构、不动产和关联企业等。一般而言，避免双重征税协定涵盖了所得税代扣，利息、股息或特许权使用费的税赋，遗产税，增值税（VAT），就业收入和其他税收。除税收外，该协定还规定了税收豁免、争端解决机制、限制和其他相关事项。

目前，中国已与100多个国家签订了避免双重征税协定。为了设计合理的交易结构，投资者应该研究与特定国家的条约，并确认交易是否被包括在协定内，是否可以行使其他权利。

避免双重征税协定不仅以规范税收为目的，而且鼓励跨境贸易，支持税收信息交换，并确保各方遵守税收法规。

（三）双边投资协定（Bilateral Investment Treaty，BIT）

从20世纪80年代起，中国与100多个国家签署了双边投资协定。虽然许多已经被更复杂和烦琐的贸易协定取代，例如避免双重征税协定和其他双边条约，但双边投资协定仍然很重要，特别是对于那些税法和监管环境不够成熟的新兴国家的投资而言。这些协定也有助于巩固中国与其他发达国家之间的双边投资条件。

双边投资条约能够保证公平待遇、投资保护、赔偿损害和资金自由流动；可以通过外交途径协助争端解决，提供有关当事人所处法律和税收环境的有用信息。如果投资者的权利被侵犯，则双边投资协定授予其诉诸国际仲裁的权利。

双边投资协定是打破贸易壁垒的有效工具，如关税、配额、补贴和其他非关税措施，包括安全要求或反倾销措施。这些壁垒也可能不直接由双边投资协定来解决，而由其他协议来议定。

（四）国家税务总局的 59 份税收指南

在全面审查中华人民共和国与投资东道国的国际条约和经济关系后，投资者应当研究双方的内部税收制度。2017 年 5 月以来，为了加快实施"走出去"战略，推进"一带一路"建设、使中国投资者熟悉投资国家的税收制度，国家税务总局共发布了针对"一带一路"倡议的 59 份"中国居民赴某国家（地区）投资税收指南"（简称"税收指南"）。这些指南涵盖了亚洲、欧洲、非洲、大洋洲的国家和地区（见表 5-1），其中包括"一带一路"之路沿线的主要国家和地区。随着中国与其他国家和地区就"一带一路"倡议的各项条款的进一步谈判，以及从海外投资目的地持续收集的税收信息，这一清单将定期更新。

表 5-1 国家税务总局发布的"税收指南"包括的国家和地区名单

地域	国家和地区
亚洲	阿联酋、阿曼、巴基斯坦、巴林、不丹、菲律宾、格鲁吉亚、哈萨克斯坦、韩国、吉尔吉斯斯坦、柬埔寨、卡塔尔、科威特、老挝、黎巴嫩、马来西亚、蒙古国、孟加拉国、缅甸、尼泊尔、沙特阿拉伯、斯里兰卡、塔吉克斯坦、泰国、土耳其、文莱、乌兹别克斯坦、新加坡、亚美尼亚、也门、伊朗、以色列、印度、印度尼西亚、越南、中国香港
欧洲	阿尔巴尼亚、爱沙尼亚、奥地利、白俄罗斯、保加利亚、波兰、俄罗斯、黑山、捷克、克罗地亚、拉脱维亚、立陶宛、罗马尼亚、马其顿、摩尔多瓦、塞尔维亚、斯洛文尼亚、乌克兰、匈牙利
非洲	埃塞俄比亚、南非
大洋洲	新西兰

这些指南能够帮助投资者理解和适应特定国家和地区的地理、政治、经济和税收情况。"税收指南"还分享了中国企业管理税务事务的主要经验，以及纳税人的税收实践和与税务相关的法律法规。

由于目标国家和地区税收制度的多样性，因此上述指南各不相同，但总体结构大体是一致的。"税收指南"的第一章介绍了国家和地区概况，包括政治、地理、经济、社会；投资环境概述包括近年经济发展情况、资源储备和基础设施、重点/特色行业、投资政策、经贸合作、投资注意事项等。其第二章介绍了税收制度和税收管理方法，简要介绍该国家和地区的主要税种，并对转让定价、成本扣除规则和反避税规则进行了说明。因为围绕投资领域的税收是多元化的，所以这一部分至关重要。虽然一些国家有简单的和对投资者友好的税收制度，但有些制度需进行复杂的操作，例如回购税、社会保障税、银行保险交易税等。

在"税收指南"中，对投资者有用且最重要的章节涵盖国际税收问题，以及中国与东道国家和地区的关系，包括主要税收考虑因素。这些因素包括税收抵免、转让定价方法和要求、潜在的税收风险、跨境交易、间接税负计算等。"税收指南"的最后一章包括税收管辖权的争议解决机制，争议的主要原因、仲裁程序、预防措施、预先裁决和税务审计程序。这些问题将在下一节详细论述。

连同"税收指南"，中国"一带一路"网一并发布了我国与"一带一路"沿线国家的关系描述，当前或已完成的中国投资项目，"一带一路"合作各方的计划以及未来战略的备忘录。

二、税务尽职调查背景下的正确交易架构选择

在获取了相关国家的具体信息后，投资者们要开始准备进行真正的投资决策，以选择正确的交易架构。税务尽职调查要求企业既熟悉相关国家的整体税务环境，又掌握目标公司的内部税收属性。从税务的角度来讲，企业需要从两个方面做好税务尽职调查。

（一）评估

企业需要评估税收会对每个交易架构产生何种影响，并对交易是如何被征税的进行评价。在考虑拟采用的交易架构时，较为经典的模式是股权收购

和资产收购。尽管决策会依据交易的具体环境进行更改,但在通常情况下,卖方倾向于股权收购,买方倾向于资产收购。

（二）审查与目标公司相关的税收

出于评估和预测的目的,企业需要考虑相关税收信息。首先,理解目标公司的商业模式和公司股权结构是非常必要的。其次,买方应通过与知识丰富的人员交谈（公司的税务专家）或阅读纳税申报单等来收集税务相关信息。这有助于投资者评估和量化企业的历史税务状况并制订未来的税收计划。它还能帮助企业熟悉目标公司各个税种的征收水平。再次,模拟可能的交易结构并评估税收对不同交易结构的影响。最后,将纳税相关信息与其他考虑因素结合起来,做出最符合商业利益的决策。

股权出售发生在买方和目标公司股东之间。在股权交易期间,公司不确认任何损益。相反,股东会以售价和原始价格之间的差异确认收益或损失。

股权收购受到卖方股东的青睐,因为这种模式只产生企业所得税,所以避免了资产收购时出现的双重征税（企业所得税与股东资本利得税）现象。此外,一些国家鼓励长期投资,对持有一年以上的股权征收较低的资本利得税。当买方可以利用税收损失等税收属性时,他们也可能更喜欢股权出售。另外,由于资产的不良税基,买方也可能不选择股权收购。如果公司资产按历史价值纳税并且不能折旧至公允价值,那么财产税可能高于资产出售收入。在考虑税收影响时,投资者应该研究被投资国的房产税税率和企业所得税税率特征（税率是多少以及是否通过低税率来鼓励长期投资）。

此外,买方在开始股权收购时应当小心,公司可能因不当行为而被国家税务总局追究责任。通过查看国家税务总局关于目标公司负债情况的报告,可以确定并解决此类问题。

资产收购通常出现于各方已就特定资产或负债的转移达成一致之后。对于这种交易架构,目标公司将把损益确认为销售价格与资产的纳税基础之间的差额。这一策略有利于买方消除未披露的税务风险，并使其仅选择其希望承担的资产和负债（而不是全部资产和负债）。从卖方的角度来看，资产出售具有税收陷阱，如双重征税或折旧回收。

除了上面讨论的两种交易架构之外，还有很多其他的交易模式。股权购买和资产购买的结合被称为混合交易，最简单的混合交易结构是卖方将股权出售给买方，以要求豁免资本收益，然后再将资产出售给买方以赎回股权。为了实现双赢，在特定的商业谈判、假设和税收影响下，也可融入其他的交易模式。

案例 5-1　中联重科并购意大利混凝土机械制造商 CIFA

交易金额：3.76 亿欧元

目标国家：意大利

行业：机械制造

案例背景：中联重科股份有限公司（简称中联重科）成立于 1992 年，主要从事工程机械、农业机械等高新技术装备的研发制造，公司先后在深圳、香港两地上市，成为业内首家同时在 A 股和 H 股市场上市的公司。公司 2008 年实现销售额 150 亿元，年增长率达到 60% 以上。中联重科自成立后，先后收购了英国保路捷、湖南机床厂，重组湖南省浦沅集团有限公司，收购长沙高新技术产业开发区中标实业有限公司和陕西新黄工机械有限责任公司。中联重科认为收购比直接建厂更有效，将并购作为公司发展的核心战略。

CIFA 成立于 1928 年，是一家历史悠久的意大利家族企业，是欧洲领先的混凝土设备制造商。在混凝土机械市场排在德国 Putzmeister 和 Schwing 之后，位居世界第三。该公司在意大利有 7 个生产基地，在全球 70 多个国家和地区有营销网络，其产品在西欧、东欧等地占有较高的市场份额。该公司的核心竞争优势是产品全面、性价比高。2007 年 10 月，CIFA 的大股东因为需要现金偿还一部分债务，决定出售 CIFA 股权。

2008年1月，中联重科收到CIFA正式的邀请投标程序函之后，中联重科董事长詹纯新和弘毅资本投资总裁赵令欢立即飞往意大利约见CIFA的股东，并迅速完成了弘毅投资、高盛集团和曼达林基金的联合收购团队的搭建。2008年6月20日，中联重科最终与CIFA达成收购意向，以现金方式完成对CIFA的全资收购。收购后，中联重科持有60%的股权，高盛、弘毅、曼达林持有40%的股权。交易总金额为3.755亿欧元，对应的企业价值倍数（EV/EBITDA）9.6倍。中联重科支付1.6亿欧元，其中2亿美元为借款，使用公司自有资金支付5 000万美元。

案例分析：中联重科收购CIFA是中国企业海外并购的经典案例，有以下几方面的经验可供借鉴。

（1）擅于与第三方机构沟通和紧密配合。在投资并购过程中，中国的弘毅投资作为中联重科的财务顾问，成功协助中联重科组建了弘毅投资、高盛集团和曼达林基金的联合并购团队。弘毅投资作为国内的专业投资机构，了解国内资本市场和中联重科的并购战略；高盛集团作为老牌的国际一流投行，在各个国家有着人脉网络和资源，熟悉国际并购的规则；曼达林基金是意大利本土投资机构，更了解意大利的本土资本市场和标的企业情况。外部第三方团队从交易架构、交易流程、商业谈判、估值等各个环节给中联重科提供了强有力的支撑，确保了中联重科并购的成功。

（2）设计合理的交易架构。为了完成本次收购，投资方在中国香港设立了两家特殊目的公司（Special Purpose Vehicle，SPV），在卢森堡设立了两家SPV，在意大利设立了一家SPV。这个交易架构设计的目的就是充分利用双边税务协定，降低税收成本，提供资金流动性和融资便利性。依照中意之间的税务协定，资本或获利所得离开意大利要征收高达30%的预提所得税，而通过设置恰当的SPV，可以规避或减少预提所得税金额。在本次收购中，意大利和卢森堡皆为欧盟国家，彼此免除预提所得税。

（3）充分利用多种金融工具降低企业的现金成本。现金流是企业的生命线，在并购过程中，企业需要尽量降低现金的支出，通过发债、借款、引入战略投资者等多种方式来降低企业的资金成本。本次交易总金额为3.755亿欧元，而中联重科仅支付5 000万美元自有资金就完成了收购。弘毅投资、高盛集团和曼达林基金作为战略投资人都参与了本次收购，并持有40%的股权。作为利益共同体，三家机构会全力协助中联重科完成并购交易，并在并购后的整合中发挥积极的作用。中联重科的发债、借款则通过中国香港的SPV完成。公司借款2亿美元，为企业提供低成本资金，降低了企业现金流的压力。

很多中国企业在海外投资并购时完全依赖自有资金，缺乏利用多种财务工具的能力。这方面需要向中联重科学习，该公司通过多种财务手段降低了企业短期资金压力和收购成本。在本案例中，更为重要的是充分利用交易架构的设计，降低企业的税收成本。中国企业在海外投资并购一定要充分利用这方面的便利条件，提前做好税务筹划工作。

第二节　并购交易中的便利性评价和成本评估

除了税收影响之外，在进行并购交易尽职调查和估值时，还必须考虑两个因素：便利性和成本。每一个希望通过"一带一路"倡议签署重要合同或计划收购其他公司的投资者，都希望交易达成之后，企业未来的盈利能力和交易的安全性是有保障的，并且会考虑每一个可能影响交易结构的细节。在评估交易的便利程度和相关成本（显性和隐性的成本）时，投资者应该研究两个问题，即在特定国家或行业中，企业在什么运营成本和便利水平上运营以及可能的交易架构带来相关的成本和交易的便利程度。

与商业相关的潜在成本和各国政府机构的一般信息可以从我国为投资者发布的评估不同国家特征的国家简报中获得，包括政治、经济和行业特定的信息和监管水平。

一些国家在行业准入或进行特定交易时有严格的规则。跨国交易涉及公司法、市场法规和公司规章。这些简报为理解公司设立的程序和可能影响交易的法规提供了指导。在某些情况下，超过目标企业所在国家政府的相关法规或行业限制的投资，必须向该国财政部报告。对于一些国家来说，如果并购的比例超过其行业中有关外资股权和债权转让的规定，则需要获得目标企业所在国国家储备银行的批准。一些国家限制境内外资流动，并制定了有关申报的规定和程序。申报会导致交易时间延长。一些国家的法律制度比较复杂，可能导致决策过程不透明。在这种情况下，为了减少不确定性并获得最大收益，企业需要咨询当地税务、法律或行业专家，这将导致交易总成本的增加。

为了评估目标企业所在国家和地区的政府办事效率和商业运作的难易程度，中国投资者可以查看"经商便利指数"（Ease of Doing Business Index）。该指数由世界银行根据企业年度数据编制，对世界各地的企业运营的难度和创业活动的便利性进行了评估和比较。

"经商便利指数"排名显示了世界各地商业监管的质量和简便性，以及知识产权保护的质量。该指数构建的目标是提供关于政府对经济增长影响的研究数据。自2001年11月，世界银行成立营商环境小组以来，该小组已经发布了800多项研究成果，研究结果表明，改善经营规则和经济增长之间存在着密切的联系。

与其他类似研究不同，"经商便利指数"仅研究和量化与商业有关的法律法规和规则，不考虑更基本的条件，如基础设施、通货膨胀、犯罪、商业盈利能力等。

"一带一路"投资者应在评估交易结构之前对目标企业所在国家的政治和文化进行评估。整合资源、打破文化壁垒以及人员调整都将产生"隐性成本"，企业在制定有效的决策时应该将这些考虑在内。

一般而言，复杂的财务估值技术会将国家或行业特定的系统性风险纳入其中，但实际上，一些"一带一路"国家没有金融市场，有些国家即便有，也还处于欠发达状态，这些风险无法量化。在这种情况下，投资者应该相信自己的直觉，并从理论上考虑在政治或文化环境恶化的情况下可能产生的成本。

市场预期是很多公司没有考虑到的非传统因素。由于不确定性和平均交易规模较大，因此市场预期会影响并购交易的价值，其对于跨境并购交易来讲是最为重要的参考因素。交易完成后，买方市值增长表明市场比买方评估的更乐观。相反，市场的负面反应表明买方可能需要重新评估公司并购交易后的财务状况。在这两种情况下，买方的市值都会在并购公告发布时发生变化，这是并购交易的间接收益或成本。

在评估目标企业所在国家的整体商业环境和政府办事效率之后，中国企业应该对每个交易结构的便利性和成本进行实际评估。在实践中，这些取决于交易的特点和其他多种因素，交易可以以多种方式进行，但出于研究目的，我们只考虑以下三种一般交易结构。其他模型可以参考这三种主要结构创建。

一、资产购买

资产购买是投资者消除隐藏和未知成本的最佳做法。同时，在购买协议中可以明确约定买方在购买资产时承担的债务，这可以使买方避免意外或未知的负债。但是，包括环境法或税法在内的一些法律可能会对买方提出要求。

当买方只想获得整个公司的特定业务部门或单个工厂时，通常会使用这种结构。然而，由于需要花费额外的精力去识别和购买与本商业项目相关的每项重要资产，此过程可能产生较大的时间成本并带来不便。尽管某些资产（例如设备）可以通过销售清单或其他类似文件轻易转移，但其他资产（如知识产权或房地产）需要特别的转让机制和手续。一些资产，包括许多许可证，根本不可以转让。

为了将某些资产从卖方转移到买方，可能需要第三方同意，原因是许多合同经常明确声明，如果没有第三方的同意，卖方不能出售。为避免因花费时间去识别和取得同意而拖延交易，各方应提前识别所有需要的第三方同意事项并提前获得第三方的同意。

资产收购最重要的优势是只要多数股东确认即可，即通常只需要超过50%的股东同意。

二、股权收购

因为股权收购不需要第三方同意或其他与资产收购相关的法律文件,所以股权收购更快、更容易。买方考虑的问题在于,除非所有股东愿意出售其股票,否则买方将不会得到全面控制权。股东人数过多增加了出现耽搁、长期谈判和其他复杂情况的风险。

在股权收购过程中,目标公司的资产和业务流程保持不变,避免了第三方同意程序的不利影响,但在某些情况下,一些资产所有权合同可能涉及"控制权变更"条款,要求该公司之前的所有者同意将所有权转让给新股东后才能进行交易。

三、合并

在传统的合并类型中,通常是两家现有公司联合成一个商业实体。对于这种交易结构,目标公司的股东可能会收到现金、买方的股权或两者兼而有之。在所有权转移方面,合并的并购交易类似于将所有资产和负债转移给买方的股权收购。从卖家的角度来看,合并的优点在于它只需要大多数目标股东的同意。合并使买方能够获得目标公司的商业秘密、技术、客户、市场份额和供应商等。

对于走向全球并投资于完全未知的商业环境的公司而言,买方可以通过合并的交易模式,获得当地专业人士帮助,以保证业务流程的成功和持续。另外,在合并各方之间可能会出现文化差异,各方需要充分沟通和交流以取得文化和业务的融合。

第三节 估值:科学还是艺术

如果你问自己:"什么是估值:艺术还是科学?"最真实的答案是:"两者兼而有之。"

一方面，现代金融理论的模型通常与数学和统计学等精确科学密切相关。但是如果我们从另一方面来看，那么存在一个不可否认的人为因素：心理学、社会学和精神分析学等学科在金融世界中也扮演着重要角色。人们的非理性行为以及缺乏明确的规则和公理使得估值和投资与艺术类似。

让我们回顾长期资产估值模型（CAPM），计算移动平均线或其他覆盖图和指标的方法以及许多其他因素。很显然，这样的财务模型有着明确的科学基础，它们是基于不可否认的数学和统计学定律得出的。除此之外，在金融领域，还使用了许多基于精确科学的各种各样的模型、指标和技术。

艺术是现实的另一种表达。现在我们回想人为造成的各种市场崩溃现象，它们是理性的结果吗？不是！

人们在听取利益相关者的意见后，其行为与有关人士所预测的内容完全一样。在这种情况下，只有本能和纯粹的情感起作用。从所有非理性的商业策略、经济崩溃或者飞跃的角度看，金融是一门艺术。（有趣的是，这门艺术的创造者是大投资者、市场庄家、权威分析师，而不是私人投资者。）

设想一下，如果科学的金融市场被假期、新闻甚至天气影响，会发生什么？如果金融是一门艺术，你会怎么认真对待它？

一个成熟的投资者的特点在于他明白规则并不总是在金融市场上运作。即使所有规则都表明经济应当增长，我们也必须记住人们是非常不理性的，在财务分析时必须考虑到人为因素，并记住估值既是艺术又是科学。

"如果只有一个公式，一个办法，我们都是亿万富翁。"

科学与持续性、公正性、一致性和永恒的结果联系在一起。它可以在一本教科书中进行研究，在实验中进行测试，并获得预测的结果。如果估值和投资仅仅是一门科学，那么我们将能够取得有保证的成功和回报，并消除所有失败的风险。因此，估值比科学更像艺术，没有保证投资绝对成功的公式和教科书。

虽然投资估值技术有很多种，但有几种公认的估值技术会被更频繁地使用，并且可能对"一带一路"倡议框架中的投资更有效。它们是：

（1）可比公司分析（Public Comps）：可比公司分析表明，同行业和相似规模的公司具有相似的估值倍数，从而在评估过程中可以使用其他公司的业务指标。

（2）现金流量贴现分析（DCF）：该方法可以预估公司未来的现金流量，它通过使用所需的折现率对公司进行折现以获得公司的净现值（NPV）。对财务效益的估算涉及计算项目的净折现收益指标，定义为未来的资金流入和流出均按预计贴现率各个时期的现值系数换算为现值后，再确定其净现值（考虑到通货膨胀）。如果净现值大于0，建议投资该项目；如果指标小于0，最好拒绝。由于对投资效率的评估，公司可以理解投资的回报状况，即了解已经投入的资金和利润的比例。在评估投资吸引力时，不仅计算净现值指标，还会计算投资回收期、收益指数和内部收益率。对所有指标的价值进行全面评估，可以了解项目的有效性。也就是说，投资回报将被评估。

（3）先例交易分析（M & A Comps）：先例交易分析表明，过去为类似公司支付的价格可用于估算给定公司的价格。

成功的投资不仅仅需要Excel（电子表格），还需要深思熟虑、直觉和创造力。大多数商学院所关注的那些基于长期投资成功案例而形成的理论被认为是无用的。

案例5-2　上海梅林投资新西兰银蕨农场牛肉有限公司

交易金额：3.11亿新西兰元

目标国家：新西兰

行业：畜牧业

案例背景：上海梅林正广和有限公司（以下简称上海梅林公司）是光明集团旗下公司，公司于1997年在A股上市，旗下拥有梅林、冠生园、正广和、银蕨农场牛肉有限公司（Silver Fern Farms Beef Limited，简称SFF）、苏食、爱森、大白兔、佛手、华佗、96858等知名品牌。公司主要从事肉类食品制造及食品分销业务。

SFF成立于1948年，是新西兰最大的肉类加工企业、仅次于恒天然公司的第二大农产品出口商。牛肉、鹿肉业务占新西兰市场份额第一位。SFF的客户遍布全球，质量较高。SFF公司的加工能力过剩、原料不足，需要现金流来偿还债务、补充流动资金。获得上海梅林公司的资金后，SFF进一步优化生产设施和产能。上海梅林公司顺利完成本次海外收购后，迅速成为中国最大的牛羊肉综合产业集团，满足中国日益增长的对高品质肉类的需求。

案例分析：2015年9月15日，上海梅林公司下属全资子公司上海梅林（香港）有限公司作为收购主体，对SFF增资3.11亿新西兰元，增资后上海梅林公司将持有50%股份。

上海梅林公司合并财务报表。本次收购资金来源于自有资金和银行贷款，本次交易需要新西兰海外投资办公室（Overseas Investment Office，OIO）审批通过后才能生效。本次交易的拟购买资产为SFF及其下属子公司的全部经营性资产和50%业务的权益。本次交易定价以经上海市国资委的授权机构备案确认的SFF集团的资产估值报告的估值结果为基础，交易双方按照市场化原则协商，并根据交易协议约定的价格调整机制而最终确定。评估报告显示，SFF的股东权益为6.2亿新元，扣除债务后公司的企业价值为3.5亿新元。考虑到公司2013年和2014年业绩不佳，上海梅林公司的出价相当于公司企业价值的八八折。

整个收购过程一波三折，2016年9月20日新西兰OIO批准了该交易。

为什么我们需要评估投资项目的有效性，评估投资项目有效性的实施方法有哪些？实际上，项目投资中的问题可能难以解决。对国外投资决策实践的研究表明，在大多数西方公司中，投资评估方法可以作为决策信息。

投资项目的有效性评估由几个阶段组成。

阶段一：确定项目投资的目标和宗旨。一般而言，项目投资的目的是确定总投资和付出成本，从投资者角度确定项目的吸引力，确定公司的投资可行性，评估投资风险并证明投资者和合作伙伴进入项目适宜性。

阶段二：成本分析。本阶段包括两项活动，旨在分析投资成本和生产成本，包括其计算和预算，项目阶段的资金分配以及盈利能力的比较分析。

阶段三：评估投资效益。该阶段的第一部分为项目总体绩效指标计算，第二部分为参与项目的有效性分析,包括参与成员的确定和项目融资方案的选择。评估的第一部分可以反映项目的社会效果,以及对涉及地区预算的财务影响。

阶段四:融资策略的形成。它分为几个子阶段,包括确定融资来源、潜在投资者的组成、参与条件、设计投资进度表、确定其实施的后果、计算合并现金流以支付所有项目成本。

案例 5-3　美的集团收购德国库卡

交易金额:292 亿元人民币

目标国家:德国

行业:机器人

案例背景:美的集团(000333)创建于 1968 年,1980 年进入家电行业。美的集团在成立后,先后完成了十几起收购,快速积累资本,扩大规模,发展成为行业的领头羊。美的集团 2018 年实现销售收入 2 597 亿元人民币,净利润 202 亿元人民币。尽管近年来家电行业利润率不断降低,美的集团依旧保持稳定的增长,这得益于美的的智能制造和机器人措施。美的提出"智能制造 + 工业机器人"的"双智"战略,从 2012 年开始通过布局机器人来提高劳动生产率和自动化水平。

库卡集团(KUKA)成立于 1898 年,是世界领先的工业机器人制造商,拥有百年历史,堪称德国制造业的典范。1996 年,德国库卡从库卡集团中独立出来,与 ABB、发那科、安川合称机器人行业"四大家族","四大家族"占据全球工业机器人 60% 以上的市场份额。德国库卡以自动化为核心,主要客户来自汽车、物流、塑料、医疗设备等领域,也是全球第一家为洗衣机、冰箱提供自动化焊接的企业。公司拥有核心技术优势,80% 的收入来自欧美地区。

美的集团希望通过对德国库卡的并购,加快其智能化的战略转型,获取德国库卡的核心技术,补齐自己的"短板",充分发挥协同效应,进一步扩大市场份额。同时,德国库卡可以利用美的在中国的品牌影响力、销售资源帮助其在中国市场扩张，提升其中国区业务的比重。

案例分析：2017年1月，美的集团境外全资子公司MECCA以每股115欧元的价格，全面收购德国库卡，收购价格为37亿欧元，折合人民币292亿元。美的集团发布要约收购德国库卡实施情况报告书，"本次要约收购价格不以评估报告或者估值报告为依据，本次收购未进行资产评估及估值"。事实上，如果按照德国库卡在2015年7.43亿欧元的净利润来看，美的集团收购德国库卡的市盈率约40倍。相比于其在国内上市的估值40倍~80倍，基本上是区间的下限。

如果用海外收购的常用估值方式EV/EBITDA、企业价值/销售额的倍数来计算EV/EBITDA的倍数为18.2倍，企业价值/销售额倍数为1.6倍。我们也来对比一下2015年欧姆龙收购Adept Technology和泰瑞达收购优傲机器人两个可比交易的收购价格，后者的EV/EBITDA高达23.5（Adept Technology的EBITDA为负值，无法比较），企业价值/销售额分别为3.6倍和8.9倍。美的的收购德国库卡的价格也不算高。

2007年以来标志性的战略投资者收购德国上市公司的收购溢价数据显示，收购溢价率在30%~69%之间，平均值为46%。相对于美的董事会做出要约收购决定公告前一天收盘价的溢价为36.24%，美的的收购溢价基本在合理范围。

然而，从德国库卡2018年的财务数据看，德国库卡的净利润下滑81.2%，收入下降6%~8%，表现差强人意。短期来看，情况不容乐观。对于这笔收购成功与否，现在下结论还为时过早，还要看德国库卡公司未来几年的表现。这个案例也从另外一个侧面提示我们收购只是开始，更重要的是收购后的整合。关于投后整合我们会在下面的章节进一步讨论。

对于参与"一带一路"建设的投资者来说，估值是并购交易中不可或缺的一部分。选择哪种交易结构很大程度上取决于每笔交易对买方和卖方的价值。尽管卖方试图获得最高和最理想的价格，但买方需要进行彻底的尽职调查并评估每种情况的每个细节。一般来说，三个主要标准在决策中起着至关重要的作用：业务的未来前景，与特定业务、行业或国家相关的风险以及资本成本。

基于企业未来的前景做出的数值假设对企业未来现金流量的净现值的影响很大，某些重要参数的微小变化也会导致净现值出现较大的波动。对于贴现现金流量分析需考虑诸如收入、劳动力成本、利息支出、税收等多个敏感因素。因此，在做出假设时，该模型的每个因素的波动性和确定性无法完全考虑到。例如，拥有强大工会的国家劳动力成本可能增加，银行业环境不稳定或经济形势变化将导致利率上升，政府增加税收等。另外，中国投资者也应该考虑他们的收益如何在他们的国家得到处理，以及税收无法抵免的情况。

另一个无法完全量化的假设是与特定商业、行业或国家相关的风险。尽管像资产定价模型这样的一些方法提供了风险处理和评估的方法，但它是通用模型，并不总是适用于实践，特别是在不发达、不稳定的市场中，无风险折现率或系统风险无法正确测量。一些"一带一路"国家没有自己的股票市场或竞争性行业，在数学上对风险进行评估是不切实际的。

由于上述原因，"一带一路"投资者应不断努力形成定量估值模型，并需要相信自己的直觉，必须将理论知识应用于实践，并根据定量和推测性数据做出决策。为了做出成功的决策，投资者应该了解中国和目标企业所在国家之间的政治和经济关系，这两者之间的双边协议，中国对境外投资的税收规定，目标企业所在国家的经济和政治状况以及未来预测，特定行业特征和与商业相关的最重要的信息。只有将定量分析与上述理论知识结合，将科学与艺术结合，才能促成并购交易的成功评估和完成。

第六章

"一带一路"国家投资
并购的交易文件

第一节 交易文件代价不菲

资产和财富最终会呈现在法律文件上,本章将以并购交易的流程为时间轴,简要介绍在境外投资并购交易的整个流程中,收购方需要签署的主要法律文件。中国企业在境外进行投资并购时,花钱最多的往往是交易文件的制作。笔者亲历过的场景:为了关键的条款和定义,甚至是几个字的定语,双方律师唇枪舌剑,按小时收费的律师费账单数额惊人,一晚上数万元很正常。无论如何,笔者最终发现,跨国公司的交易风控体系实质上依赖于交易的法律顾问团队,通常就是"1~2位合伙人"+"1~2位资深律师"+"N位律师助理"的组合。财务顾问的风控意见最终也要在交易文件上体现。尤其是,购买方必须意识到并购可能存在风险,必须采取一切必要的措施来降低潜在风险,加强管理。

并购交易通常很重要,值得为量身定制一份合同一掷千金,因为合同中会涉及收购方的大量投资、对目标公司的控制权和所有权的变更,以及对卖方资产的重大变更。它不仅仅包括资产的集合,还有对业务的控制。并购交易通常会涉及各种资产:知识产权、不动产、监管许可。这种有形和无形资产组合的转让通常伴随着与各种个人的合同和非合同关系的变更或转让,从股东、董事、经理到员工和代理人,从客户和供应商到贷款人和监管机构,而且通常对收购方及其管理者的运营和声誉产生更大的影响。

典型的并购交易涉及的不是一个合同,而是一套合同。

最终顺利完成交易,双方需要签署一系列的法律文件。交易相关方需要签署的法律文件均可分为两大类:前期交易文件和后期交易文件。按重要性分类,也可以分为主交易文件和辅助性交易文件,主交易文件对开展主交易的条件、成交价格、交割方式等加以界定；而辅助性交易文件，则是一系列为配合主交易文件实现目的而签订的文件。上述所谓"主交易文件"和"辅助性交易文件"，具体而言应包括哪些文件，取决于交易目的、性质、对象、模式等因素。谈判阶段以签署买卖协议（SPA）为终点。签署后，开始准备交割，通常包括收集必要的法定和交易特定批准。

主交易文件和辅助性交易文件之间，围绕主交易的目的、逻辑、流程和关键节点等形成无缝的法律之环，且环环相扣。

一、生效或交割前提条件的设置

生效或交割前提条件的设置，即将某些法律文件的签署，或适当生效（如在一定时间内生效并持续有效等），或适当履行等（如出售方在特定时间内履行某些债权协议等），作为主交易文件生效或主交易文件下付款或交割的前提条件。

二、交叉违约条款或终止合约条款的设置

在相关法律文件之间设置交叉违约（cross-default）或交叉终止（cross termination）条款。这意味着，一旦某一方在某一法律文件或协议下出现违约，则应认为该方同时在相关联动的协议下也出现了违约行为，从而启动该联动协议下的违约救济条款。交叉终止条款的机制，与交叉违约的机制相同。

三、保持相关法律条款的一致性

在主交易文件和辅助性交易文件之间，注意保持关键法律条款的一致性。例如，除非特别必要，否则主交易文件与辅助性交易文件，在适用法律、争议解决方式等事项的约定上，应保持一致，以避免出现冲突或不一致。在这些关键事项上约定不一致，将可能导致交易一方在权利受损时无法得到实际的法律救济。

第二节 交割文件靠法律和财务尽职调查

本质上,投资并购的标的就是一辆"二手车",而且还在十万八千里之外,所以,要抱着不买的心态去端详才行。

尽职调查的目的概括起来就是"发现风险、量化风险、控制风险"。发现风险是尽职调查的第一要务。收购方应分析尽职调查报告揭示的风险,做出终止交易或继续交易的决定。如果继续交易,则通过设定先决条件、调整交易价格、设置托管账户,以及在交易文件中设置合理风险分配或损害赔偿机制,强化陈述和保证条款等方法来控制风险。看看央企中国交通建设股份有限公司(以下简称中国交建)如何买巴西的"二手车"。

案例6-1 中国交建收购巴西公司Concremat

交易金额:未披露

目标国家:巴西

行业:建筑

案例背景:2017年1月,中国交建成功收购了巴西Concremat公司80%的股权。Concremat是巴西乃至南美地区最大的工程设计咨询企业。

在收购Concremat过程中中方聘请Luis Berger公司为技术顾问,毕马威会计师事务所(以下简称毕马威)为财税顾问,Stocche Forbes公司为法律顾问,分别从技术、财税和法律三个方面对风险进行梳理,判断是否会出现deal breaker(阻止交易完成的重大风险)。若在尽职调查过程中没有发现deal breaker,下一步就要对既有的技术、财税和法律风险进行量化,用具体金额体现出来。量化风险后,就需要在交易文件中对风险进行控制。

案例分析:买方的尽职调查过程是全面审慎的。从团队组建、确定流程、执行尽职调查到出具报告，中介机构发挥了专业作用。

一、组建团队：先内后外

开展尽职调查前，首先要组织买方自己的尽职调查团队。除公司内部人员外，买方通常还会聘请外部专业顾问协助进行尽职调查。由于巴西官方语言为葡萄牙语，语言障碍明显，法律法规独具特色，税种繁多，计税方法尤其复杂，买方聘用了对当地情况最了解的巴西律师事务所，毕马威的巴西团队及 Luis Berger 的南美当地团队做外部顾问，以求尽职调查的高效和彻底。

二、确定流程：系统针对

通常卖方会向买方开放网上资料室。除此之外，买方也可以主动拟定信息需求清单，明确向卖方提出所需要的信息，使尽职调查更具针对性。如有必要，买方还会进行现场尽职调查，包括高管访谈和项目现场调查。对 Concremat 公司的尽职调查也基本按照上述流程进行。

三、执行尽职调查：全面覆盖

（一）技术尽职调查

技术尽职调查包含行业、人力资源、技术、经营四部分。

（二）财税尽职调查

财税尽职调查包括财务、税务和劳工三方面。

财务部分包括财务报表（包括资产负债表、损益表、现金流量表，均为剥离后）及各项体现经营情况的指标（流动比率、债务股本比、股本回报率等）。

（三）法律尽职调查

股权架构、合同情况（设计咨询合同、投资协议、保险合同）、诉讼情况（民事、环境、税务及劳工诉讼）、所有权益（不动产、知识产权）、反垄断审批。

一、法律尽职调查

专业的人做专业的事，法律尽职调查更是如此。尽职调查的英文是 Due

Diligence，字面意思看就是"适当的勤奋"，即在任何情况下，律师都有必要勤奋地进行全面细致的尽职调查。尽职调查的范围取决于几个因素，如交易的规模、交易的保密性、业务归属的行业和当事人的配合程度。尽职调查过程通常由内部项目团队推动外聘律师来执行。例如，在收购中，律师将准备交易文件，并且条款、条件、陈述、保证和免责声明的范围必须根据尽职调查的结果进行调整。

在一个典型的法律尽职调查中，律师将起草并提交一份针对每个交易的初步调查清单。一位经验丰富、知识渊博的律师对调查的反应，在可能需要彻底审查的潜在关键问题上做出的结论或给出的建议是无价之宝。尽职调查的全面清单也有助于将提供文件或信息的人的注意力集中在一起，并减少监督的可能性。具体来说，尽职调查的用途又因卖方视角、买方视角、律师视角的不同而不同，中国买家一般面对的是买方做尽职调查。

在庞杂的尽职调查信息面前，任何专业人士都会不知所措，委托方必须与尽职调查团队一起去发现风险，与此同时，也会发现价值。即：（1）是否存在影响交易不能进行的重大法律风险；（2）是否存在对交易的估值或其他交易条件有重大影响的重大法律风险。因此，法律尽职调查是交易流程中很重要的一环，它为买方的商业决策和交易条件的谈判提供重要依据。

（一）法律尽职调查的受限制因素

法律尽职调查并非"火眼金睛"，法律尽职调查工作有四个方面的局限。

1. 认知障碍

法律尽职调查的目的是发现过去和现在的"重大性"的风险，然而，符合"重大性"标准的事项发生风险，往往在调查期间看不出来。2004年上海汽车集团股份有限公司收购韩国双龙汽车最终导致巨额亏损就是典型案例，尽职调查中关于韩国工会对投后整合的重大障碍缺乏认识。

2. 时空倒逼

实践中，进行法律尽职调查的时间极其有限，无论是内部决策还是政府审批，给拟定调查报告的时间都比较紧张，如何在短时间内尽快抓住重点，成为买方面临的重要问题。因此，法律尽职调查更多要仰仗经验丰富的中介机构。2016年光大资本投资有限公司联合暴风集团股份有限公司以43.88亿元人民币收购意大利体育传媒公司MP & Silva（以下简称MPS）65%股权，2019年发生重大风险就是典型案例。

3. 成本受限

海外并购最大的中介机构开支就是律师费，很多民营企业不太愿意支付高昂的法律尽职调查费用。毕竟企业的成本预算是有限的，而国有企业，预算审批有规范的流程。如果涉及费用上调，就想方设法控制尽职调查的工作量。

4. 方法单一

法律尽职调查是以审阅卖方提供的文件为主的工作，由于跨境并购距离遥远，文件极多，实务中通行的做法是由卖方开放数据库（DATA ROOM），供尽职调查律师审阅其中的扫描文件。面对巨大的文件数据处理，难免会有疏漏。

（二）法律尽职调查的一般关注点

海外尽职调查既然受限不少，根据其难点和特点，一般情况下尽职调查内容的关注点在：股权结构和股东权益、重大合同、质押、劳工情况、知识产权和专有技术、纳税情况。

1. 股权结构和股东权益

目标公司的股权结构和股东持股情况是尽职调查的一项最基本的内容。2016年，笔者主导了对一家海外金融科技公司D轮投资的尽职调查。对方提供股权文件（股东名册等）后，笔者最关心的是前面三轮投资者的情况。背后的逻辑是，如果前三轮投资者都是专注于金融科技的头部基金，后续投资则更多地会关心估值。通过查阅其董事会会议记录，笔者发现给团队股权激励是需要董事会认可的。另外，与中国公司不同，不少国家的公司的股东权益有多样化安排，这些公司往往发行了一系列权利交错的优先股（Preferred Shares）、可转股债权（Convertible Bonds）、权证、期权等。在公司对外出售股权时，优先股股东往往享有很大的权利包括否决权，在利益分配上也享有各种优先权。如果投资并购谈判的对象是目标公司的管理层或创始人，他们往往不持有优先股，收购方更应审阅公司章程、股东协议等文件，了解各个股东的权利和利益，以避免任何股东挑战交易的合法公平性，使得交易无法进行或增加收购成本。

2. 重大合同

尽职调查的另一项重要内容是目标公司将要或者正在履行的重大合同。尽职调查需要审查目标公司已经履行完毕的合同是否存在潜在的争议。比如，笔者曾经看到过采购合同上约定"以买方满意为支付余款的条件"，这样就会带来应收账款的风险。投融资、采购、销售和技术方面的重大合同也都是尽职调查的重点。收购方在发现问题时，若有必要，可要求目标公司与各合同当事方及时沟通。

3. 质押

质押包括抵押和不动产。西方国家有着成熟、完善、权威的查询系统，质押和抵押可以通过支付较少的费用由第三方专业机构根据收购方的要求完成基本的查询工作。但是，部分"一带一路"国家没有权威的查询系统，对相关的尽职调查买方必须高度重视。对于投资不动产，如涉及敏感地区，有时必须进行实地考察。以澳大利亚农田投资并购案为例，因为某外国公司收购的不动产的位置距离澳大利亚军事基地较近，澳大利亚的外资投资审查委员会（FIRB）便以国家安全为由要求拆分该部分资产甚至否决整个交易。如果早做实地考察，可以避免这种结果。

4. 劳工情况

很多国家的劳工法律纷繁复杂，需对工会、集体合同、养老金、员工福利等问题进行详细的评估，充分了解收购后的经营成本和风险。比如，并购法国企业，对解聘员工有严格的限制。笔者在布鲁塞尔的隆路国际律师事务所实习时，发现不少欧盟国家有罢工期间照常给员工发工资的法律规定。另外，目标公司的高管往往以各种形式持有公司权益，一旦发生收购行为，这些期权或股权可能会加速实现，有可能导致收购成本的增加。

5. 知识产权和专有技术

中国企业在很多海外并购中看重对方的知识产权。光大资本、暴风集团海外并购折戟，从媒体披露的情况看，MPS的主要版权资源在2018年至2021年到期，核心资产意甲的版权在2018年到期，英超的版权在2019年到期，而且现有的版权合约中存在大量未付版权费的问题。上述事实对MPS经营有着重大影响，直接导致了MPS被债权人申请破产，这些问题应该在尽职调查阶段被发现并被进行重点讨论。目前无法得知并购基金聘请的专业机构是否发现上述问题以及并购基金对该类问题的风险判断和决策过程。

以上案例说明，知识产权的地域性较强，收购方需要根据其收购的目的、涉及技术的性质等判断是否仅对重点市场（如欧美地区）进行查询。必要时，还需要专利律师、代理机构人员、评估机构人员、内部的技术人员等组成团队进行评估。

6. 纳税情况

税务尽职调查通常着重审阅目标公司税收是否合规、是否存在税务处理方面的未决事项和潜在风险因素。税务尽职调查可以发现潜在的致命税务缺陷，判断是否要继续交易进程。不少"一带一路"国家税收合规做得并不理想。笔者曾经接触的某南美国家，据说该国国内企业普遍存在税收合规风险，如果中国企业在并购标的公司后不萧规曹随，盈利情况会大幅下降。通过税务尽职调查可以发现目标公司的税收环境和税负水平，分析目标公司真实的盈利能力、现金流，揭示目标公司存在的税务风险和潜在问题。

总之，对于尽职调查中发现的问题和风险，收购方可以采取多种措施，包括要求对方在签约前予以更正，在交易文件中做出陈述与保证，或作为交割的先决条件。对于风险不确定的事项，可考虑由一流的律师事务所出具法律意见书。在支付条款方面，也可通过分期付款、延期支付（Holdback）、账户监管甚至对赌条款等方式控制风险。风险控制条款的设计应根据尽职调查的结果和交易的相关情况调整。

案例 6-2 三胞集团收购以色列家政护理公司

交易金额：未披露

目标国家：以色列

行业：健康

案例背景：从 2014 年开始，三胞集团及旗下企业陆续发起了一系列海外并购：三胞集团旗下南京新街口百货商店股份有限公司（简称南京新百）收购英国老牌百货集团 House of Fraser；三胞集团收购以色列最大的养老服务企业 Natali，收购美国上市公司麦考林，收购在美国拥有近 300 家门店的专业新奇特连锁 Brookstone。2015 年，三胞集团控股的宏图高科收购港交所主板上市公司、营销网络遍布全球的女性新奇特产品专业提供商万威国际。近期，三胞集团又收购了以色列最大的家政护理公司 A.S.Nursing Company。至此，三胞集团的商业版图愈加全球化。

案例分析：该并购涉及的主要风险有如下两个。

（1）三胞集团的诉讼风险。报告期内，三胞集团及其子公司涉及多项未决诉讼。原告当事人有个人、企业和工会组织，诉讼请求包括报酬索赔、人身损害赔偿等方面。其中，三胞集团及其子公司所涉及的个别诉讼金额较大。卖方方面，以色列劳工组织 Yadid Association 对包括 A.S.Nursing Company 在内的以色列 20 家护理公司所提起的集体诉讼。以色列集体诉讼流程漫长，诉讼通常持续数月甚至数年。虽然相关诉讼信息已在报告书中详细披露，但考虑到法律诉讼的持续影响，倘若不能合理有效地处理相关问题，将会对三胞集团的经营发展产生一定风险。

（2）三胞集团在以色列租赁房产不能续租的风险。报告期内，三胞集团主要的经营场所均为租赁取得，全部用于办公、仓储、培训等需求。截至 2016 年 9 月 30 日，三胞集团及其子公司存在多处租赁合同即将到期的情况。根据以色列本地关于房屋租赁的法律法规，房屋租赁合同到期后，在出租人和租房者协商同意的条件下，可以自动续租，直到一方不再认同房屋租赁关系。虽然根据三胞集团的子公司 Natali 和 A.S.Nursing Company 多年的经营经验，房屋租赁情况并未对其生产经营产生较大影响，但如果三胞集团出现大量不能续租的房屋，将可能对三胞集团的日常经营造成影响。

二、财务尽职调查

财务尽职调查能够帮助买方尽快熟悉境外目标公司的财务情况，合理估计目标公司的价值，从而为竞标及谈判做好充分准备，并帮助其预判交易完成后投后管理的财务和业务整合事项。财务尽职调查已成为几乎所有投资并购业务交易在签订协议前应谨慎行事的共同事项。每项投资都有其自身的风险水平，如果没有深入的研究，投资者可能无法正确理解风险。

海外并购的标的如果是资产，比如从澳大利亚农民手里买块地，财务尽职调查就不重要，但是，在"二手车"股权投资中，必须通过财务尽职调查搞清楚交易的财务风险，并根据风险程度及性质的不同，采取合适的应对策略。

笔者对 2017 年经历的一次财务尽职调查印象非常深刻，这家企业在"一带一路"国家投资经营，财务尽职调查涉及对印度及其他海外市场销售以及销售预测的数据。如果只看历史数据，也许可以认可公司销售有增长。但是，当笔者要求调阅所有海外合同，仔细查阅合同条款，就发现历史增长并不能印证销售预测的假设：2018 年海外市场销售收入占据总销售收入的一半。而且，最大的挑战是海外业务毛利只有国内业务的一半左右，这就意味着产品在海外卖得越多，利润增长越慢。2019 年，其公开的《招股说明书》证实我两年前的判断，摘要如下：从客户所在地来看，公司报告期内主营业务收入主要来源于境内客户，近三年来海外客户销售收入占主营业务收入比例分别为××、××和××，海外客户销售收入占比逐年下降。

案例 6-3　三胞集团的汇率风险

> 外汇风险。本次交易完成后，标的公司的日常运营中将涉及美元、以色列新谢克尔等外币，而本公司的合并报表记账本位币为人民币。如果未来我国汇率政策发生重大变化或者未来人民币兑外币汇率出现大幅波动，三胞集团可能面临一定的汇率波动风险。

系统化的财务尽职调查流程有助于确保买家不被蒙在鼓里。尽职调查的基本考虑事项有如下几个。

收入、利润和利润趋势：数据中有最近的趋势吗？上升，下降，稳定？

市场竞争对手和行业：研究和比较竞争对手的利润，了解目标公司究竟如何。

管理和所有权：研究公司的经营者，即谁在经营？

资产负债表分析：分析负债与权益比率。公司负债太多了吗？

风险：了解整个行业和公司特定的风险。是否存在突出的风险？

预期：未来的利润估计是多少？

从交易实践来看，财务尽职调查重在发现风险和价值，能够帮助买方尽快熟悉境外目标公司的财务情况，合理估计目标公司的价值，从而为竞标及谈判做好充分准备。它会帮助买方预判交易完成后投后管理的财务和业务整合事项。

财务尽职调查主要包括以下五个关键因素。

（一）终止交易

如目标公司业务环境发生重大变化，最新数据与初始信息相差较大，预测收入、利润率等财务指标不太可能实现。笔者曾参与一个项目，当时笔者要求调出公司所有涉及国际市场的合同，笔者发现未来增长的预测根本没有基础，并且尾款存在不能收回的风险。

（二）估值调整

即使是欧洲、美国的海外标的基础财务信息质量比较好，也会出现严重会计差错。光大资本在暴风集团并购案中的失误就是典型案例，事实上，体育传媒公司MP&Silva（MPS）的65%股权根本不值47亿元。有些"一带一路"国家，标的隐藏了重大财务风险，因此需要通过仔细的财务尽职调查确定可持续的盈利水平，作为估值计算的基础。

（三）交易保护

在尽职调查过程中，可能会发现一些或有负债及承诺事项有发生风险，这种可能具有不确定性，无法直接进行价格调整，但购买方需要在股权购买合同中约定相关条款来保护己方。例如，为避免税收方面的潜在风险，买方要约定条款，在约定期间内目标公司发生任何交易时间前的税务追索成本，均由卖出方承担。但是，如果风险发生在交易款已经全部付清后，只能通过法律手段主张权利了。

（四）价格调整

在海外并购中，欧美卖方一般不接受业绩对赌机制，境外卖方通常会要求诸如运营资金调价机制、净资产调价机制、锁盒（Locked Box）等其他价格调整机制。这些对于估值日和交割日之间的价格调节机制，中介机构需要通过财务尽职调查详细分析测算。买方也可以通过分期付款机制降低价格，减少风险。

（五）投后整合

这是中国买方最缺失的能力，在财务尽职调查过程中中介机构要协助买方分析交易后的整合事项，但是，有些方面，如过渡期IT系统的花费等，这些中介机构也不一定熟悉，购买方交易团队需要全面关注。

对于暂时处于财务困境的目标公司，财务尽职调查还会关注与企业重组有关的问题（如员工养老金、关厂成本等），目标公司在债务重组及交易后的未来几年内的资金需求，从而判断是否需要后续投资。

第三节　前期交易文件

由于收购方投入的人力、物力、财力相对较大，承担的风险也较大，出售方也担心信息保密的问题，为使双方获得具有法律约束力的保障，最常用到的文件包括保密协议、条款清单等。

一、保密协议/保密承诺函

在交易的初始阶段，因标的资产、股权或业务等的拥有人，或目标公司的股东等（以下统称为"出售方"）需向收购方披露有关交易标的的相关信息。因此，按照惯例，在该出售方披露相关信息前，出售方会要求签署保密协议等。对披露信息保密的义务涉及：将机密信息的使用限制在特定目的，规定向第三方披露的条款和责任，共同投资者、银行和其他金融机构、顾问和董事会、监管机构、法院和法律或证券交易所规定要求的其他披露等。

案例 6-4　保密协议模板

保 密 协 议

披露方：　　　　　　　　　　　接受方：
注册地址：　　　　　　　　　　注册地址：
法定代表人/授权代表人：　　　法定代表人/授权代表人：
本协议由披露方与接受方在友好协商的基础上，因特别的目的达成如下保密协议。

定义和解释

本协议中，除非上下文另有规定，以下词语具有下列含义：

（1）披露方：指披露保密信息的一方，在本协议中指甲方。同时也包括甲方的附属公司，关联方是指，就任何人而言，直接或间接通过一个或多个中间人控制、被该人控制或与该人处于共同控制之下的任何其他人；"控制"（包括"控制""被控制"和"与共同控制"）是指直接或间接拥有，指通过拥有有表决权的证券、通过合同或其他方式指导或促使指导某人的管理和政策的权力。对某人的提及包括公司、信托、合伙企业、非法人团体或其他实体，无论其是否包括一个单独的法律实体。

（2）保密信息：指披露方披露的，无论是以口头、书面、电子或其他任何媒介方式出现的，与披露方商务、运营、技术、财务等有关的一切资料，包括但不限于营销计划、商业或财务资料、贸易信息、合同、技术知识、法律文件、产品演示、产品原型、模型、样品、方法、规格、专有数据、软件程序、软件源文件和公式等以及其他一切与披露方有关的资料。此外，披露方与接受方双方讨论和谈判等正在发生或计划中的事实、状态和谈判各方的信息以及根据本协议做出的总结、分析、会议纪要等也均属于保密信息。

（3）接受方：指根据披露方许可接受保密信息的一方，在本协议中指乙方。同时也包括乙方的关联成员及职员，即与乙方及乙方任何一方有关的所有董事、顾问、官员、职工、雇员、法律顾问、财务顾问或其他形式的所有有关人员等。

（4）确定目标：指针对披露方、接受方双方就事宜而进行的相互讨论、通信、谈判直至本协议涵盖的业务或者交易达成约束性协议。

任何由披露方提供或披露的包含有保密信息的所有材料，包括但不限于文件、手册、说明书、流程图、项目列表和数据文件的电子稿、打印稿、复印件、备份文件等（以下简称材料）应当是，且将一直是披露方的财产，披露方享有唯一所有权。本协议不构成披露方对接受方的任何独家权利，披露方提供保密信息不意味着转让信息上的任何权利，也不形成披露方对接受方的任何要约和承诺，接受方不得将保密信息用于任何权利之注册或登记。

接受方同意并承诺，对披露方披露的保密信息实行严格保密责任，采取一切可行的手段保护保密信息的安全，避免保密信息的泄露。接受方未经披露方事先书面同意，只能按照本协议约定的确定目标去使用披露方的保密信息和材料，不得为其他任何目的而使用、披露、交流保密信息的全部或部分内容，不得以任何方式将该保密信息的任何方面泄露或透露给任何人。

接受方采取前项保密措施所赋予的注意程度与谨慎防范措施应不低于接受方对自己类似保密信息保护所赋予的最高注意程度，对披露方向接受方透露的包含保密信息的任何资料或数据，予以严格保密。

接受方承诺在其发现存在不当使用或不当处置披露方保密信息等违反本保密协议的行为情况时，应立即以书面形式通知披露方，并同意按照披露方的要求协助披露方处理上述情况。

接受方为实施确定目标的需要，经披露方事先书面同意，可以向接受方的相关人员披露保密信息，但披露的信息和人员都必须严格受限于"有获知的必要"的原则。在保密信息披露前，接受方应以书面形式向披露方提供上述拟获悉保密信息人员的名单，并需与以上所有人员签订保密协议，且该等人员所负的保密义务程度不得低于接受方在本协议中应负的保密义务。经接受方披露获悉保密信息的相关人员不得再将保密信息向任何其他人员披露。

如接受方与第三方订立有专有信息交换协议，并且该协议的条款和条件的严格程度不低于本协议，接受方应将该专有信息交换协议提交披露方，并应在取得披露方的事先书面同意后才能向前述第三方披露保密信息。

本协议中的任何内容都不应被视为授予或许可接受方任何有关秘密信息的权利，也不应被视为披露方有义务授权或许可接受方或任何其他实体为本协议所约定确定目标以外的任何目的使用保密信息。

在披露方与接受方就确定目标（包括但不限于项目信息、合作方式、投资金额、信息披露等）达成一致意见之前，任何一方均不得宣称或披露双方就此项目进行合同的意向或任何其他合作信息。

披露方对披露的保密信息的准确性和完整性不负有保证义务，也没有及时更新保密信息的义务，接受方利用披露方披露的保密信息进行商业行为或其他任何行为，给披露方、接受方或任何第三方造成损失的或引起任何第三人主张权利的，由接受方自行承担责任。本协议所约定的确定目标未完成或本协议终止后，接受方应依照披露方的指示，立即返还或永久性销毁从披露方处取得的所有包含保密信息的任何材料，包括但不限于保存在任何介质中的保密信息的任何原件、复印件、重印件、复制品、备份件（包括计算机系统自动进行的备份）、衍生资料（包括但不限于基于保密信息做成的汇报、报告、PPT、会议纪要等资料）或者记录和笔记（包括对秘密信息的任何分析），并在本协议终止后的五日内由接受方负责人向披露方书面证实其对本条款的遵守。如接受方未销毁或未完全销毁并由此给披露方造成损害的，由接受方承担由此产生的一切责任。

如本协议约定的确定目标完成，接受方在披露方事先书面允许的范围内保留保密信息或含有保密信息的材料，确保不向任何第三方透露。

接受方同意，为保护披露方及其业务，本协议规定的接受方的义务都是必须的且合理的。接受方明确同意，如果接受方违反本协议的任何约定，或因接受方的原因导致本协议项下的保密信息被任何第三方获知，则接受方应当赔偿披露方由此遭受的所有损失，包括但不限于任何直接的或/及间接的，有形的或/及无形的财产或/及非财产方面的损失，以及披露方因调查接受方的违约行为而支付的合理的律师费等损失。接受方对因其职员、顾问、银行等任何相关人员而造成的任何保密信息泄露承担责任。

本合同的订立、效力、解释、履行及争议解决等问题均受中华人民共和国法律、法规管辖并依其解释。双方对本协议有关条款产生的争议，或任何因本协议引起的或与之相关的争议，包括本协议的存续、有效性或终止有关的争议，合同双方应当努力协商解决。如协商不果，则合同任何一方有权将争议事项提请中国国际贸易仲裁委员会进行仲裁，并按该会在仲裁当时有效的仲裁规则裁决。仲裁裁决对双方均有约束力。

如果本协议中的任何条款成为或被作为无效或不能强制履行，所有其余条款仍然具有法律效力。

本协议经甲乙双方签字并盖章后即时生效，有效期为叁年。

本协议一式两份，甲乙双方各执一份。

甲方（签字并盖章）　　　　　　　　乙方（签字并盖章）
法定代表人/委托代理人　　　　　　　法定代表人/委托代理人
签字　　　　　　　　　　　　　　　签字
　年　　月　　日　　　　　　　　　　年　　月　　日

二、投标文件/报价函

在许多并购交易中，出售方为了争取到最好的出价，通过招标或竞争性谈判的方式选择收购方。国际市场上许多著名的交易，以及我们作为律师处理过的多起交易，均是通过此种方式进行的。在此种交易方式下，收购方需要向出售方提交投标文件（针对较为正式的招标程序而言），或约束性报价函（对一般的竞争性谈判等而言）。上述文件的共同性在于，就其法律性质而言，其均为收购方提出的要约，在该文件的有效期内，其对收购方自身有法律约束力，如交易价。当然，买方也会在此函件里约定一系列常规的前提条件，降低自身的交易风险。

三、保证金协议

有时，出售方会以收购人/报价人提交一定金额的保证金为前提条件，向相关报价人开放一定时长（如1～3个月等）的独家谈判期。此时，双方就有必要签署一份保证金协议。在该保证金协议中，须清楚界定保证金的性质、保证金返还的条件、独家谈判期的时长和结束条件等。没有海外并购经验的中国国有企业，要签订这样的协议，涉及决策流程的挑战，毕竟在交易尚未明晰的情况下，要支付一笔费用。

四、条款清单

交易双方经常谈判到深夜的条款清单是并购交易的惯例内容，一旦交易双方进入相对实质性的谈判阶段后，双方对交易的具体商务条件，如交易价格、付款安排、交割条件等事项进行谈判，并以"条款清单"的方式将双方商务人员达成的共识予以条款化以便在正式合同中直接套用。因其重要性，双方律师会深度参与条款清单的谈判和草拟，因为条款清单是整个交易中非常关键的文件之一。但通常而言，条款清单并非正式的合同，并无法律约束力。

相比于同样不具有法律约束力的意向书，二者主要的不同点在于：意向书的记录一般较为笼统模糊，而条款清单对于商务条件的描述通常是非常清晰具体的，初具主交易文件的雏形。条款清单是买方在完成初步尽职调查后提供的更正式的文件。条款清单通常概述了提议报价的要点，包括具体条款、交易结构和提议的时间安排。它们表示买方希望进入一个专属期，在额外尽职调查和满足某些条件的情况下完成交易。

案例 6-5　条款清单实例

项目条款清单

年　月　日

本条款清单旨在列明（购买方）与（出售方）手中收购　　　　的意向性条款和条件。

本条款清单的条款和条件将在经过各方协商一致后达成的有法律约束力的最终协议（以下简称最终协议）中体现。本条款清单仅表达了各方的意向，不能视作是约束性协议或谅解，除第 8 条至第 12 条对各方有约束力并将在本条款清单终止后继续有效外，其余条款均不构成对各方有法律约束力的义务。

一、拟议交易

购买方将指定一家为＿＿＿＿，根据最终协议的条款和条件，从出售方手中收购（第2条所述的）物业（"交易"）。

在签署本条款清单后，各方意图继续尽最大努力、秉持善意的原则进行协商，以期尽快达成与本条款清单的内容一致的最终协议。

二、物业

出售资产将包括下列资产的权属、权利：

三、价格

物业的购买价格为＿＿＿＿，由购买方与出售方在尽职调查完成后根据尽职调查的结果确认。

四、先决条件

各方应当就交易交割前的各项事务和交割的先决条件进行协商，该等先决条件应包括但不限于以下：

（1）购买方尽职调查已完成，且满意；

（2）购买方应已就交易取得所在国政府审批；

（3）购买方应已就交易取得所有中国政府审批和内部审批；

（4）物业未发生任何重大不利变化且出售方在最终协议下做出的陈述与保证在签署日和交易交割时均真实、准确且完整。

五、保证和赔偿

出售方的陈述与保证应包含性质与本类交易相同的交易下惯常所见的陈述与保证。该等陈述与保证应于签署有约束力的最终协议时做出并生效，并在交易交割时依然保持真实、准确。

最终协议应当包含出售方和购买方惯常应承担的赔偿责任。

六、信息开放

出售方应允许购买方的代表（包括法律顾问、财务人员、技术团队和环境顾问）进入物业并及时提供所有合理要求的文件和信息以便购买方完成必要的调研，包括但不限于对物业开展的尽职调查。

七、成本和费用

各方同意各自承担其因准备、协商和签署本条款清单而发生的成本和费用。

八、保密

由一方("披露方")在本条款清单下或基于此或在协商期间向另一方("接收方")披露的所有信息，均构成披露方的保密信息。

除用于为记录或实施交易所必要的用途("批准用途")外，接收方不得为其他目的使用或复制该等信息。

接收方不得将该等信息披露给任何人士，但以下情况除外：

（1）向接收方或其关联法人的雇员、法律顾问、审计师或其他顾问在"需要知道"的限度内所做的披露，但前提是该等人士不得在批准用途以外使用、披露或复制该等信息；

（2）经披露方同意的披露；

（3）在法律或与本条款清单相关的法律程序要求的情况下，在必要的限度内所做的披露；

（4）信息非因接收方违反对披露方的保密义务而归属或进入公共范畴。

各方应根据本条的规定，将本条款清单的存在和其中的条款视为另一方的保密信息对待。

九、排他

出售方不得（直接或间接）就交易或与处置物业相关的其他潜在交易，邀请、发起、征求、接受或继续与其他方的洽询、讨论或提案，并同意仅与购买方就同类交易接洽，以及在其接收到有关该类交易的任何收购意向、信息请求或其他性质的要约或请求的情况下将相关情况告知购买方。

排他期为自本条款清单签署之日起的6个月。作为出售方同意排他谈判的对价，购买方同意在签署本条款清单之日向出售方一次性支付一笔不可退的金额为＿＿的费用。出售方在此认可并确认该笔费用构成促使其履行其在本条款清单项下义务的有价值且充分的对价。

十、生效及终止

本条款清单经签署生效并于排他期届满时自动终止。

十一、可分割性

本条款清单应被视为是可分割的,如果任何条款被认为是无效或不可执行的。

十二、适用法律和管辖

本条款清单应适用××国现行有效的法律。

各方服从该地区法院的非专属管辖权。

兹证明,各方代表于文首日期签署本条款清单。

第四节　正式交易文件

案例6-6　江苏鱼跃医疗设备股份有限公司关于参股美诺医疗集团有限公司（Amsino Medical）暨关联交易进展的公告

投资协议的主要内容

一、交易主体

投资方：江苏鱼跃科技发展有限公司（简称鱼跃科技）、江苏鱼跃医疗设备股份有限公司（简称鱼跃医疗）。

其他签署方：<u>Amsino Medical Group Company Limited</u>（简称Amsino Medical）、<u>Richwell Assets Limited</u>、<u>Richard Ya Lee</u>。

二、投资方式与框架

（1）鱼跃科技和鱼跃医疗（以下简称鱼跃方）与标的公司、标的公司创始股东签署协议,按照每股1.538 2美元的认购价格,分别以现金方式向标的公司增资1 327.368 2万美元,总计增资金额2 654.736 4万美元。

（2）本次投资完成后,鱼跃科技持有标的公司8 629 255股普通股,占标的公司所有已发行普通股数的19.33%,鱼跃医疗持有标的公司 8 629 256 股普通股，占标的公司所有已发行普通股数的 19.33%。

（3）本次投资完成后鱼跃方将持有公司的普通股。投资后，公司股份结构如下：

序号	股东名称	股份类型	股份数	占比
1	Richwell Assets Limited	普通股	15 824 912	35.45%
2	Richard Ya Lee	普通股	9 681 156	21.69%
3	鱼跃医疗	普通股	8 629 256	19.33%
4	鱼跃科技	普通股	8 629 255	19.33%
5	其他股东	普通股	1 873 780	4.20%
合计			44 638 359	100.00%

注：根据相关协议，标的公司应当在鱼跃方认购款金额支付后的 30 个自然日内完成优先股回购，本次投资完成后标的公司将无优先股。

三、条件与交割

（一）投资条件

只有当下述每一项交割条件均得以满足（或被鱼跃方书面豁免）的前提下，鱼跃科技和鱼跃医疗才有义务向公司支付认购款的全部金额：

（1）公司已经在签署日取得和完成为签署和履行本协议和其他交易文件一切必要的内部同意、批准、授权和其他行动。

（2）公司、创始股东在本协议、鱼跃方认购普通股相关协议中做出的所有陈述和保证在所有方面应真实、准确且不具误导性。

（3）优先股回购补充协议在签署日经公司与优先股股东正式签署并生效。

（4）创始股东、公司已经与鱼跃方就鱼跃认购款经修改与重述的公司章程条款达成一致。

（5）截至鱼跃方支付认购款之日，未发生任何导致公司无法继续经营的重大事件，或禁止本次投资或使得本次投资非法或无效的任何适用法律、法院判决或政府命令。

（6）认购文件中列出（除以上投资条件以外）的其他交割条件，为免疑义，如认购文件的交割条件比上述投资条件有更详细约定的，以认购文件的交割条件为准。

（二）投资交割

（1）在公司签署投资协议后最晚于2017年5月30日之前，且在本协议设定的先决条件全部满足的情况下，鱼跃方将一次性向公司支付鱼跃认购款的全部金额。

（2）公司应当在认购款支付后的30个自然日内完成优先股回购，并且在优先股回购完成后5个自然日内完成股份交割手续以及相应的商业登记变更手续（包括但不限于公司股份、股东以及董事会成员变更登记）。各方在此同意，股份交割取决于以下每一条件的满足（除非鱼跃方书面同意豁免）：

①鱼跃方向公司发出股份交割通知；

②优先股股东持有的公司股份已经完全被公司回购；

③公司和创始股东在本协议中做出的所有陈述和保证截至股份交割之日在所有方面应真实、准确且不具误导性。

④公司和创始股东在交易文件下无任何违约。

⑤公司、创始股东和公司的其他股东已经批准就股份交割后经修改与重述的公司章程，以及其他相关股东权利文件。

⑥本交割条款所有条件满足时，公司将立即向鱼跃方发行本协议约定数量的普通股，并相应更新公司股东名册。

四、公司治理

在本次投资交割之后，公司的董事会应由五（5）名董事组成，其中创始股东有权委派三（3）名董事，鱼跃科技与鱼跃医疗各自有权分别委派一（1）名董事。公司董事长和CEO由Richard Ya Lee担任。

一、主交易文件

主交易文件可以是股权转让协议、资产转让协议、业务转让协议、增资协议等。主交易文件是整个交易中最为关键的法律文件。通常而言，主交易文件中最为重要的条款为：卖方的陈述与保证、交割前提条件、卖方责任限制等。

在主交易文件签署阶段，还包括签署主交易文件后，立即采取的某些措施，通常在签署主交易文件前很长时间就开始准备。这些措施不仅包括努力获得足够的资金以支付给卖方，还包括实际转让的必要步骤以及准备法定/监管文件。

（一）卖方的陈述与保证

卖方的陈述与保证，是指卖方保证销售的对象没有"缺陷"。在股权交易文件签署日，对于目标公司的权属、公司记录、财务、税务、重大合同、不动产、重大设备、知识产权、合规、诉讼（包括非诉讼的争议和调查程序）、披露信息等方面做出的陈述与保证。除非另行说明的情况，卖方通常会在交割日重复做出同样的陈述与保证。卖方违反陈述与保证的后果通常是买方有权要求卖方赔偿损失。

卖方陈述保证大多是补充尽职调查不能解决的风险，尽职调查普遍不能覆盖每个方面，比如说知识产权不能被验证，还有合规性问题，如数据保护，反腐败（FCPA）等。

（二）交割前提条件

通过尽职调查而获知的风险，不能通过陈述与保证来解决，而是要设置卖方交割前的义务。交割前提条件，一般简称为交割条件，在股权转让协议签署之后，是否进行股权的交割（股权转让和价款支付），取决于若干先决条件得到满足或豁免，这些条件就是交割条件。

交割通常受制于某些交割条件，这些条件可能是交易特定的和/或法律要求的。常见的先决条件包括：政府审批（包括中国政府境外投资审批和目标国政府的审批）；重大合同的相对方对于交易的同意（如能源类项目中，购电协议下购电方的同意）、重大不利影响等。

例如，法定/监管条件尤其是并购控制批准、监管批准，特别是交易监管部门的批准等。例如，非欧盟/欧洲自由贸易区买家收购德国公司25%的股份也须经德国经济和技术部批准。

交易的特定条件可以是第三方放弃因控制权变更（股权交易）而终止重大合同的权利，第三方同意转让重大合同或资产（资产交易），卖方完成重大准备行动等。如果约定的期限内这些条件还没被满足或豁免，那么任何一方都可以终止协议，且双方互相不承担责任（约定分手费或反向分手费的情况除外）。相反，如果条件如期满足，则双方有义务必须按合同约定进行交割。

（三）卖方责任限制

赔偿条款与买方知情关联。买方的知情通常会免除卖方的责任。因此，卖方最好的准备是在签署前适当披露。尽职调查过程中因披露而产生的"认定知情"是否排除责任取决于达成的协议。

最低起赔限额：买方索赔金额只有达到一定最低额才有资格获得赔偿。总索赔需要超过某个阈值，可以是免赔额形式，卖方只需赔偿超过阈值的金额；或者卖方必须赔偿包括阈值金额在内的全部损失。

赔偿的最高限额：卖方责任的总体限制，是指卖方全部赔偿责任不超过一定限额，一般而言，按购买对价设定一定比例。

赔偿的期限限制：买方必须在期限内进行索赔，否则不能再进行索赔，买方通常被要求以书面形式通知卖方赔偿，不得无故拖延。

二、托管账户协议

为保证主交易文件下相关付款的安全和正常进行，交易各方通常会通过设立托管账户的方式来安排付款。由此，交易各方就需要与各自选定的账户托管人共同签署适当的《托管账户协议》。在《托管账户协议》中，应有托管账户的设立条件、托管银行（或其他托管人）将相应款项支付给出售方的具体条件和节点等事项。

三、商标／技术授权使用协议、商标／技术转让协议等

如主交易的性质为业务转让，则通常会涉及商标和／或技术授权使用协议、商标和／或技术转让协议等。通过签署此类协议，收购方可获得为运营目标业务而必需的针对相关商标或技术的使用权或其他权利。

四、原股东协议之补充协议

如主交易的性质为股权转让或增资行为，则收购方在交易行为完成后将成为目标公司的新股东。因此双方需要签署相应的协议文件，即针对目标公司原股东协议的补充协议，来确认收购方的新股东地位，并界定新股东与原有股东之间的关系。当然，如收购方通过获得目标公司原有股东所持的全部股权而成为目标公司的唯一股东，则无须签订上述协议文件。在此情况下，收购方只需根据目标公司所在地相应法律法规的相应要求，在相关商事登记机构办理股东登记即可。

第七章

"一带一路"国家投资并购境内外监管与合规

第一节 监管环境变化

2017年8月18日,《国务院办公厅转发国家发展改革委商务部人民银行外交部关于进一步引导和规范境外投资方向指导意见的通知》(国办发〔2017〕74号)政策文件发布,文件全文共六部分,明确了当前在引导和规范我国企业参与境外投资方面的指导思想、基本原则、鼓励开展的境外投资、限制开展的境外投资、禁止开展的境外投资以及保障措施。在指导思想方面,强调以"一带一路"建设为统领,深化境外投资体制机制改革,进一步引导和规范企业境外投资方向,促进企业合理有序开展境外投资活动,防范和应对境外投资风险,推动境外投资持续健康发展,实现与投资目的国互利共赢、共同发展。

在基本原则方面,提出"四个坚持"原则,一是坚持企业主体,按照商业原则和国际惯例开展境外投资,企业在政府引导下自主决策、自负盈亏、自担风险;二是坚持深化改革,坚持以备案制为主的境外投资管理方式,在资本项下实行有管理的市场化运行机制,按"鼓励发展+负面清单"模式引导和规范企业境外投资方向;三是坚持互利共赢,引导企业充分考虑投资目的国国情和实际需求,注重与当地政府和企业开展互利合作;四是坚持防范风险,合理把握境外投资重点和节奏,积极做好境外投资事前、事中、事后监管,切实防范各类风险。

2017年12月26日,国家发展改革委(以下简称"国家发改委")发布了《企业境外投资管理办法》(国家发改委2017年第11号令),于2018年3月1日起施行。相较之前的《境外投资项目核准和备案管理办法》(国家发改委2014年第9号令),国家发改委2017年第11号令简化事前管理环节,进一步覆盖事中、事后监管。最值得关注的亮点是"小路条"制度的取消。所谓"小路条"制度，是指按国家发改委 2014 年第 9 号令规定，中方投资额 3 亿美元及以上的境外收购或竞标项目，投资主体在对外开展实质性工作之前，应向国家发改委报送项目信息报告。国家发改委收到项目信息报告后，对符合国家境外投资政策的项目，在 7 个工作日内出具确认函。当然，对中国境内投资主体来说，国家发改委 2017 年第 11 号令也对其有所约束，且看以下两条：

第二条 本办法所称境外投资，是指中华人民共和国境内企业（以下称"投资主体"）直接或通过其控制的境外企业，以投入资产、权益或提供融资、担保等方式，获得境外所有权、控制权、经营管理权及其他相关权益的投资活动。

第六十三条 境内自然人通过其控制的境外企业或香港、澳门、台湾地区企业对境外开展投资的，参照本办法执行。

境内自然人直接对境外开展投资不适用本办法。境内自然人直接对香港、澳门、台湾地区开展投资不适用本办法。

值得注意的是，国家发改委 2017 年第 11 号令扩大了适用范围，其第六十二条规定，投资主体直接或通过其控制的企业对香港、澳门、台湾地区开展投资的或通过其控制的香港、澳门、台湾地区企业对境外开展投资的，参照执行。对境外投资，国家发改委 2017 年第 11 号令做到了惠及全国。

2017 年两会期间，全国人大代表、安踏集团董事局主席丁世忠提交了《关于进一步完善法律法规支持民营企业跨境并购的建议》。他建议制定全国统一的、专门的《企业跨境并购法》，或出台一部《民营企业跨境并购条例》，以规范企业并购行为；明确规定政府行政机构在并购工作中的职能、并购程序、并购主体的权利与义务；并购中资产评估、产权归属以及税务的管理，并购过程中债权债务的处理，以及职工身份和劳动安排等问题。丁世忠从民企跨国并购需要得到支持的角度，做出这种表述，显然是在企业实务经营中有具体的需求所致。它对于国内民营企业开展全球化业务，具有非常现实的意义。

第二节 境内监管：发展改革管理部门、商务部门、外汇管理部门

在我国现行的法律体系下，对境内企业开展境外投资进行监管的部门主要有发展改革管理部门、商务部门及外汇管理部门。从2016年到现在，境外投资监管领域出台了一些新的政策。

国家发改委2017年第11号令第二条不仅明确了境外投资的定义，还对投资活动进行了列举，这有助于投资主体判断其境外活动是否属于境外投资的范畴。

根据国家发改委2017年第11号令规定，境外投资活动主要包括但不限于下列情形：

获得境外土地所有权、使用权等权益；

获得境外自然资源勘探、开发特许权等权益；

获得境外基础设施所有权、经营管理权等权益；

获得境外企业或资产所有权、经营管理权等权益；

新建或改扩建境外固定资产；

新建境外企业或向既有境外企业增加投资；

新设或参股境外股权投资基金；

通过协议、信托等方式控制境外企业或资产。

国家发改委2014年第9号令第二十五条规定：投资主体实施需国家发改委核准或备案的境外投资项目，在对外签署具有最终法律约束效力的文件前，应当取得国家发改委出具的核准文件或备案通知书；或可在签署的文件中明确生效条件为依法取得国家发改委出具的核准文件或备案通知书。国际市场上通常不将政府审批作为协议生效条件，而将其作为交割条件。实际上，境内企业实施的不少跨境并购交易也将政府审批作为交割条件而非生效条件，因此在一定程度上存在规定和现实脱节的问题。国家发改委2017年第11号令第三十二

条将核准备案从国家发改委 2014 年第 9 号令的生效条件变更为项目实施条件。该条规定：属于核准、备案管理范围的项目，投资主体应当在项目实施前取得项目核准文件或备案通知书。根据该条规定，"项目实施前"，是指投资主体或其控制的境外企业为项目投入资产、权益（已按照国家发改委 2017 年第 11 号令第十七条办理核准、备案的项目前期费用除外）或提供融资、担保之前。

一、鼓励开展 + 负面清单

"鼓励开展的境外投资"这个提法是在国办发〔2017〕74 号文中首次作为一项制度提出来的。对外直接投资（ODI）相对应的是外商直接投资（FDI），FDI 领域其实已经实施了负面清单制度，ODI 领域也引入了这一制度。目前，最核心的负面清单就是国办发〔2017〕74 号文列出的一些重要的限制类、禁止类的境外投资。除此之外，国务院国有资产监督管理委员会（以下简称"国资委"）提出了中央企业对外投资的负面清单，包括某些行业禁止类，所以在对外投资监管方面，主要是以鼓励开展 + 负面清单的方式进行的。

（一）敏感行业有较大调整

在国家发改委 2014 年第 9 号令的基础上，国家发改委 2017 年第 11 号令调整了"敏感国家和地区"及"敏感行业"的范围，并明确将涉及敏感国家和地区、敏感行业的境外投资项目统称为"敏感类项目"。对于敏感行业，国家发改委 2017 年第 11 号令除了简单列举以外，还授权国家发改委发布敏感行业目录。2018 年 1 月 31 日，国家发改委发布《境外投资敏感行业目录（2018 年版）》，首次以单独的敏感行业目录形式公布境外投资的敏感行业，目录将武器装备的研制生产维修、跨境水资源开发利用、新闻传媒以及根据国办发〔2017〕74 号文需要限制企业境外投资的行业（包括房地产、酒店、影城、娱乐业、体育俱乐部及在境外设立无具体实业项目的股权投资基金或投资平台）列为境外投资敏感行业，如表 7–1 所示。

表7-1 敏感行业的变化

国家发展改革委2014年第9号令	境外投资敏感行业目录	变化
➢基础电信运营 ➢跨境水资源开发利用 ➢大规模土地开发 ➢输电干线 ➢电网 ➢新闻传媒	➢武器装备的研制、生产、维修 ➢跨境水资源开发利用 ➢新闻传媒 ➢根据国办发〔2017〕74号文，需要限制企业境外投资的行业： 1. 房地产 2. 酒店 3. 影城 4. 娱乐业 5. 体育俱乐部 6. 在境外设立无具体实业项目的股权投资基金或投资平台	➢删除：基础电信运营、大规模土地开发、输电干线、电网 ➢新增：武器装备的研制、生产、维修，以及房地产、酒店、影城、娱乐业、体育俱乐部、在境外设立无具体实业项目的股权投资基金或投资平台等需要限制企业投资的行为 ➢保留：跨境水资源开发利用、新闻传媒

（二）境外投资的导向清晰

国办发〔2017〕74号文对境外投资的监管引入了类似外商直接投资中的"负面清单"模式，将境外投资分为鼓励类、限制类和禁止类三类境外投资。

1. 鼓励类境外投资

国办发〔2017〕74号文对鼓励类境外投资项目做了列举，如有利于"一带一路"建设的基础设施建设项目，有助于带动我国优势产能、优质装备和技术标准输出的项目，与境外高新技术和先进制造业企业投资合作及在境外设立研发中心的项目，境外油气、矿产等能源资源勘探和开发项目，农林牧副渔等领域投资合作项目，商贸、文化、物流等服务领域的境外投资项目。此外，还支持符合条件的金融机构在境外建立分支机构和服务网络，依法合规开展业务。

2. 限制类境外投资

限制类境外投资包括五种情形，分别是：

（1）赴与我国未建交、发生战乱或者我国缔结的双多边条约或协议规定需要限制的敏感国家和地区开展境外投资；

（2）房地产、酒店、影城、娱乐业、体育俱乐部等境外投资；

（3）在境外设立无具体实业项目的股权投资基金或投资平台；

（4）使用不符合投资目的国技术标准要求的落后生产设备开展境外投资；

（5）不符合投资目的国环保、能耗、安全标准的境外投资。

其中，前三种情形须境外投资主管部门核准。

3. 禁止类境外投资

国办发〔2017〕74号文禁止境内企业参与危害或可能危害国家利益和国家安全等的境外投资，并列明五种情形，包括：

（1）涉及未经国家批准的军事工业核心技术和产品输出的境外投资；

（2）运用我国禁止出口的技术、工艺、产品的境外投资；

（3）赌博业、色情业等境外投资；

（4）我国缔结或参加的国际条约规定禁止的境外投资；

（5）其他危害或可能危害国家利益和国家安全的境外投资。

二、备案为主 + 核准为辅

备案为主，核准为辅。这个制度不是新制度，国家发改委和商务部已经同步执行，总体而言体现了行政放权的指导思想。

（一）发展改革管理部门备案核准的划分以及权限分工

境外投资其实分两部分，一类是对外直接投资，另外一类是境内企业、自然人通过其控制的境外企业或港澳台地区企业开展投资。现在，对外直接投资分为敏感类和非敏感类，敏感类就是双敏感，包括敏感国家、地区和敏感行业，如果拟投资的项目被划入敏感类里，须国家发改委进行核准。如果是非敏感类项目，还要看对外投资主体，如果是中央企业，即国资委直接履行出资人职责的国企，就直接到国家发改委备案；如果是地方企业，且是大额非敏感类项目，要到国家发改委备案，如果是小于3亿美元的投资，那就到省级发展改革管理部门备案。

对间接投资，同样分为敏感类和非敏感类，前者到国家发改委备案，后者大额的，到国家发改委实施事前报告，这是一项新的制度，不再是备案，在发改委的在线申报系统当中，录入相关的项目信息就完成了报告的步骤。小于3亿美元的，无须履行国家发改委2017年第11号令下的监管程序。

国家发改委2017年第11号令下各类境外投资项目应履行的事前监管程序具体见表7–2。

表7–2　国家发改委2017年第11号令中各类境外投资项目应履行的事前监管程序

项目类型	境内投资者投资额	投资主体直接开展的境外投资项目（涉及境内投资主体直接投入资产、权益或提供融资、担保）	投资主体通过其控制的境外企业及港澳台地区企业开展的境外投资项目（不涉及境内投资主体直接投入资产、权益或提供融资、担保）
敏感类项目	无论大小	国家发改委核准	国家发改委核准
非敏感类项目	3亿美元及以上	国家发改委备案	国家发改委大额非敏感类项目情况报告
	3亿美元以下	中央企业：国家发改委备案 地方企业：省级发展改革管理部门	无须履行核准、备案和报告事前程序

（二）商务部门备案核准划分及权限分工

接下来是商务部体系备案核准划分及权限分工。如果你所在企业既是中央企业，又涉及双敏感项目，此时就需要由商务部来核准，如果不涉及敏感项目，只需到商务部备案；对于地方企业，如果涉及双敏感项目，是由省级商务部门初步审核，然后再由商务部做最后的核准，如果是非敏感项目，只需要到省级商务部门进行备案。商务部门的具体核准和备案权限主要以企业属于中央还是地方企业，以及是否涉及敏感国家和地区、敏感行业为标准进行划分，具体划分标准请参见表7–3。

表 7-3　敏感行业划分标准

企业类型	项目类型	审批机关		备注
		商务部	省级商务部门	
中央企业	涉及敏感国家和地区、敏感行业	核准		
	其他项目	备案		
地方企业	涉及敏感国家和地区、敏感行业	核准	初审	对属于核准情形的对外投资，地方企业需通过所在省级商务主管部门向商务部提出申请
	其他项目		备案	

（三）外汇管理部门的登记程序

外汇管理局是外汇登记部门，尽管严格意义上它不能算是一个投资监管部门，但在境外投资的重要环节，即资金出境的环节，都要外汇管理局审批。事实上，它的重要性不亚于前面提到的发展改革管理部门和商务部门。根据国家外汇管理局 2015 年发布的《国家外汇管理局关于进一步简化和改进直接投资外汇管理政策的通知》（汇发〔2015〕13 号）的附件《直接投资外汇业务操作指引》，境内机构境外直接投资前期费用登记和外汇登记主要程序如表 7-4 所示。

表 7-4　境内机构境外直接投资前期费用登记和外汇登记主要程序

银行办理事项	审核材料	办理原则	备注
境内机构境外直接投资前期费用登记	（一）汇出境外直接投资前期费用的，需提交以下材料： 1. 境外直接投资外汇登记业务申请表。 2. 营业执照和组织机构代码证。 （二）境内机构为其境外分支、代表机构等非独立核算机构购买境外房产的，需提交以下材料： 1. 境外直接投资外汇登记业务申请表。 2. 境外设立分支、代表机构等非独立核算机构的批准/备案文件或注册证明文件。 3. 境外购房合同或协议。 4. 其他真实性证明材料。	1. 境内机构（含境内企业、银行及非银行金融机构，下同）汇出境外的前期费用，累计汇出额原则上不超过 300 万美元且不超过境内机构投资总额的 15%。 2. 境内机构汇出境外的前期费用，可列入其境外直接投资总额。 3. 银行通过外汇局资本项目信息系统为境内机构办理前期费用登记手续后，境内机构凭业务登记凭证直接到银行办理后续资金购付汇手续。	不以取得"企业境外投资证书"为前提。

续表

银行办理事项	审核材料	办理原则	备注
境内机构境外直接投资外汇登记	1. 境外直接投资外汇登记业务申请表。 2. 营业执照或注册登记证明及组织机构代码证（多个境内机构共同实施一项境外直接投资的，应提交各境内机构的营业执照或注册登记证明及组织机构代码证）。 3. 非金融企业境外投资提供商务主管部门颁发的《企业境外投资证书》；金融机构境外投资提供相关金融主管部门对该项投资的批准文件或无异议函。 4. 境外投资者以境外股权并购境内公司导致境内公司或其股东持有境外公司股权的，另需提供加注的外商投资企业批准证书和加注的外商投资企业营业执照。	4. 境内投资者在汇出前期费用之日起6个月内仍未设立境外投资项目或购买境外房产的，应向注册地外汇局报告其前期费用使用情况并将剩余资金退回。如确有客观原因，开户主体可提交说明函向原登记银行申请延期，经银行同意，6个月期限可适当延长，但最长不得超过12个月。 5. 如确有客观原因，前期费用累计汇出额超过300万美元或超过境内投资者投资总额15%的，境内投资者需提交说明函至注册地外汇局申请（外汇局按个案业务集体审议制度处理）办理。	须取得备案机关的"企业境外投资证书"和"备案通知"。

三、重事中、事后监管

国家发改委2014年9号令和商务部2014年3号令都比较侧重于事前监管，就是核准、备案和报告。国家发改委2017年第11号令出台之后，在这些环节上做了相应的细化。同时，国家发改委2017年第11号令以及《商务部 人民银行 国资委 银监会 证监会 保监会 外汇局关于印发〈对外投资备案（核准）报告暂行办法〉的通知》（商合发〔2018〕24号），把报告制度作为一个重点，从而实现对境外投资的投资中和投资后的监管。"核准备案必报告"是指项目后续进展要有相应的报告表提交给国家发改委；向商务部门提交年度报告，内容包括完成进展、实际交易金额、目标所在地的项目开始实施这些阶段性的信息都需要进行报告。然后，有些突发事件和重大事件，包括工程出现了意外的重大事故，以及与项目所在国的一些外交争议，这些都属于重大不利情况，也需要报告到商务部。若规定的这些事中和事后报告投资方做不到，或者说主管部门通过在线检索、约谈、抽查，发现投资方没有履行这些报告制度，就要承担相应的后果。最典型的是将其违规信息录入全国信用信息共享平台，更严重的结果是相关部门暂停为其办理对外投资备案核准手续，包括新办的项目，同时采取相应措施。

（一）发展改革管理部门监管

国家发改委 2017 年第 11 号令第四十三条、第四十四条、第四十五条，分别新增了重大不利情况报告、项目完成情况报告、重大事项问询和报告等制度。此后，国家发改委的监管不再限于事前监管，在事中和事后环节均增加了相应的报告和监督机制。根据国家发改委 2017 年第 11 号令第四十四条规定，属于核准、备案管理范围的项目，投资主体应当在项目完成（指项目所属的建设工程竣工、投资标的股权或资产交割、中方投资额支出完毕等情形）之日起的 20 个工作日内通过网络系统提交项目完成情况报告表。

境内企业开展境外投资均需向发展改革管理部门履行境外投资项目的核准/备案手续，报告有关信息，并配合监督检查。主要法律依据为国家发改委 2017 年第 11 号令，根据此文件，监管对象的范围包括境内金融和非金融企业，事业单位、社会团体等非企业组织，境内自然人通过其控制的境外企业以及港澳台地区企业对境外开展投资，相比国家发改委 2014 年第 9 号令，国家发改委 2017 年第 11 号令的监管对象范围有所扩大，并首次将境内企业设在境外的主体以及境内自然人通过其控制的境外企业或港澳台地区企业对境外的投资行为纳入监管范围。

（二）商务部门/金融监管部门监管

境内非金融和金融企业在开展境外投资时需分别向商务部门或主管金融监管部门履行境外设立企业的核准/备案手续。非金融企业由商务部门依据现行有效的《境外投资管理办法》（商务部令 2014 年第 3 号）实施核准/备案管理，并向获得核准或备案的企业颁发"企业境外投资证书"；金融企业则由其主管金融监管部门（中国证券监督管理委员会，简称"证监会"，中国银行保险监督管理委员会，简称"银保监会"），分别依据其相关规定开展境外投资的核准/备案手续。

提醒注意的是，对于中央企业从事境外投资，由国资委根据《中央企业境外投资监督管理办法》（国务院国有资产监督管理委员会令第35号）进行监督管理。

（三）外汇管理部门外汇管理

境内投资主体获得发改部门和商务部门/主管金融监管部门的对外投资核准/备案手续后，根据外汇管理部门的要求办理境外直接投资外汇登记。国家外汇管理局于2015年2月28日发布的汇发〔2015〕13号，取消了境内企业境外直接投资的外汇登记核准，改为"银行办理、外管监督"的模式，即由银行直接审核办理境外直接投资项下外汇登记，外汇管理部门通过银行对境外直接投资外汇登记实施间接监管。

境内自然人直接对境外或港澳台地区企业的投资并不在国家发改委2017年第11号令的监管范围，根据我国现行法律法规，发展改革管理部门和商务主管部门并未对境内自然人直接境外投资做出明确、具体的规定，而由外汇管理部门长期主导自然人境外投资的管理。国家外汇管理局于2014年7月14日公布的《国家外汇管理局关于境内居民通过特殊目的公司境外投融资及返程投资外汇管理有关问题的通知》（汇发〔2014〕37号，简称"37号文"）是境内自然人境外直接投资的主要法律依据。根据37号文，由外汇管理部门对境内居民个人设立的特殊目的公司及相关外汇登记事宜进行管理，境内居民以境内合法资产或权益向特殊目的公司出资前，应向外汇管理部门申请办理境外投资外汇登记手续，在办理境外投资登记手续后，方可办理后续业务。但需要注意的是，37号文仅适用于以返程投资为目的的境内自然人境外投融资行为，并不涉及境内自然人境外的实业投资。

（四）《对外投资备案（核准）报告暂行办法》的主要内容

在国家发改委发布2017年第11号令之后，商务部、中国人民银行、国资委、原银监会、证监会、原保监会及外汇管理局等七部委于 2018 年 2 月 8 日联合发布《商务部 人民银行 国资委 银监会 证监会 保监会 外汇局关于印发〈对外投资备案（核准）报告暂行办法〉的通知》（商合发〔2018〕24 号），暂行办法于发布之日起生效。暂行办法建立了各部门"管理分级分类、信息统一归口、违规联合惩戒"的对外投资管理模式。

根据暂行办法，商务主管部门、金融管理部门依据各自职责负责境内投资主体对外投资的备案或核准管理，国资委负责履行出资人职责的中央企业对外投资的监督和管理。暂行办法进一步明确了各部门对不同主体的境外投资进行核准/备案的职责划分。暂行办法规定，由商务部统一就对外投资核准/备案和报告信息进行汇总，各部门定期向商务部通报对外投资核准/备案和报告信息，商务部定期将汇总信息反馈前述各部门共享共用，初步建立了各部门间的内部信息汇总和共享机制，有助于各部门根据汇总信息开展监测报告、分析预警、有效干预等工作。

同时，对于境内投资主体的违规行为，暂行办法也明确了相应的惩戒措施，如境内投资主体未按照暂行办法规定履行核准/备案手续和信息报告义务的，商务部会同相关主管部门视情可采取提醒、约谈、通报等措施，必要时将企业违规信息录入全国信用信息共享平台，对企业的行政处罚通过国家企业信息公示系统记于企业名下并向社会进行公示；如发现境内投资主体存在偷逃税款、骗取外汇等行为，相关监管部门应将有关问题线索转交税务、公安、工商、外汇管理等部门依法处理。

第三节　境外监管：反垄断审查和政府审批

一、反垄断审查

反垄断法的立法基础是由企业并购（兼并、收购），推导出企业在进行垄断，其逻辑链条往往是这样的：行业领先者吃掉次级领先者——这个行业领先者变成"一家独大"——从此行业缺乏竞争。所以，并购只对资本有利、对企业利好。

反垄断法是监督商业中经济权力分配的法规，它是确保企业健康竞争、行业繁荣、经济得以增长的重要法规。反垄断法，适用于几乎所有的行业和部门，涉及各个层次的业务，包括制造业、运输业、分销业和营销业。反垄断法禁止许多限制贸易的商业行为，例如：价格操纵、可能削弱某些市场竞争热情的企业合并，以及旨在获得或持有垄断权的掠夺行为。反垄断法的目的是防止经济力量过分集中于大企业或大集团。因为这些企业或集团有可能利用垄断的支配地位或经济优势，对自由竞争产生不利影响，并最终损害消费者的利益。

以下两笔引起高度关注的中国央企的海外投资并购，都涉及了海外反垄断审查：

2016年3月11日，中国外交部发言人在例行记者会上表示，中方欢迎欧盟批准中法企业合作建设英国欣克利角核电站，期待项目不断取得进展。据报道，欧盟已批准法国电力集团与中国广核集团有限公司合作建设欣克利角核电站。欧盟反垄断监管机构调查结果认为，有关合作不会妨碍英国电力市场竞争。中国外交部发言人表示，中方欢迎欧盟做出上述决定。

2017年4月4日，美国联邦贸易委员会（FTC）批准中国化工集团有限公司收购先正达的交易。FTC批准此交易的前提是，中国化工集团有限公司要剥离除草剂百草枯、杀虫剂阿维菌素和杀菌剂百菌清三种产品在美国的业务。FTC认为，先正达拥有上述三种产品，并在美国占有重要的市场份额。同时，中国化工集团有限公司的子公司安道麦是美国数一数二的通用农药供应商。如果不剥离，合并交易很可能在美国造成垄断，令消费者不得不为这些产品支付高价。

反垄断执法机构对于并购交易进行评估之后，存在三种可能：禁止、附条件批准或批准。由以下两个上市公司实例可以看出对并购交易进行反垄断审查的必要性。

案例 7-1　河北宣化工程机械股份有限公司通过南非反垄断审查的公告

证券代码：000923　证券简称：河北宣工　公告编号：2017-36

河北宣化工程机械股份有限公司关于重大资产重组通过

南非反垄断审查的公告

本公司及董事会全体成员保证信息披露内容的真实、准确和完整，没有虚假记载、误导性陈述或重大遗漏。河北宣化工程机械股份有限公司（以下简称：公司）近日收到南非竞争法庭（"the Competition Tribunal of South Africa"）出具的无限制条件的批复意见，公司本次重大资产重组事项已通过南非反垄断审查。公司本次重大资产重组事项尚需中国反垄断审查部门、中国商务部门、发改部门的境外投资审批/备案，中国证监会的关于本次发行股份购买资产并募集配套资金暨关联交易事项的核准等，相关部门批准后方可实施。公司将根据本次重大资产重组的进展情况及时履行信息披露义务，敬请广大投资者注意投资风险。

特此公告。

河北宣化工程机械股份有限公司董事会

2017 年 5 月 26 日

案例 7-2　洛阳栾川钼业集团获得土耳其竞争主管机关无条件通过的公告

洛阳栾川钼业集团股份有限公司关于收购自由港集团下属

Tenke 铜钴矿项目获得土耳其竞争主管机关无条件通过的公告

洛阳栾川钼业集团股份有限公司（以下简称"公司"）已于上海证券交易所网站及公司网站刊登了《洛阳栾川钼业集团股份有限公司重大资产购买报告书（收购境外铜钴业务）（草案）》，披露了公司全资子公司 CMOC Limited（洛阳钼业控股有限公司）收购自由港集团下属 Tenke 铜钴矿项目（以下简称"本次收购项目"）的相关事宜。

公司于 2016 年 8 月 19 日收到土耳其竞争主管机关的通知，土耳其竞争管理委员会根据相关法令无条件批准公司收购自由港集团下属 Tenke 铜钴矿项目。

土耳其竞争主管机关的审批为本次收购项目实施所需履行的程序。公司本次收购项目尚需取得的其他有关批准详见公司披露的《洛阳栾川钼业集团股份有限公司重大资产购买报告书（收购境外铜钴业务）（草案）》。

公司将密切关注该事项的进展情况，积极推进相关工作，严格按照有关法律法规的规定和要求，及时履行信息披露义务。

特此公告

洛阳栾川钼业集团股份有限公司董事会

2016 年 8 月 22 日

二、东道国政府审批

（一）以澳大利亚为例

1. 澳大利亚海外投资审核委员会

跨国并购导致外国投资者进入相关市场，不少东道国政府的审查已经成为必要程序。2016 年，大康牧业放弃收购澳大利亚 S.Kidman & Co., Ltd 股权，否决交易的就是澳大利亚海外投资审核委员会（Foreign Investment Review Board，FIRB），标的 Anna Creek 的总面积逾 10 万平方千米。该 FIRB 执行的制度源于澳大利亚投资法规《1975 年外国收购与接管法》（又称为 FATA）和"外国投资政策"，负责执行 FATA 的政府机构为海外投资审核委员会，故而该项审批制度被称为 FIRB 批准。

案例 7-3　大康牧业关于要约收购 S.Kidman & Co Ltd 股权的进展公告

关于要约收购 S.Kidman & Co Ltd 股权的进展公告

一、进展概述

2016 年 4 月 29 日，澳大利亚财长以国家利益为由对于大康牧业股份有限公司控股子公司大康澳大利亚控股有限公司（Dakang Australia Holdings Pty Ltd，以下简称"大康澳洲"）向澳大利亚海外投资审核委员会（以下简称"FIRB"）提出收购 S. Kidman & Co Ltd（以下简称"Kidman 公司"）80% 股权的申请做出了初步否决的声明，并要求收购方于澳大利亚时间 2016 年 5 月 3 日前做出相应回复。2016 年 5 月 3 日，湖南大康牧业股份有限公司（以下简称"公司"）与 Kidman 公司、大康澳洲、Australia Rural Capital Ltd（澳大利亚农资公司，本次要约收购 Kidman 公司 20% 股权的当地一家在澳大利亚证交所（ASX）上市的公众公司，以下简称"ARC"）以及 Anna Creek Pty Ltd（安纳西有限公司，以下简称"安纳西"）签订了 Termination Deed（终止协议，以下简称"协议"或"本协议"），就上述相关方于 2016 年 4 月 19 日签订的签署附条件生效的 Bid Implementation Agreement（要约收购实施协议，以下简称"BIA"）进行终止。

二、协议的主要内容

协议各方一致同意终止除保密义务以及其他常规义务之外的 BIA 协议及其他相关协议，包括：竞买方同意撤回要约；大康澳洲同意撤回 FIRB 申请；Kidman 公司退回保证金；以及大康澳洲、ARC 以及 Kidman 公司会就本次收购在今后的 3 个月内继续进行洽谈，共同寻求可以得到 Kidman 公司董事会、股东以及澳洲财长认可的可行方案。

三、其他说明及风险提示

（1）公司将在未来三个月积极努力与交易对手方磋商，形成可被认可的收购方案，公司或子公司与 Kidman 公司的 BIA 所述的要约总金额不会发生变化，但是未来三个月的磋商谈判非排他性，即有关本次

Kidman 公司的要约收购不会排除其他竞争报价或谈判对手。

（2）鉴于公司已于 2016 年 4 月 30 日将《关于签署附条件生效的〈Bid Implementation Agreement〉的议案》《关于 S.Kidman & Co Ltd 股权收购的可行性研究报告》提请公司 2015 年年度股东大会进行审议，本着公司不放弃尝试，努力形成切实可行的获得澳大利亚 FIRB 批准的 Kidman 公司要约收购方案，同时在不变更 BIA 协议的要约收购金额的前提下，请公司全体投资者谨慎并注意上述议案的投票表决。

（3）本次要约收购事项仍存在较大的不确定性，烦请各位投资者注意投资风险。

四、备查文件

公司与 Kidman 公司、大康澳洲、ARC 以及安纳西签订的 Termination Deed。

特此公告。

湖南大康牧业股份有限公司董事会

2016 年 5 月 4 日

2. 澳大利亚农地投资法规

澳大利亚海外投资审核委员会 17 号指南——农业用地投资。

（1）农业用地投资

当外国投资者持有的农业用地总价值超过 1 500 万美元时，其（不包括外国政府投资者）在农业用地上的投资计划一般需要获得批准，但来自澳大利亚贸易协定合作伙伴国家的投资者可以例外。外国政府投资者对农业用地的所有收购都需要获得批准。

外国人士对农业用地权益的所有收购，无论其是否需要批准，无论其价值多少，都必须向澳大利亚税务登记局申报外国所有权登记。

本指南为计划投资澳大利亚农业用地的外国投资者提供参考，包括需要申报的农业用地收购行为、审批程序及合规性等。

（2）重大需申报行为

如果满足相关门槛条件，外国人士获取澳大利亚农业用地的收购权益是一项重大需申报行为。当外国投资者（及其合伙人）持有的农地权益及收购农地权益的对价合计总价值超过 1 500 万美元时，视作满足门槛条件。计划签署含有需申报行为相关协议的外国人士，必须在签署协议前通知财务主管。

对农业用地的投资是一项需申报行为，也是一项重大行为。这意味着财务主管可以：

·决定不反对该行为，并给予不强加条件的无异议通知；

·决定不反对该行为，前提是遵守一项或多项条件，确保该行为不会违反国家利益，并给予附强制条件的无异议通知；

·决定认为此行为将违背国家利益，并做出禁止所提议重大行为的命令。

如果违背国家利益的重大行为已经实施，财务主管可以作出解除该行为的处置令，或者施加强制条件。

（3）农业用地投资门槛

适用的门槛值取决于外国人士的国籍，以及该投资者是否为外国政府投资者。

·对于外国政府投资者，适用 0（零）美元门槛。

·对于非外国政府投资者（来自智利、新西兰、泰国和美国的投资者除外），门槛金额为累计 1 500 万美元。

为达到累积门槛值，外国投资者（及其合伙人）持有的农地权益及收购农地权益的对价合计必须超过 1 500 万美元。

（4）保障澳大利亚人的机会——公开透明的销售过程

作为国家利益测试的一部分，决策者需要考虑澳大利亚居民购买给定的农业用地的机会，因而需要考虑销售过程的公开性和透明度。

一般来说，对于非公开出售的农业用地，以及没有"广泛上市（marketed widely）"至少 30 天的农地，都不能获得认购批准。这一要求的目的是确保澳大利亚居民在任何农地销售过程中有充足的投标机会。

公开透明的销售过程意味着：

·利用澳大利亚投标人可以合理访问的渠道（如在广泛使用的房地产上市网站或大型地区 / 国家报纸上刊登广告）公开出售或发布广告；

·该资产已公开出售或广告至少 30 天；

·在仍可供出售的情况下，有平等的机会对该资产进行投标或出价。

·申请人有责任证明他们是怎样获知该资产已被广告出售，以及收购是否符合公开透明的销售流程规定。申请人可能会被要求提供销售过程的相关证明。

此项要求的例外情况包括收购申请人：

·收购的资产是通过在过去 6 个月以上述方式销售或广告的私人出售资产，但未销售或销售失败的；或者

·拥有大量的澳大利亚所有权份额（50% 或更多），尽管含有外国所有权成分，可以视作是澳大利亚本地竞标者的机会；

·遵从国家或联邦法律，按要求进行收购，例如，采矿缓冲区。

案例 7-4　关于农地投资的两个案例

案例 1　广告进行时

Michele 是一名希望收购 Joe 农场的外国人士。起初她在本地报纸上看到了 Joe 农场的广告，并与刊登广告的地产经纪人联系，得知该地产已上市 2 个月。

Michele 向地产经纪人证实，该地产已通过多种渠道广告至少 30 天，包括在线渠道、农村地产经纪商，以及当地和全国媒体广告。如果 Michele 向海外投资审核委员会申请收购 Joe 的农场，销售过程基本不会引发国家利益问题。

案例 2　5 个月前发过广告

外国投资者直接联络 Susan，希望能购买她的农场。Susan 的农场目前并没有上市销售，但曾在 5 个月前发布销售广告，因未能售出而被撤下市（未接到购买者出价或不接受出价）。

外国投资者 Green Forestry Co. 接洽了 Susan，由于他们在 Susan 的农场附近拥有大量用于林业业务的土地，并且现在有资金可用于扩大业务。

Green Forestry Co. 向海外投资审核委员会申请收购该资产。由于该资产在过去 6 个月内曾公开广告销售，此收购行为满足公开销售过程要求。

（5）发展条件——住宅开发

标准发展条件将适用于所有用于住宅开发的农业用地收购。收购的条件是在五年内开始开发。

（6）特定投资者豁免

农业用地门槛及农地重大申报行为框架不适用于来自智利、新西兰、泰国和美国的非外国政府投资者。

- 这种情况下，如果所要收购的土地权益既包含农业用地，又包含其他类型的澳大利亚土地，适用于商业用地和住宅用地等其他类型土地的框架依然适用。
- 在确定目标实体是否为土地实体时，这些国家的投资者可能会忽视专门用于初级生产环节的土地权益。如果该行为是澳大利亚外国投资框架下的另一种重大或需申报行为，则框架依然适用（如在澳大利亚实体中获得的重大利益超出门槛值）。
- 对于计划收购专门用于初级生产环节土地的泰国投资者，如果该土地价值超过 5 000 万美元，则该收购为重大需申报行为。

（7）风能或太阳能电站的所有者或经营者豁免

风能或太阳能电站所有者或经营者对农业用地的特定收购不受农业用地门槛值限制。《2015 年海外并购及收购条例》第 5 节中对"风能或太阳能电站"的定义为：依据《可再生能源（电力）法案 2000 号》规定认可的，风力发电站或太阳能发电系统。

若太阳能和风能发电站的所有者和经营者在购置含有风力或太阳能发电站的农用土地权益时，其唯一目的是在此土地上运营此风能或太阳能电站。根据法案可以无视该土地为农业用地的事实。

在这种情形下，即便该土地符合农业用地的常规测试，也可被视为非农业用地，以适用于其他类型土地的筛查和指定门槛。举例来说，如果它被视为非空置商业用地，则参照这种土地的适用门槛。详情参见澳大利亚海外投资审核委员会 14 号指南。关于风能和太阳能电站的更多信息请参照澳大利亚海外投资审核委员会 50 号指南。

（8）农业用地的定义

农业用地是指澳大利亚境内用于或可以合理用于初级产品生产的土地，

包括部分用于初级生产的土地，或只有部分可以合理用于初级生产的土地。

农业用地还包括不时可能被水覆盖的土地（如农场大坝或溪流）。但是，以沉水作物与动物为唯一初级生产产品的土地，或可以合理用于此类业务的土地不属于农业用地。如河口和海湾的养鱼或牡蛎养殖场，河口和海湾不属于农业用地。

当土地包含了从事或能够从事初级产品生产业务的建筑或建筑的一部分时，若建筑物与土地没有直接联系，则该土地不属于农业用地。例如，从事初级产品生产业务的某行政办公室位于市中心某办公楼某层，该办公室不属于农业用地的定义范围。

（9）初级生产业务

对初级生产业务的定义与1997年所得税评估法（ITAA 1997）第995-1（1）小节中的定义相同。该定义包括：培植或繁殖植物；以销售其本身或其身体产品为目的而饲养动物；从事开展与捕捞鱼类及其他海洋动物直接相关的活动；在以砍伐为目的的种植园或森林中种植抚育树木；或在种植园或森林中砍伐树木。

初级生产从业者的定义包括以下业务：

·在实体环境中培育或繁殖植物、真菌或其产品或部件（包括种子、孢子、球茎和类似物）；

·以销售其本身或其身体产品为目的而饲养动物（包括自然增长）；

·利用生产的原材料生产乳制品；

·从事开展与捕捞鱼类、海龟、儒艮、海参、甲壳类动物或水生软体动物直接相关的活动；

·直接从事珍珠或珍珠贝的提取或培育活动；

·在以砍伐为目的的种植园或森林中种植抚育树木；

·在种植园或森林中砍伐树木；

·运送在种植园或森林中砍伐的树木或其部分至：

——首先要被碾磨或加工的地方；

——将要把它们运送到首先被碾磨或加工处的地方。

在考虑某项活动是否属于初级生产业务时应该考虑各种指标，包括：

·该活动是否有显著的商业目的或特征；

·该人是否以正在从事的活动赚取利润，并有从活动中获利的前景；

·该活动是否有重复性和规律性；

·该人是否以与该业务中一般贸易类似的方式开展该活动；

·该人是否以营利为目的、以类似商业的方式计划、组织并进行该活动。

如果该活动更适合被描述为业余爱好、休闲形式或体育活动，则非经营活动。

更多信息请参阅税收裁定 TR 97/11：《所得税：我是否从事初级生产业务？》。

有关放牧含义相关信息，请参阅税收裁定 IT 225 号：《初级产品—放牧收入》。

（10）"可合理用于"概念

土地能否合理用于初级生产经营，取决于土地的实际情况和周围环境。可能提供合理指标说明土地可以（或不可以）被合理使用的因素（单独或相互影响作用）包括以下几点：

·该土地在其区域规划内允许被用于初级生产：这些可能为土地是否可合理用于初级生产业务提供了合理的指标。举例来说，如果区域规划允许从事初级生产活动而无须当地监管主体的进一步批准，则表明该土地可合理用于初级生产业务。但是，农村居住区内的土地，其区划要求明确规定不允许进行初级生产活动，或只批准在特殊情况下进行，则不属于合理用于初级生产业务的土地。

·土地使用历史：如果近年来这块土地曾用于初级生产活动，则很可能表明该土地能合理用于初级生产活动，除非在此期间该土地出现过一次或多次重大变化（如重大的永久性环境退化，水资源枯竭或污染，早期初级生产活动基础设施的搬迁或损失等）。若近年来土地并未用于初级生产活动，并不一定意味着未来不能将其合理地用于初级生产业务。这方面的例子包括土地出于以下原因没有被用于初级生产业务：

——长期极端气候事件，如长期干旱；

——近期自然灾害，如山火或洪水；

——其他活动，如矿产勘探和开发，在此之后可以预期或法律要求的土地修复工作意味着整体或部分土地可合理用于初级生产业务。

• 土地特征（如气候、作物产量、土地面积、偏远地区、土壤质量、库存量、地形、植被和水资源）：土地必须有足够规模以供在部分或全部土地上开展独立经营的初级生产活动，一公顷或更少的土地不能被视为农地。土地远离货物运输和其他基础设施，包括关键的农业服务提供者，可能意味着该土地无法合理地用于初级生产业务，直到此类基础设施和/或服务可供当地使用为止。

• 租约、许可条件或限制：根据租赁或许可证占用农业用地的权利，其条款期限（包括任何延期或续展）很可能超过五年时，可能会附加土地使用条件或限制。

——在明确允许进行初级生产活动的情况下，无论承租人或许可证持有人在租赁期限或许可期限内的意图如何，土地都可被认为能合理用于初级生产业务。

——如果承租人或许可证持有人不允许将其用于初级生产业务，也不应孤立认为该土地不能合理用于初级生产业务。如上所述的其他因素，以及这种限制租赁或许可证的理由都将与评估有关。举例来说，如果出租人保留了他们经营初级生产业务土地的相邻土地，并对承租人的使用做出限制，以便他们能在租期结束时重新将土地用于其经营（土地经过休耕，生产力得到了提高），则该土地能够合理用于初级生产业务。

通常市区范围内的住宅不被认为是可合理用于初级生产业务的土地，尽管这类土地上可以进行小规模密集型的初级生产活动，或者某些情况下会发生与初级生产业务相关的行政活动（如果土地面积大于一公顷，请参阅下述除外条款）。但如果在土地上进行初级生产业务的非附属活动，那这类土地就是农业用地。如商品蔬菜园或培育植物作为植物苗圃的一部分。

（11）除外条款

《2015年海外并购及收购条例》第44节明确排除了完全不能或不能主要用于初级生产业务的土地，满足下列一种或多种条件。

• 区划要求政府批准初级生产业务的土地。

——如果根据区划该土地可用于某种初级生产而无须批准，它就被认为是农业用地。若潜在投资者预备利用该土地从事另一种初级生产业务，无须考虑是否需要批准。

·区划要求允许用于初级生产业务，已向有关政府当局提出以下相关申请并正在等待最终决定。

——该土地将被划分为不允许用于初级生产业务的土地；

——批准在该土地建立矿山、石油、天然气井、采石场或者其他类似作业（开采行为）；

——批准在该土地建立与采矿作业相关的基础设施（如用于处理采矿作业所提取的材料的基础设施和矿工食宿等）；

——批准在土地上储存采矿作业的废料；

——批准（包括认可）在该土地上建立或经营风能或太阳能发电站（地表或地下）。

·完全或主要用于采矿作业、建设与采矿作业有关的基础设施，或储存采矿作业废料的土地。

·已经政府当局批准允许大规模用于采矿作业、建设与采矿作业有关的基础设施，或储存采矿作业废料的土地（目前尚未用于非采矿或生产租赁）。

——获批准单独取得该土地，或者相比其他土地，该土地的全部或主要用途更满足此类批准条件。

·用于风能或太阳能电站建设，或获批允许建立风能或太阳能农场的土地，或者收购该土地的目的仅为满足政府批准建设太阳能或风能农场的条件。

——在上述情况下，土地将被视为空置或非空置的商业用地。如果风能或太阳能发电站位于陆地表面，那么这块土地将被视为非空地。更多信息参见澳大利亚海外投资审核委员会14号指南和澳大利亚海外投资审核委员会50号指南。

·根据联邦法律、国家或领土或具有法律约束力的协议规定全部或主要用于环境保护的土地。

·全部或主要用于野生动物保护区或动物改造区的土地。

·位于已获政府当局批准为产业园区内的土地。

·面积在一公顷或以下的土地。

·已获政府当局批准,为市民提供旅游、户外教育或户外康乐设施的土地。

该规则还排除了仅用于以下初级生产业务的土地:直接从事捕鱼、养殖珍珠或其他水生生物,包括植物和动物产品的相关行为。

(12)农用土地豁免证书

外国人(包括外国政府投资者)可以申请豁免证书,以涵盖收购农地权益的计划。

以下情形可以考虑申请农用土地豁免证书:

·三年内计划收购总额不超过1 000万美元;

·将要收购的土地的区域或地区可以被明确界定。

一般情况下,豁免证书的授予条件是将单笔交易的最高价值限制在1 000万美元(即产权价值,而非地产价值),并在此期间对收购进行定期报告。

上述限制仅供参考。取决于各类因素,实际限额可能低于这些限制,包括但不限于:

·豁免证书的地区限制;

·收购方的业绩记录;

·土地的未来使用,包括一切资本投资计划;

·近期海外投资审核委员会批准的总价值,包括独立或通过豁免证书批准的。

标准开发条件将适用于所有收购用于住宅开发的农业用地豁免证书,即豁免证书的条件是在五年内开始发展。

需要申报澳大利亚税务登记局外国所有权登记的外国投资者,在豁免证书到位期间进行的任何适用的收购和处置行为,分别应遵守《2015年水权或农业用地使用权外资登记法案》相关规定,履行告知要求。

关于豁免证书的更多信息参见澳大利亚海外投资审核委员会21号指南。

(13)费用

费用在申请时支付,正确付款后开始处理。

关于海外投资申请付费的更多信息,参见澳大利亚海外投资审核委员会30号指南。

（14）处罚

违反澳大利亚境外投资规则的行为将遭受严厉处罚（包括民事和刑事处罚）。

（15）更多信息

更多信息详见澳大利亚海外投资审核委员会官网 www.firb.gov.au。

（二）以美国为例

国家安全审查立法机构中最有名的是美国外国投资委员会（CFIUS）。自 1988 年起，总统或 CFIUS 在超过 2 000 个案件中仅正式否决了少数几个交易，但是近年来，CFIUS 否决中国投资者申请的投资的案例逐渐增加。

案例 7-5　深圳市新纶科技股份有限公司关于终止收购美国阿克伦聚合物系统公司股权的公告

深圳市新纶科技股份有限公司关于终止收购美国阿克伦聚合物系统公司股权的公告

深圳市新纶科技股份有限公司（以下简称"公司"）于 2018 年 5 月 10 日召开的第四届董事会第二十九次会议审议通过了《关于终止收购美国阿克伦聚合物系统公司股权的议案》，鉴于美国外国投资委员会（CFIUS）将对公司收购美国阿克伦公司 45% 股权事项实施限制，本次交易无法按原定计划实施，公司董事会同意终止对美国阿克伦聚合物系统公司股权的收购事宜，具体情况如下：

一、交易基本情况

为进一步提升公司在光电显示产业链上的研发创新能力，通过资源整合布局下一代柔性显示材料市场，经公司董事会审议通过，公司全资子公司新纶科技（香港）有限公司（以下简称"香港新纶"）收购美国 Akron Polymer Systems，Inc.（阿克伦聚合物系统公司，以下简称为"阿克伦公司"或"标的公司"）45% 股权。具体内容详见公司于

2017年12月12日披露的《关于收购美国阿克伦聚合物系统公司45%股权的公告》（公告标号：2017-132）。

二、交易终止原因

由于标的公司曾经参与涉及美国军用材料的相关项目，本次交易需通过美国外国投资委员会（CFIUS）审查批准后方可交割。根据香港新纶与标的公司签署的《股权收购协议》，如果CFIUS已经通过书面或口头方式通知购买方或标的公司，表明CFIUS打算发送或已向美国总统发送报告，建议总统暂停或禁止本协议项下拟进行的交易或对本协议项下拟进行的交易施加重大限制，并且标的公司或购买方任一方认为无法接受该限制，可由购买方或标的公司任一方提出终止。该信息已在公司2017-132号公告中进行相应披露。

截至2018年5月，经反复多次沟通，CFIUS始终明确表示将对本次交易实施限制，本次交易无法按照原定计划顺利实施。为保障上市公司及股东权益，经与标的公司股东协商，公司决定终止本次股权收购。

三、终止收购的影响

（1）本次交易各方均承诺，本次终止交易不会导致相互之间发生索赔、诉讼事宜。交易各方为实施本次交易而发生的审计、评估、法律等费用，由交易各方自行承担。

（2）本次交易终止不影响公司继续与阿克伦公司进行合作，公司将依托与阿克伦公司在深圳市设立的合资公司——聚纶材料科技（深圳）有限公司继续在光电显示领域拓展业务。

（3）由于股权收购未能完成，预计将对相关技术的引入带来一定障碍，敬请广大投资者注意投资风险，公司将积极做好与海外合作方的沟通协商，避免对公司业务带来不利影响。

特此公告。

深圳市新纶科技股份有限公司董事会

2018年5月11日

美国外国投资委员会（CFIUS）是由美国联邦政府多个政府部门组成的联席委员会，由美国财政部代表担任 CFIUS 主席，成员包括美国国务院、国防部、司法部、国土安全部等机构的代表。CFIUS 于 1988 年根据《1950 年国防生产法》的《Exon-Florio 修正案》设立。CFIUS 的授权法规根据《2007 年外国投资和国家安全法》进行修订。

1.CFIUS 的权限

CFIUS 可对下列"应审查交易"行使职权：

（1）导致外国人士对美国业务产生"控制"的一项合并、收购或其他并购交易。

美国业务包括外国公司在美国的运营。

（2）交易将导致外国人士获得控制权。

关于外国人士的界定将重点关注最终控制人，是否使用特殊目的公司或控股公司不影响对外国人士性质的分析。

（3）控制权。

控制权并不仅仅取决于持股比例，需要根据公司治理等因素进行具体分析。

CFIUS 申报为自愿申报，但交割前的申报为交易提供了"安全港"，如果交易未办理事前申报，在交易交割后，CFIUS 仍可能对交易进行审查，并且可能促使美国政府强制交易方取消交易，或者迫使外国交易方剥离相关美国业务。

2.CFIUS 优先考虑的问题

（1）确保美国国防工业基地安全。

（2）保护关键技术。

（3）保护关键基础设施。

（4）保护美国技术领先。

（5）确保政府和国防供应链安全。

（6）遵守重要的美国国家安全政策（如反恐、防止核扩散、出口管制）。

（7）能源安全。

（8）政府所有权。

实践中，CFIUS 还可能考虑若干其他因素，包括收购人/实体的国籍。

3.CFIUS 潜在关注的领域

CFIUS 对交易的关注逐渐从核心国家安全事项和"关键基础设施"的交易扩大到包括更广义的"核心技术"和高科技行业，如图 7-1 所示。

图 7-1　CFIUS 潜在关注的领域

4.CFIUS 近期数据统计

CFIUS 定期公布其审查交易的统计数据（但交易具体详情仍然保密）。CFIUS 还向国会提交年度报告，如表 7-5、图 7-2 所示。

表 7-5　CFIUS 2014~2016 年审查交易的统计数据

单位：个

受审查交易、撤回交易以及总统决定的统计数据									
年份	申报总数	触发调查的交易数量	触发调查的交易比例	提交总统的交易数量	申报被拒绝的交易数量	申报被撤回的交易数量	撤回并重新提交的交易数量	申报撤回并因CFIUS相关的国家安全原因而放弃的交易数量	申报撤回且未说明原因的交易数量
2014	147	51	35%	0	1	12	7	2	3
2015	143	66	46%	0	1	13	9	3	1
2016	172	79	46%	1	0	27	15	5	7

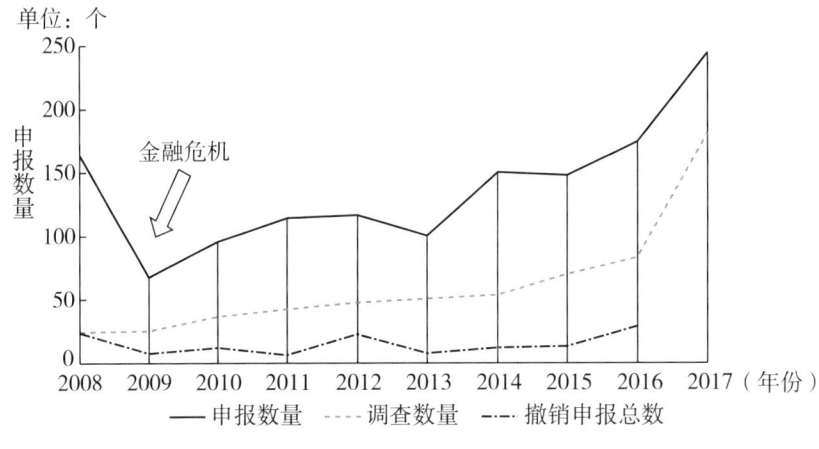

图 7-2 CFIUS 审查交易的趋势图

5. 聚焦中国的案例

（1）环宇通讯收购案（2016年）

三安光电拟收购环宇通讯，CFIUS 以危及国家安全为由开展审查，为避免 CFIUS 进一步展开国家安全方面的审查，双方合意设立合资经营公司。

（2）Lumileds 收购案（2016年）

由于未能提出令 CFIUS 满意的缓解国家安全问题的提案，中方投资人拟以 29 亿美元出售飞利浦 Lumileds 业务的交易被拒。

（3）飞兆半导体收购案（2016年）

飞兆半导体以可能遭 CFIUS 审查风险为由拒绝接受华润微电子有限公司及华创投资的拟议收购。

（4）爱思强收购案（2016年）

中方投资者福建宏芯投资基金拟收购德国半导体公司爱思强公司（爱思强在美有一家子公司）。

CFIUS 建议总统否决该交易，理由是"只需突破一些技术难题，爱思强的产品就可用于军事用途"。

德国国家安全部门也对交易进行了审查并提出了质疑。

（5）Lattice 收购案（2017年）

Canyon Bridge Capital Partner，一家据称有中方政府背景的私募公司，拟收购美国半导体公司 Lattice Semiconductor Corporation。

Canyon Bridge Capital Partner 与 Lattice Semiconductor Corporation 进行了 8 个月的谈判，以期 CFIUS 能批准本次交易。CFIUS 全面调查后，企业历经了数轮撤回及重新申请。

Lattice Semiconductor Corporation 提出了一系列风险缓解方案，试图解决任何国家安全方面的担忧，但是未果，最终未能说服 CFIUS 或美国总统。

（6）高通收购案（2018 年）

新加坡公司博通拟以强制收购方式收购半导体生产商高通公司，交易价值在 1 170 亿至 1 420 亿美元之间。

2018 年 1 月 29 日高通单方面向 CFIUS 提出自愿接受调查申请，"主动邀请 CFIUS 就博通拟以征求委托书形式进驻高通董事会多数席位介入审查"。

在同博通及高通沟通后，CFIUS 于 2018 年 3 月 4 日出具了一份临时裁令，在这份裁令中，除其他事项外，CFIUS 要求高通延期举行股东大会（原定于 3 月 6 日召开），博通拟在该股东大会上取得高通董事会席位。该裁令旨在维持博通及高通双方现状。

2018 年 3 月 11 日，CFIUS 向 SEC 发出通知，称博通的行为违反了临时裁令。第二日，即 2018 年 3 月 12 日，特朗普总统签发总统令，叫停博通对高通的收购案。

（7）速汇金收购案（2018 年）

蚂蚁金服对速汇金（MoneyGram International）的收购案于 2018 年 1 月正式宣告终止。这起交易最终没有达成的根本原因是，尽管双方多次提出缓解方案，但 CFIUS 仍以担忧国家安全为由拒绝批准交易。

（8）Xcerra Corporation 收购案（2018 年）

CFIUS 拒绝批准湖北鑫炎拟以 5.8 亿美元收购 Xcerra Corporation 的交易。Xcerra 是半导体生产加工过程设备生产商。但 2018 年 1 月，美国有关部门批准了中国半导体设备公司北方华创微电子装备有限公司以 1 500 万美元收购美国半导体生产商 Akron Systems LLC.。

应对境外审批审查，首先，企业应充分了解有关国家和地区的外资并购监管要求；最后，正确评估该项审批对交易可能产生的影响，比如对国家安全审查、反垄断审查以及国有控股企业的特殊限制都要全面、恰如其分地评估审批;最后,与有关监管当局积极做好正式和非正式的沟通,争取监管方对交易影响的理解和对并购交易的认可。

案例 7-6　中远海控收购东方海外剥离长滩码头

交易金额:63 亿美元

目标国家:美国

行业:港口

案例背景:2012 年 3 月,东方海外与美国长滩港签署一份价值 46 亿美元、时效长达 40 年的长期租约。东方海外将与长滩港合作投资 12 亿美元将两个旧码头合并重建成一个全新的现代化码头,预计 2019 年 6 月完工。建成后的新码头将有效增强吞吐能力,利用全球最先进的货物处理技术,预计吞吐量将翻一番,年吞吐量可达 330 万标准箱(TEU)。此外,通过增设更多码头内铁路线、使用电气化货物装卸设备和岸电系统,将使空气污染减半,届时此码头将成为北美最具竞争力、最有效率及最环保的集装箱码头。

此前的 2018 年 6 月 29 日,中远海控收到国家市场监督管理总局反垄断局做出的《经营者集中反垄断审查不予禁止决定书》,决定对其收购东方海外股权交易不予禁止,交易各项先决条件全部满足。随后,联合要约方于 2018 年 7 月 6 日向东方海外所有股东发出要约的综合文件,Faulkner Global 及上港集团 BVI 以每股 78.67 港元作价,正式向东方海外全体股东要约,接纳要约的最后日期为 2018 年 7 月 27 日。

2018 年 7 月 6 日,中远海控发布公告称,为确保在要约收购完成后,东方海外的上市地位得以维持,中远海控全资子公司 Faulkner Global 与 PSD Investco、Crest Apex 及融实国际等三家机构达成股权转让协议。根据该协议,若东方海外在要约收购完成后的公众持股量低于 25%,Faulkner Global 将最多出让东方海外全部已发行股份的 15.1% 给上述投资者,PSD Investco、Crest Apex 及融实国际将最多分别认购东方海外全部已发行股份的 7.73%、4.99% 及 2.38%。

案例分析：中远海控（601919.SH；01919.HK）全资子公司 Faulkner Global 携手上港集团 BVI 于 2017 年 7 月 9 日宣布向收购东方海外（国际）有限公司（东方海外，00316.HK）全体股东发出要约收购的一年后，该案获得 CFIUS 放行，意味着该起收购案接近完成。

那么，这笔交易是如何通过 CFIUS 审核的呢？背后的实质是：

中远海控全资子公司 Faulkner Global、东方海外已与美国国土安全部和司法部签订了《国家安全协议》，承诺向无关联的第三方出售东方海外持有及运营的位于美国的长滩集装箱码头的实体，并在出售完成前把长滩港集装箱码头的实体由以东方海外为受益人的美国信托托管。基于以上《国家安全协议》的签署，各方已收到 CFIUS 于 2018 年 7 月 6 日发出的信函，CFIUS 确定目前本次要约收购不存在未解决的美国国家安全事宜。

第四节 境内上市公司信息披露及合规

上市公司海外并购，除应当遵守发改委、商务部、国家外汇管理局和国资委等部门的监管要求外，还要符合中国证券监督管理委员会（以下简称"证监会"）和证券交易所有关上市公司治理、重大资产重组以及信息披露等特别规定。

上市公司海外并购面临多个监管部门的审批，因此确定相关监管部门报批的顺序格外重要。为提高审批效率，进一步优化企业兼并重组市场环境，中华人民共和国工业和信息化部（以下简称"工信部"）、证监会、发改委及商务部于 2014 年 10 月联合制定了《上市公司并购重组行政许可并联审批工作方案》，就中国证监会与一般的境内企业境外投资所需审批先后顺序问题做出明确规定。由工信部牵头，会同多部门推行上市公司并购重组并联审批，将发改委的境外投资项目核准和备案，商务部的外国投资者战略投资上市公司核准、经营者集中审查等三项审批事项改为并联式审批，审核时间大大缩短，上市公司海外并购效率得到提升。

中国证监会制定了一系列规则规范上市公司的交易行为，具体包括《上市公司重大资产重组管理办法》（2016年修订）、《上市公司收购管理办法》（2014年修订）、《上市公司证券发行管理办法》、《上市公司非公开发行股票实施细则》（2017年修订）等。根据《并购重组审核分道制实施方案》，上市公司的并购重组自2013年10月8日起正式实施分道制审核。对于上市公司并购满足豁免、快速审核类要求的，属于现金收购情形的，中国证监会豁免审核，直接核准；对于涉及发行股份购买资产情形的，中国证监会取消预审环节，直接提交并购重组委审核。

上市公司的任何交易行为均需要符合信息披露的要求，因此，上市公司在进行海外并购时，需要特别注意信息披露的要求。在上市公司购买境外资产过程中，上市公司应按照《上市公司信息披露管理办法》和证券交易所的规则等相关规定，并结合具体情况，履行相应的信息披露义务。《上市公司重大资产重组管理办法》《上市公司收购管理办法》以及上海证券交易所（简称"上交所"）和深圳证券交易所（简称"深交所"）的股票上市规则等文件中亦对某些具体事项的披露做出了明确规定。同时，上交所的信息披露指引和深交所的信息披露备忘录还对具体事项披露的内容和格式，以及涉及的停复牌的事项做出明确规定。

南京新百通过全现金形式收购英国老牌百货企业 Highland Group Holdings Limited 旗下的 House of Fraser Ltd 约89%股权，是A股零售企业有史以来最大的一笔境外直接收购案。House of Fraser Ltd 有超过160年历史，是英国历史最悠久的皇家授权百货连锁商店，在英国和爱尔兰设有超过60家门店。收购后，南京新百将 House of Fraser Ltd 引入中国市场，打造"东方福来德"品牌百货。

案例 7-7　南京新百收购 Highland Group Holdings Limited 股权公告

关于公司收购 Highland Group Holdings Limited 股权暨对外投资的公告

一、对外投资概述

（1）对外投资的基本情况：根据南京新百与 Highland Group Holdings Limited 及/或交易对方签署的《股权购买协议》，南京新百拟通过支付现金收购 Highland Group 约 89% 的股权（以下简称"标的资产"）。

（2）Highland Group 是一家位于英国的百货公司集团，成立于 2006 年 6 月 14 日，总部位于英国伦敦。Highland Group Holdings Limited 旗下的经营实体 House of Fraser Ltd（以下简称"House of Fraser"）是在英国及爱尔兰等地结合百货门店、网络以及手机等多渠道销售的百货经营企业，其 House of Fraser 百货品牌拥有超过 160 年历史，提供的产品类别覆盖男装、女装、童装、美容、潮流饰品及家居饰品等。作为一揽子交易，南京新百分别与标的公司的 A 类普通股及优先股股东、B 类普通股股东和优先普通股股东及/或标的公司签署《A 类普通股及优先股购买协议》《B 类普通股购买协议》和《优先普通股购买协议》（以下统称《股权购买协议》）。由于优先普通股、优先股、A 类普通股及 B 类普通股在投票权和受益顺序上均有差异，因此支付对价不同，详情参考"交易对方基本情况简介"。本次交易完成后南京新百取得标的公司投票权的比例为 88.89%，取得标的公司合计股数的持股比例为 88.96%。

（3）本公司计划在英国设立全资子公司作为收购主体，并由其以自有资金及债务融资的方式支付 155 330 878 英镑现金收购 Highland Group Holdings Limited 股权架构中优先普通股（以下简称"PO 股"）600 500 股、A 类普通股（以下简称"A 股"）8 888 890 股、优先股 151 111 110 股以及 B 类普通股（以下简称"B 股"）526 316 股；本次交易完成后，本公司将持有标的公司约 89% 的股权。本次交易的交易价款系由交易各方协商一致后确定，同时参考具有证券相关业务资格的评估机构出具的预评估结果。根据《股权购买协议》，标的资产的基础对价约为 15 533 万英镑。以 2014 年 1 月 25 日为评估基准日，本次交易标的公司全部股权的预评估值为 20 167 万英镑，对应 89% 股权的预评估值约为 17 949 万英镑。标的资产的基础对价较预评估值无溢价。

（4）该事项经本公司第七届董事会第六次会议审议批准。会议以 9 票同意、0 票反对、0 票弃权，审议并通过了《关于签订〈股权购买协议〉的议案》。根据上海证券交易所《股票上市规则》及《南京新街口百货商店股份有限公司公司章程》的规定，本次收购暨对外投资事项需要提交股东大会审议。

（5）本次交易中各交易对方与公司及公司控股股东、实际控制人之间不存在任何关联关系，本次交易不构成关联交易。

（6）本次交易的成交金额占南京新百 2013 年度经审计的合并财务会计报告期末净资产额的比例已超过 100%。根据《上市公司重大资产重组管理办法》，本次交易构成重大资产重组，需经中国证监会核准。

（7）截至本公告日，本次交易涉及的尽职调查、审计、评估等工作正在开展之中。公司将尽快召开董事会审议本次重大资产购买相关事项，并披露本次《重大资产购买预案》。

二、相关方基本情况介绍

（一）交易对方基本情况简介

本次交易的交易对方包括 Highland Group Holdings Limited 股权结构中的 PO 股股东、优先股及 A 股股东以及 B 股股东，其中：

1. PO 股股东情况

PO 股在标的公司利润分配和破产清算剩余财产收益清偿中均享有第一顺位的优先求偿权，不享有投票权。截至目前，PO 股共 600 500 股，Bank of Scotland plc 100% 持有该类别股票。Bank of Scotland plc 为一家依据苏格兰法律设立的公司，成立于 1695 年，总部位于爱丁堡，是苏格兰地区历史最悠久的银行。Bank of Scotland plc 在英国境内外提供零售银行、公司银行、资产管理、私人银行等一系列金融服务。现隶属于英国最大的金融机构之一 Lloyds Banking Group。

股东名称	所持股票数（股）	在整个 PO 股中所占比例
Bank of Scotland plc	600 500	100%
合计	600 500	100%

2. 优先股及 A 股股东情况

优先股不参与标的公司利润分配，在破产清算剩余财产收益清偿中处于第二顺位，不享有投票权。A 股在标的公司利润分配中处于第二顺位，在标的公司破产清算剩余财产收益清偿中处于第三顺位，并且是唯一享有投票权的股份类别。每一 A 股代表一个投票权。

根据《股权购买协议》的约定，BG Holding ehf 和 Kevin Stanford 均有义务在交割日将不受任何质押或抵押限制的所持标的公司股权转让给南京新百。

3. B 股股东情况

B 股股东均为标的公司管理层，在标的公司利润分配中与 A 股同处于第二顺位，在标的公司破产清算剩余财产收益清偿中处于第四顺位，不享有投票权，不可公开转让。

（二）标的公司基本情况简介

标的公司是一家国际知名的百货公司集团，其经营实体 House of Fraser 运营超过 164 年，是英国历史最悠久的皇家授权百货商店。House of Fraser 被私有化之前长期在伦敦证券交易所主板上市，并且入选 FTSE100 成分股。标的公司经营自有品牌、采购品牌及特约品牌三类产品的销售，类别主要覆盖男装、女装、童装、美容、潮流饰品及家居饰品等。House of Fraser 的供应商涵盖各类国际知名品牌，包括 PRADA、HUGO BOSS、DIESEL、Ralph Lauren 等。其特约品牌商中，前 15 位企业均为合作逾十年之久的商业伙伴。另外，House of Fraser 旗下多个自有品牌，如 Howick、Dickins & Jones、Linea 也以时尚的设计和亲民的价格赢得广泛的市场影响力。House of Fraser 在英国境内开设了 59 家门店，在爱尔兰开设了 1 家门店，在中东城市阿布扎比开设了 1 家特许经营店，总销售面积超过 490 万平方英尺。由于 House of Fraser 品牌的悠久历史，标的公司大部分门店都位于所在城市的核心商圈，如伦敦的 Oxford Street，格拉斯哥商业街，曼彻斯特 King Street 等，主要面向追求中高端百货品牌的中产消费者。

此外，House of Fraser 还面向全球消费者建立了统一的网上销售平台 HouseofFraser.co.uk，通过网络订单、邮件订单、线上下单商场提货等多种方式增进顾客的购物体验。2014 财年标的公司总营业额为 1 191 60 万英镑（未经审计），市场份额稳居英国百货行业前列。

Highland Group Holdings Limited 是 House of Fraser 的控股公司，也是本次交易的被收购主体。本次交易为市场化收购，交易价款系由交易各方协商一致后确定，同时参考具有证券相关业务资格的评估机构出具的预评估结果。以 2014 年 1 月 25 日为评估基准日，本次交易标的公司全部股权的预评估值为 20 167 万英镑，较最近一期账面净资产（未经审计）的增值率为 89.90%。股权定价的增值原因为：（1）House of Fraser 历史悠久，拥有丰富的品牌资产、商圈资源以及供应商伙伴关系；（2）House of Fraser 自私有化之后各项财务指标逐步改善，未来有较大的增长空间；（3）欧洲零售市场正在复苏，市场对百货零售行业估值正在修复。最终评估结果仍有待资产评估师确认，并将在《重大资产购买报告书》中予以披露。

（三）本次交易前后股权结构变动

对于标的公司的特约品牌销售，财务报表中营业收入统计的是销售佣金净收入，总营业额则统计特约品牌的销售商品收入，二者计算口径存在差异。

（四）本次交易是否涉及关联关系说明

本次交易中各交易对方与公司及公司控股股东、实际控制人之间不存在任何关联关系，本次交易不构成关联交易。

三、《股权购买协议》主要内容

（一）支付对价

股份数量为每个交易对方持有的 PO 股、优先股、A 股及 B 股的合计数量。本次交易完成后南京新百取得标的公司合计股数的持股比例为88.96%。双方约定在《股权购买协议》下，受让方拟支付155 330 878英镑现金（此为基础对价）收购转让方所持有的Highland Group约89%的股权，包括PO股600 500股、A股8 888 890股、优先股151 111 110股以及B股526 316股。其中，定金为10 000 000英镑，受让方须在签署本协议的10个工作日内将定金汇入指定的账户内；上述基础对价还存在调整条款，最终支付对价还取决于一系列调整因素，包括额外酬金、标的公司2014财年息税折旧摊销前净利润未达预期的扣款、闲置资金利息等。

（二）交割的前提条件

各方完成交易之义务，以下述各项条件在交割之时或之前实现或由买方放弃，或只待交割便得以实现为条件：

1. 监管条件

（1）江苏省发展和改革委员会接受有关本次交易的备案；

（2）中国商务部对本次交易予以核准；

（3）中国国家外汇管理局江苏省分局对本次交易办理登记；

（4）中国证券监督管理委员会对本次交易予以核准（"监管条件"）。

2. 股东批准条件

持有不少于三分之二表决权的南京新百股份股东，在正式举行的特别股东大会上（亲自或者通过委托代理人进行表决的方式），同意本次交易（"股东批准条件"）。参照2014年4月14日汇率（1∶10.2911），约合人民币1 598 525 599元。

（三）托管

交易各方在签署《股权购买协议》后，同意尽快委任一名托管代理人，并采取所有必要或合理的措施与托管代理人共同签署一份托管协议，约定本次交易托管的相关条款。在符合相关条款的前提下，如果交割时，尚未发生托管触发事件，则价格为6 000 000英镑的终止费将存入托管账户。

（四）协议的生效

《股权购买协议》于交易各方签署时生效。

（五）协议的终止

交易各方签署的《股权购买协议》终止条件包括：（1）交易双方书面合意终止；（2）自动终止：交割条件未满足或于CP最终期限日23∶59之时或之前被放弃，除非根据相关其他条款另行同意；（3）受让方有权在交割日或交割日前终止本次交易，倘若：（a）德勤会计师事务所对标的公司2014财年合并财务报告出具有保留意见的审计报告（或未能送达任何审计报告）；（b）John King、Mark Gifford 及 Nigel Oddy 中的任何一人辞职或收到标的公司及其下属子公司发出的终止雇佣通知。

（六）违约责任

违约方应赔偿非违约方损失，守约方亦可申请强制履约。

索赔时间限制。转让方不应当因违反任何转让方保证（与基本保证有关的索赔除外）承担责任，除非受让方于交割之后18个月内向转让方送达索赔的通知。

最小索赔金额。转让方不应当因违反任何转让方保证（任何与基本保证有关的索赔的情形除外）针对任何个别索赔（或一系列基于实质上完全相同的事实或情形产生的索赔）承担责任，如果任何有关该索赔或一系列索赔，或针对其他转让方的类似索赔或一系列索赔协议规定或认定（不论相关条款有何规定）的责任金额不超过100 000英镑。如果有关任何该索赔或一系列索赔，或针对其他转让方的类似索赔或一系列索赔，规定或认定的责任金额超过100 000英镑，在受其他规定约束的前提下，相关转让方应当就索赔或一系列索赔按照协议规定或认定的金额承担责任，而不仅限于就超过的部分承担责任。

合计最小索赔金额。转让方不应当因违反任何转让方保证（任何与基本保证有关的索赔的情形除外）针对任何索赔承担责任，除非转让方应或原本应承担责任（不论相关条款有何规定）的针对违反转让方保证的所有索赔（包括之前的索赔）的合计金额超过2 000 000英镑。

如果上述所指的所有索赔按协议规定或认定的责任金额超过 2 000 000 英镑，在符合相关条款的前提下，相关转让方应当就索赔或一系列索赔按照协议规定或认定的金额，而不仅限于超过的部分承担责任。

最大责任限度。在受相关条款约束的前提下，违反转让方保证的所有索赔（任何与基本保证有关的索赔的情形除外）以及任何与英国公平贸易署或竞争委员会调查有关的索赔的合计责任金额不得超过 6 000 000 英镑，且每一转让方针对违反转让方保证索赔（除针对基本保证的索赔之外）以及与相关调查有关的索赔承担的合计责任金额不得超过 6 000 000 英镑的相关比例。上述索赔承担责任，所有的赔偿金额都需要从托管账户贷方账户里的余额中支出。每一转让方就与违反基本保证有关的索赔承担的合计责任金额不得超过对价的相关比例。

（七）协议的准据法和争端解决

本协议、按照本协议将要签订的文件，以及因本协议或此等文件产生或与本协议有关的任何非合同义务将适用英国法。各方不可撤销地同意，英国法院将具有专属管辖权，以解决因本协议或按照本协议将要签署的文件而产生或有关的任何争议。因此，任何因本协议或按照本协议将要签署的文件而产生或有关的任何法律程序，应提交该等法院。各方不可撤销地接受该等法院的管辖，并放弃基于地点或基于法律程序已在不方便的地点提起为由，而对程序提出任何异议。

第八章

"一带一路"国家投资并购的投后管理

"投后管理是中国对外投资最大的短板,我们不重视投后管理,也缺乏投后管理的能力、水平和经验,缺乏投后管理的人才。"中投公司总经理屠光绍在 2017 年 11 月 20 日的"2017 年外滩国际金融峰会"上直言,"对外投资不是简单地找到一个好项目,把钱放进去。你放进去以后怎么进行有效的投后管理,甚至比你做的投资决策可能更重要。有这方面实践经验的投资者都有这个共同的认识。"

越来越多的全球案例显示,投资并购后的整合是并购成功之路上的重要一环。在很多企业并购案例中,尽管对外投资企业花了很多时间制定了符合公司未来发展需要、切实可行的战略,选择了适合的标的,付出了合理的代价,但如果不能成功地整合目标公司,那么交易将不能为企业带来价值。毕马威在 2013 年全球 CFO(首席财务官)的调查中惊讶地发现,七成以上的并购交易并未实现预期价值,而有一半以上的并购交易受访者表示正是因为整合阶段的种种困难,导致企业预期的协同效益难以实现。整合管理失败的主要表现是:关键人才流失、客户关注度不够、组织混乱及分化、文化冲突、竞争应对不力。

很多发起并购交易的中国公司,甚至根本就没有并购整合的团队,也有很多中国公司发起并购之前没有做专利尽职调查、环评调查、商业尽职调查,对并购标的缺乏深入的研究和分析,那么并购失败的结局就不可避免。

第一节 并购整合后面临的挑战

若忽视投后管理和整合,就会破坏海外民众对中国企业的好感和信任,直接影响海外投资项目的收益和国家利益。企业并购失败往往可以归结于"三不两过"：不遵守东道国法律法规，不重视企业的社会责任，不尊重当地宗教文化和社会习俗；过度追求短期利益，过度竞争而忽视合作。

综合来看，中国公司海外并购后整合面临的主要是以下四方面的挑战。

一、企业文化整合风险

在"一带一路"国家投资并购中，文化整合风险是排在第一位的风险。文化的整合涉及企业的方方面面，对企业的发展起着不可估量的影响。企业文化包括价值观取向、行为准则和传统习惯等。企业内部的固有文化受到外来企业冲击和破坏时，会产生本能的排斥反应。中国企业应该主动与被收购企业沟通，以便加强了解，遵循求同存异的原则，理解并尊重企业之间的文化差异，通过双方渗透式融合，而不是简单、粗暴地以一种文化来取代另外一种文化。中国文化和"一带一路"国家文化有着较大的差异，企业文化也千差万别，如果双方文化上没有融合，最终会导致整个并购的失败。

二、战略层面的整合风险

并购完成后，企业所面临的外部环境、内部资源都发生了变化，需要依据新的内外部环境制定新的战略规划，涉及公司的发展战略、产品战略、市场战略和资本战略等方面的重构。中国企业需要从市场、经营、资金、技术等方面重新配置资源，对销售、成本和利润进行持续的跟踪和评估，才能充分发挥协同效应。如在TCL收购汤姆逊之后，液晶电视的出现导致传统电视销量的大幅下降，TCL没有依据市场的变化调整公司战略，给公司带来很大的亏损。

三、经营层面的风险

并购完成后，目标公司原有的供应商和客户可能会对新公司的能力产生怀疑和不信任，导致市场认可度的下降，销售额可能会急剧下降，被收购企业的业务也无法持续稳定的运营下去。由于中国企业国际化经营管理经验不足，缺乏国际化的管理人才，对目标国家和市场熟悉程度不够，容易产生决策上的失误，使并购后的企业陷于困境之中。

四、人员整合风险

中国企业可能会对目标企业人力资源体系做出变革，会导致公司核心员工，特别是高层员工的流失。人才流失会导致企业生产效率下降和客户流失，造成业务萎缩。对于轻资产的公司，收购的目的就是获取核心员工和市场，核心员工和市场流失某种程度上意味着收购的失败。有时候，企业从降低成本角度考虑会裁掉一部分员工，有些国家的工会很强势，裁员会使其产生抵触情绪，工会甚至会抵制裁员方案，做出一些不利于企业的行为。

第二节　并购整合的内容和方法论

并购整合可以分为四个层次：第一个层次是获得目标企业的产权（包括股权、资产等）和被动获取收益的权利；第二个层次是获得目标企业的控制权和主动获取收益的权利；第三个层次是实现战略、经营和财务的整合；第四个层次是管理和文化的整合。

企业并购的价值创造源自并购整合过程中的能力管理，要达到"1+1>2"的效果，在企业战略、文化、人力资源、业务流程等领域的整合中都必须关注三项根本性的任务，即能力的保护、能力的转移与扩散以及能力的发展。

一、并购整合的内容

并购整合包括以下几个方面的内容：战略整合、人力资源整合、财务资源整合、商誉和其他无形资源整合及文化整合。其中,文化整合是企业海外并购整合过程中面临的最大挑战。文化因素作为并购活动中的"软指标",从某种程度上来说,其重要性甚至超过了财务、技术市场等要素。

(一)战略整合

战略整合管理包括企业使命与目标、企业总体战略、经营战略与职能战略的整合。企业并购后整合是否成功取决于两个企业间战略性能力的转移,而其战略性能力的转移取决于并购双方战略能力的相互依赖性。目标企业的战略应该与并购企业的战略相互配合、相互融合,否则就难以发挥出正协同效应。但是,目标企业也应根据自身情况制定适当的战略,如并购公司全面削减成本战略或全公司范围的人事政策调整,可能就不利于一个以研究开发为特色的目标企业在产品创新上建立竞争优势。

(二)人力资源整合

并购后的人力资源整合管理是企业并购成败的关键所在。笔者所在的东软集团就是一家软件企业,进行投资并购的主要目的就是获取人才和市场。中国企业相当多的海外并购是为了获得企业的"软资产"。所谓的"软资产"是指被收购企业员工的知识价值与客户的关系,以及正在开发的具有技术优势和潜在市场机会的新产品或新服务。因此,挽留被收购企业中的关键人才是一项重要而紧迫的任务,收购企业需要制订和实施一个综合性的、周密的重新聘用计划。在整合过渡期内,由于出现大量的人员流动以及普遍的人员重叠,有必要对新组织的人事结构进行调整,重新确定各个层次管理人员的权限。并购方可以留用原企业的主管,通过各种报表及时掌握该组织的经营情况,实施间接控制。并购企业需要让员工清楚、及时地了解整个并购的大致情形、并购活动对于新企业的战略意义、企业的发展前景和方向、工作规划,以及某方面的主管和负责人。并购企业通过分析被并购企业员工的诉求,提出富有吸引力的目标和承诺,可以增强其对并购方的信任和依赖感。

(三)财务资源整合

在企业并购过程中,财务人员可以采用购买法和权益结合法两种方式合并财务报表。购买法仅将合并日后被并企业实现的利润纳入利润表,而权益结合法将被并企业整个年度的利润并入并购企业的利润表。如果被并购公司的经营活动也会随之被并购,被并购公司的存货需要按照并购公司的存货计价标准进行调整。

(四)商誉和其他无形资源整合

在并购活动中,公司的命名方式有四种:采用收购公司的名称、保留被收购公司的名称、采用两公司名称的组合、使用全新的名称。当被并购公司拥有著名商标时,并购公司会保留其商标。一般而言,消费者只关心商标品牌,而不关心所有者的变更。

(五)文化整合

在并购整合过程中,文化整合占据了最核心的地位。管理风格和公司文化的差异是影响并购成败的主要原因。很多看起来能够带来并购协同效应的公司,可能存在着严重危害双方和睦共处的文化。中国企业完成海外并购后的文化整合至关重要,对于并购活动是否有效起着决定性的作用。80%的并购整合失败都源自文化因素。根据并购双方文化的强弱关系,企业并购文化整合模式可以分为四类:文化注入式、文化融合式、文化融入式和文化促进式。企业文化战略是决定企业文化整合的效果的关键,应考虑并购双方文化的强弱关系,选择恰当的文化整合战略。

"一带一路"国家投资并购的文化整合,面临国家文化和企业文化双重差异带来的挑战。同时,这两种文化差异给海外并购整合带来的风险大小,还受到并购双方文化认同度和并购一体化程度的影响。并购活动的问题很大一部分源于人员因素,这是由于不同企业的雇员并不确定并购会给自身的工作带来怎样的影响,也可能是因为存在文化的不适应,以及安全感的下降和信任的缺乏。这些因素导致员工对并购产生敌意。并购产生的另一个结果是让雇员对组织的认同感消失,导致工作满足感的下降和雇员的流失。收购公司与目标公司组织文化差异越大,海外并购组织文化整合风险越大。随着并购整合的不断实施,海外并购文化整合风险可能随着协同效应的实现而变得越来越小,也可能随着矛盾的激化而变得越来越大。另外,研究也发现并购前积极的合作经历有助于降低双方之间的文化整合风险,积极的合作经历最终会产生更好的并购绩效。

二、并购整合的方法论

企业应在宣布交易的同时启动整合,精选整合团队的领导人员,设定整合时间表和止损点。对标的公司按照买方企业的资源和管理体系进行流程改造和嫁接,力争和买方企业做到流程"无缝对接",尽量使经营管理协同效应最大化。与此同时,并购方还需要通过明确目标与制定激励措施来保持标的公司业务的正常运转。

项目管理方式是管理整合过渡阶段的合适的方式。对于整合项目管理组织,有效且实用的结构应包含以下三个层次:指导委员会、并购管理小组和各种类型的职能工作小组。指导委员会由两个企业的高层管理者组成,给整合工作提供战略与政策方面的指导,保证整合的目标与并购的目的相一致;并购管理小组由 3~5 名专职人员组成,推动整合工作向前发展,保持管理工作的整体性和持续性,集中解决和协调来自组织各方面的问题和矛盾;职能工作小组解决财务、人力、信息技术等方面并购整合工作中的具体问题。在整个投后整合(Post-merger Integration,PMI)即并购后的整合的实施过程中,不断沟通和交流是十分必要的,这样才能减少误解和冲突,整合文化,构建企业未来的沟通目标。

根据中国企业"一带一路"国家投资并购的成功经验,我们总结出中国企业成功的投后管理通常包含以下六个方面的内容。

（一）明晰并购愿景，制定整合战略和路线图

制定清晰的整合战略是并购项目成功实现整合的基础。公司应根据不同的交易动因和公司实际情况，对被并购对象提出明确的发展目标，即未来成为一个什么样的企业。在"一带一路"国家投资并购方面经验丰富的企业往往在筛选投资目标的阶段就会考虑这些问题，比如被收购资产在公司整体战略中处于什么地位？应发挥什么作用？在管控模式上是应该保留被收购企业原有的管理体系，还是改造被收购企业，将其纳入自己的管理体系？回答了这些问题，也就基本确定了整合工作的大方向，企业可以在此基础上制定整合工作阶段目标并形成清晰的整合战略。

东软集团在做投资并购时，通常会仔细思考自己的优势在哪里，并购完成后是否能够有效地整合。东软集团的收并购主要集中在大健康领域，先后收购多家医疗IT、社保软件、健康管理领域的公司。因为这三个领域是东软集团的优势业务领域，收购完成后很快能够实现整合，助力标的企业提升业绩，实现协同效应。

（二）设立专职整合团队参与并购项目全过程

在很多海外并购项目中，中国企业在交割前和交割后是由完全不同的两个团队负责的，在交接工作时经常出现信息缺失的情况。由于两个小组的人员思路不同、处理问题的方式也不同，容易给被并购方留下中方企业交割前后态度和做法不一致的印象。此外，并购交易和整合团队的人员配备要求也不一样，交易团队主要由战略、财务、法务以及外部专家顾问组成，而并购后整合工作需要大量组织变革、运营和生产管理、人力资源管理、技术研发等方面的专家。考虑到这样的情况，一些中国企业设置了专职的整合团队，负责开发整合方法论、设计整合流程、开展整合工作、积累和传播整合经验。

在实际项目中，整合团队的职责主要包括：

（1）评估整合风险、确定整合目标；

（2）挖掘整合风险点，为交易谈判提供支持；

（3）管理、指导实际整合工作，协调各业务团队的工作，成为交易双方沟通的桥梁。

并购交易与整合环节联系紧密，但工作内容和目标存在明显差异。拥有丰富并购项目经验的公司通常会分别设立专职的交易和整合团队，二者相互配合，平行推进工作。整合团队会介入项目的全过程，保证并购和整合不脱节，这也有利于被并购方建立并加强对于收购方的信任，最大限度地减少整合过程中可能出现的组织结构、业务、人员管理和文化等方面的冲突。

东软集团的业务团队从一开始就会参与并购交易，甚至很多并购项目就是业务团队推荐给集团总部的。业务团队对目标公司的优势和风险点有着非常清楚的认识，因此公司领导也非常重视业务团队对于并购交易的意见。在并购过程中，业务团队会充分评估整合风险，提前与被收购方进行充分的沟通，为将来投后整合打下良好的基础。而一旦收购完成，业务团队就会对目标公司进行全面整合。

（三）建立合理、高效的管控体系

海外业务管控一直是中国企业境外项目运营的一个薄弱环节。在选择业务管控模式时，企业需要综合考虑业务战略、股权架构、协同效应和潜在风险等因素。根据集团参与度和业务协作度的不同，企业可以选择的四个基本管控模式分别是：直接运营、战略运营、战略设计、财务控制。针对每一种管控模式，企业需要在公司治理构架、纵向职能体系构建、核心人员管理、业绩追踪、服务与运营提升这五个方面明确具体的管理原则。

东软集团收购德国哈曼（Harman）的导航团队后，展现了对原公司历史、文化和员工的尊重。在完成收购后，东软集团没有撤换任何管理团队成员，只派遣了一名财务总监参与公司的管理，并将集团罗马尼亚的业务并入该公司。目标公司的高管也经常到访中国，和总部业务团队频繁交流，感受母公司的文化。并购完成后，目标公司管理团队和员工的情况非常稳定，业务也不断发展，团队人数五年间也增长了一倍。

（四）整合双方优势资源，实现交易协同效应

企业在开展并购项目时，通常会期望交易能够实现协同效应，即双方通过开展合作、共享业务资源实现优势互补，使并购后公司的总体效益大于并购前两个企业效益之和，即"1+1>2"。在进行项目可行性分析、筛选投资目标和开展尽职调查工作时，企业需要深入分析所购买资产是否能够满足公司发展战略需求，明确协同效应来源，制定发挥协同效应的目标。交易后整合阶段是落实协同效应的关键时期，企业需合理设计交易后被并购资产的管控模式和管理原则、运营模式、财务管理体系，整合双方优势资源，形成并发挥协同效应。通常来说，并购协同效应包括运营协同和财务协同两方面。运营协同又包括收入协同和成本协同。收入协同可通过整合双方市场、客户资源等方式实现，成本协同可以通过采购成本节约、销售与管理成本节约等方式实现。财务协同可以通过资本市场和上市融资、资金统一管理与分配等方式实现。协同效应的来源包括规模经济效益、销售渠道和客户资源整合、产业链上下游业务相互支持、新技能或研发团队形成合力等。

在制订了协同效应实施计划之后，企业还需要跟踪、监控计划执行情况，根据市场变化、计划实施效果以及实际操作中积累的经验和教训，对协同效应实施计划进行定期和不定期的动态调整，以保证实施计划能够有效指导业务开展。

中国企业"一带一路"投资并购成功的一个很重要的方面就是能够通过投资并购实现业绩的增长，特别是中国市场的业务增长。如在吉利收购沃尔沃后，沃尔沃在中国的销售取得了高速的增长，而且沃尔沃很多先进的技术、管理方法也带动吉利中国业务的快速增长，实现"1+1>2"的协同效应。相比较而言，TCL收购汤姆逊的彩电业务，不但没有实现中国业务的增长，而且原来欧洲和北美的业务也裹足不前，把TCL拖入泥潭。

（五）应对企业文化融合挑战，顺利实施员工整合

"一带一路"国家投资并购涉及中外企业文化的融合。当中国企业并购国外

企业时，由于双方文化背景相差较大，在工作方式、价值观念、领导风格和行为规范等方面存在较大差异，如果处理不当，这些差异很容易引起中外双方的冲突和对立，从而影响企业运营的方方面面。"一带一路"国家投资并购项目文化融合的一个重点领域是员工整合，而员工整合的关键点在于与对方员工就整合战略、整合目标和整合方案进行深入沟通，在理解并充分考虑员工关注问题的前提下，通过全方位沟通打消对方顾虑、赢得对方支持，使之产生认同感和归属感。

从长期来看，文化融合还需在高管融合、观念融合、人力资源制度、日常管理等几个方面加强工作，从根本上建立起"文化宽容、差异融合"的新的企业文化。

考虑到"一带一路"国家文化的多样性，成功的并购一定要求文化的充分融合。中国企业在进行"一带一路"国家投资并购之前就要做好功课，充分研究目标公司所在国和公司的文化，在融合过程中，充分尊重国家和公司文化的二重差异性。如吉利收购沃尔沃时采取了"沃人治沃"的策略，充分尊重沃尔沃的高管、员工和公司的文化传统，而不是移植吉利中国总部的管理文化。同样的，东软集团收购德国哈曼的导航团队也采取同样的策略，取得了成功。

（六）建立高效沟通机制，赢得利益相关方认可

在并购整合工作中，中国企业往往忽视与各利益相关方沟通的重要性，信息披露较少，不善于交流，缺乏公共关系管理经验。在"一带一路"国家投资并购项目中，企业应认识到各利益相关方的诉求可能存在差异，比如客户希望新公司仍然保持产品和服务的质量，客户体验不会受到影响；合作伙伴希望了解公司未来业务调整方向，如经营战略、商业模式、供应商管理等，以考虑是否需要调整与新公司的合作方式；员工则关心在企业所有权转移过程中，岗位设置、工作职责、薪资福利、业务汇报线等会不会发生变化；其他利益方，如政府机构、分析师和媒体等，则可能更为关注企业社会责任、盈利预期和未来投资计划等问题。

信息不通畅会带来隔阂，隔阂会引发对立情绪，而打破这样的隔阂其实并不难。企业首先需要明确在当地投资所涉及的各利益相关方，确定公关策

略，以及要向这些利益相关方传递的企业品牌形象和信息。有条件的企业还可以设立公关部，配备专业人员或是向公关服务提供商寻求专业指导意见。在与各方进行沟通时，企业应注意强调交易本身的信息，包括企业投资战略、对被并购目标的定位和未来规划、协同效应的来源，以及将为东道国带来的就业和经济发展机会等内容。这将有助于社会各方了解企业并购的商业目的，而不是把注意力集中在非商业因素上。

第三节　并购整合的评估与管理

整合是指调整公司的组成要素，使其融为一体的过程。并购整合，是将两个或多个公司合为一体，由共同所有者拥有的具有理论和实践意义的一门艺术。PMI 所包含的内容是极其丰富的。其中，战略整合、财务整合、人力资源整合和文化整合由于其地位的重要性，是人们研究最多的领域。交易缺口（Transaction Gap）和转化缺口（Transition Gap）是并购失败的两个原因。前者可以通过并购谈判、讨价还价来弥补；后者需要通过商业流程整合、信息系统整合和生产整合等并购后整合活动来弥补。布鲁斯·沃瑟斯坦（Bruce Wasserstein）明确指出，"并购成功与否不是仅依靠被并购企业创造价值的能力，而是更大程度上依靠并购后的整合"，并购整合不当就会造成财富毁灭。

对于并购的整合程度，学术界有两种理论：协同效应，成功的整合会带来超出预期的业绩收益；摩擦效应，并购方较深的整合程度对并购成功有不利影响，会破坏当初吸引并购方的目标方资源。企业整合的风险包括内部资源风险，即企业内部生产者因组织、管理、战略能力等带来的风险；外部资源风险，主要是企业外部消费者受市场区隔、产品定位等影响带来的风险。

相关性在并购整合风险中一直被关注。2003 年，迈克尔·波特（Michael E. Porter）对世界 500 强公司进行研究，认为 70% 以上的公司不能实现对不相关资源的成功整合，在收购 5 年内，这些企业会选择重新把并购的企业剥离出去。只有并购双方技术差异适度，既有一定的差异而又在并购方的接受能力范围之内，并购后的技术整合才可能是有效率的。但是对于相似性所导致的并购公司探索性学习的动力下降，从而带来技术整合与新技术产出水平的不确定性，应当进行高度的防范。例如2009年四川腾中收购美国悍马，由于后续的技术整合、技术保障以及发展模式均面临极大的问题，最终于2010年2月宣布并购失败。相比较而言，吉利也同样对美国悍马表达了收购意向，但是吉利认为悍马与自身的战略发展方向并不契合，随后选择了澳大利亚变速系统国际公司（Drivetrain System International，DSI）。收购DSI大大强化了吉利的自动变速器技术研发和生产能力。经过整合，吉利的技术能力得到显著提升。2010年，吉利收购沃尔沃，提高公司在汽车环保、安全、节能方面的水平。

  在并购整合时，收购方要对双方差异做出正确判断，并且合理利用互补机制，如果选择了错误的战略，即对差异性大的资源采用集中战略，对差异性很小的资源采用分散战略，会造成并购后公司内部冲突加剧、资源浪费，进而导致公司整体业绩下降。如果并购双方的差异性不大，目标公司极有可能接受新的资源配置；反之，雇员会更倾向于保持原有的社会认同，以至于新的资源不是那么容易整合。在这种情况下，只注重整合速度会对并购后的业绩有害，可能造成内部的冲突和不安定。

  在做整合之前，中国企业需要先客观评价标的资产的整合难易程度，并对自身消化整合能力进行正确的认识和评估，这样才能知己知彼，有针对性地制定并购整合战略和战术。很多中国企业关注硬性因素，而忽视软性因素，最后导致整合失败。对于硬性因素，可以采用雇用各种顾问、在当地提前设点熟悉市场等各种方式来解决，但对于软性因素带来的整合风险，难以在短期的尽职调查中了解清楚。这方面因素潜藏于日常沟通中，而且矛盾往往日积月累最终才会爆发，例如劳资关系导致的罢工、社区关系紧张、宗教文化差异乃至交流误解导致的冲突等。这要求并购方在日后的整合管理中更有耐心，对标的企业、员工、社区、客户等持有更开放的心态，更愿意真正去了解并尊重当地的文化，而非带着那种"来者通吃"的霸气，或者"谁出钱谁是大爷"的土豪作风。

如图 8-1、图 8-2 所示，在并购之前，中国企业需要从硬性、软性因素和能力两个维度对自我能力进行评估，同时需要从硬性、软性因素和风险两个维度对标的企业整合难度进行评估。

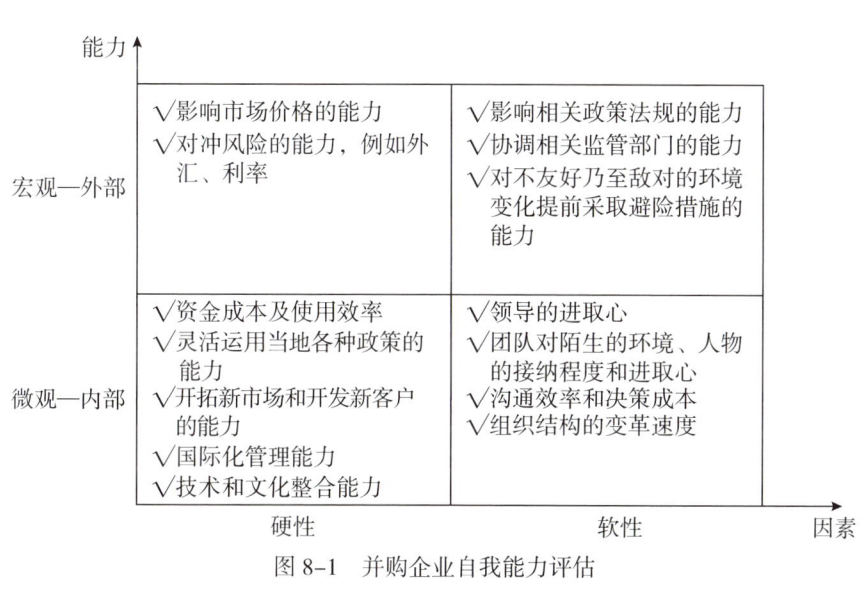

图 8-1　并购企业自我能力评估

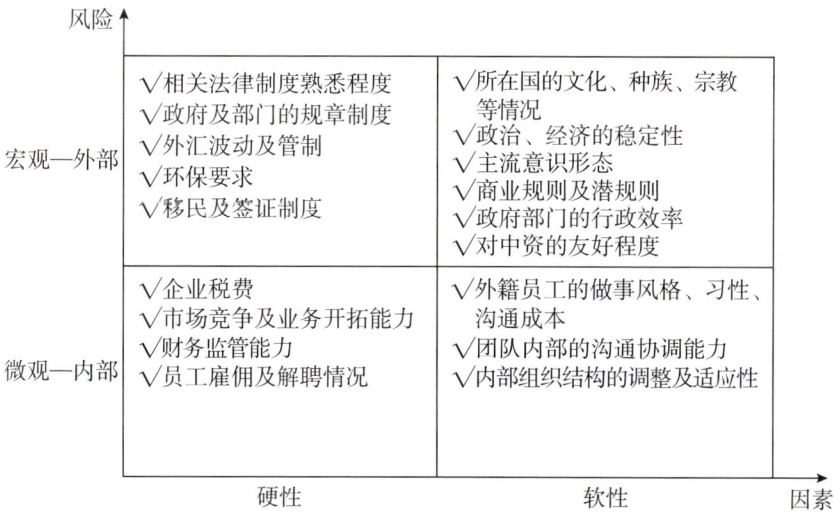

图 8-2　标的企业整合难度评估

在对自身和标的企业做出评估后，企业需要制定投后管理模式，不同的管理模式各有利弊。同是积极管理董事会,全面介入管理层,有成功的案例,也有失败的案例;纯粹有限的管理董事会,不介入管理层的财务投资模式,也有成功的案例。因地制宜、因人而异似乎是投后管理艺术的精髓。

中国企业在"一带一路"投资并购整合中可以借鉴日本企业的经验。日本企业倾向于让海外公司自主经营一段时间,如2~3年。日本公司会花比较多的精力在治理结构设计、长期激励方案、决策权限界定、不同委员会职责和会议日程设计等方面,通过合理的治理结构和有效的绩效管理方式降低交易风险。

日本企业通常会采用奖金类的保留方案,保留标的企业的管理层和关键员工。保留奖金通常匀速兑现,即交割后的第一年支付50%,第二年支付50%。对于业绩指标,通常日本企业会在交割后3~4个月,对标的企业有一定了解后调整考核指标。在对标的公司业务了解有限的情况下,日本企业通常会沿用前1~2年的绩效指标,等到对海外业务逐步了解后再决定是否调整业绩指标,以及如何与总部联动起来。

日本企业也很注意"平衡放权和管控",通过科学设计公司治理结构来达到有效的管理。日本企业关注战略方向、资源有效利用等大方向的把控,在"充分放权"和"过度干涉"之间寻求平衡。对于两个公司文化的差异,日本企业通过工作中的磨合逐步识别差异所在,并在工作中逐步加强彼此的理解。

案例 8-1 京瓷收购 AVX

交易金额:不详

目标国家:美国

行业:电子

案例背景:AVX 公司当时在电容器领域处于世界领先地位。为了把京瓷发展成为综合性的电子零部件公司,稻盛和夫向 AVX 公司董事长提出收购的要求,AVX 公司董事长爽快地答应了。收购采取了"股票交换"的方式,把当时纽约证券交易所 AVX 的股票高评 50%,以 30 美元的价格与时值 82 美元的京瓷股票进行交换。AVX 公司董事长提出 30 美元价格太低,希望以 32 美元成交。当时京瓷美国公司的社长和律师都强烈反对，他们认为轻易答应这类要求，对方会得寸进尺。稻盛和夫认为这位董事长对他的股东负责，于是同意了对方的要求。

然而，当双方股票进行交割时，道琼斯指数大幅下跌，京瓷的股票也跌了10美元，变成了72美元。看到这种情况，AVX公司董事长提出把原来的82对32的交换条件改为72对32。京瓷一方异口同声，主张驳回对方的要求。但是，稻盛和夫还是接受了不利的变更条件。他认为收购合并是两个完全不同的企业合二为一，是企业和企业"结婚"，应该最大限度为对方考虑。

收购之后，京瓷的股票一路上扬，AVX公司的股东获利丰厚，他们的喜悦之情感染了公司员工。一般而言，被收购公司的员工对收购公司总是抱有抵触和不满，但是AVX的员工们却因为京瓷接连的高姿态，一开始就抱有友好的态度，而且很自然地接受了京瓷的经营哲学。

案例分析：由稻盛和夫创办的京瓷，是日式经营的代表，同时也是日企进行海外并购的先驱。从20世纪70年代以来，京瓷所进行的海外并购多达40多起。许多日本公司收购美国公司，但后来由于亏损不得不纷纷撤退或出售，而京瓷却获得丰厚的回报，这与京瓷的创始人、经营者稻盛和夫不只考虑自己的利害得失，而为对方着想的理念分不开。

京瓷选择被并购企业时的标准有着共通点——由于某一方面的原因而陷入经营困境。收购这样的企业，一方面固然会有交易成本低廉的优势，但另外一方面，在后续的经营改善方面会面临更大的挑战，尤其是在跨文化、跨地域的情况下，这样的难度相当大。但是从京瓷海外并购的实际效果来看，几乎每宗并购都能够使被并购企业成功重建，这其中的关键是京瓷独到的并购后整合、管理的模式和技巧，通过将京瓷的东方式经营管理理念注入陷入困境的西方企业，成功地革新企业文化，从而实现突破性的转变。

这些方法中重要的一项，也是京瓷经营文化的基础：扩大企业内部的沟通范围，优化沟通效果，提升员工的参与感，引入"日常改善"的理念。20世纪70年代，京瓷在最初的一宗并购项目中，从美国仙童公司手中买下圣地亚哥的一家工厂。当时，该工厂由于长期经营不善，已经陷入连年亏损的境地，局面非常混乱：管理层高高在上，远离业务一线，为应付日益困难的经营局面，唯有在各种降低成本的细枝末节上打转；员工也全无热情可言。京瓷入驻后，首先向对方传授现场改善的做法和经验，同时将工作重心放在缩短管理层和员工之间的距离，增加沟通的频率。除此之外，为了改善整体的沟通效果，京瓷还将办公区改建成开放式的，以增进沟通的效果，化解管理层和员工之间的隔阂。

同样，在收购AVX的过程中，京瓷也展现了对AVX原有历史、文化和员工的尊重。在完成收购后，京瓷不仅没有改变AVX的公司名称，没有撤换任何管理团队成员，反而将当时业绩突出的京瓷北美电子部件事业部并入AVX公司，并将刚组建的京瓷北美工厂与AVX进行整合。这种对于AVX发展前景的信心和诚意表现，得到AVX员工极大的认可和支持，同时也为后续在AVX推行的改善措施奠定了良好的基础。被收购后，AVX公司继续成长，不到5年，又在纽约证券交易所再次上市。在再上市的过程中，京瓷通过出售股票获得了丰厚的回报。

第四节　投后管理经典案例分享

笔者根据多年海外并购经验，同时参考了成功的并购案例，发现能够实现有效整合、成功实现协同效应的企业都具有一些共同的特点，包括：（1）能够认识到海外并购整合工作的重要性，"并而不整"将难以实现协同效应和交易目标；（2）在签约前，对业务模式和整合战略加以充分考虑，"谋定而后动"；（3）尽早启动整合工作，使双方工作团队充分磨合，为业务对接奠定基础；（4）制定"管控模式"要从如何更有效地实现业务发展目标出发，最终体现在公司治理、组织架构和决策授权体系的设计方案中；（5）认识到文化差异的存在，以开放的心态迎接挑战，建立有效的沟通机制，赢得对方的认同感和归属感；（6）以"一带一路"国家投资并购为契机，提升企业国际化经营与管理能力，建立国际化人才的培养机制，并在并购战略的基础上，制定长期财务目标。

吉利汽车和光明集团作为两家典型的中国海外并购成功的企业，中国企业在进行"一带一路"国家投资并购时可以借鉴其成功经验；而TCL并购汤姆逊则作为反面案例为中国企业"一带一路"国家投资并购敲响警钟。

案例 8-2　吉利收购沃尔沃

交易金额：18亿美元

目标国家：瑞典

行业：汽车

案例背景：2010年，沃尔沃正处于企业存亡之际。高不成低不就的沃尔沃在北美备受市场冷落，在外是虚有其名的空架子，人们虽然知道沃尔沃很出名，但就是不愿意购买它；在内有着"世界上最安全的汽车"之称，但是接连亏损。从沃尔沃诞生那一刻开始，沃尔沃的造车技术，就已经被整个行业认可，沃尔沃从来不缺乏同行的赞扬，以至于最开始在欧洲市场受到排挤的时候，汽车巨头福特，二话不说就慷慨解囊，将其全资收购。但福特也没有预料到，收购完成后，沃尔沃依旧无法重新焕发活力，接受不了连续亏损的福特决定抛售沃尔沃股份，把这个"烫手山芋"甩出去。

2010年8月2日，吉利在伦敦举行对沃尔沃公司全部股权收购的最终交割仪式。此次并购是我国经典的海外并购案例。从今天的角度来看，当年的收购无疑是正确的。沃尔沃2014年的销量首次超过2007年以来的年度销售纪录，而中国已经成为沃尔沃全球最大的市场。2015年沃尔沃汽车全球销量首次突破50万辆，利润同比增加2倍，不仅收复了欧洲市场，在美国市场的表现也有起色。2017年全球销量创下历史新高，达到54.3万辆，收入增长10%，利润大涨66%。同时，此次并购还带动了沃尔沃总部瑞典哥德堡的经济发展，带动了当地零配件行业的发展。吉利与沃尔沃资源相似性、互补性及整合行为的高度匹配，是吉利成功收购沃尔沃的关键。

2017年12月27日，吉利收购沃尔沃集团8.2%的股权，加快其全球化的布局。沃尔沃集团拥有10万名员工，在18个国家设厂，产品覆盖190个国家和地区，拥有沃尔沃、沃尔沃遍达、UD、特雷克斯卡车、雷诺卡车、新星客车、佩沃客车、迈克卡车等品牌。该笔投资是在吉利投资沃尔沃汽车后7年完成的，标志着吉利已经完成对沃尔沃汽车的整合，借助沃尔沃集团这个更大的平台，开始在更大范围和更广泛的领域布局。

案例分析：在并购整合完成后，不但沃尔沃的销量实现增长，吉利也受益匪浅。吉利汽车一直以来都被认为是低端产品，企业的转型升级和与国际市场接轨受到限制，沃尔沃优秀的品牌价值能够充分带动吉利汽车实现战略转型。尽管吉利在国内市场发展较快，但其汽车设计制造和研发能力与世界水平仍有较大差距。沃尔沃能够为吉利提供先进的汽车制造技术，帮助吉利迅速缩小与世界高端轿车品牌之间的差距。通过并购沃尔沃，吉利引入了国际先进的内部管理团队，自主培养了一批拥有国际管理经验的团队，获得了欧美市场的销售渠道和网络，吉利的全球化战略得到了有力的保障。

吉利对沃尔沃的并购整合也不是一帆风顺的，双方整合经历了很长的磨合期。在交割几年后，沃尔沃的表现并不尽如人意。而到2012年，沃尔沃在华销售量下滑10%，这导致吉利更换了沃尔沃的领导班子。2012年至2014年，吉利和沃尔沃还有其他整合动作：（1）2012年底，吉利和沃尔沃签订了3份技术转移合作协议，旨在实现协同效应；（2）2013年，二者宣布在瑞典设立吉利—沃尔沃联合研发中心，以此开拓中端市场，几乎同时，沃尔沃宣布裁员1 000人，以避免再次出现亏损；（3）2014年9月，沃尔沃推出了被收购后的首款新车XC90。

吉利对沃尔沃的整合行为包含以下五方面成功的经验。

第一，目标方的独立性：吉利在并购整合后没有忙着剥夺沃尔沃的独立管理权。交易完成后，吉利按照"沃人治沃"的方式管理沃沃，允许沃尔沃内部保留单独的运作体系，不干涉沃尔沃的运营管理，保留高管团队，并且对工会承诺不转移工厂和不裁员。李书福表态"吉利是吉利，沃尔沃是沃尔沃"，体现了这一整合原则。吉利也没有直接大量应用沃尔沃的技术，可以想象，如果吉利大量应用沃尔沃的技术，沃尔沃的品牌形象和销量一定大打折扣。

第二，文化的融合性：吉利"以人为本"的企业文化同瑞典的主流文化及沃尔沃的企业文化具有高度融合性。吉利保留了瑞典的哥德堡团队精英及工厂、研发中心、工会协议和经销商网络，体现了对沃尔沃国际形象的尊重和支持双方文化融合的态度。

第三，品牌的独立性：沃尔沃属于豪华汽车品牌，吉利是低端车品牌，并且缺乏拥有国际市场运营经验和能力的人才。并购之后，吉利尊重沃尔沃品牌，并保持了沃尔沃的独立。吉利经营沃尔沃是接受和学习沃尔沃现有的管理经验，而不是主宰它。吉利同样保证并购后沃尔沃的品牌和运营的独立性，充分发挥原品牌的核心价值。

第四，刻意放慢整合速度：在并购后相当长一段时间里，双方就产品研发的理念和技术方向进行不断磨合，在双方达成共识后，吉利才于2012年开始在张家口设立沃尔沃发动机国产化项目，引入一系列先进的涡轮增速小排量发动机。吉利选择较慢的整合速度，是基于与沃尔沃双方在文化、管理观念等方面相似性很小的情况。

第五，人才和技术的整合：尽管吉利收购了沃尔沃100%的股权，但是没有收购沃尔沃100%的知识产权。沃尔沃的平台和发动机是与福特、马自达共享的，吉利不能直接应用沃尔沃的技术和生产标准。也就是说沃尔沃的核心技术还掌握在沃尔沃手里，吉利只能通过各种办法获得沃尔沃的技术和人才。吉利花费200亿元开发沃尔沃的架构，架构开发由双方共同完成，吉利研发能力得到很大的提升。吉利的领克、博越都大量运用沃尔沃的技术，取得了不错的销量。沃尔沃的一些高管和技术人员加入吉利，带来了沃尔沃先进的创意、理念和技术。吉利在瑞典设立欧洲研发中心，该中心有20多个国家和地区的1 600名专家，吉利通过欧洲研发中心可以不断汲取欧洲百年造车精华，不断提升自身的产品和技术水平。

案例 8-3　光明集团的海外并购

交易金额：不详

目标国家：澳大利亚、新西兰、以色列、西班牙等

行业：食品

案例背景：2006 年 8 月 8 日，光明食品（集团）有限公司（以下简称光明集团）成立，由上海益民食品一厂（集团）有限公司、上海农工商（集团）有限公司、上海市糖业烟酒（集团）有限公司、锦江国际（集团）有限公司的相关资产集中组建而成。

成立之初，光明集团的年收入为 414 亿元人民币。至开启海外并购之前的 2009 年，年收入达 508 亿元人民币。2010 年，收购新西兰新莱特乳业开启了光明集团海外并购的序幕。自此以后，光明集团在 5 年内完成了 8 宗海外并购项目。光明集团先后收购了 Salov 集团的多数股权及其子公司翡丽百瑞、新西兰乳业巨头新莱特、澳大利亚玛纳森食品集团、法国 DIVA 葡萄酒公司、以色列乳业巨头特鲁瓦、西班牙米盖尔等国际知名企业，在全球布局了以食品为核心的多个产业领域，并致力于全球资源的整合配置，打造光明食品全球制造、全球分销的体系。在海外并购项目的推动下，光明集团在 2014 年的收入已超过 1 200 亿元人民币，较 2009 年增长 136%。

案例分析：在海外并购过程中，光明集团已经总结出了一套行之有效的海外并购方法。

第一，标的选择。光明集团海外并购项目的选择遵循以下 5 个标准。（1）符合光明集团的发展战略，收购后能产生"1+1>2"的效果。以光明收购国际知名橄榄油品牌翡丽百瑞为例，翡丽百瑞是一家有百年历史的家族企业，在欧美橄榄油市场具有绝对的领导地位，企业发展平稳，业务每年保持稳定增长。光明经过对各项风险点的评估，认为该公司是适合收购的标的；而该公司选择被收购的原因也是希望借助光明集团的资源更好地开发中国市场，获得更快的增长，因此最终

促成双方合作。收购后，该公司在中国市场上实现了每年三位数的增幅。（2）标的企业的管理团队比较优秀，能有效管理企业，减少光明集团的管理成本。（3）风险可控，光明集团会仔细评估项目的每个风险点，包括财务情况、当地法律法规、养老金等多个因素。例如，在收购英国第二大早餐麦片品牌维他麦公司（Weetabix Food Company）时，养老金缺口金额一直是双方争论的焦点，最后狮王资本出资3 000万英镑弥补光明集团，减少了光明集团接收后因养老金缺口问题遭受的风险。（4）加快海外企业的上市步伐，充分利用全球资本市场为光明集团的国际化战略服务。（5）与团队形成协同融合，建立长期的合作关系。

第二，合理规划。光明集团在投资之前就考虑了收购标的企业之后企业价值提升到一定规模后怎么办，是上市、整合，还是将其资产注入已有上市公司。全过程价值链管理使得光明集团海外收购的增值手段多样化，确保收购资产能保值增值。

第三，分级管理制度。光明集团并购的企业分布在世界各地，距离中国较远，不可能所有的事情都汇报给总部，由总部来处理。光明集团把企业各种决策分等级，不同等级的事务交由不同级别的管理层来决策，只有当事务等级足够高，才会提交给董事长来决策。这样一来，大大缩短了决策链条，提高了决策效率。

第四，人才培养和管理制度。光明集团虽然在不断尝试海外并购，但国际化管理人才缺乏一直是其瓶颈。在实践过程中，光明集团通过几条途径来解决管理人才缺乏的问题：（1）选派了解西方管理理念的高管加入当地管理团队，积累经验，储备人才；（2）与国际人才公司合作，招聘海外高管；（3）留住原股东和被并购企业管理团队。例如，在收购维他麦公司的过程中，光明集团与原来控股股东狮王资本共同管理维他麦公司，狮王资本以40%的小股东身份继续持有维他麦，留下部分管理团队。对于维他麦的管理团队，光明集团采取股权和现金激励措施，颁布奖惩制度，明确企业和员工努力的目标。

案例 8-4　TCL 并购汤姆逊公司的彩电业务

交易金额：5.6 亿美元

目标国家：法国

行业：家电

案例背景：2003 年 11 月 4 日，TCL 集团与法国汤姆逊公司正式签订协议，重组双方的彩电和 DVD 业务。合资公司取名 TCL 汤姆逊电子公司，简称 TTE 公司。TCL 占六成以上的股份，处于控股地位。汤姆逊在 TTE 持有 33% 的股份，且将 9 000 名汤姆逊员工并入新公司。新组建的合资公司在欧洲、美洲和亚洲拥有十几家生产基地，年销售彩电达到 1 800 万台，TCL 成为全球最大的彩电供应商。

当时，汤姆逊公司的彩电和 DVD 业务亏损 2.54 亿欧元，但是 TCL 集团董事长李东生并不以为意，喊出了 18 个月盈利的口号。然而在执行过程中，面对 CRT（阴极射线管）技术的换代以及员工的整合等问题，TCL 依旧将中国式管理照搬到法国。

此后三年里，TCL 在欧洲市场全面陷入被动，既没有打开销售陷入困境的局面，对原有的烂摊子也束手无策，企业内部关系也矛盾重重，资金、人才、技术、管理、品牌、渠道等一系列问题全部涌现出来。并购完成后，TTE 连年出现巨额亏损，3 年净亏 40 亿元人民币，股票戴上了 ST 的帽子。欧洲彩电业务巨额亏损成为吞噬 TCL 集团利润的黑洞，以致失败后李东生感叹："我们原来的团队显得过于乐观，整合效应并没有发挥，企业还是按原来的习惯运作。"TCL 并购汤姆逊彩电业务，联想并购 IBM 个人电脑事业部，这是 2003 年左右中国企业国际化的标志性事件。但是与联想并购 IBM 个人电脑事业部后 2012 年成为全球第一大电脑厂商相比，TCL 并购汤姆逊彩电业务毫无疑问是失败的。

案例分析：TCL 并购汤姆逊的案例中，暴露了中国企业在"一带一路"国家投资并购的几个常见的问题。

（1）缺乏必要的准备和尽职调查。TCL收购汤姆逊仅用了8个月时间，缺乏细致的准备和对目标企业的充分了解。相比较而言，联想并购IBM花了多长时间呢？从接触开始算起是3年，谈判拉锯是13个月。TCL并购汤姆逊，最大的动力是成为全球第一彩电生产商。李东生本人，将并购汤姆逊视为千载难逢的做大做强的机会，TCL仅仅花了4个月时间接触，就决定并购汤姆逊，所以才会对自己花大价钱请的第三方机构给出的风险警告视而不见。(当时，摩根士坦利对这一并购持中性看法，而波士顿咨询则持反对意见，认为风险偏大。)

（2）对法国政策不了解，导致人事成本巨大。在《TCL国际化：李东生出海惊魂》中，作者提道："TTE很快陷入了'招人招不到，裁人裁不了'的尴尬情形。一方面原因是彩电行业在欧美属于夕阳行业，这方面的人才很少，也很难招；另一方面是欧洲裁员十分复杂，除了提前3个月通知外，还要支付高额的补偿金，如果裁员超过10人，补偿数额要由资方与工会谈判决定。所以，TCL在欧洲收购企业后，因为工会压力，国际整合迟迟到不了位。而在国内，这是根本不可能碰到的情形。"

在复盘这次并购的时候，李东生说，自己没有想到的是，在欧洲解雇一个员工这么难，这极大地推高了公司的运营成本。李东生在自己的微博中透露，在欧洲解聘人员，对于那些老弱病残员工必须优先安排工作。也就是说，如果你要解雇员工，必须先解雇那些有能力的、年轻的、能做事的，因为这些人能够轻易找到工作。这就与解雇的初衷矛盾，本来是想解雇那些能力不足的，留下能力强的轻装上阵，而按照法律要求，要解雇先得解雇能力强的，那不是自断手脚吗？

（3）文化难以融合。TTE副总裁童雪松在2005年末接受《中国经营报》采访时透露："TCL曾设想把中国设计的模具与汤姆逊共享，以此节约模具设计的巨大成本开销。虽然按照这些模具生产的彩电在美国很畅销，但法国人却怎么也看不上这些模具。"这种尴尬TCL遇到了很多，"例如有些法国人有语言上的优越感，不愿意说英文，TCL又没有什么人会讲法语，双方的沟通非常困难，一个简单的事情开很长时间的会，往往也达不成共识。"

（4）资金链运作问题。交易现金以及整合过程中的运营资金是通过银行贷款和企业上市融资获得。并购完成后，经营、投资和筹资现金均为负数，总体现金及现金等价物水平均出现了巨幅下降。

（5）海外并购成本和汤姆逊品牌价值估计错误。并购成本包括咨询中介费、评估费、谈判费、向被并购方企业支付的价款和管理整合的费用，这些费用超过了TCL的预期。TCL原来以为汤姆逊RCA品牌在北美市场发展得比较成熟，有进一步提升的空间，但实际上RCA品牌的生机几乎消磨殆尽，在北美市场出现巨额亏损。由于交易前对并购交易成本和整合成本估计不足，导致了TCL经济效益急剧下降，公司出现经营危机。

（6）对彩电发展潮流预期不准。当时，彩电制造商已经推动从背投彩电向平板电视的更新换代，而汤姆逊把全部的研究经费都投在背投产品的技术开发上。TCL在彩电技术变革的时期对汤姆逊进行收购无疑是一种冒险。如果在收购之前进行充分的市场调研，也许就不会出现这样的问题。"汤姆逊为什么要卖掉自己的彩电业务？全球第一台彩电就是它生产的，在欧盟向中国电视机企业提起的反倾销诉讼中，汤姆逊就是幕后主使之一。它享受了专利的红利，所以就不愿投资开发平板电视，但平板电视是未来的消费潮流，卖掉电视业务就可以甩掉包袱。即使如此，TCL在并购它时连'过时'的技术都没获得，人家不卖。"TCL集团原彩电新闻发言人刘步尘说。2012年年初，李东生在谈及并购汤姆逊的教训的时候说："我们并购的时候有一样东西没看准，就是未来电视会往哪个方向走，究竟是等离子还是液晶电视，当时更多人认为是等离子，但是汤姆逊有很强的DLP（数字光处理）技术，我们认为汤姆逊的背投更胜等离子，一脑门子扎下去，结果赔了大钱。"

TCL并购后千疮百孔、百无一是，很显然缺乏整合能力，而这通常也是中国企业海外并购中的一大通病。TCL并购汤姆逊彩电业务的案例无疑为中国企业的"一带一路"国家投资并购提供了极强的警示和借鉴价值。

附录

"一带一路"国家投资并购案例集

案例一　华信收购俄罗斯石油公司 14.16% 的股权（失败）

关键词：集成油、集成气、股票、风险

收购方：中国华信能源有限公司（CEFC China）

目标公司：俄罗斯石油公司（Rosneft Oil Russia）

【时间线】

· 中国华信能源有限公司（以下简称华信）于 2017 年同意从嘉能可集团（以下简称嘉能可）和卡塔尔投资管理局（QIA）买入俄罗斯石油公司价值 91 亿美元 14.16% 的股份。

· 在将股票销售给华信的计划失败后，2018 年 4 月，卡塔尔投资局宣布将接替华信收购俄罗斯石油公司 14.16% 的股权，为此支付 44 亿美元。

· 2018 年 5 月 4 日，俄罗斯石油公司发出通知，取消了向华信出售 14.16% 股权的协议。

· 华信已经花费了大约 4 亿美元在这次收购上，并且这些钱将不会被退还。

【交易主体介绍】

华信拥有将近 5 万名员工，年收入超过 400 亿美元，曾荣获中国最具影响力的企业、十大最具国际化竞争力的中国领军企业等称号。华信已经连续四年上榜《财富》世界五百强，2017 年排名第 222 位。

俄罗斯石油公司成立于 1995 年 9 月 29 日，是俄罗斯石油业的领导者和全球最大的上市石油公司。业务范围包括油气勘探和生产，上游海上钻井项目，油气提炼和原油，国内及国外的天然气和产品营销。公司拥有约 32 万名员工，2017 年位列《财富》世界 500 强公司第 158 位。

嘉能可是全球最大的多元化自然资源公司之一，也是90多种商品的主要生产商和经销商，拥有约150个采矿和冶金基地以及大量石油生产资产和农业设施。

嘉能可的工业和营销活动遍布全球，公司员工数接近16万人，在50多个国家和地区设立了90多个办事处。嘉能可的客户大部分属于汽车、钢铁、发电、石油和食品加工领域，但他们也为商品的生产者和消费者提供融资、物流和其他服务。

QIA是卡塔尔国于2005年成立的，是卡塔尔主权财富基金，也是中东地区最大的主权财富基金，截至2018年9月，总资产规模为3 200亿美元。其资金主要来源于卡塔尔石油收益，目的是通过向新的资产类别多样化转型来加强该国的经济实力。在30多年前卡塔尔投资的基础上，其不断增长的长期投资组合有助于补充该国在自然资源方面的巨额财富，提供长期稳定的回报。

【交易回顾】

嘉能可和卡塔尔投资管理局于2016年12月以113亿美元买入俄罗斯石油公司19.5%的股权。由于交易结构复杂，嘉能可和卡塔尔投资管理局实际仅持有4.5%的股权，这是二者联合出售14.16%股权的原因。

2017年9月，华信宣布收购嘉能可和卡塔尔投资管理局持有的俄罗斯石油公司14.16%的股权，交易对价91亿美元。此次收购一经交割，华信将成为俄罗斯石油公司第三大股东。双方还签署了战略合作协议和原油长期供应合同等协议。协议约定双方将在石油上下游产业链、金融服务、资产交易等方向开展深入合作。但是由于中国华信能源有限公司董事会主席叶简明被曝已被有关部门调查，华信陷入严重的债务危机和纠纷。

俄罗斯《每日商报》(*Vedomosti*)报道称，根据协议，华信2018年4月未能支付收购俄罗斯石油公司股份的首笔款项。首笔款项占交易总值的20%，约为18亿美元，其余款项原定于2018年9月底支付。媒体表示，中国华信能源有限公司在收购上已经花费了约4亿美元，这笔钱不会被退还。

2018年4月，卡塔尔投资管理局宣布收购俄罗斯石油公司的14.16%股权。交易完成后，卡塔尔投资管理局将拥有俄罗斯石油公司18.93%的股份，成为俄罗斯石油公司第三大股东，嘉能可将保留0.57%的股权。整个交易对价37亿欧元（约为44亿美元）。

与此同时，俄罗斯石油公司计划在 2018 年至 2020 年从公开市场回购价值 20 亿美元的股票。俄罗斯石油公司表示，已任命瑞银为独立代理人，负责执行其公开市场份额回购计划。2018 年 8 月，瑞银集团董事会批准了在 2020 年年底前购买至多 20 亿美元股票的计划。俄罗斯石油公司在一份声明中说："董事会批准的计划旨在在市场大幅波动的情况下提供优异的股东回报。"

【总结】

我们的结论是，华信的这一收购案件不成功。中国收购方的行动、能力与雄心不符。在这种情况下，大量的金钱和时间被浪费了。

从 2014 年到 2016 年，华信的资产规模几乎逐年翻番，营业收入也逐年增加，从 174.06 亿元人民币增至 2 472.55 亿元人民币。尽管企业收入增长迅速，但净利润绝对值仍未跟上总收入的增长。反映其盈利能力的资产回报率逐年下降，从 7.4% 下降至 2.9%，净利润率长期低于 2%。

中国企业在"一带一路"国家投资并购需要与公司自身体量和能力相匹配。但中国很多民营企业战略过于激进，希望通过投资并购快速实现业务的大幅增长。伴随着一系列激进的并购举措，公司内部深层次的矛盾不断暴露，导致公司现金流的情况恶化，最终导致交易失败，甚至将企业拖入深渊，从此一蹶不振。

案例二　中石油收购阿拉伯联合酋长国阿布扎比陆上石油公司8％的股权

关键词：能源、石油

收购方：中国石油天然气股份有限公司（CNPC）

目标公司：阿拉伯联合酋长国阿布扎比陆上石油公司（ADCO）

【时间线】

• 2017 年 2 月 19 日，中国石油天然气集团有限公司（以下简称"中石油"）与阿拉伯联合酋长国阿布扎比国家石油公司（ADNOC）签署了股票收购协议，中石油获得阿布扎比陆上石油公司（ADCO）8% 的股权及 ADCO 陆上油田开发项目 8% 的权益，期限为 40 年。

【交易主体介绍】

中石油是中国最大的石油和天然气生产商和供应商、全球主要的油田服务提供商之一，也是全球知名的工程建设承包商，其原油产量占全国的52%，天然气产量占全国的71%。中石油在近70个国家和地区设有办事处，还在非洲、美洲等国家和地区拥有石油和天然气资产及利益，正在寻求发挥更大的国际作用。

ADNOC是世界领先的石油和天然气公司之一，完全由阿布扎比酋长国政府拥有。该公司成立于1971年，活跃在石油和天然气行业的所有领域。它有17家专门的子公司和合资企业，在上游和下游部门都有业务。ADNOC活跃在世界各地，每天生产约300万桶原油。近年来，为满足工业燃气用户日益增长的需求，ADNOC扩大天然气田的工作取得了重大成就，并且提高了注气要求。

在开展所有业务活动的同时，ADNOC致力于可持续发展，确保人民需求与地球资源之间的和谐平衡，支持在所有项目中推行环境保护原则，而其HSE（健康、安全和环境管理体系的英文简称）业绩不仅是海湾区域一级，而且是国际一级。

ADCO是ADNOC集团内的主要陆上生产商，每天生产160万桶石油和15.9亿立方米天然气。ADCO由ADNOC持有60%的股权，其他股东包括英国石油（10%）、法国道达尔（10%）、中石油（8%）、日本石油开发公司（5%）、中国华信（4%）和韩国GS能源（3%）。

【交易回顾】

ADCO陆上油田开发项目是阿布扎比政府批准的开放式招标项目，ADNOC持有60%的股份，而另外40%的股份则留给外国伙伴。中石油出资65亿迪拉姆（合17.7亿美元）的注册资金获得ADCO陆上油田开发项目8%的权益，同时获得项目联合作业公司ADCO 8%的股份。

阿拉伯联合酋长国是中国在中东的第二大贸易伙伴，阿拉伯联合酋长国与中国之间的贸易额从2015年的548亿美元增加到2016年的600亿美元。

【总结】

我们的结论是，这笔交易是一笔相对成功的交易。

作为全球第二大能源消费国，中国在2016年是原油的主要进口国。总部位于北京的咨询公司恩亚能源（Sia Energy）估计，受补充库存需要、汽油需求强劲和燃料出口畅旺的影响，中国2016年的原油进口将增长86万桶，增幅近13%。

这一具有里程碑意义的协议标志着中石油与ADNOC的关系进入一个重要新阶段。作为协议的一部分，中石油将通过在ADNOC建立量身定制的技术中心，在设计和开发成熟油田的技术应用方面发挥积极作用。

这笔交易加强和深化了阿拉伯联合酋长国与中国之间的关系，双方以共同的价值利益、共同优化能源的机会，寻求最大的经济价值，支持ADNOC和中石油的长期发展。这将是一种互利的伙伴关系，双方能够保持强劲的生产水平，从一个非常有吸引力、长期和可持续的机会中获得最大的回报。

> 跟进：2017年年底，中国石油工程建设公司与ADCO签订了15.2亿美元的EPC总承包合同，涉及Bab油田综合设施开发项目。2018年3月，中国石油与ADNOC签署协议，中国石油以11.75亿美元的价格收购ADNOC两个油田10%的股权。
>
> 2018年7月19日，ADNOC和中石油的子公司中国石油集团东方地球物理勘探有限责任公司（BGP）达成了价值58.8亿迪拉姆（约合108亿元人民币）的合作协议。通过这一协议，ANDOC向BGP授予了一项重要的二维地震反射波勘测业务，以勘探阿布扎比尚未开发的油气资源。双方还打算继续寻求更多的合作机会，在国际上就下游投资领域进行联合投资。

案例三　海航实业收购新加坡CWT

关键词：物流、重命名

收购方：海航实业集团有限公司

目标企业：CWT Limited Singapore

更名为：CWT International Limited

【时间线】

·2013年，大型跨国公司海航集团旗下的海航实业集团股份有限公司（以下简称"海航实业"）入股新加坡领先的综合物流解决方案提供商CWT Limited（CWT），后来成为控股股东。

·2017年9月，海航实业通过自愿性全面要约方式收购CWT，在综合物流服务、国际大宗商品贸易和金融服务领域获得了更大的优势。自2017年12月起，CWT Limited更名为"CWT International Limited"。

【交易主体介绍】

海航实业是香港联交所主板上市公司，是一家高增长的投资者、开发商，以开拓潜在的全球投资市场为使命。其最大股东海航集团是一家领先的企业集团，上榜《财富》全球500强，其核心业务涵盖航空、控股、旅游、资本和物流。稳固的财务基础，包括强大的资本和流动性，确保了海航集团履行承诺的能力。

CWT集团创立于1970年，主要业务是为集装箱码头提供仓储和集装箱货运服务，通过全球领先的综合商品服务和服务合作伙伴网络，为全球多样化的客户群提供服务支持。CWT结合了行业领域的能力、全球规模优势，以及在商品营销、金融服务和综合物流方面的业务，为客户提供了全面的业务解决方案，帮助客户取得了成功，业务蓬勃发展。

【交易回顾】

海航实业宣布，截至2017年11月2日下午5时（新加坡时间），其拥有、控制或同意收购的CWT股份总数和有效接受要约，总额为5.89亿股，约占已发行CWT股份总额的98.1%。海航实业在新加坡收购后更名为CWT国际有限公司。

海航实业以10亿美元收购了新加坡物流和大宗商品公司CWT，CWT的商品营销、金融服务和物流运营也将成为集团的核心业务。海航实业并购CWT堪称是一笔"蛇吞象"的交易。2016年年底，海航实业的收入和毛利润为1.83亿港元和0.63亿港元。相比较而言，CWT的收入和利润达到509亿港元和7.11亿港元。

海航集团收购 CWT 被新华社称赞为"小而美"项目的典范。2017 年 10 月下旬，海航实业股份股价在一天内飙升 26%，此前有媒体称该企业收购 CWT 是中国"一带一路"十大投资并购案例之一。

海航集团董事会认为，并购后的公司名称变更将更好地反映集团战略，与集团的业务和发展战略保持一致，公司名称变更符合公司和整个股东的最佳利益。

【总结】

我们的结论是，这笔交易是一笔相对成功的交易。海航集团的自主品牌已成为海外扩张的先锋，并以强大的本地化战略开拓了全新的市场。CWT 主要利润来源于物流服务和金融服务，这与海航集团的业务协同效应明显。通过对 CWT 的收购，海航实业可以增强盈利能力。新加坡作为国际物流枢纽，更加有利于海航实业全球业务的拓展。海航实业可以利用 CWT 渠道和网络进一步拓展其在全球供应链物流的服务能力。在收购 CWT 之前，海航集团旗下天海投资以 60 亿美元完成了对全球最大的供应链服务商英迈国际（Ingram Micro）的并购。海航集团不断扩大在物流领域的布局，尽管收购过程相对成功，但是海航集团也面临着如何深度整合收购标的的难题。

东南亚已经成为中国企业海外投资的一个重要区域，笔者分析有以下四方面的原因。第一，良好的政商关系：东南亚国家与中国有着良好的关系，东南亚国家对中国在当地的投资持欢迎态度。第二，文化认同度高：东南亚国家华人比例高，文化和中国更为接近，中国企业收购和整合时更为容易。第三，东南亚人口规模大，经济发展速度快：东南亚地区总人口超过 6 亿，巨大的人口基数为中国企业业务拓展提供了可能。随着中国人力成本提高，很多欧美企业将制造业向东南亚转移，带来了当地经济的快速发展和购买力的提高。中国很多产业已经饱和，东南亚市场对于中国企业来说是一个新的增长点。第四，投资成本较低：相比于欧美的投资成本，东南亚地区的投资成本较低。新加坡作为东南亚最发达的国家，有很多一流的医药、物流、科技、金融企业，这些企业也成为中国企业投资并购的首选标的。

跟进：2017年12月11日，海航集团已行使法定权利，从新加坡物流公司CWT的异议股东手中收购所有股份，进而结束这一10亿美元的收购项目。海航财务顾问代表海航集团发布公告称，对尚未接受要约收购的CWT股东的报价为每股2.33新加坡元（合1.73美元）。价格与对其他CWT股东的报价相同，这笔交易的估值为13.99亿新加坡元（合10.4亿美元）。

案例四　阿里巴巴再投20亿美元双倍下注来赞达

关键词：网上购物、手机

收购方：阿里巴巴集团

目标公司：东南亚电商来赞达（Lazada）

【时间线】

· 2018年3月19日，阿里巴巴集团（以下简称"阿里巴巴"）宣布将在来赞达再投资20亿美元，以加快东南亚最大电子商务平台的增长计划，并深化其与阿里巴巴生态系统的整合。

【交易主体介绍】

阿里巴巴是1999年由马云创立的，宗旨是让天下没有难做的生意。阿里巴巴的目标是建设未来电子商务的基础设施，让客户在阿里巴巴见面、工作和生活，并成为一家至少持续102年的公司。阿里巴巴在200多个国家和地区运营，每个月有超过5亿人使用其购物应用程序。

来赞达，2012年成立，是东南亚排名第一的网上购物平台，经营范围覆盖印度尼西亚、马来西亚、菲律宾、新加坡、泰国和越南。作为东南亚电子商务生态系统的先驱，来赞达通过其市场平台为超过14.5万名本地和国际卖家以及3 000多个品牌商提供量身定制的营销、数据和服务解决方案，为该地区的5.6亿消费者提供服务，提供从消费类电子产品到家居用品、玩具、时尚产品、运动器材和日用品等众多产品。来赞达专注于提供卓越的客户体验，通过自己的第一和最后一英里（约 1.6 公里）配送部门提供多种物流服务、支付方式，包括货到付款、全面的客户服务和无障碍退货。目前，阿里巴巴持有来赞达多数股份。

【交易回顾】

2018 年 3 月 19 日，阿里巴巴宣布，将向来赞达再投资 20 亿美元，以加快实施东南亚最大电子商务平台的增长计划。包括这一新的计划，阿里巴巴共向来赞达投资 40 亿美元。阿里巴巴在 2016 年以 10 亿美元的投资控制了来赞达，并在 2017 年又投资 10 亿美元，将持股比例进一步提高到 83%。

2018 年的投资凸显了阿里巴巴对来赞达业务成功的信心，也凸显了东南亚市场的增长前景，该地区是阿里巴巴全球增长战略的关键部分。

亚马逊 2017 年就开始进军东南亚市场，但仅仅在新加坡进行了试水。Shopee 也属于较早进军东南亚的公司，由 Sea 投资，前身为 Garena，在美国 IPO 筹资超过 10 亿美元。阿里巴巴并没有将其在东南亚的发展限制在支持来赞达，还向印度尼西亚电商公司 Tokopedia 投资了 11 亿美元。印度尼西亚是东南亚最大的经济体，也是世界第四人口大国。竞争对手已经在该地区投入数十亿美元建设广泛的物流基础设施。2017 年，亚马逊在新加坡推出了两小时送货服务，而京东也在印度尼西亚建立了自己的物流网络，并于 2018 年 1 月宣布对越南电商平台 tiki.vn 进行投资。

预计此次投资将推动来赞达融入阿里巴巴生态系统，并使来赞达能够利用阿里巴巴的资源，以创新的方式进一步为消费者提供服务，增强东南亚商家的竞争力。此次投资凸显了阿里巴巴致力于为东南亚本土人才提供广阔平台，为东南亚数字经济发展做出贡献的雄心。

在巨额现金和股价飙升的支持下，为确保其在价值迅速增长的电商市场中获得更大份额，阿里巴巴在亏损的来赞达中投入了新的资金，这凸显了阿里巴巴全球化的雄心。

【总结】

我们的结论是，这是一笔相对成功的交易。

2017 年是阿里巴巴及其支付子公司蚂蚁金融（Ant Financial）在东南亚迅速扩张的一年，同时也是其与全球最大的在线零售商亚马逊对峙的一年，还面临京东挖掘该地区新消费者的挑战。

由于拥有年轻的人口、较高的移动普及率以及目前占该地区零售额 3% 的在线业务，东南亚地区受到了阿里巴巴的高度重视。事实上，凭借 6.4 亿消费者、不断壮大的中产阶级和不断提高的智能手机普及率，东南亚正逐渐成为科技巨头的主要战场。咨询公司弗若斯特沙利文（Frost & Sullivan）预测，该地区电子商务的商品总值将从 2016 年的 205 亿美元上升到 2021 年的 655 亿美元。

已经有大量证据表明阿里巴巴和来赞达之间的关系有所加强。2018 年来赞达开始在东南亚各地提供淘宝的产品，阿里巴巴已经用自己的高管取代了来赞达的科技团队领导层。此外，阿里巴巴为发展云业务，还在该地区建设数据中心，在基础设施方面投入巨资，促进了电子商务和支付服务的发展。蚂蚁金融也收购了其他几家东南亚支付企业的股权。自阿里巴巴首次投资以来，来赞达取得了显著发展。

案例五　KS ORKA 收购印度尼西亚地热能源 95% 的股权

关键词：能源、地热、资金筹集

收购方：浙江开山压缩机股份有限公司

工具公司：KS ORKA

目标公司：印度尼西亚地热能源（PT Sokoria Geothermal Indonesia，SGI）

【时间线】

·2016 年 8 月，浙江开山压缩机股份有限公司控股合资公司新加坡 KS ORKA 签署协议，从 PT Bakrie Power（PTBP）和 Xped Ltd.（原名 Raya Group）收购印度尼西亚 Sokoria Geothermal Indonesia（SGI）95% 的股份。

·2017 年 1 月 16 日，KS ORKA 完成了对 SGI 地热项目的收购，KS ORKA 打算加快 SGI 项目的开发，第一个地热发电机组于 2018 年 12 月上线。

【交易主体介绍】

SGI 持有印度尼西亚 Sokoria 地热项目（SGPP）的开发权利。SGI 项目的开发将为弗洛雷斯岛提供稳定的、长期的电力供应，满足当地的用电需求，促进当地经济的发展。地热是一种日益重要的可再生能源。印度尼西亚被称为"火山之国"，据报道，印度尼西亚拥有世界 40% 的潜在地热能源，估计总容量为 28 000 兆瓦。

KS ORKA 是冰岛公司 Hugar Orka ehf 与浙江开山压缩机有限公司的合资公司。KS ORKA 将冰岛地热项目开发专业知识与开山的发电厂技术和制造专业知识相结合，形成了亚洲唯一垂直整合的地热和废弃能源公司。

【交易回顾】

2016 年 8 月，KS ORKA 签署协议，从 PTBP 和 Xped 收购 SGI 95% 的股份。SGI 拥有印度尼西亚 Sokoria 地热发电项目的开发权，该项目位于印度尼西亚东努沙登加拉的弗洛雷斯岛，为 30 兆瓦地热发电项目，包括安装发电厂、变电站、发电机和涡轮机，以及铺设输电线路。

该交易是有条件并购交易，KS ORKA 与 Xped、PTBP 签署了有条件的股权购买协议。按照协议约定，KS ORKA 贷给 SGI 150 万美元，用于支付特许经营权费用、土地使用税和相关的发展费用，Xped 和 PTBP 以持有的 SGI 98% 的股权作为担保。如果三个月内，交易前提条件达成，KS ORKA 将以 1 美元每股收购 Xped 和 PTBP 95% 的股权。否则，Xped 和 PTBP 需要归还贷款。股权交割后，KS ORKA 将主持 SGI 地热勘探和开发项目。如果勘探结果满足要求，KS ORKA 将支付 200 万美元给 Xped 和 PTBP；如果不满足，按照勘探的实际情况，会相应减少付款金额。

目前，印度尼西亚是仅次于美国和菲律宾的世界第三大地热能源发电国。2007 年，地热能占印度尼西亚能源供应总量的 1.9%，占印度尼西亚电力的 3.7%。2011 年，爪哇、北苏门答腊和北苏拉威西六个地热田的装机容量就接近 1 200 兆瓦。

随着"一带一路"倡议的推进，在创新驱动的发展战略指导下，浙江开山压缩机股份有限公司成功开发了拥有自主知识产权的螺杆膨胀发电技术，以"一井一站"开辟了地热发电技术的新路子。

第一个地热发电机组于2018年12月上线。该项目的实施与印度尼西亚国家电力公司（PLN）计划完成的弗洛雷斯电网整合工作同时进行，钻探工作正在进行中。

【总结】

我们的结论是，这笔交易是一笔相对成功的交易。目前，浙江开山压缩机股份有限公司正在全面实施以独立开发的地热井口电站技术为核心，向可再生能源运营商转型的战略。这种对外投资是其向可再生能源运营商转型战略的一部分，这将有助于提高公司未来的营业收入和利润。该项目非常适合展示该公司在地热发电方面的螺杆膨胀发电技术，还可以取代印度尼西亚电网中高成本的柴油燃烧发电。如果协议顺利实施，对于浙江开山压缩机股份有限公司和KS ORKA尽快实现每年开发500兆瓦地热发电容量的目标，以及开拓全球地热市场，具有重要意义。

在"一带一路"国家投资并购时，交易交割是否成功有时取决于诸如政府审批、实际勘探、知识产权许可等条件，因此存在着较大的不确定性。在这样的情况下，交易前提条件的设置能最大限度地保证收购方的利益。整个交易可以划分为几个阶段，在满足一定条件的前提下，收购方支付一定的费用，交易进入下一个阶段。如果交易前提条件无法满足，交易自行终止。交易前提条件设置取决于双方实力的对比和博弈，中国买家在投资并购时有时需要支付保证金，由于买方原因导致交易无法进行时，保证金将不再退回。本案例中交易条款设计非常有利于买方，KS ORKA的利益得到最大限度的保护，值得中国企业学习。

案例六　中国欢聚时代参与新加坡视频社交平台Bigo D轮融资

关键词：TMT、进一步投资

收购方：中国欢聚时代

目标公司：BIGO Inc. Singapore

【时间线】

· 2014年，中国欢聚时代（简称YY）持有BIGO Inc.（Bigo）27.8%的股份。

· 2018年6月5日，YY以2.72亿美元认购了Bigo D轮优先股，成为Bigo最大股东。

· 2019年3月，YY完成对Bigo的全资收购，交易总金额约为14.5亿美元，其中包括3.43亿美元现金以及相应的YY股份。

【交易主体介绍】

YY是中国领先的直播流媒体平台。平台上的用户通过创造、分享和享受广泛的娱乐内容和活动，为充满活力的社区做出贡献。YY使用户能够通过在线直播媒体实时互动，并为用户提供独特的身临其境的娱乐体验。YY于2012年11月在纳斯达克上市。2018年YY全年总营收达人民币157.64亿元，同比增长36%，净利润为人民币16.42亿元，同比增长18.4%。

Bigo成立于2014年，旗下有直播平台Bigo live、短视频社交平台Like、游戏直播APP Cube TV和多款社交APP产品。公司业务主要集中在东南亚、南亚、中东和美洲。截至2018年底，Bigo live拥有2.25亿注册用户，超过4 000万活跃用户，用户平均每天在平台上花费40分钟。公司2017年10月正式实现盈利，当年总营收高达3亿美元。Bigo的投资人还包括平安海外控股、贝塔斯曼亚洲投资基金等一线风险投资机构。

【交易回顾】

YY宣布，在总部位于新加坡的社交媒体平台Bigo的D轮融资中，该公司投资了2.72亿美元，成为其最大股东。此外，YY还获得了在投资协议完成日期一周年后可行使的选择权，以市场公允价格购买额外的Bigo股票，以最终获得超过Bigo 50.1%的投票权的权利。其他投资者也与YY一起参与了D轮融资，其中包括YY董事长兼代理首席执行官李学凌先生，他利用个人资金投资了Bigo。Bigo是一个快速发展的基于视频的全球社交媒体平台。Bigo总部位于新加坡，旗下有全球领先的直播平台Bigo live，以及视频编辑和共享平台Like。Bigo为全球年青一代用户创建了一个基于视频的在线社区，在东南亚、南亚和中东等新兴市场建立了强大的影响力，为进一步的全球扩张铺平了道路。

虽然Bigo最初在东南亚推出，但它已经超越了该地区，总共设立了20个地方办事处。Bigo live是iOS上"社交网络"类别中的十大应用之一，不仅在东南亚国家如此，在沙特阿拉伯、巴基斯坦和新西兰也是如此。

通过最新的投资，YY已成为Bigo最大股东。YY与Bigo的联系一直可以追溯到Bigo成立之日。Bigo live应用程序于2016年3月推出后就迅速疯传。

Bigo live在完成C轮融资之后，市值超过4亿美元，且进一步拓展业务范围，已经超越了网络直播，增加了更多的应用。其中包括Cube TV，一种以移动游戏为重点的流媒体服务软件，以及用于编辑和共享短片的应用程序Like。此后，Bigo的注册用户在短短一年多的时间里增加了近两倍，从7 000万增加到2亿。

但早在Bigo正式推出之前，YY就参与了该公司的工作。2014年，YY就已经持有Bigo 27.8%的股份。当时Bigo的首席执行官正是李学凌。此外，Bigo的联合创始人、首席技术官胡建强也是YY的员工。

Bigo似乎对AI下了很大的赌注，在新加坡启动了这项技术的研究，并计划为其配备100名AI专家和工程师。Bigo在自己的平台上对这项技术进行了测试。在YY的支持下，Bigo 2017年的收入达到了16亿美元，给其竞争对手带来了更大的压力。此前，Bigo的融资公告紧随竞争对手M17娱乐公司首次公开募股（IPO）之后。M17娱乐公司的目标是筹集约1.15亿美元。作为一家得到盈利母公司支持的私营公司，Bigo比无利可图的M17娱乐公司有融资优势，一旦上市，M17娱乐公司将面临盈利的压力。截至2018年3月31日，M17娱乐公司的直播流媒体应用仅有3 300万注册用户，与Bigo相比是微不足道的。

【总结】

我们的结论是，这笔交易是一笔相对成功的交易。鉴于中国直播业务的发展已经趋于稳定，YY借助Bigo进行全球扩张具有重要的战略意义。《南华早报》援引iResearch的数据称，自2016年12月以来，中国的总体直播收视率一直在下降。尽管如此，YY在2018年第一季度的财务业绩表示，其收入、月活跃用户（MAU）和月度付费用户都有所增加。

中国市场变化很快，消费者的兴趣也在快速变化。我们认为短视频的兴起可能会对直播产生一些影响，另一个原因可能在于政府政策的变化。事实上，印度尼西亚政府部门最近已经使用了 Bigo 的 AI 技术解决方案，以帮助他们进行网络监控。有了 AI 监控系统和遍布全球的监控人员团队，政府能够在人力有限的情况下识别平台上 96% 的不当内容。Bigo 最近还在新加坡开设了一个研发中心，该中心是负责公司未来研发进展的主要基地。

欢聚时代董事长兼代理首席执行官李学凌先生说："我们非常高兴地宣布完成对 Bigo 的收购。这是 YY 集团的一个重要里程碑，表明了我们对全球化战略的信心和承诺。YY 和 Bigo 在中国和海外的强势业务的结合，将帮助我们创造更高质量的直播内容，扩大国际影响力，并为我们的全球用户社区提供世界一流的用户体验，从而使 YY 成为世界领先的视频社交平台公司。"

中国互联网产业高速发展，已经从最开始借鉴美国的互联网公司的模式，也就是所谓 C2C（copy to China）模式，演变成 CFC（copy from China）。中国互联网企业正在把在中国成功的模式，加入海外的互联网产品中。阿里巴巴、腾讯、小米、YY 等互联网企业在海外市场中已经取得了巨大的成功，将推动更多的中国互联网企业加入这一行列中。

案例七　上汽集团对通用汽车印度哈洛尔工厂的收购

关键词：汽车、分享

收购方：上海汽车集团股份有限公司

目标公司：印度哈洛尔工厂，通用汽车公司

【时间线】

·2017 年 6 月，上海汽车集团股份有限公司（简称上汽集团）宣布将接管通用汽车在印度古吉拉特邦的哈洛尔工厂，并计划在未来 5 年内投资 200 亿卢比（约 21 亿元）。

【交易主体介绍】

上汽集团是中国 A 股市场上最大的汽车上市公司，总股本为 116.83 亿股。上汽集团努力把握产业发展趋势，加快创新驱动型产业转型，从传统制造企业成长为全方位的汽车产品和旅游服务提供商。

General Motors Halol Plant 是通用汽车公司的工厂，位于印度古吉拉特邦的哈洛尔。它为印度市场生产各种雪佛兰汽车，年产能为 110 000 辆，员工总数约为 1 100 人。

【交易回顾】

通用汽车已经进入印度市场二十多年，但是从未实现盈利，市场占有率约 1.2%。因此通用汽车不得不调整在印度的战略布局，考虑将哈洛尔工厂出售。

2017 年 6 月，上汽集团宣布将接管通用汽车位于印度古吉拉特邦的哈洛尔工厂。在印度市场，上汽集团将在当地政府的支持下雇用约 1 000 名本地员工。该工厂于 2019 年投产，年产能在 50 000 辆至 70 000 辆之间。

上汽集团指出，其将成为中国首家在印度生产汽车的汽车制造商。目前，印度是世界第四大汽车市场。预计到 2020 年，印度将成为世界第三大汽车市场。此外，上汽集团在印度的发展将由其子公司独立运营，这使得上汽集团在印度市场更加灵活。

在印度通用汽车公司完成了哈洛尔工厂的移交后，上汽集团加快了哈洛尔工厂的改造和国产化。2017 年，上汽集团整车出口和海外销售达 17 万辆，比上年同期增长 31.8%，整车出口销售量继续在全国排名第一。上汽集团 2019 年已进军印度市场。前期经过并购，哈洛尔工厂的改造在 2018 年有序推进，供应商园区也在加快建设，首款互联网汽车产品正在按计划开发，于 2019 年投产。

上汽集团将通过新成立的当地子公司 GM Motor India 销售标志性的英国 GM 品牌下的汽车，GM 品牌是上汽集团全球乘用车战略的主要焦点，在亚太地区建立了组装和分销业务。

【总结】

我们的结论是，这笔交易是一笔相对成功的交易。上汽集团的自主品牌已成为上汽集团拓展海外市场的先锋。此次收购将为上汽集团在印度汽车市场的发展奠定基础。

印度和中国是人口最多的两个发展中国家，相比于中国的人口结构，印度的人口结构更有优势，年轻人占比更大。印度 65% 的人口是年轻人，平均年龄 29 岁。近些年，印度采取了一系列改革举措，改善了营商环境，印度经济发展迅速，已经成为全球投资的热点区域。2018 年，海外投资者在印度投资了 395 亿美元，已经超过在中国的 328 亿美元。而且中国企业也看好印度未来的经济发展，小米、阿里巴巴、华为、联想、复星、OPPO、vivo 等企业都在印度市场投下重资。

案例八　长电科技并购星科金朋

关键词：IC 封装测试行业、现金支付

收购方：江苏长电科技股份有限公司

目标公司：星科金朋（STATS ChipPAC Ltd., Singapore）

【时间线】

· 2015 年初，江苏长电科技股份有限公司（以下简称"长电科技"）宣布收购 STATS ChipPAC。

· 2016 年 5 月 9 日，长电科技宣布完成对 STATS ChipPAC 的并购，交易总金额为 47.8 亿元人民币（合 7.8 亿美元）。

【交易主体介绍】

长电科技为客户提供全面而广泛的产品组合，包括分立式、引线式、引线键合、倒装芯片、微机电系统（MEMS）和传感器、集成无源器件（IPD）、模塑互联系统（MIS）、高级晶圆级封装（WLP）、硅通孔（TSV）和系统封装（SIP）解决方案。长电科技总部位于中国江阴，拥有广泛的全球制造基地，在中国、新加坡和韩国设有运营中心，并在亚洲、美洲和欧洲设有客户支持办事处。

STATS ChipPAC 为通信、消费和计算机等成熟市场的半导体公司以及汽车电子、物联网（IoT）和可穿戴设备等新兴市场的半导体公司提供创新的包装和测试解决方案。

【交易回顾】

长电科技对 STATS ChipPAC 的合并和收购是一项战略行为，改变了全球半导体行业的竞争格局。该项目横跨新加坡、韩国、美国、中国台湾等多个国家和地区，涉及多个利益相关方，交易结构的设计烦琐而严格。为满足相关地区外资并购的政策和规定，长电科技对收购目标进行了划分和重组。

2016 年 5 月 9 日，JCET-SC 宣布完成对新加坡密封制造商 STATS ChipPAC 的并购。收购宣布时，在行业中造成了巨大的反响。因为根据收入数据，STATS ChipPAC 在全球密封领域排名第四，而长电科技排名第六。这种收购重组案件极其复杂，从拟议的收购到具体的操作，再到收购结束，需要近一年半的时间。

收购主要分为两部分。

第一部分：长电科技联合国家集成电路产业投资基金股份有限公司（以下简称"产业基金"）和芯电半导体（上海）有限公司（以下简称芯电半导体）在苏州设立长电新科，三方的股权比例为 50.98%、29.41%、19.61%，合计出资 5.1 亿美元。长电新科又与产业基金成立第二层公司长电新朋，合计出资 5.2 亿美元，长电新科持有长电新朋 98.08% 的股权，产业基金持有剩余 1.92% 的股权。随后，长电新朋在新加坡成立子公司 JCET-SC（新加坡），作为收购 STATS ChipPAC 的收购主体。之后，JCET-SC 以每股 0.465 77 新加坡元的价格收购了 STATS ChipPAC 100% 的股份，总投资约 7.8 亿美元。7.8 亿美元包括长电新朋 5.2 亿出资、产业基金给长电新朋的 1.4 亿美元贷款、中国银行 1.2 亿美元的贷款承诺函。

第二部分：长电科技和 STATS ChipPAC 达成协议，在提出要约的同时重组其台湾子公司。在运营方面，STATS ChipPAC 在新加坡成立了一家新的独立公司——Bloomeria，两家台湾子公司的资产被剥离给 Bloomeria，从而使两家台湾子公司的资产不包括在收购案件中，以满足中国台湾地区的政策要求。

收购完成后，STATS ChipPAC 成为 JCET-SC 全资子公司，公司从新加坡交易所退市。

【总结】

这是一次稳健的战略收购。从并购的技术水平来看，有几个独特的方面值得学习，例如如何选择战略联盟，如何实现联合投资者之间的利益平衡等，涉及复杂的并购过程和交易结构设计。STATS ChipPAC 的业务遍及新加坡、韩国、美国等多个国家和地区。这意味着，长电科技对 STATS ChipPAC 的收购必须遵守有关国家和地区并购的政策和法规，而且操作程序极其复杂，其中最重要的是收购目标的分离和重组。

长电科技秉持可持续发展和双赢理念，崇尚员工、客户、股东和社会和谐发展，被评为"中国重点高新技术企业""中国半导体十大领军企业"。目前，长电科技的封装技术专利数量在美国和中国都是同行业第一，市场份额位居世界第三。

案例九　京新药业向以色列Mapi公司投资1 000万美元

关键词：医药工业，增效

收购方：浙江京新药业股份有限公司

目标公司：Mapi Pharma Ltd. Israel

【时间线】

· 2015 年 12 月，浙江京新药业股份有限公司（以下简称"京新药业"）宣布使用自有资金，以 10.8 美元每股的价格认购 Mapi Pharma Ltd.（以下简称"Mapi"）92.59 万股股份，总投资 1 000 万美元。

· 2018 年 8 月 16 日，京新药业宣布对 Mapi 增资 1 000 万美元。

【交易主体介绍】

京新药业是一家集研发、制造、销售为一体的上市制药公司，在中国化工制药企业中排名前 100 位。

Mapi 成立于 2008 年，是一家以开发临床阶段的中枢神经药物为主的制药公司，从事高门槛和高附加值生命周期管理（LCM）产品的开发，这些产品针对的是大型市场及包括复杂活性药物成分的非专利药品（原料药）和配方。Mapi 的优势是强大的化学和制药研发能力，对全球市场和监管需求的深刻了解，以及在其业务所在的所有国家和地区促进合作的能力。Mapi 总部设在以色列，在以色列和中国设有研发机构，并在以色列贝尔谢巴以南的 Neot-hovavo 生态工业园设有生产设施。Mapi 拥有强大的知识产权实力，为原料药和配方提交了大量专利申请。

【交易回顾】

在 2015 年投资 1 000 万美元后，京新药业又对 Mapi 公司增资 1 000 万美元，公司持有 Mapi 的股份由 5.87% 增加到 9.71%。新的资金主要用于 Mapi 开展神经性疼痛和多发性硬化等适应症的药物研发和市场推广。截至 2018 年 8 月，京新药业已经完成了 7 笔海外创新药公司的投资，通过布局海外创新企业，提升公司的研发能力，推动业绩快速增长。

以色列处于发展阶段的制药公司 Mapi 已经从中国同行京新药业获得了一轮 1 000 万美元的融资。Mapi 正在从新一轮融资中划拨资金，用于开发两种新产品，一种用于治疗精神分裂症，另一种用于治疗疼痛。

Mapi 致力于高门槛、高附加值生命周期管理药品、复杂原料药及配方的开发。募集的资金将支持 Mapi 的未来发展，并使公司的渠道能够扩大到更多的药物、持久性创新的产品的研发。

【总结】

Mapi 与中国企业利用双方的优势建立了新的合作模式。京新药业的投资是产品开发协议的一部分，Mapi 将专门为京新药业开发产品，并将为京新药业在中国市场的注册、制造和营销提供支持。但尽管如此，Mapi 仍将拥有全球知识产权和营销权。

目前，中国制药企业与国外企业的合作具有这样的特点：中方直接从国外购买相应的创新产品和技术，从而参与新药的投资与合作开发；合作领域主要是癌症药品，主要是外国大公司的非核心领域；合作模式主要是中国企业获得中国地区的独家转让权，全球范围的转让几乎没有。但是从辉瑞、罗氏等国际制药巨头的发展道路来看，投资或收购早期项目是一条很好的发展道路。预计未来将有越来越多的中国制药企业走上国际投资和并购之路。

但是，从以往合作的角度来看，中国医药企业的外商投资和并购合作模式需要探索。一些直接收购项目的机会已经消失，更稳健的模式是跟随国际并购基金参与股权投资，以争取风险低于收益。

案例十　京新药业以500万美元收购P2B的股权

关键词：医药产业，股份

收购方：浙江京新药业股份有限公司

目标公司：Pharma Two B Ltd.（P2B）Israel

【时间线】

· 2017年3月22日，京新药业宣布以500万美元资本投资Pharma Two B Ltd.（以下简称"P2B"），收购其不超过5%的股权。

【交易主体介绍】

P2B是一家以色列的生物制药公司，致力于"非市售剂量""低毒""优效"复方制剂的研发。该公司的主营产品为P2B001，该产品为革新型的复方制剂，适应症为帕金森综合征，现处于临床试验阶段。

【交易回顾】

2017年3月22日，京新药业宣布投资500万美元，收购P2B不超过5%的股权，并在中国市场拥有P2B001革新型复方制剂产品的权益，P2B001预计将于2021年左右在中国上市。通过此次投资，京新药业已成为以色列P2B公司的股东，有利于巩固合作关系，为京新药业保留潜在优势。

【总结】

京新药业在目标企业的技术调查方面做了大量工作，同时，投资领域也是其熟悉的医药产业和治疗领域。通过国内外的比较和研究，京新药业最终因看好 P2B 的技术而进行了投资。

京新药业占据全球创新高地，通过从丹麦、以色列、美国等国家收购医药企业的个别冠军，促进企业的快速发展。据统计，京新药业 2018 年实现营业收入 29.44 亿元人民币，同比增长 32.66%；净利润 3.7 亿元人民币，同比增长 39.97%；扣除非净利润 3.16 亿元人民币，同比增长 653.97%。未来，京新药业还计划进行 10 亿元人民币的大规模投资和收购，进一步改善产业布局。

案例十一　吉利收购马来西亚的宝腾和莲花汽车

关键词：汽车工业，股权

收购方：浙江吉利控股集团有限公司

目标公司：宝腾控股有限公司（Proton Holdings Berhad，PHB），莲花汽车（Lotus Cars），宝腾母公司（DRB-HICOM）

【时间线】

·自 1996 年以来，宝腾控股有限公司（以下简称"宝腾"）一直是莲花汽车的拥有者。

·2017 年 5 月，马来西亚宝腾母公司宣布计划将旗下宝腾 49.9% 的股权和莲花 51% 的股权出售给吉利。

·该交易于 2017 年 6 月签署，从那时起，莲花不再是宝腾的子公司。

·2017 年 9 月 29 日，浙江吉利控股集团有限公司（以下简称"吉利"）与 DRB-HICOM 联合宣布了宝腾控股（Proton Holdings Berhad）和宝腾汽车（Perusahaan Otomobil Nasional Sdn Bhd）的董事会成员及部分高管成员名单。

【交易主体介绍】

吉利是一家私人控股的全球汽车集团，总部位于中国东南部的浙江省杭州市，是中国最大的独立汽车品牌之一。集团成立于 1986 年，最初是一家冰箱制造商，20 世纪 90 年代开始生产摩托车，1997 年凭借吉利汽车品牌进入汽车行业，2002 年推出了第一辆汽车，并于 2010 年从福特汽车收购了沃尔沃。该公司销售吉利汽车、莲花、领克、宝腾和沃尔沃等品牌的乘用车，以及伦敦电动汽车公司和远程汽车品牌旗下的商用车。2017年，吉利在全球销售超过180万辆汽车，总销售收入达到2 782亿元人民币（同比增长33%），净利润达到188亿元人民币（同比增长61%）。公司总资产超过2 000亿元人民币，连续七年入选《财富》全球500强企业。

宝腾是一家总部位于马来西亚的公司，活跃于汽车设计、制造、分销和销售领域。宝腾成立于1983年，是马来西亚唯一的全国性汽车品牌公司，直到1993年Perodua出现。"PROTON"是Perusahaan Otomobil Nasional（国家汽车公司的马来西亚语）的缩写。宝腾最初由DRB-HICOM拥有，少数股权由三菱集团成员持有。2004年，三菱已将其持有的宝腾股权全部出售，2012年，宝腾被DRB-HICOM全部收购。

【交易回顾】

吉利汽车的母公司吉利控股收购了宝腾49.9%的股份和莲花51%的股份。收购完成后，吉利控股将拥有吉利汽车、领克、沃尔沃、伦敦电动汽车、宝腾和莲花六款汽车品牌，涵盖低端和中端品牌、奢侈品牌和特殊品牌。吉利原来的主要市场在中国和欧洲，现在进一步扩展到东南亚。

2017年5月24日，吉利宣布收购马来西亚汽车制造商宝腾49.9%的股份，获得进军东南亚市场的平台。作为交易的一部分，吉利以5 100万英镑（6 620万美元）从宝腾收购了英国汽车制造商莲花51%的股份。但DRB-HICOM（宝腾的母公司）掌握50.1%的股权，这意味着宝腾仍是马来西亚的品牌。

宝腾拥有两家工厂，其中包括马来西亚丹绒马林的一家未充分利用的工厂，每年能生产15万辆吉利汽车。宝腾还在马来西亚拥有现成的销售网络，吉利可以用它来销售汽车。

田建华说，马来西亚将允许吉利开发右手驱动车型，并有可能随着收入的增加引进沃尔沃汽车，他估计，马来西亚的汽车保有率约为中国的五分之一，发展潜力大。

【总结】

我们的结论是,这笔交易是一笔相对成功的交易。如果吉利收购沃尔沃,是为了沃尔沃的品牌和技术,那么收购宝腾则是为了进入东南亚市场。对吉利来说,马来西亚只是一个跳板,印度尼西亚甚至整个东南亚才是吉利未来的重要战场。非日本品牌汽车企业在东南亚一直举步维艰,而这笔交易为吉利在东南亚建立了分销网络。同时宝腾也获得了一个经济实力雄厚的合作伙伴,并可能获得更先进的技术。

随着宝腾和莲花的加入,吉利加快了全球化步伐,并在东南亚建立了一个滩头阵地。吉利的目标是到2020年为东南亚市场生产50万辆汽车。除了作为进入东南亚的切入点外,宝腾还为吉利进入全球范围内的右手驾驶(RHD)市场,包括马来西亚、英国、印度和澳大利亚,提供便利。

这项投资是在中国和马来西亚最近签署的价值数十亿美元交易的基础上进行的,但宝腾是一种以民族自豪感包裹的资产,是马来西亚独立后工业化和经济增长的象征。

对于汽车出口萎缩,业界普遍认为贸易壁垒和区域经济动荡是主要原因。此外,我国奇瑞和江淮等自主品牌的主要出口国是俄罗斯、巴西等国家,但由于这些国家的货币贬值和经济衰退,我国汽车的出口销售额逐步下降。然而,"一带一路"倡议为我国汽车公司的出口带来了福音。例如,印度是"一带一路"沿线的一个国家,2016年我国对印度的车辆出口同比增加了近五倍。此外,东盟是中国最大的贸易伙伴。与其他国家和地区相比,我国自主品牌车辆向东南亚出口更有优势。一是因为中国与东盟签订了《中国—东盟自由贸易协定》,营造了良好的贸易环境,且对90%的商品实现了零关税。第二,东盟十国之间有着关税优惠协定。据2014年6月泰国《世界杂志》报道,东盟十国之间的贸易关税接近于零,只剩下少数敏感商品仍未实施零关税,并且东盟将继续推行零关税措施。在这一点上,吉利收购马来西亚宝腾的意图,是非常清楚的。

案例十二　复星集团以2.9亿新谢克尔收购阿哈瓦的全部股权

关键词：美容行业，100%

收购方：复星集团

目标公司：阿哈瓦（AHAVA）死海实验室有限公司

【时间线】

·2016年4月10日，中国企业复兴集团签署了一项协议，以2.9亿新谢克尔（约合4.96亿元人民币）收购了阿哈瓦的全部股权。

【交易主体介绍】

复星集团成立于1994年，是中国领先的医疗集团。复星集团秉承改善人类健康的使命，业务涵盖医疗产业链的所有关键领域，包括医药制造和研发、医疗服务、医疗器械和医疗诊断，以及药品分销和零售。复星集团始终将创新视为业务增长的动力。

阿哈瓦于1988年创建于死海区域，并被全球公认为死海黏土皮肤护理品牌。作为以色列政府授权的公司，阿哈瓦有权开发死海资源，可以凭借其优良的配方和精湛的技术，充分利用死海资源。同时，通过配合各种天然植物精华，阿哈瓦迅速发展壮大，成为以色列独一无二的珍贵国家级高新技术公司。

【交易回顾】

2016年4月10日，在耶路撒冷大卫城堡酒店举行了重要的签约仪式：中国领先的投资集团复星集团与以高恩控股为代表的阿哈瓦股东签署了一项协议，以2.9亿新谢克尔收购阿哈瓦的股份。

复星集团副董事长兼首席执行官梁信军与高恩控股首席执行官盖伊·雷夫（Guy Regev）在以色列政府高级官员和双方公司代表的见证下签署了协议。

复星集团对以色列市场充满信心，并不断在各个领域寻找合适的投资机会。复星集团相信，阿哈瓦是一个以信誉和实力打造的成功品牌。复星集团很高兴成功完成此次交易，为各方取得双赢的成果。

复星集团希望通过投资以色列企业，在未来进一步深化中国企业与以色列企业的合作。复星集团在以色列市场的投资始于 2013 年，当时它收购了以色列领先的激光美容设备公司飞顿激光有限公司（Alma Lasers）。自复星集团投资以来，飞顿在中国的发展取得了显著的成果，并成功地将中国市场发展成其最大的单一市场。

【总结】

中国的经济增长将越来越多地受到消费的驱动，消费领域最重要的是家庭财富的保护和增值，追求健康管理和幸福生活。因此，复星集团未来将更坚定地关注资产方面的 B2F（企业对家庭）商业模式，投资于丰富、健康、快乐的行业。复星集团将利用内外的核心资源，凭借工匠精神打造产品，为家庭提供丰富、健康、快乐的一站式综合解决方案，为客户提供良好的服务，创造丰富的价值。

阿哈瓦是一个矿物护肤品品牌，最初创建于死海地区，享有世界声誉。其顶级面部护理产品包括死海 Osmoter 系列面部精华、矿物质精华、皮肤活化保湿凝胶等。这些产品深受世界各地消费者的喜爱。阿哈瓦在希伯来语中的意思是"爱"，而复星一直在积极实践其"中国动力嫁接全球资源"的投资模式，该模式将向世界提供代表"来自以色列的爱"的阿哈瓦产品。

以色列总人口只有不到 900 万，科技对 GDP 的贡献超过 90%。以色列的优势行业，包括医疗、节能材料、新型材料、高科技等，与中国企业的契合度非常高，中国企业已经成为仅次于美国企业的以色列主要投资商。复星集团、水晶光电、和邦生物、三胞集团、巨人网络等多家中国企业已经在以色列完成多笔并购交易。随着中国经济的转型升级，中国企业海外并购的重心从原来的资源和能源等行业，转向医疗、消费、高科技等行业，以色列拥有全球领先的技术和创新人才，吸引了越来越多的中国企业到以色列投资并购。

案例十三　水晶光电战略投资以色列Lumus

关键词：高新技术产业，可转换债券
收购方：浙江水晶光电科技股份有限公司
目标公司：Lumus Limited Israel

【时间线】

· 2016年5月17日，浙江水晶光电科技股份有限公司（以下简称水晶光电）以自有资金300万美元认购Lumus Limited（以下简称Lumus）发行的18个月期无担保可转换债券。

· 2016年11月15日，水晶光电宣布以自有资本220万美元收购Lumus股东雅可夫·阿弥泰（Yaakov Amitai）先生持有的100 000普通股，以500万美元认购93 355股新的C轮优先股，将全资子公司持有的300万美元的无担保可转债转换为67 362股C轮优先股。

【交易主体介绍】

水晶光电是2002年8月2日成立的国家级高新技术企业，2008年9月19日在深圳证券交易所上市。水晶光电是国内专业从事光学成像、LED、微显示和反射材料的研究、开发和制造的企业。公司在光机设计、开发能力和光学元器件加工领域具有一定的技术积累。公司下设三家全资子公司——浙江晶景光电有限公司、江西水晶光电有限公司、浙江方远夜视丽反光材料有限公司，一家控股子公司——浙江台佳电子信息科技有限公司，并参股日本光驰株式会社、浙江浙大联合创新投资管理合伙企业（有限合伙）、宁波联创基石投资合伙企业（有限合伙）。

Lumus是一家创业高科技公司，在穿透式视频眼镜领域具有领先的设计能力，并且拥有大量欧美客户资源。

【交易回顾】

2016年，Lumus宣布已获得1 500万美元的B轮融资，由盛大集团和水晶光电领投。Lumus 融资的资金将用于公司研发、生产能力的提高和市场的拓展，以便和 Hololens、Meta 等产品竞争。完成交易后，水晶光电将持有 Lumus 260 715 股股份，占交易完成后总股本的 3.06%。借助 Lumus 在穿透式视频眼镜和欧美客户资源方面的优势，这项投资将有助于水晶光电加速其在虚拟显示领域的发展。

【总结】

水晶光电是一家以薄膜光学产品、蓝宝石和反光材料为核心技术的光学元件企业，已成为索尼、三星、柯达等企业的主要供应商。近年来，水晶光电正积极地布局 VR/AR 等智能显示领域。在收购 Lumus 后，水晶光电试图在智能眼镜业务中实现从零部件供应商到解决方案供应商的跨越式转型。水晶光电通过参与 C 轮优先股的认购和受让原有股东的股权，成为 Lumus 的战略投资者。此次并购不但有助于加强双方在技术领域的深入合作，也有助于水晶光电利用 Lumus 优质的欧美客户资源，进一步拓展海外市场。不同于很多中国公司收购目标公司的控制权的方式，水晶光电采用参股的方式，成为 Lumus 小股东，既降低了公司的收购成本，又为未来更为深入的资本合作打下基础。

不得不承认，以色列的 AR 技术确实受到国内投资者的欢迎。2016 年，阿里巴巴向以色列 AR 公司 Infinity AR 投资了 1 500 万美元。

案例十四　安踏以 3.32 亿元人民币收购 FILA 在中国地区的商标使用权和经营权

关键词：商标使用权和经营权、商业模式

收购方：安踏体育用品有限公司

目标公司：百丽国际

【时间线】

· 2005 年 9 月，斐乐（FILA）进入中国市场。

· 2007 年，百丽国际以 4 800 万美元收购 FILA 品牌在中国内地及香港、澳门地区的所有权益。

·2009年8月,百丽国际将FILA中国的品牌特许权以3.32亿元人民币的价格出售给安踏体育用品有限公司(以下简称"安踏")。

【交易主体介绍】

安踏是中国领先的运动服装品牌,并被选为"中国奥委会的2009—2012运动服饰合作伙伴"。安踏拥有自己的设计、研发、制造和营销团队,在全国有6 000家零售店销售。收购前,安踏是中国本土品牌,无法真正与国际品牌竞争。安踏的市场主要是中国的二线和三线城市,而一线城市往往被阿迪达斯和耐克等国际品牌占领。

百丽国际成立于1991年,是中国最大的女鞋零售商,在中国拥有22%的女鞋市场,生产、分销和零售多种鞋类品牌,如Belle、Staccato、Teenmix、Tata、Fato、Jipi Japa、Joy & Peace和Bata。

FILA创建于1911年,是世界前十大运动品牌,先后开发了高尔夫、网球、健身等系列产品,呈现一个经典、时尚、性感、高品质的意式形象。

【交易回顾】

百丽国际将出售其85%的Full Prospect股份,后者拥有FILA集团在中国内地以及香港和澳门地区的商标特许经营权。FILA集团保留与Belle合资的Full Prospect的剩余股权。百丽还将作价5 000万港元出售FILA集团旗下零售业务在香港和澳门地区的特许经营权。百丽国际的优势在女鞋,缺乏国际高端运动品牌的拓展经验,由于经营不善,FILA品牌的影响力和高端形象日益边缘化,而安踏认为收购全球运动服装品牌代表了进军高端运动服装市场的机会,对于FILA在中国的品牌认知也具有重要战略意义。

安踏收购后一个很重要的决定就是将FILA的品牌定位由原来的高端运动品牌转变为"回归时尚",目标客户为25岁至35岁的年轻人,并在加入时尚的元素后,保留FILA原有运动品牌的特点。在产品环节上,安踏针对中国人的体型特点设计出新产品,并不断加入新的创新元素,同时从经销商手里收回所有的门店,改成直营的模式。

安踏有针对性地对FILA原有的商业模式进行改变,逐渐显现出非常好的效果。收购后的5年,FILA年销售额的增长率超过50%,在2014年,实现扭亏为盈。截至 2017 年底，FILA 在中国的市场门店数达到 1 086 家，未来 5 年预计将保持 30% 的增速，销售收入占集团收入的 20%。

【总结】

收购 FILA 既是安踏的机遇，也是挑战。一方面，它可以帮助安踏进入更高端的市场，并加入一线品牌团队。此外，收购 FILA 可能是安踏提升品牌知名度和认可度的机会，从而提升品牌资产。另一方面，FILA 和安踏的品牌形象之间存在巨大差距，安踏可能很难维持 FILA 在全球市场的地位。此次收购让安踏有机会向其行业的"巨头"学习，并可能在未来几年内进入国际市场。然而，安踏首先必须证明其能够运营全球规模的品牌并保持其成功，从而在国内证明自己。安踏选择收购商标使用权和经营权，相比于收购整个公司，成本更低，整合起来也更容易。中国有着全球最大的单一市场，消费升级正在悄然进行，中国体育市场的成长空间巨大，也是全球巨头逐鹿的战场。

在成功收购 FILA 的基础上，安踏又成功地收购了韩国的户外品牌 Kolon、登山运动品牌 Sprandi 和冬季运动品牌 Descente，实现"单聚焦、多品牌、全渠道"的经营管理模式。

案例十五　光大国际以 1.23 亿欧元收购 NOVAGO

关键词：环境保护

收购方：中国光大国际有限公司

目标公司：NOVAGO Poland

【时间线】

· 2016 年 6 月 23 日，中国光大国际有限公司（以下简称"光大国际"）签署了初步销售协议。

· 2016 年 8 月 31 日，光大国际宣布以 1.23 亿欧元完成对 NOVAGO 的收购，其中包括 1.18 亿欧元（约 8.62 亿元人民币）的股权价值和 500 万欧元的土地储备资源。

【交易主体介绍】

光大国际是中国光大集团旗下实业投资旗舰公司。光大集团由中央汇金投资有限责任公司和财政部共同发起成立。中国光大集团在2018年《财富》全球500强中排名第322位。

NOVAGO是波兰最大的固体废物处理公司。该公司于2016年被福布斯评为波兰最具活力的公司之一，2015年被比泽尔·比泽内苏（Gazele Biznesu）评为波兰成长最快的公司。

【交易回顾】

该笔交易是中国在波兰最大的投资项目，双方并购谈判前后持续了几个月。

光大国际称，此次海外收购是中国光大集团在2016年6月习近平主席访问波兰后积极实施的第一个中波合作项目。光大国际于2016年6月23日签署初步收购协议，并于波兰当地时间8月29日顺利完成交付。

在波兰举行的收购和交付仪式上，波兰发展部副部长多马嘎尔斯基在讲话中说，他希望这笔投资能给双方带来利润，并相信合作会成功。他深信，来自中国的这一投资是一项非常好的投资，可以为波兰带来新的就业机会和新的技术发展，这种创新投资将得到波兰政府的大力支持。

纵观技术合作及中欧和东欧市场数据，成立于1992年的NOVAGO是波兰最大的独立固体废物处理公司。其业务包括垃圾处理、垃圾填埋回收、沼气生产、垃圾衍生燃料（RDF）生产、沼气热电联产等。

NOVAGO在华沙和奥尔什丁这两个核心商务区的市场份额超过30%，在波兰4个省拥有6家领先的综合垃圾处理厂。2015年，NOVAGO处理了89万吨固体废物，在2015年被选为比泽尔·比泽内苏最具活力的波兰企业，在2016年被选为福布斯最具活力的波兰公司之一。2015年营业收入超过1.35亿波兰兹罗提（约2.2亿元人民币）。

NOVAGO副总裁东布罗夫斯基解释说，合并谈判持续了几个月，经过双方的一系列会谈和分析，光大国际决定收购NOVAGO。之后，NOVAGO高管还访问了光大国际在上海和香港的环保项目，以更深入地了解收购者的实力。

此次合并收购，主要有助于双方在技术层面的合作，还有助于光大国际开拓中欧和东欧市场。

被收购后，NOVAGO 不仅可以继续发展波兰现有的技术，还可以发展光大国际在中国设计的新技术，这对 NOVAGO 来说是一个很好的机遇。今后，更先进的废物处置设备不仅将应用于波兰，也将应用于中欧和东欧。

光大国际有四个业务部门：环境能源、环境用水、环境保护和环境科学技术。截至 2016 年 6 月 30 日，光大国际已实施 187 个环保项目，总投资约 485.68 亿元人民币；已完成项目总投资约为 214.57 亿元人民币；在建项目投资约 102.98 亿元人民币，筹建中项目投资约为 168.13 亿元人民币。

光大集团于 2017 年年初成立了国际业务部，专门从事国际市场开发，并先后获得波兰固体废物项目和越南项目。未来，中亚、西亚、北亚和东南亚市场将成为光大集团关注的焦点。

【总结】

我们的结论是，这是一个完美的选择，也是一个成功的合作范例。

此次收购是光大国际首次在欧洲收购固体废物处理企业。这不仅是中国在波兰最大的投资项目，也是 2017 年中国在东欧和中欧环保市场上最大的收购项目。

在"一带一路"国家进行投资布局是光大国际的一项重要战略。光大国际希望利用 NOVAGO 在波兰的影响力，在垃圾焚烧方面的经验，在环保、新能源和设备制造方面的技术，积极推动其在中欧和东欧的发展。

CHAPTER 1

THE CURRENT SITUATION AND TREND OF CHINA'S INVESTMENT AND M&A ALONG THE "BELT AND ROAD" COUNTRIES

Section 1
Overview of the "Belt and Road Initiative"

On September 7th, 2013, during the visit to Central Asian countries, President Xi Jinping proposed to construct the "Silk Road Economic Belt" cooperatively for the first time. In October of the same year, he proposed to build the "21st Century Maritime Silk Road" jointly. These two proposals constituted the major "Belt and Road Initiative".

The "Belt and Road Initiative" consists of two parts. One part is the "Silk Road Economic Belt", which includes three major paths: one is from the northwest and northeast of China through Central Asia and Russia to Europe and Baltic Sea, another is from the northwest of China through Central Asia and West Asia to the Persian Gulf and the Mediterranean Sea, and the third is from the southwest of China through the Indochina Peninsula to the Indian Ocean. The other part is the "21st Century Maritime Silk Road", which includes two major paths: one is from the Chinese coastal ports through the South China Sea and the Straits of Malacca to the Indian Ocean and to Europe, and the other is from the Chinese coastal ports through the South China Sea, extending to the South Pacific.

The Belt and Road includes the following six international economic cooperation corridors: New Asia-Europe Continental Bridge, China-Mongolia-Russia, China-Central Asia-West Asia, China-Indochina Peninsula, China-Pakistan, Bangladesh and China-India-Myanmar.

The "Belt and Road Initiative" is of great significance to China and helps to promote China's economic growth. It is expected that the "Belt and Road Initiative" will create a new market for Chinese goods, and China's high-quality production capacity can be effectively guided to the regions of Belt and Road. China has announced to provide low-cost loans to participant countries.

Since China launched the "Silk Road Economic Belt" and the "21st Century Maritime Silk Road" initiative in 2013, the "Belt and Road Initiative" has been advancing in exploration, perfecting in development and growing in cooperation. The progresses and results are far beyond expectations. With the growing "friends circle" of the "Belt and Road Initiative", the "Belt and Road Initiative" has become a major international cooperation initiative with the concept of turning ideas into actions and turning dreams into reality.

The followings are major events of the "Belt and Road Initiative":

—In September 2013, Chinese President Xi Jinping first proposed the idea of jointly building the "Silk Road Economic Belt" during his speech at the Nazarbayev University in Kazakhstan.

—In October 2013, Xi Jinping proposed to establish a closely integrated China-ASEAN community and provide guidance for the construction of the "21st Century Maritime Silk Road" to promote maritime cooperation.

In a speech at the parliament of Indonesian, Xi Jinping proposed to establish the Asian Infrastructure Investment Bank (AIIB) to fund infrastructure construction and promote regional connectivity and economic integration.

—In February 2014, Xi Jinping and Russian President Vladimir Putin reached a consensus on the "Belt and Road Initiative" and the connection with the Russia's Eurasian rail link.

—In October 2014, 21 first-time intent-founding member states signed *The Memorandum on the Preparation of the AIIB* and decided to establish the Asia Infrastructure Investment Bank.

—In November 2014, during the APEC meeting in Beijing, Xi Jinping announced China would invest 40 billion US dollars to establish the Silk Road Fund to provide investment and financing support for infrastructure construction, resource development, industrial cooperation and financial cooperation in the countries along the Belt and Road.

—In March 28, 2015, the National Development and Reform Commission, the Ministry of Foreign Affairs, and the Ministry of Commerce jointly issued the *Vision and Action for Promoting the Construction of the Silk Road Economic Belt and the 21st Century Maritime Silk Road*.

—In May 2015, the "Guiding Opinions on Promoting International Capacity and Equipment Manufacturing and Cooperation" was released.

—In December 2015, the Asian Infrastructure Investment Bank was formally established.

—In May 2017, the first "Belt and Road Forum for International Cooperation" was held in Beijing.

—In June 2017, *Vision for Maritime Cooperation under the Belt and Road Initiative* was released.

—In October 2017, the "Belt and Road Initiative" was written into the *Constitution of the Communist Party of China*.

—On January 22, 2018, the second ministerial meeting of the Forum of China and the Community of Latin American and Caribbean states opened up in Chile. The meeting adopted the *Santiago Declaration*, *Joint Action Plan for Cooperation between China and Latin American and Caribbean States (Priority Areas) (2019 – 2021)* and *The Special Declaration on the "Belt and Road Initiative"*.

—On May 16, 2018, the "Belt and Road Initiative" tax cooperation conference was closed in Astana, the capital of Kazakhstan. Participants discussed and jointly released *The Astana "Belt and Road" Tax Cooperation Initiative*.

—In May 2018, China-EU Dialogue on the "Belt and Road Initiative" was held in Brussels, where the EU headquarters is located.

—In July 2018, the 8th Ministerial Meeting of the China-Arab States Cooperation Forum was held in Beijing.

——In July 2018, the State Administration of Foreign Exchange's "Belt and Road Initiative" National Foreign Exchange Management Policy Research Group released the *Overview of the "Belt and Road" National Foreign Exchange Management Policy*.

——In November 2018, the first China International Import Expo was held in Shanghai.

——In December 2018, the first meeting of the Advisory Council of the Belt and Road Forum for International Cooperation was held in Beijing.

——In April 2019, the Second Belt and Road Forum for International Cooperation was held in Beijing.

Section 2
Review of China's Investment and M&A in the "Belt and Road" Countries

On March 11, 2018, Zhong Shan, Minister of Commerce, mentioned China's cumulative direct investment in the Belt and Road countries exceeded 60 billion US dollars, involving agriculture, manufacturing, infrastructure and many other fields. A number of infrastructures such as railways, highways and ports were built one after another. A number of energy and resource cooperation projects were smoothly promoted, and a number of manufacturing projects were completed and put into production. China has built 75 overseas economic and trade cooperation zones in the Belt and Road countries, with a cumulative investment of more than 27 billion US dollars.

1. Review

Figure 1-1 compares the growth rate of China's foreign trade from 2013 to 2017 and the growth rate of China's foreign trade with the Belt and Road countries. China's trade and investment in the Belt and Road countries have generally maintained growth. From 2013 to 2018, the total trade volume of goods between China and the countries along the Belt and Road exceeded USD 6 trillion, with an average annual growth rate of 4%. According to the data analysis, South Korea, Vietnam, Malaysia, India, Russia and other countries are China's most important the Belt and Road Initiative trading partners.

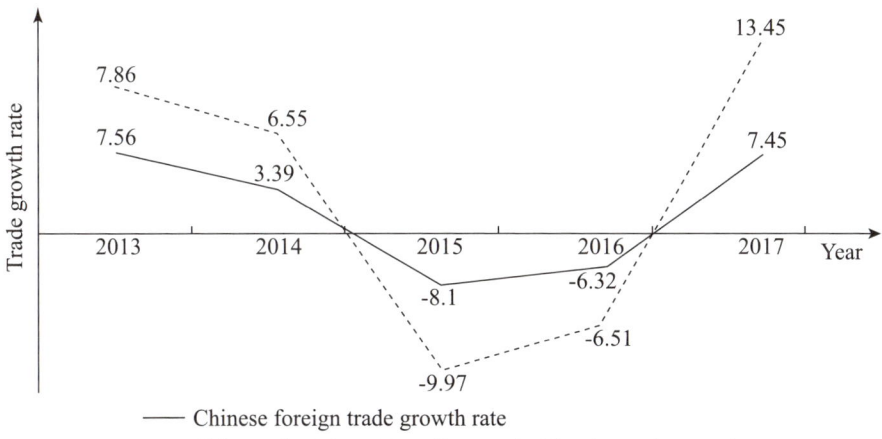

Figure 1-1　Comparison of China's foreign trade growth rate and China and the "Belt and Road" countries' foreign trade growth rate

From 2013 to 2018, China's direct investment in countries along the Belt and Road exceeded USD 90 billion, with an average annual growth rate of over 5%. In the same period, the contract value of China's newly signed foreign contracted projects exceeded USD 600 billion, with an average annual increase of 11.9%. A number of key projects, including the Addis Ababa—Djibouti Railway, the China-Laos Railway, and the Port City of Colombo, Sri Lanka, have brought about an orderly advancement and served as an effective demonstration.

From the perspective of the investment industry, the State Administration of Foreign Exchange, the Ministry of Commerce, and the Ministry of Finance have issued a series of policies restricting irrational foreign investment. The structure of China's foreign investment has also changed, with an increase of M&A in the chemical, power, manufacturing and energy industries. More than 60 M&A projects of more than USD 100 million have pushed the real economy and new and high technology to the world stage. In the next five years, the investment of Chinese enterprises in the Belt and Road countries will continue to grow rapidly. The investment field will expand from large-scale infrastructure, energy and resources projects to tourism, e-commerce, and humanities education and exchanges.

Participants in the Belt and Road project investment are diversified. In the early days of the Belt and Road Initiative, state-owned enterprises led the Belt and Road construction. At present, however, the participation of private enterprises and foreign-funded enterprises are increasing. The characteristics of state-owned enterprises and private enterprises in the countries along the Belt and Road are mainly as follows: the amount of investment by state-owned enterprises is higher than that of private enterprises, while the number of investors among privately owned enterprises exceeds that of state-owned enterprises.

M&A is the main form of Chinese companies' overseas investment. In the peak period of 2016, Chinese companies had more than two overseas M&As every day. Through overseas M&A, Chinese companies have acquired high-quality brands, technologies, markets, and resources, reducing costs and increasing global influence. Compared with domestic asset prices, overseas asset prices are lower, and Chinese companies can allocate high-quality resources internationally through overseas M&A. According to statistics, in 2018, Chinese companies initiated 125 overseas M&As, and the amount of M&A reached 28.8 billion US dollars, mainly concentrated in science and technology, manufacturing, medical health, TMT (technical, media and communication acronyms of 3 English words), finance, consumption and other fields. The proportion of M&A in the fields of energy, electricity and raw materials, which accounted for a relatively large proportion, began to decline, and listed companies have become the main force of M&A. The main advantage of listed companies' M&A is that they have financing platforms and there are valuation differences between domestic and foreign markets. Among enterprises participating in overseas M&A, the proportion of private enterprises has further increased. In the future, the number of M&A investment by Chinese enterprises along the Belt and Road countries will grow rapidly. The reasons are: on the other hand, the strength of Chinese enterprises is increasing; they hope to allocate resources from all over the world. On the other hand, countries along the Belt and Road have full confidence in China's economic development.

The regions invested by M&A along the "Belt and Road" countries are mainly concentrated in South Asia, Southeast Asia and West Asia, with India, Singapore and Israel ranking in the top three. At the same time, we can also see that more and more Chinese companies are considering investment and M&A in Central and Eastern Europe.

2. The reasons for the rapid growth and change of the "Belt and Road" countries' investment and M&A

(1) The rapid growth of China's economy

Since China's reform and opening up, China's economy has maintained a growth rate of more than 8% for a long time. China becomes the world's second largest economy. In 2018, there were 120 Chinese companies ranked among the world's top 500 and the number is very close to 126 of the United States. The strength of Chinese companies has also laid a foundation for the success of Chinese companies' overseas M&A. The expansion of the scale of enterprises also indicates that traditional internal growth cannot continue to increase the value of enterprises, and overseas investment and M&A has become a common and effective means of performance growth.

(2) China's huge domestic market demand

China has a population of 1.4 billion and is the largest market in the world. By investing in M&A in countries along the Belt and Road, Chinese companies acquire high-quality overseas resources, technologies, markets and talents, and then graft them to the Chinese market to accelerate development. "Global M&A, China Integration" has become the guiding ideology for overseas M&A of many companies. After that, they further increased the intensity of overseas M&A through the success of the Chinese market. The history of many well-known Chinese companies, such as Haier Group, Midea Group, Geely Holding Group, Fosun Group, Pengxin Group, etc., is also a history of Chinese companies' global M&A.

(3) High valuation of China's capital market and lack of quality assets

China's capital market valuation is higher than mature capital markets such as the US and Europe. Through overseas investment and M&A, Chinese companies can acquire overseas assets at a lower P/E ratio and then integrate the premium into the listed company. The stock price rise after the acquisition (the P/E ratio is rising) means that companies can acquire more overseas quality companies with higher valuations, thus forming a virtuous circle. However, the behavior of many companies' premium purchases has pushed up the company's business reputation. If the acquisition performance target is not achieved, the business reputation impairment brings about a sharp decline in earnings and stock prices.

(4) The demand of China's economic transformation and development

The production capacity of many industries (infrastructure, real estate, manufacturing, etc.) in China is in a state of saturation. Initially, enterprises moved from the coastal areas to the central and western regions and the economic development gradient provided the possibility for industrial transfers. In the next step, the transfer direction of enterprises may be along the Belt and Road countries. The rapid growth of China's investment and M&A in Southeast Asia, South Asia and West Asia also confirms this speculation.

At the same time, Chinese companies need to move upstream to the value chain and it is more urgent to acquire overseas technology, talents and markets through investment and M&A. Singapore, Israel and some countries in Europe have a good industrial base and innovative capabilities and many of the target companies can meet the needs of Chinese enterprises for industrial upgrading. We have also seen that these countries have always been hot spots for investment and M&A in the Belt and Road Initiative. As a matter of fact, traditional resource-based investment and M&A projects still maintain a certain proportion and this is inseparable with the China's economic development demand.

3. Investment of Chinese-state-owned enterprises in the "Belt and Road" countries and regions

In the past few years, Chinese state-owned enterprises have seen a large number of important investment and M&A cases in the Belt and Road countries and regions. China Vanke Co. ,Ltd. and other companies acquired Global Logistic Properties for USD 11. 6 billion, Shanghai Fosun Pharmaceutical (Group) Co. ,Ltd. (Fosun Pharma) acquired 74% of Indian pharmaceutical company Gland Pharma Limited (GLand Pharma) for USD 1. 09 billion, Alibaba increased its holding of Southeast Asian e-commerce Lazada to 83% stake for USD 1 billion, SAIC Motor acquired General Motors Company's Halol plant in India... In addition, enterprises like Alibaba, Fosun Pharma, Tencent, Sancell, Sinopec and CGN have more than one investment and M&A transaction in the Belt and Road countries and regions. It shows the confidence of these private enterprises and state-owned enterprises in the Belt and Road Initiative. According to the monitoring data of Morning Whistle Group, in 2017, the number of Chinese-funded overseas M&A transactions fell by 23% and the disclosure amount decreased by 13. 54%, while the number of M&A transactions along the Belt and Road increased by 21. 82% year-on-year, and the disclosure transaction amounts increased by 47. 40%. Since 2013, the Belt and Road construction has continued to make progress. Table 1 – 1 the top 50 Chinese companies' for Bell and Road Investment and M&A[1].

---

[1] Morning Whistle Group: A Chinese capital cross-border M&A service provider.

Table 1 – 1　The top 50 Chinese Companies for Bell and Road investment and M&A

Buyer	Time	Target	Transaction Amount (million dollars)	Target Country
Alibaba and Ant Financial	2016/4/12 2017/6/28	Indonesia Lazada Group SA	2 000.00	Singapore
	2014/5/28	Singapore Post	248.94	Singapore
	2017/3/3	Paytm	177.00	India
	2015/10/7	40% stake in One97	680.00	India
	2016/6/18	Ascend Money	—	Thailand
	Total	5	3 105.94	
CEFC CHINA	2017/9/8	Rosneft Oil	9 100.00	Russia
	2015/12/14	Kazakhstan National Petroleum International	—	Kazakhstan
	2015/9/7	Travel Service	—	Czech Republic
	2017/2/19	Abu Dhabi Company for Onshore Oil Operations	900.00	United Arab Emirates
	Total	4	10 000.00	
Fosun Group and Fosun Pharma	2016/4/10	AHAVA	76.38	Israel
	2017/5/24	Delhivery	30.00	India
	2017/10/27	Bond IT	14.25	Israel
	2017/10/3	Gland Pharma	1 091.00	India
	Total	4	1 211.63	
Tencent Holdings	2016/12/21	Sanook.com	—	Thailand
	2016/8/17	Hike Messenger	175.00	India
	2017/10/9	OLA	400.00	India
	Total	3	575.00	

Continued

Buyer	Time	Target	Transaction Amount (million dollars)	Target Country
Sanpower Group and Nanjing Xinbai	2016/7/1	Cordlife Group Ltd	64.30	Singapore
	2017/7/12	Lotan Nursing Service	18.51	Israel
	2014/12/9	Natali Seculife Holdings Ltd	70.00	Israel
	Total	3	152.81	
Sinopec	2015/12/17	Sibur	1 338.00	Russia
	2017/2/19	8% stake of Abu Dhabi Co-mpany for Onshore OilOperations	1 800.00	United Arab Emirates
	Total	2	3 138.00	
China General Nuclear Power Group	2016/11/3	Malicounda Solar Power Station	—	Senegal
	2016/3/23	Malaysian Power Assets	2 300.00	Malaysia
	Total	2	2 300.00	
China Merchants Group	2017/7/29	Operation rights of Hambantota Port	1 120.00	Sri Lanka
	2016/12/9	Port of Colombo	1 100.00	Sri Lanka
	Total	2	2 220.00	
China Mobile	2014/6/9	Ture Corporation PCL	877.10	Thailand
	2014/4/23	Pakistan 3G, 4G license	516.00	Pakistan
	Total	2	1 393.10	
China Shipping (Group) Company	2016/9/29	Abu Dhabi Khalifa Port Phase II Container Terminal	738.00	United Arab Emirates
	2017/5/15	KTZE-Khorgos Gateway	38.00	Kazakhstan
	Total	2	776.00	
Geo-Jade Petroleum Corporation	2014/4/8	North Caspian Petroleum JSC	37.50	Kazakhstan
	2014/8/8	Maten Petroleum	525.00	Kazakhstan
	Total	2	562.50	

Continued

Buyer	Time	Target	Transaction Amount (million dollars)	Target Country
Everbright	2016/9/1	NOVAGO	135.62	Poland
	2016/10/7	Tirana International Airport	—	Albania
	Total	2	135.62	
Zhejiang Kaishan Compressor Co.,Ltd.	2016/8/16	OTP Geothermal	60.00	Singapore
	2016/8/8	PT Sokoria Geothermal Indonesia	—	Indonesia
	Total	2	60.00	
Vanke, Houpu Investment, Hillhouse Capital Group, BOC Group	2017/12/1	Global Logistic Properties (GLP)	11 718.95	Singapore
Giant Interactive Group and Other Consortiums	2016/9/23	Playtika	4 400.00	Israel
Sanonda Shares	2016/9/14	ADAMA	2 775.54	Israel
Bright Dairy & Food	2015/3/31	Tnuva	2 167.20	Israel
Offshore Oil Engineering	2014/7/10	Yamal	1 600.00	Russia
Shanghai Electric Power, GCL Group	2016/11/1	K-Electrical	1 600.00	Pakistan
Silk Road Fund	2016/3/16	Yamal LPG project	1 400.00	Russia
Beijing Holdings	2016/11/9	Verkhnechonskneftegaz	1 100.00	Russia
CITICPE	2016/4/19	Biosensor International Group	1 050.00	Singapore

Continued

Buyer	Time	Target	Transaction Amount (million dollars)	Target Country
Bright Oil	2014/2/18	Anadarko Petroleum Corporation Bohai Bay Oil field	1 046.00	China
HNA Group	2016/12/11	CWT	1 000.00	Singapore
COSCO Pacific	2015/12/10	Kumport Container Terminal	940.18	Turkey
JCET	2014/11/6	STATS ChipPAC Ltd.	780.00	Singapore
COFCO Group	2016/3/3	Noble Industry	750.00	Singapore
Shanghai Pharmaceutical	2017/10/19	Kantler's China business	557.00	China
Lianli Copper	2016/1/5	Kazakhstan Copper Resources	480.00	Kazakhstan
Industrial and Commercial Bank of China	2015/5/22	Tekstil Bankasi	316.00	Turkey
China Rongsheng Heavy Industry Group Holdings Co., Ltd.	2014/8/21	Central Point Worldwide Inc.	281.74	Kyrgyzstan
Guangdong Agricultural Reclamation Group	2016/9/21	Thaihua Gum	269.71	Thailand
The Export-import Bank of China	2017/1/17	Invitel Group	214.37	Hungary
Sinochem International	2016/3/28	Halcyon Agri Corporation	174.75	Singapore
Huawei Technology	2016/12/8	Toga Networks, Hexa Tier	150.00	Israel

Continued

Buyer	Time	Target	Transaction Amount (million dollars)	Target Country
Yunnan Water	2017/3/17	Galaxy NewSpring	136.50	Singapore
Hengyuan Petrochemical	2016/1/12	Shell Refining Company in Malaysia	130.00	Malaysia
ZTE	2016/12/6	NETAŞ TELEKOMÜNIKAS-YONAŞ	130.00	Turkey
China Fortune Land Development	2017/6/5	Two plots of the AMI	102.16	Indonesia
Jingdong Century Trade	2017/8/27	Go-Jek	100.00	Indonesia
Sichuan Hebang Biotechnology	2015/10/16	S. T. K Stockton Group	90.00	Israel
Nanjids. com	2016/6/15	Cartelo Crocodile	89.96	Singapore
Shanghai Stock Exchange, Shenzhen Stock Exchange, China Financial Futures Exchange, and China-Pakistan Investment Corporation	2016/12/27	40% equity of Pakistan Exchange	85.00	Pakistan
Tatwah Smartech	2017/4/18	Topbest Coast Limited	73.00	Cyprus
Xi'an Shangu Power	2015/7/11	EKOL	51.90	Czech Republic
Kanghong Pharmaceutical	2017/10/20	100% equity of IOPtima Ltd.	46.72	Israel
Shandong Ruyi	2017/11/23	Bagir	16.50	Israel
SAIC	2017/7/9	Halol factory	—	India

Continued

Buyer	Time	Target	Transaction Amount (million dollars)	Target Country
WH Group	2017/6/1	Hamburger Pini, Pini Polska, Royal Chicken	—	Poland
China Construction Bank	2016/9/29	PT Bank Windu Kentjana International Tbk	—	Indonesia

Section 3
Characteristics of Global Investment and M&A Development under the "Belt and Road Initiative"

Since the launch of the Belt and Road Initiative in 2013, Chinese companies have invested more and more in M&A activities along the Belt and Road countries. We have also observed that global investment and M&A under the Belt and Road Initiative show the following five new features.

1. The internationalization of Chinese companies is the trend of the time

As China joins the global economic competition, Chinese companies need to allocate resources on a global scale to extend the supply chain system to the world. Chinese companies can transfer procurement, production and sales to the rest of the world to create an ecosystem that runs through the industry chain. The focus of overseas M&A of Chinese companies has gradually shifted from the developed countries in Europe and the United States to countries along the Belt and Road. New economies such as Central Asia and Southeast Asia have become new hotspots for Belt and Road M&A. Global financing is critical for corporate investment and M&A and several banks have issued bonds at home and abroad. In terms of funding sources, more and more local low-cost funds are actively participating in M&A projects.

2. The new pattern of "state-owned enterprises taking the lead, private enterprises following up"

Participants in the Belt and Road project are showing the trend of diversity. In the early days, state-owned enterprises led the construction and investment of Belt and Road. At present, the participation of private enterprises and foreign-funded enterprises is also increasing. State-owned enterprises are paying more attention to layout. State-owned enterprises took the lead in large-scale investment and M&A projects and private enterprises followed suit. Compared with state-owned enterprises, the professionalism of private enterprises' investment and M&A in the countries along the Belt and Road needs to be improved and it is necessary to use intermediary agencies to control risks. In addition, in order to reduce the risk of overseas investment and ensure sustainable development in the local area, it will become a common form of investment for various companies to find suitable local partners and establish joint ventures.

3. The investment model

Chinese companies have advantages in railways, electricity, infrastructure, etc., which complements the resource advantages and market demands of countries along the Belt and Road. The future investments in these areas are expected to further increase. Cross-border M&A is rapidly developing in recent years and becomes the main way of investing. Compared with other investment models, cross-border M&A does not require a long construction period. Therefore, it has become the preferred method for many multinational companies who want to accelerate the market expansion and enter the target market in a short period of time. The investment model mentioned in this book mainly refers to cross-border M&A.

4. Promoting the development of real economy has become the focus of overseas investment

After the State Administration of Foreign Exchange, the Ministry of Commerce and the Ministry of Finance issued a series of requirements to strengthen the authenticity and compliance with foreign investment regulations, and since 2017, irrational investments in real estate, hotels, entertainment and other fields have been curbed. While industries encouraged by our country such as medicine, advanced manufacturing and high technology have become new investment hotspots.

5. International talents will become the key to future investment and M&A growth along the "Belt and Road" countries

Chinese companies' participations in overseas mergers and acquisitions need people having good professional background, financial literacy, business acumen, skills specially acquired for international assignments and cross-cultural communications, and languages and traditions of the countries that they will have to operate with. The failure of many cases for investment and M&A along the Belt and Road countries is mainly due to the failure of cross-cultural communication, the relevant personnel's not understanding the international rules and the target companies' not truly integrating with Chinese companies. Chinese enterprises can only ensure the success of M&A and maximize the return on investment by doing a good job in involving talents reserved in advance and adjusting talent policies according to the M&A enterprise objectives.

CHAPTER 2

INVESTMENT AND M&A OBJECTIVES IN THE "BELT AND ROAD" COUNTRIES

Section 1
Five Determining Factors of Overseas Investment and M&A

M&As have let the growth of enterprises. According to statistics, more than half of M&As have failed. In the following, with the media disclosing overseas M&A cases, it explains the five factors that determine the success of overseas M&As.

1. Strategy guides enterprises

" 'Chinese Enterprises going global' is based on strategic objectives within their capabilities, instead of just outbound 'going out'", said Jiang Kui, general manager of Shandong Heavy Industry Group (SHIG)①, according to the successful experience of implementing overseas M&A in recent years. Shandong Heavy Industry Group's overseas M&A roadmap shows as follows. In January 2009, when the French economy fell into a trough, Weichai Power bought Moteurs Baudouin for EUR 2.99 million. In January 2012, while the Italian economy was struggling, Weichai Power purchased Ferretti Group. In September 2012, Germany was trapped in the European Debt Crisis, and Weichai Power purchased KION Group 25% stocks and Linde Hy-

---

① Shandong Heavy Industry Group is a wholly state-owned company established by Weichai Holding Group, Strong Construction Machinery, Shandong Automobile Industry Group etc. Weichai Power is a subsidiary of Weichai Hololing Group.

draulics 70% stocks.

In 2016, SUMEC Machinery & Electric Co. ,Ltd. , one of the subsidiaries of SUMEC Group Corporation, bought Innomotive Systems Hainichen GmbH (ISH), which was founded in 1992 and produced auto parts as a supplier to leading German car makers such as Daimler, BMW and Volkswagen. The strategic goal of "Great Auto Parts" business segment in SUMEC Group has played a positive role in guiding overseas expansion, laying a good foundation for industrial synergy at a higher level and higher platform. Before M&A, it is necessary to formulate the corporate strategy of the enterprise, based on which the investigation of the business and resource status of the target company would be conducted. The acquisition of the target enterprise would be considered when the target company can integrate well with the company's strategy. After the strength of the acquired firm is enhanced, finally the competitive advantage will be enhanced through the acquisition.

2. Follow the trend of industry development

From the entry of global automobile companies into China to the globalization of China's automobile industry, this is the macro trend of the new round of automobile industry. It is also the only way for Chinese automobile companies to grow bigger and stronger. "Internationalization", as an important method for the Chinese auto industry to respond to the country's policy of expanding openness and enhancing the strength in the international market, is a key driving force to boost the ability to upgrade the system, integrate and optimize resources, and enhance the competitiveness.

SUMEC Group seized the opportunity of the global auto industry and market, clarified the positioning and development model, integrated into the big platform, fully utilized its advantages of trade, production, industry technology and finance, and continued trying in the direction of "Great Auto Parts" industrial layout and overseas M&As, as well as making efforts to improve and strengthen the "Great Auto

Parts" industry roadmap. ISH which was taken over by SUMEC Group, provided a world-class benchmark for the manufacturing transformation and global layout of the "Great Auto Parts" business of SUMEC Group with its high level of automation, lean management and expertise.

3. Conduct thorough due diligence on the target company

Great opportunities founded are in overseas M&A, but there are also many risks. The biggest problem in the overseas M&A processes is risk management. Under such circumstances, it is necessary to complete due diligence. Due diligence is generally divided into three aspects: financial, legal and commercial. Sometimes the investigation of intellectual property rights are also required. Due diligence, as a bargaining base for protecting the interests of buyers during important negotiations, has to be taken seriously, otherwise Chinese companies will probably lose their initiative. Many M&A failures are caused by the absence of detailed investigation of the target company in advance. In the process of M&As, due to information asymmetry, it is difficult for the buyers to have a full understanding of target companies. But many buyers take it for granted that they understood target companies well and valued them through the assumption of ideal operation of target companies. However, many companies found that after closing, the situation did not go as expected. Moreover, there might be major problems in the target companies being neglected, which led to the failure of M&As.

4. Integration after M&A and investment depends on the team

After its successful acquisition of ISH in 2016, SUMEC Group recruited senior executive in the industry as the CEO and established a senior management team. Mr. Jiang Kui, general manager of Shandong Heavy Industry Group said that although they are both located in Europe, Ferretti Group and KION Group which Shandong Heavy Industry Group acquired have very different governance structures. The differences are: one is about the cultures; another is about histories; Ferretti Group is a family enterprise while KION Group has experienced industrial and financial shareholder rotation with higher level of publicity. The third is that Weichai Power has different percentage of shares in the two companies. Weichai Power is the main shareholder of Ferretti Group and has control over the decision-making body. For KION Group, Weichai Power is the single largest shareholder and in a relatively controlled position. Therefore, the managements of the two companies by China's headquarter are different.

5. Rapid and effective integration after M&A

Since the acquisition of ISH, SUMEC Group has strictly observed German local law and regulations, and fully respected ISH's management mode, culture and values. By adopting a series of measures that are conducive to long-term operation, business integration and employee development, and carrying out necessary asset optimization, SUMEC Group promoted the system of organizations, processes, personnel and culture, which has effectively guaranteed the smooth and efficient operation of ISH. In 2016, ISH successfully turned losses into profits, which was recognized and praised by the local governments and employees.

On June 9th, 2017, Mr. Wang Weidong who is the Minister Counsellor of the Chinese Commercial Counsellor's Office in Germany attended the 25th anniversary of ISH in Hainichen, Saxony and delivered a speech. He said, "In the past 25 years, ISH has gradually developed into an industry leader. I am proud of the success of the company. Tremendous changes can be witnessed during the 25-year development of ISH, especially when ISH and SUMEC Group reached a strategic partnership last year. A new historical starting point has been established. I would like to express my sincere wishes with three sentences. Firstly, it would be good to face the changes that have taken place after cooperation with Chinese enterprises and seek new development opportunities in the process of change. Secondly, together with Chinese enterprise, it is essential to build mutual trust and practical cooperation, and jointly face fierce competition. Thirdly, we are committed to innovation and become the golden partner of innovation cooperation.

Section 2
Objectives of Investment and M&A in the "Belt and Road" countries

Before Chinese enterprises invest in the Belt and Road countries, they must be clear about what the objectives of Investment and M&A are and why they need to invest. We believe that "access to resources, technology and market" is the most common objective of overseas Investment and M&A.

Special attention needs to be paid to country risks before breaking down objectives. Generally speaking, national risk concerns politics, economy and finance, and business environment (administrative efficiency, tax system, legal system, investment environment). China's large foreign-oriented financial institutions will make country risk rating for the target countries and the three major international rating agencies, Moody, Standard & Poor's and Fitch, will also rank sovereign risks.

1. Objective one: obtaining resources

China is now a global leading producer in lithium battery manufacturing, accounting for more than 50% of the world. At present, the widest use of lithium battery in China is new energy vehicles. With the rapid development of the new energy vehicle market, the global demand for the upstream material lithium has increased significantly. World-class lithium resources are located in South America and Australia. Lithium is in the heyday of the industry, and the price of lithium metal rose by 100% ~ 150% in 2017. According to statistics from Morning Whistle Group, Chinese enterprises have finished nearly 20 lithium resources M&A projects overseas only in 2017. The methods of acquisition are divided into two types: acquisition of equity and signing off-take contracts, while most Chinese enterprises chose the former. Among those M&A cases, 15 projects brought in about RMB 3.748 billion in total.

Tianqi lithium has grown into a domestic industrial giant in the core materials in lithium battery due to the tremendous growth of domestic demand for lithium chemical products in the new energy power battery market. On May 18, 2018, Tianqi Lithium announced that it planned to acquire 23.77% of Sociedad Qulmicay Minerade Chile S. A. (SQM) shares at a cost of RMB 25.9 billion. In September 2016, Tianqi Lithium purchased SCP, a lithium producer in Chile, for USD 209 million. In May 2014, Tianqi Lithium invested USD 500 million to acquire 51% of Windfield, the parent company of Talison of Australia, and indirectly controlled the company.

2. Objective two: acquiring techniques

The following example illustrates how a leader in health protective gloves manufacturing took the advantage of the capital market and the leverage of industrial capital, to penetrate the industry of the high-end medical devices, won the international leading position in the industry, reached the top lists of manufacturers of the three types of medical equipment-heart stents, which made it a leading domestic enterprise in the field.

According to "China Venture Capital & Private Equity Annual Ranking 2017" from Zero 2 IPO Research, CITICPE is listed in the top 10 of private equities in China. On April 19th, 2016, Bank of China issued a total of USD 580 million in M&A loans to CITICPE for the privatization of Biosensors International Group, and assisted CITICPE in completing the cash input of annexation loan, as well as the payment of privatization, promoting the delivery of the project. The acquisition of the Biosensors International Group by CITICPE is a classic case in which Chinese private equity funds privatized large overseas listed companies in the capital market and acquires international high-end medical device manufacturing technology. CITICPE successfully implemented privatization acquisition of Biosensors International Group through funds it manages. The total transaction price was equivalent to USD 1.05 billion.

Biosensors International Group is the world's fourth-largest heart stent company, only ranking after Abbott, Boston Scieific and Medtronic. It has the world's leading heart stent development technology, such as the world's first biodegradable polymer DES (EXCEL stent), the world's first polymer-free drug-eluting stent DCS (BioFreedom stent), which shortens DAPT treatment time to one month. Biosensors International Group is headquartered in Singapore and was listed on the main board of the Singapore Exchange in 2005 with a market capitalization of approximately SGD 1.3 billion. CITICPE entered the heart stent market with the acquisition of Biosensors International Group, and created its first step of the cardiovascular industry chain ecosystem. The accelerated aging process and increased incidence of cardiovascular disease have contributed to the continued growth of PCI surgery, with an estimated global growth rate of approximately 5% ~ 10% while China accounting for approximately 15%. With strong research, development, and sales ability, Biosensors International Group ranks the 4th in the world in terms of heart stent sales and the third in China. With the launch of new products, the market share is expected to increase.

In May 2018, Bluesail Medical Co., Ltd. (referred to as Bluesail Medical) issued the "Announcement on the issue shares and pay cash to purchase assets and raise supporting funds, and the completion of transfer of underlying assets of connected transactions" (the "Announcement") to acquire CBCH II 62.61% shares and issued shares to purchase 100% of CBCH V shares. Among them, 100% of the original shareholders of CBCH V are Beijing CITIC Investment Center (Limited Partnership), referred to as Beijing CITIC in short. Beijing CITIC is a fund of CITIC Industrial Fund. After the transaction was completed, Beijing CITIC held 19% of Bluesail Medicall and became its second largest shareholder. According to the "Announcement", Bluesail Medical signed performance counter bet with Zibo Bluesail Investment Co., Ltd. (hereinafter referred to as lanfan investment), Beijing CITIC and the management respectively, promising that the net profit realized in 2018, 2019 and 2020 will not be less than RMB 380 million, RMB 450 million, and RMB 540 million respectively.

3. Objective three: occupying the market

According to "Global Giants of Luxury 2017" released by Deloitte, one of the world's four largest accounting firms, SMCP Group, owned by Ruyi Group, ranked the 51th over the top 100 of Global Luxury, and the Japanese main board listed company RENOWN ranked the 58th. In 2016, the two companies owned by Ruyi Group have a combined turnover of USD 1.34 billion. Ruyi Group becomes the only company in China that has entered the top 100 global luxury through holdings. Ruyi Group spent 1.3 billion euros acquiring 84% of SMCP Group, which was the largest M&A transaction in China's fashion sector.

Table 2-1 Ruyi Group's M&A

Time	Underlining	Country/Region	Amount
2010	RENOWN	Japan	JPY 4 billion
2012	YeonSeung	South Korea	—
2012	GWA	India	—
2013	Carloway	Scotland	—
2014	PeineGruppe	Germany	—
2016	SMCP	France	EUR 1.3 billion
2017	Aquascutum	UK	USD 117 million

Continued

Time	Underlining	Country/Region	Amount
2017	Invista	US	USD 2 billion (appr.)
2017	Trinity Group	Hong Kong, China	USD 284 million
2018	Bally	Swizerland	USD 700 million (appr.)

Many overseas M&As in Ruyi Group were not executed by the listed company (stock code: 002193, stockshort name: Ruyi Group), because the listed company's overseas M&A involve overseas assets or counterparties, and its information disclosure, accounting audit, consideration payment and tax supervision which are special. However, the current special supervision of overseas M&A lacks targeted requirements and exemption rules. From the shareholding structure, in addition to Ruyi International Fashion Industry Investment Holding Co., LTD., Ruyi Group includes the Yinchuan Financial Holdings Co., Ltd., ITOCHU Corporation, McConnel Dowell and ITOCHU (China) Group Co., Ltd. The latter four hold 26%, 11.72%, 6.59% and 2.20% of the share of Ruyi Group.

In many cases, two of the above three targets will appear at the same time. The acquisition of Air International Group by a listed company Aotecar is a typical case.

Case 2-1 Aotecar acquired Air International Group, the global 8th largest automotive air conditioner maker

Transaction Amount: USD 135 million
Target Country: Australia
Industry: Automobile
Case Background: Aotecar is a leading manufacturer of automotive air-conditioning compressors in China and is the world's largest manufacturer of scrolltype automotive air-conditioning compressors. Aotecar established a

wholly-owned subsidiary in Hong Kong, China as the main body of the acquisition of Air International Group. On October 1st, 2015, it completed the relevant procedures for the equity closing of this transaction with AITS L. P. Air International Group is one of the world's leading manufacturers of HVAC systems (Heating, Ventilating and Air Conditioning). It provides HVAC and PTC (Powertrain Cooling System) products for vehicle manufacturers, such as GM, Volkswagen and Chrysler. By 2015, Air International Group has 15 subsidiaries, including two joint ventures in China and India, namely Southern Air International and Air International Thermal Systems (AITS) Air International Group holding 50% of the joint venture companies. Meanwhile, through continuous endogenous growth and extended development, the international performance of Air International Group has made great progress. The annual compound growth rate of operating income in the past five years is as high as 17%, outperforming the global market average.

Case Study: The acquisition has two objectives: market capture and technology acquisition. Automotive electric air-conditioning compressor is the heart of automotive air-conditioning. After the acquisition of Air International Group, the automotive air-conditioning system business of Air International Group will become complementary of the air-conditioning compressor business of Aotecar. Aotecar will continue to focus on air-conditioning compressor business while a number of cooperation with Air International Group on products being visible. Products from Air International Group can help Aotecar to form a complete product portfolio in the field of automotive air-conditioning, and to have the ability to provide high-quality automotive air-conditioning compressors and automotive HVAC systems to domestic and foreign vehicle manufacturers. At the same time, Aotecar and Air International Group will share their customer channels. With overseas customers and channel network from Air International Group, Aotecar can seek opportunities for overseas business, and with the assistance of air-conditioning international, Aotecar can enter the high-end market and become a global supplier of world-class vehicle companies.

The CEO of Air International Thermal Systems Todd Sheppelman said: "Our new relationship with Aotecar New Energy Technology Company is very exciting for all of us. This acquisition will further enhance our investment capabilities. As we grow further, our capabilities and skills are improved, which allows us to better support our growing customer base and global footprint."

At present, it has formed the five giants in the automotive HVAC system around the world, which are DENSO Group from Japan, Valeo Group from France, HVCC from Korea, Mahle Group from Germany and Delphi Technologies from the USA. Air International Group is catching up and continues to expand its market share by improving technology, opening up markets and optimizing global layout. In the Chinese automotive air-conditioning market, in addition to the five giants, Air International Group also occupies a large market share.

CHAPTER 3

MODELS AND FINANCING ARRANGEMENTS OF INVESTMENT AND M&A ALONG THE "BELT AND ROAD" COUNTRIES

Investment and M&A represent the one of the cores in the Belt and Road Initiative. Statistics show that from 2000 to 2016, a total of more than 13 100 cross-border M&A transactions with a total value of USD 1. 31 trillion were completed in the countries along the Belt and Road. It is necessary for Chinese companies who are interested in participating in the Belt and Road investment and M&A to understand the Belt and Road construction of different investment and M&A models, understand their advantages and disadvantages, and adopt the most reasonable trading model in each case. M&A of many Chinese companies do not entirely rely on their own funds and need to be financed from the third parties. Therefore, financing arrangements are also a key issue that Chinese companies need to address in the Belt and Road investment and M&A process.

This chapter introduces the Belt and Road investment and M&A model and financing arrangements. The chapter is divided into three sections. The first section proposes a reasonable transaction structure and funding arrangement of the successful investment and M&A for countries along the Belt and Road. The second section introduces two common M&A models: asset acquisition and equity acquisition. The third section introduces investment risks and financing trends in countries along the Belt and Road.

Section 1
The Transaction Structure of Investment and M&A along the "Belt and Road" Countries

A reasonable trading structure design is critical to the success of M&A projects in countries along the Belt and Road. Key factors in the transaction structure include the transaction subject, tax arrangements, payment types and acquisition forms. The design of the transaction structure needs to be adjusted according to the commercial purposes of the two parties, the tax arrangement and the laws and regulations of the host country. The transaction structure of each project is different and there is no rule of passage. A poorly designed trading structure can have a disastrous effect on sellers, buyers and lenders. The investment and M&A transactions along the Belt and Road require a large amount of funds to be effectively deployed among multiple countries. In addition to using their own funds, Chinese companies need to raise funds from international investors, financial and investment institutions to obtain sufficient funds and complete transaction. A reasonable trading structure and good financing model are critical to the success of the investment merger. Therefore, for Chinese companies, finding a safe, innovative trading structure and financing model that best promotes M&A transactions always represents a challenge. In the appendix, we summarize 19 classic M&A cases along the Belt and Road. Chinese companies preparing for investment and M&A along the Belt and Road can refer to these cases as their guide while designing the transaction structure and effectively arrange funds. Interested readers can learn more in these cases.

Section 2
Model of Asset Acquisition and Equity Acquisition

Asset acquisition and equity acquisition are the two main forms of investment and M&A. This section describes the advantages and disadvantages of these two acquisition methods and further describes them through specific cases.

In any M&A transaction, one of the top issues for all parties to the transaction is the type of ownership transfer mechanism used – the form of acquisition. Asset acquisitions and equity acquisitions are two major forms of investment and M&A. These two acquisition methods have their own advantages and disadvantages, and need to be reasonably arranged based on the specific characteristics of each project. Sometimes, the best trading structure is obvious, and the parties can quickly reach an agreement to complete the investment and M&A transaction. However, in most cases, the parties need to spend a lot of time and resources to try to agree on the form of the acquisition.

Following are two ways to transfer assets or stocks and related liabilities from the target company to the acquiring company, which usually are referred as an "asset acquisition" and "stock acquisition."

a. Purchase of assets: The seller sells all or part of the target assets to the buyer in exchange for the buyer's stock, cash or a combination of stock and cash. The buyer may choose to bear all, part or no liability of the seller. Usually, the buyer does not bear the liabilities of the seller's target assets.

b. Purchase of shares: The shareholders of the target company sell the shares of the target company to the buyer. The shareholders of the target company can accept the buyer's stock, cash or a combination of stock and cash. Usually, the buyer assumes the liabilities of the target company.

Equity acquisitions and asset acquisitions are two major forms of M&A that Chinese companies use in order to invest in countries along the Belt and Road Initiative, obtain eligible overseas targets and take over the ownership or control of the target company and target assets. Asset and stock acquisition methods are widely used in logistics, real estate, gaming, infrastructure, food, energy, healthcare and finance.

1. Asset acquisition

An asset purchase transaction usually involves the seller company selling the assets it uses in the course of its business operations to the buyer. The assets purchased generally contain all of the company's assets, and in certain cases the assets transferred include only certain selected assets. In the following three cases, the acquisition of assets may be the most practical way to complete such transactions: a. the acquirer is only interested in a specific product line, b. the acquirer is only interested in multiple product lines in one department of the parent company, c. the acquirer is interested in the product line of the department where the seller is not an independent legal entity.

In an asset transaction, when the seller retains ownership of the company's shares, the buyer usually clarifies that only part of the liability is sold to the buyer as a defined asset and liability in the purchase agreement. Therefore, the buyer usually requires that the buyer does not assume any obligation other than the stated liability in the asset purchase agreement. Asset acquisition has clear benefits for both buyers and sellers. Table 3-1 summarizes the benefits of asset acquisitions to both parties.

Table 3-1 The benefits of assets to both parties

Benefits	Buyer	Seller
Transaction has a great flexibility to clarify the types of assets and liabilities included in the transaction	√	√
Reducing the risk of the buyer taking on unknown liabilities	√	
No need to buy unnecessary assets	√	
Being able to dispose only some of the assets in the asset package		√
The ideal solution for handling non-performing business-related assets		√
Selling only assets related to a specific business unit	√	√
The ideal solution for buyers who have great doubts about the debt of the target company	√	√
No minority shareholders	√	
Continuing to retain the legal entity of the company while selling the ownership of the assets		√
Allowing reassessment of the market value of acquired assets within the deadline of accounting standards	√	
Possibility of the exemption of shareholders' approval	√	

Although asset acquisitions have the advantages mentioned in table 3 − 1, there are still several shortcomings in purchasing assets from the perspective of the buyer and seller. From the buyer's point of view, the disadvantages are as follows.

a. Loss of the seller's net loss and tax credit.

b. It is impossible to transfer the rights of assets such as licenses, franchises, patents, etc. to the buyer.

c. If the assets sold are used as collateral for the loan, the consent of the lender is required for the transfer.

In asset transactions, the seller faces the taxation issues associated with the double taxation system. In addition, sellers usually need to submit to the government the relevant legal documents of transferring ownership of assets and liabilities to the buyer, which may incur additional costs.

In the framework of asset acquisitions, the chapter further discusses the following two types of sub-transactions: acquiring assets in cash and purchasing assets in stock.

(1) Acquiring assets in cash

In the process of acquiring assets in cash, the buyer acquires the seller's assets by paying cash and may choose to accept part or all of the debt of the seller's assets. As long as the seller's board of directors' votes to sell all or "substantially all" of the company's assets, the seller's shareholders must approve the transaction. After receiving the buyer's cash, the seller can:

a. reinvest all into operations;

b. reinvest partially and use the rest as dividends paid to shareholders;

c. liquidate the company and distribute all the cash to the shareholders.

When all the assets of the seller company have been acquired, the principal entity of the seller company will no longer exist if the shareholders of the seller approve the liquidation of the company. When the seller completes the asset sale, it will transfer the cash obtained from the buyer to the shareholder of the seller through liquidation.

(2) Purchasing assets in stock

The alternative form of cash-for-equity is to exchange stocks for stocks, that is, the shareholders of two independent companies concentrate the owner's equity in the buyer's company, and the buyer holds the combined assets and liabilities of the two companies. In this case, when the seller's board of directors and shareholders approve, the seller's shareholders will receive the buyer's stock in exchange for the seller's assets and liabilities. In the process of purchasing assets in stock, the seller needs to dissolve the company after obtaining the approval of the shareholders. After the transaction is complete, the seller company will no longer exist.

2. The stock acquisition

A stock (share) acquisition transaction refers to the purchase of shares of a target company. In stock trading, the buyer does not choose to purchase specific assets and liabilities, but instead, purchases the entire company's equity. After the transaction, the buyer becomes the owner of the company instead of the seller, and the company's business operation continues, the seller has no ongoing rights or obligations to the assets, liabilities or operations of the original company's business. Because all known and unknown liabilities are transferred to the buyer, and the seller can avoid continuing to assume responsibility, this type of sales is often favored by the seller's shareholders. Prior to the stock acquisition, the buyer needs to ensure that the company has a clean operating history or that there are no major difficulties in completing the sale of the assets, such as: a. restricting the transfer of certain assets from the seller to the buyer, b. whether a third party consent is required so that assets can be transferred.

In cash-for-stock or stock-for-stock transactions, the buyer buys shares directly from the seller's shareholders. If the target is a private entity, the acquisition is completed by an equity purchase agreement between the acquirer and the target shareholder. For listed companies, because of the large number of shareholders, the acquisition company needs to make an offer to the shareholders of the target company. Whether the acquisition is regarded as friendly or hostile, is determined based on whether the offer is supported by the board of directors and the managers of the target company. Buying stocks is the most commonly used method in hostile acquisition. If the buyer fails to persuade all the seller's shareholders to sell their shares, the minority seller's shareholders will continue to hold shares in the seller's company, and the target company will become a non-Wholly-owned subsidiary of the buyer. As the seller's equity transfer will be completed through public bidding, the approval of the seller's shareholders is not required in the transaction. Table 3-2 summarizes the benefits of stock acquisition to both parties.

Table 3–2　The benefits of stock acquisitions to both parties

Benefits	To buyer	To seller
All assets can be transferred with the equity of the target company, thereby reducing the number of documents completed	√	
Right to use the name, license, franchise, patent, etc. of the target company is retained	√	
Continuity of the contract and the recognition of the corporate brand can be maintained	√	
Seller has no continuing rights or obligations to the assets, liabilities or operations of the original company's business		√
Ability to defer tax payment		√
No complications related to the disposal of assets, that the seller doesn't wish to retain and is not purchased by the buyer		√

Despite the above advantages, equity transactions also have the following disadvantages. Disadvantages to buyers include: a. unknown or undisclosed liabilities, b. unfinished union agreements or employee benefit plans, and c. the presence of some shareholders that may generate huge administrative costs and obstacles to implementation when the strategic adjustments are implemented. Disadvantages that sellers will face include: a. the ability to choose which assets to retain, and b. the loss of all the potential tax credits.

Case 3-1 and Case 3-2 are examples of Fosun Pharma's acquisition of the equity of Indian pharmaceutical company Gland Pharma and China Merchants Group's acquisition of Hambantota Port for 99 years.

Case 3 – 1 Fosun Pharma acquired Indian pharmaceutical company Gland Pharma

Transaction Amount: USD 1. 09 billion
Target Country: India
Industry: Medical

Case Background: In 2017, Fosun Pharma announced plans to acquire 86. 08% stake in Gland Pharma for no more than $1. 261 billion. However, the deal has raised concerns among the Indian government. India allows foreign capital to invest up to 100% of its domestic pharmaceutical industry, but requires government approval when higher than 74%. According to the Indian Cabinet Economic Affairs Committee (CCEA) challenged the proposal, Fosun Pharma decided to reduce the shareholding ratio to 74% while the valuation did not exceed USD 1. 09 billion. Under the new terms, Gland Pharma's founding shareholders had the right to put options within one year after the expiration of the share purchase agreement (SPA) deadline and sell the remaining shares for $355 million. Gland Pharma also established a new board of nine members, and Fosun Pharma was given a right to appoint most of its members.

Case Study: Fosun Pharma's acquisition of Gland Pharma is a cash-for-stock transaction in which the buyer directly purchases shares of the seller's shareholders. Since the target is a private entity, the purchase is made through a stock purchase agreement between the acquirer and the target company's shareholders, so it is not necessary for the acquiring company to issue a takeover offer to the shareholders of the target company. Although the acquisition process has some twists and turns, the importance of this acquisition to Fosun Pharma and Gland Pharma India is obvious. The cooperation agreement between Fosun Pharma and Gland Pharma created a new channel for Fosun Pharma to sell Gland Pharma's products in the existing market. Besides, this transaction became a key point in the global layout of Fosun Pharma.

Case 3 – 2 China merchants port acquired 99-years operation rights of Hambantota Port

Transaction Amount: USD 1. 12 billion
Target Country: Sri Lanka
Industry: Infrastructure

Case Background: The port of Hambantota is a deep-Water port located on the southern coast of Sri Lanka. Its three-phase port development project involves the construction of a major industrial and service port in an affiliated industrial zone. The first phase of the port of Hambantota was completed in December 2011 and started operations in June 2012. The second phase of the construction project was completed in April 2015. The port has 10 berths and the terminal length is 3 487 meters which enables it to handle liquid bulk cargo in containers, bulk, general purpose, ro-ro and large vessels.

In July 2017, China Port Operator China Merchants Port Holdings Co., Ltd. (referred to as China Merchants Port) announced that it would acquire 85% stake in Sri Lanka's Hambantota Port for USD 974 million. According to the agreement, China Merchants Port has to invest up to USD 1. 12 billion in the port of Hambantota, of which USD 974 million will be paid directly to the Sri Lanka Port Authority to acquire 85% of the shares of Hambantota International Port Group (Private) Co. , Ltd. , whereas the latter acquired a 58% stake in the port services company. Hambantota International Port Group (Private) Limited has the sole and exclusive right to develop, operate and manage the port of Hambantota, and the port services company has the right to operate the port. The agreement is valid for 99 years and the agreement stipulates that the Sri Lankan Government and the Port Authority will ensure that no ports or terminals that compete with the services and operations of the Port of Hambantota will be directly developed within 100 km for the first 15 years.

Case Study: The Hambantota Port transaction is a case of obtaining asset use rights and development rights in cash. With the rapid development of China's economy, the infrastructure and interconnection of countries along the "Belt and Road" have become the foundation of the "Belt and Road" construction. According to the advantage of geographincal position, the port of Hambantota will have a great potetial for future expansion. The investment of Chinese enterprises will improve the conditions of port infrastructure and service capacity of the port, and drive its economic development to achieve a win-win situation.

Section 3
Investment Risks and Financing Trends along the "Belt and Road" Countries

According to the data released by the State-owned Assets Supervision and Administration Commission of the State Council in October 2018, five years since the Belt and Road Initiative was proposed, the central enterprises have invested or participated in more than 3 100 investment projects and projects in the Belt and Road countries. However, for the Belt and Road Initiative, this is only the beginning. More importantly, Chinese companies will learn to compete on the global stage, conduct international trade and investment best practices, acquire international advanced technology and scale on the international market. For Chinese companies that are interested in investing in the "Belt and Road" countries, this doesn't come without risk. Therefore, it's very important of the creation of a new investment and financing model, encouraging the government to strengthen cooperation with private capital, and establishing a diversified financing system and a multi-level capital market.

1. Participation of state-owned enterprises and private enterprises

Up to now, China's policy banks (China Development Bank and the Export-import Bank of China) and Silk Road Fund are both Chinese enterprises' funders, while the Asian Infrastructure Investment Bank and the New Development Bank are mostly the funder of the countries where the Belt and Road projects are located. By 2030, China will no longer fund all the Belt and Road projects. It is expected that more than half of the Belt and Road investment projects will be funded by the private capital, multinational banks and foreign governments. The introduction of diversified shareholders and partners is one of the key factors in the success of investment and M&A. The introduction of diversified shareholders and partners is one of the key factors for the success of investment and M&A and acquisitions. Although Chinese state-owned enterprises are in a dominant position in the development and investment of the Belt and Road projects, more and more private and foreign companies have begun to take the initiative. In addition, in order to reduce risk and achieve sustainable development in the destination country, companies are likely to establish joint ventures or other forms of partnership with local partners. As China's economic growth slows down, Chinese private enterprises are looking for new opportunities, and the products and prices they sell are also suitable for consumers in countries along the Belt and Road. At present, countries in Southeast Asia, West Asia, Africa and South Asia are the most popular investment destinations among state-owned enterprises along the Belt and Road. Under the guidance of the Belt and Road Initiative, state-owned enterprises will continue to be the "group leader". However, unlike state-owned enterprises, private and foreign-funded enterprises have invested more in developed regions such as the United States and Europe due to relatively low risks, mature market economies, and sound legal systems. Chinese private enterprises will occupy more and more market share of exit activities in the future, especially in the form of investment mergers and acquisitions. Countries along the Belt and Road are undoubtedly very attractive to Chinese private companies, and appropriate financing arrangements have become an important part of the success of the "Belt and Road" national project transactions. The positive news is that a large part of the financing arrangements now comes from the private capital. The local public-private partnerships (PPPs) will also play an important role.

The local public-private partnerships (PPPs), as a new type of financing mechanism, can help private countries along the Belt and Road initiative to attract private investors to fund their infrastructure projects. They can also be a convenient tool for ensuring risk sharing, identifying potential success projects, and building effective project monitoring systems. Therefore, there is a need to promote a public-private partnership framework in China and many countries along the Belt and Road. At the same time, open tendering of the project is also necessary. At present, financing for infrastructure projects has been seen as a challenge for many ASEAN countries. The lack of funding for national infrastructure projects remains a major problem for many of them. After the 19th National Congress of the Communist Party of China, the development of the Belt and Road and the development of "Guangdong-Hong Kong-Macao Greater Bay Area" have been prioritized. The future growth of investment and M&A activities and private equity is predictable. According to the *Asia Private Equity Insights 2018*, since the Chinese government began to curb capital outflows in August 2017, Chinese companies' M&A activity has decreased by 40%. In the first nine months of 2017, private equity-backed acquisitions grew by 129% to $48 billion. Private equity funds focus on emerging industries such as telecommunications, renewable energy, education and advanced manufacturing, which have huge growth potential in the future. With the rise and rapid development of China's technology startups, it is expected that the venture capital and private equity fund industries will also see rapid growth. In addition, under the current situation of imbalanced supply and demand in the domestic market, the development of "Guangdong-Hong Kong-Macao Greater Bay Area" has opened up a new path for the development of Chinese private equity firms. In this case, the two main challenges the market will face will be the transaction pricing and exit environments.

Due to the optimistic outlook of the market, transaction pricing is one of the biggest challenges, which gives the seller no reason to deal with its capital. Since the funds have always been focusing on the potential industries (including medicine and technology), and some of them have even set up special investment funds, it is difficult to explore high-quality transactions. The market is witnessing an increasing number of a new generation investors entering the market. Unlike previous generations of investors, the new generation is more inclined to put capital under their control. These investors are more open and willing to take on more risks. They must ensure that their financing and guarantee structures are in compliance with the relevant local laws and are well protected.

Case 3 – 3 Nesta acquired Global Logistic Properties' controlling stake

Transaction Amount: SGD 16 billion
Target Country: Singapore
Industry: Logistics assets
Case Background: In 2017, a consortium of Vanke Group, Hillhouse Capital Group, Houpu Investment and Bank of China Investment won a management buyout and took over Singapore's logistics giant GLP. Nesta Investment Holdings (LP, Nesta) bid SGD 16 billion for the acquisition of a controlling stake in Singapore's listed company GLP, with the aim of delisting the company from the Singapore Stock Exchange and privatizing it. Vanke Group became the largest shareholder of GLP, accounting for 21.4% of the shares. The remaining members represent the balance of interests among GLP insiders, namely, Houpu Investment (21.3%), Hillhouse Capital Group (21.2%), Bank of China Investment (15%), and GLP management (21.1%) . The acquisition was initiated by GLP 's largest shareholder, the Singapore Government Investment Corporation (GIC), a Singapore-based sovereign wealth fund that holds a 36.93% stake in GLP. In October 2010, GLP was listed in Singapore. In early 2017, the Singapore government investment

company asked GLP to carry out strategic operations to increase shareholder value. The company's share price rose by about 12%. Since then, GLP has raised people's expectations because of restructuring, so its share price soared and became the best performing stock in Singapore. After the acquisition was completed, GLP shares rose 21.9%, setting a new record of 3.29 Singapore dollars; Vanke Group's share price in Shenzhen rose 0.6% to 24.59 yuan, and Hong Kong stocks rose 2.4% to 23.29 Hong Kong dollars.

Case Study: This is a private equity acquisition case and is considered to be the largest private equity acquisition case in Asia's history. Through the acquisition, Vanke Group became a major shareholder of GLP, and Vanke Group and GLP are expected to have significant synergies. The deal helped Vanke improve its presence in logistics and real estate sector and enhance its presence in this region. GLP' management will support the acquisition because of price determinations, limited prerequisites, and a defined timeframe for completion.

2. The risks associated with investment and M&A

So far, Chinese policy banks have assumed the financial risks of investing in countries along the "Belt and Road", while operational risks have fallen on Chinese state-owned enterprises. With the involvement of other companies, the risks and opportunities associated with the structure of the investment transaction need to be carefully evaluated. The main risks include the followings.

(1) Due diligence risk of M&A transactions

Chinese companies will increasingly seek to acquire companies along the Belt and Road countries to accelerate access to local markets. The process of M&A is full of challenges. Firstly, the profits of many companies along the Belt and Road countries depend on their strong government relations. After the completion of the merger, there is great uncertainty in whether these companies can maintain stable and profitable business. Secondly, the overseas private holding companies can easily exaggerate their business activities, leading Chinese buyers to pay a higher premium. Finally, because companies in the countries along the Belt and Road usually have a strong local culture, cultural integration after M&A can be very difficult.

(2) Legal and regulatory risks

The legal systems of countries along the Belt and Road vary widely, making it challenging to replicate projects between countries. Different legal systems may create obstacles to investment, especially in the event of the legal disputes.

(3) Financial risks

Chinese banks have limited experience in assessing national credit risk along the Belt and Road, which is part of the reason for the surge in the government guarantees and credit insurance demand. Chinese banks need to develop the internal capabilities or find ways to work with local global banks that are more insightful or have more experience in assessing credit issues in countries along the Belt and Road.

(4) The importance of local partnerships

China's leading contractors have decades of experience in business development along the Belt and Road countries, but many other companies do not have similar advantages. Most Chinese companies need to rely on working with the well-known local partners to achieve investment success.

(5) Risks related to independent intellectual property rights (IPR)

Such risks refer to the intellectual property disputes involved in overseas M&A transactions. Some common precautions include: due diligence of intellectual property rights, analysis of risks of infringement of intellectual property rights of the third parties, intellectual property protection provisions in equity or asset purchase agreements and effective management of intellectual property rights after the completion of transactions.

(6) Tax risks and foreign exchange risks

Tax risk and foreign exchange risk refer to the change in the investment value caused by the target company's failure to perform relevant tax obligations and changes in currency exchange rates and interest rates. Acquisition of overseas target companies may result in an unpredictable tax risks such as foreign exchange risk. Precautions that can be taken to address this risk include: tax due diligence; consideration of tax regulations and depreciation of acquired assets; use of financial instruments to prevent losses due to exchange rate and interest rate fluctuations; use of RMB as a settlement currency in the M&A process.

(7) Risks related to labor law

Investors should be aware of this risk when conducting overseas operations and hiring local labor. The main risks include disputes related to wages, compensation, transfer, dismissal and different methods of dealing with labor relations due to different employment regulations. Some common precautions include:

a. Fully understand local laws and regulations concerning labor relations and dispute resolution procedures.

b. On the basis of full grasp of the background and laws, have in-depth understanding of the cultural background of labor relations, and comprehensive assessment and prediction of relevant labor risks involved in M&A transactions.

c. In the integration stage after mergers and acquisitions, Chinese investors should lift the original labor-management relations according to local laws and cultures, and resolve labor disputes in accordance with applicable laws and dispute settlement mechanisms.

(8) Relevant political risks

Political risk refers to the risk of economic losses caused by changes in the political environment of the investor's location and target location, unstable political status, and changes in laws and policies. Types of political risk include: expropriation, target country defaults, foreign exchange restrictions, strikes, wars, political riots, and insurance claims.

These risks will adversely affect business viability and the ability to obtain financing. The Chinese companies need to carefully consider these disadvantages before participating in the "Belt and Road" project. So far, Chinese companies have relied heavily on debt financing and, in some cases, private equity financing. Those companies that participate in the "Belt and Road" projects are increasingly looking to reduce interest rate risk, exchange rate risk and financing interest associated with the long-term loans. This is especially important for companies operating in the high-risk countries along the Belt and Road as they have higher cost and greater uncertainty. Therefore, it is expected that Chinese banks will be more cautious in handling capital applications, which will lead Chinese companies to seek other financing channels. The funds required for the Belt and Road construction will be obtained through a combination of private capital, multilateral banks and foreign government funds. In the complex operation of the unfamiliar Belt and Road market, legal system and financing channels, Chinese companies will increasingly need the help of local partners, technology and component suppliers to gain insights into the realities of the target country. On the other hand, this also provides an excellent opportunity for a variety of local companies in the countries along the Belt and Road.

3. Financing trends

With the transformation and upgrade of China's economic structure, the proportion of private investment in the Belt and Road investment is gradually increasing. In 2016, Chinese government significantly restricted overseas investments in the real estate and entertainment industries and encouraged investment in countries along the "Belt and Road". Considering the huge capital needs of countries along the Belt and Road, a diversified source of funding will be needed in the future. The following trends will ensure the reduction of risks the Chinese financial institutions currently are faced with.

a. Global capital participates in the investment of the Belt and Road project through banks and financing companies in Western countries;

b. A more balanced financing portfolio, including equity financing, Silk Road Fund, China Development Bank and private equity funds;

c. Local banks in countries along the Belt and Road will provide debt financing, which will minimize foreign exchange risk and promote the localization of financing for the Belt and Road projects.

In general, these trends will greatly promote the formation of a collaborative ecosystem based on the principle of "communicating, building, and sharing" along the Belt and Road countries. In addition, as China launches the Belt and Road bonds to fund large-scale investment projects, companies also have a new financing channel. In March 2018, the China Securities Regulatory Commission (CSRC) announced that China allows domestic and foreign companies to issue bonds through the Shanghai and Shenzhen stock exchanges to provide funds for the Belt and Road project. Government-backed institutions along the Belt and Road countries can also issue similar bonds in China. As of March 2018, CSRC has approved the application of seven domestic and foreign enterprises, and plans to issue a total of RMB 50 billion of Belt and Road bonds to finance investment projects. In order to meet the huge financing needs of countries along the Belt and Road, the Belt and Road bond issuance will continue to increase.

Many Chinese companies have actively used this new channel to obtain financing:

a. In June 2018, Hengyi Petrochemical Co., Ltd. issued a three-year Belt and Road corporate bond of RMB 500 million on the Shenzhen Stock Exchange. The funds raised by the bond issue will be used for the company's petrochemical project in Brunei;

b. In January 2018, private cement producer Red Lion Holdings Group Co., Ltd. (Red Lion Group) issued a three-year Belt and Road corporate bond of RMB 300 million on the Shanghai Stock Exchange. The proceeds will be used to purchase cement production equipment in Laos, which is expected to produce up to 5 000 tons per day. The Red Lion Group, which was rated AAA by China Chengxin Group, set the coupon yield of the three-year bond at 6.34%, and the subscription multiple of the bond was 2.67 times. According to the bond prospectus, the Red Lion Group's project in Laos has been listed by the National Development and Reform Commission as the Belt and Road key project in Zhejiang Province, where the Red Lion Group is located.

c. In March 2017, Russian company UC Rusal issued a three-year non-redemption bond of RMB 1 billion on the Shanghai Stock Exchange. This is the first RMB bond completed by the Belt and Road countries.

d. In January 2018, GLP announced that it had obtained the approval of the China Securities Regulatory Commission and issued up to RMB 12 billion of Belt and Road corporate bonds on the Shenzhen Stock Exchange. The funds will be used to repay the debts incurred by GLP in the acquisition of logistics assets in Europe.

The various financing tools mentioned above provide a new source of funding for the Belt and Road project, ensuring that the huge financing needs of the Belt and Road project can be fully met in the future.

CHAPTER

4

TEAM BUILDING FOR INVESTMENT AND M&A ALONG THE "BELT AND ROAD" COUNTRIES

In the Belt and Road where M&As are in full swing, Chinese buyers still face many problems such as unclear ideas of M&A, insufficient business negotiation capabilities, incomplete understanding of the market and industry, insufficient understanding of the culture of the country where the acquired company is located, insufficient due diligence of the targeted company, weak risk control ability, insufficient integration and utilization of third-party resources, inadequate capability of the post-investment integration and so on. Therefore, in the process of overseas M&A, there are often problems such as high premiums on the acquisition of the underlying assets, integration failure after the acquisition, increased risk of corporate goodwill impairment and increased losses which lead to the failure of the entire M&A transaction and cause huge losses to the Chinese buyers, even dragging the Chinese parent company into the quagmire. At the same time, due to the high degree of uncertainty in the overseas M&A market and the complicated transaction process coupled with many factors such as the insufficient overseas M&A experience, Chinese companies' overseas M&As would frequently hit the wall, be denied or reviewed.

It is undeniable that there are many objective reasons for the failure of overseas M&A, but the author believes that there are more subjective reasons of Chinese enterprises. More precisely, insufficient capacity and lack of experience of M&A team results in the failure of overseas M&A. The lack of professionals with international M&A experience is the biggest obstacle for the success of M&A of Chinese enterprises.

Case 4-1 TCL Group's M&A of Alcatel's Mobile Phone Business

Transaction Amount: 55 million euros
Target Country: France
Industry: Mobile Phone

Case Background: On April 26, 2004, TCL Group announced the acquisition of the mobile phone business of Alcatel France. The TCL Group contributes 55 million euros and Alcatel contributes 45 million euros. Alcatel will inject the brand, technology and channels into the joint venture. At that time, TCL mobile phone was once the first brand in China, and Alcatel's mobile phone sales reached more than 7 million units in 2004. Li Dongsheng hopes to fully integrate the supply chain through the acquisition of Alcatel's mobile phone business, play a synergistic effect to reduce costs and use Alcatel's technology to launch innovative products.

However, when the joint venture began operations, both parties had problems in business integration and cultural integration. With the intensification of cultural conflicts and the failure of business integration, the operation status of the joint venture company deteriorated rapidly and the talents were lost. At the beginning of the second year, the 100 million euros invested by TCL and Alcatel were running out, and the company suffered serious losses. In May 2005, TCL Group reorganized the joint venture company and gradually reversed the predicament after the integration of the joint venture with domestic business.

Case Study: There are two main reasons for the failure of the transaction: a. The company manager did not form a clear M&A method and failed to carefully select the acquisition target before the acquisition and prepare all the preparations in advance. The TCL Group's decision to acquire Alcatel was made within three months, when TCL Group had just completed the acquisition of the Thomson color TV business. The acquisition lacked sufficient research on the target company and was too hasty. b. There was an insufficient talent reserve. In 2004, at the beginning of the tide of Chinese companies participating in global investment and M&A, international talents were seriously inadequate. TCL Group began global recruitment after the acquisition of Alcatel. After the merger was completed, for a long time Li Dongsheng had still been unable to find a suitable international assistant. This led to the failure of M&A. It is clear that the human factor has a decisive influence on the final structure of investment and M&A. The main reason for the failure of many Chinese overseas M&A projects is that they have not chosen "partners" and have not used "people".

Section 1

The Formation of Investment and M&A Team along the "Belt and Road" Countries

Investment and the M&A along the "Belt and Road" countries is a complex system engineering. It is necessary to form an M&A team of various professionals with relevant experience and capabilities. Active participation, division of labor and collaboration are the key to ensuring the success of M&A transactions. Chinese companies generally lack management talents who can control large-scale overseas M&A projects, including project management, preliminary research, business negotiation, integration planning and post-investment management. Consequently, these companies have a high degree of reliance on third-party professional teams. Third-party professional teams need to participate in all aspects of the M&A transaction and give professional advice based on the progress of the project. A good third-party team is critical to the success of the M&A. In the process of project promotion, Chinese companies need to constantly adjust the negotiation strategy based on the latest information and identify the real situation of the seller's enterprise. The companies need to circumvent potential risks through setting the terms of agreement and through designing reasonable transaction architecture to reduce the cost of M&A.

Typically, the Belt and Road M&A team includes an in-house team and an external third-party professional team.

1. In-house M&A Team

The company itself directly operates the M&A team, and the team is built to be complete, including investment team, legal team, human resources team, finance team, operation team, technical team and so on. Many listed companies have set up the Corporate Development Department or the Strategic Investment Department to undertake the organization and coordination of their M&A. These departments are the main focus of the company's investment in M&A. After the project being established, the Corporate Development Department will quickly assemble a virtual project team within the company according to the project. The project leader in the internal team of the company is very important. He not only has to judge the opportunity, but also has to lead all relevant work including the due diligence, commercial negotiation, delivery, and post-investment integration. The "one head, one tail" work of the internal team of the enterprise in the M&A process needs to be completed independently by in-house team. "Head" refers to the formulation of "corporate strategy". The internal employees of the company must have a relatively accurate grasp of the real situation of the enterprise. The formulation of the enterprise strategy must conform to the real situation of the enterprise. "Tail" refers to "post-investment integration". After the company signs the equity transfer agreement, it enters the post-investment management stage and involves the integration of two independent companies. This part of the work is basically completed by relevant in-house teams. External third-party professional teams are more likely to play a role in the transaction process.

Here, we focus on the importance of post-merger integration. There are many reasons for the failure of M&A. The failure of integration after M&A is a very important reason. Forming an experienced M&A integration team is important for the success of M&A. In most cases, the company has begun to design integration plan and prepared to form the integration team. After signing the transaction agreement, both parties will build an introduction team as soon as possible to plan and arrange the aspects of corporate strategy, finance, sales, procurement, culture, human resources and technology. During the post-merger integration, the matching of manpower, cultural values, and behaviors all require the in-house team of the company to do their homework in advance and make great efforts. Generally speaking, the M&A team and the post-merger integration team are not the same team due to different focuses. After signing the equity transfer agreement, the focus of the work is transferred from the M&A team to the integration team. Considering the importance of post-merger integration, the sooner the integration team participates in the M&A project, the better the understanding of the project and the likelihood of successful integration will be after the M&A.

2. External Third-party Professional Team

External teams typically include third-party M&A intermediaries and related industry experts, including financial advisors, lawyers, audit and evaluation consultants, strategic consultants, and public relations firms. A good external third-party M&A team needs to be able to combine all aspects of strength and a variety of first-rate talents, in order to effectively deal with the various difficult issues in the M&A process.

According to Deloitte's statistics, Chinese companies' overseas M&A requires third-party organizations to provide assistance and services in four aspects: due diligence execution, M&A project development, search and screening of M&A targets, valuation and transaction negotiation, and the post-merger integration.

Third-party teams have more M&A experiences since they participated in multiple M&A projects for different companies. They can provide many valuable suggestions for corporate M&A. Transaction structures of many project are quite complex, involving different legal entities in multiple countries. Without the assistance of third-party professional teams, internal teams would be unable to complete the process. In addition, many companies do cross-industry M&A because there is no relevant business team within the company, so the external expert team is very important. Only by fully referring to the analysis of target companies by industry experts can the company make accurate judgments and correct decisions.

The selection of an external team of consultants is very important. Many Chinese companies that often do overseas M&A have expert resource pools, screening and evaluation processes of external institutions and can form external consultant teams according to specific conditions of the project and the "schedule" of external partners. The cost of the external third-party team is "rigid cost" for the company, which means that regardless of whether the M&A is completed, the cost of the external consultant team must be paid, which is a big expense for the company. In the early days of Chinese companies going global, many companies were reluctant to spend large sums of money to hire top-notch third-party teams. Due to the lack of strong professional support in the transaction process, they were in a passive position in overseas M&A and often paid the high price in M&A, encountering the so-called "China premium."

A good third-party team must give reasonable suggestions from a professional, objective third-party perspective, rather than simply cater to the company's ideas or just receive the agency fee for a quick completion of transaction. Companies must be cautious when selecting third-party teams. They should not choose third-party team based only on service fees or the principle of "personal supremacy", but also based on the professionalism of intermediaries, the degree of emphasis on the project, and relevant industry experience. Partners of the external team are very important. The work of many intermediaries is basically completed by the project manager. If the partners do not have enough participation in the project, they will not grasp the potential risk points of the project. For the enterprise, this is not only a loss of costs, but sometimes it will make the company "ride the tiger" in the transaction process, resulting in the failure of the transaction or the additional cost in the transaction process.

In Sections 3 and 4 of this chapter, we will further discuss the role of different third-party teams in M&A projects and how to deal with the relationship between internal and external third-party M&A teams.

Section 2

The In-house Team for the "Belt and Road" Countries' Investment and M&A Projects

The value and status of the company's internal M&A team is not to be blamed. Their work includes project acquisition, business negotiation, due diligence, deal closing and post-investment management. Many listed companies or some non-listed companies have established internal departments such as Corporate Development Division and Investment Division, which specialize in M&A and capital operations. Members of the investment department need to have a good industry background, excellent internal and external organizational coordination, comprehensive financial and legal knowledge, and good foreign language skills. The investment team is the key team for the entire company's M&A. The head of the M&A team is the core of the entire overseas M&A, and plays a key role in the success of the M&A. The company's internal finance, legal, risk control and business departments also need to actively participate in the Belt and Road M&A project to assess risks and benefits from different perspectives. The main responsibility of the finance team is to investigate the financial and tax situations of the acquired company, identify potential financial risks, and give the company's valuation range and tax planning recommendations. The legal team's main tasks include legal due diligence, government approval, and the drafting and review of the transaction agreement. The business team needs to give professional advice on M&A synergy, core technology, M&A, etc. The main responsibility of the risk control team is to identify potential risk points in the project and take precautions and counter measures.

Investment and M&A is the company's "top-ranking project" and the company's M&A activities depend on the future development of the company. The company's "top leader" is usually the "Supreme Commander" of the "Belt and Road" M&A project. They will pay attention to the latest progress of the "Belt and Road" M&A project and the main points of divergence between buyers and sellers and making quick decisions. In fact, there is no perfect company, only a perfect transaction. The acquired company must have such problems. With the deepening of due diligence, the target company will unveil the mysterious veil, and in many cases, there will be a situation like the "big face" in Sichuan opera. This requires the company's "top leader" to weigh the pros and cons according to the company's strategy and decide whether to make an acquisition.

The "first-hand" of different companies will have a big difference in the choice of M&A targets. Some "top leaders" like to buy large companies, and some like to buy "small but beautiful" companies. In fact, there is no absolute standard for the selection of M&A targets. It depends on the company's own situation and the effect of post-merger integration, whether it can produce synergies and enhance the value of the company. For example, Zhang Ruimin, the Chairman and CEO of Haier Group, put forward the idea of "shock fish". Haier Group's M&A of more than a dozen of "shock fish" companies achieved good results. The cases of "Haier Culture Activates Shock Fish" officially entered the Harvard University classroom, and Zhang Ruimin became the first Chinese entrepreneur to board the Harvard forum.

Case 4-2　Haier Group's M&A history

Transaction Amount: Billions of dollars
Target Country: USA, Japan, Thailand, New Zealand, Italy
Industry: Home Appliance
Case Background: Founded in 1984, Haier Group has grown from a small, insolvent company to a global appliance giant. In 2018, Haier Group's sales revenue reached RMB 266.1 billion, with 10 R&D centers, 25

industrial parks, 122 manufacturing centers and 106 marketing centers worldwide. Haier Group owns Haier, Casarte, GEA, Fisher & Paykel, Candy, AQUA, Leader and other home appliances brands. Haier Group's development strategy has been continuously adjusted with the changes of the times. It has successively proposed brand strategy, diversification strategy, internationalization strategy, global brand strategy and network strategy. In the development process, M&As have always been the most important development path for Haier Group. In the course of more than 30 years of development, Haier Group has acquired a number of world-renowned brands. In 2011, it acquired the washing machine and refrigerator business of Sanyo Co. ,Ltd. , and acquired more than 90% of New Zealand's Fisher & Paykel in 2012. In 2016, it acquired the global home appliance giant General Electric Appliances and acquired the Italian appliance manufacturer Candy in 2018. The history of Haier Group is also a history of M&A.

Case Study: Haier Group's M&A strategy has the following four characteristics.

a. Have a clear development strategy. The M&A of Haier Group serves the company's long-term development strategy. After the completion of the acquisition, the target company will quickly be integrated into its development track. According to Haier's words, Haier is eating "shock fish" . The technology, equipment, and talents of the targeted company are good. Once new management ideas and culture are injected the company will be activated soon.

b. Unique cultural integration. After Haier's M&A, it will attach great importance to the integration of culture. Haier advocates "integration" rather than "ruling. " After Haier Group acquired Fisher & Paykel, it held 2 director seats on the board of 7 people, and the remaining 5 were still the original managers.

c. The combination of "leap-forward M&A" and "gradual M&A" . For the target enterprises with existing cooperation and relatively well understanding, Haier Group will adopt the one-time acquisition method, which is "leap-forward M&A" , and for the target companies with large volume, no cooperation base and complex business, Haier Group will adopt "gradual M&A" to complete the integration in several stages. The company will not only achieve the goal of rapid integration, but also reduce the risk of M&A.

d. Give full play to synergies. For a global enterprise like Haier Group, synergy after M&A is crucial. After the completion of the M&A, Haier Group can fully cooperate with the acquired enterprises on the core elements of sales network, procurement cost and R&D resources, and effectively exert the effect of "1 +1 >2" to achieve a win-win situation.

The in-house M&A team is the executor of the M&A and the leader of the M&A transaction. The team needs to continuously understand the relationship between the parent company and the acquired company, grasp the rhythm and scale of the negotiation, and continuously optimize the integration plan formulated in the early stage of the transaction. The in-house M&A team needs to form a perfect integration of culture, human resources, and finance after the transaction is completed. This requires the in-house M&A team members to have a deep understanding of the industry, operation, culture, and capital market rules. They need to have a clear decision-making route to ensure that the infrequent factors affecting the transaction can be quickly processed to make the right decision at different points in time. The "Belt and Road" overseas M&As usually have clear and tight schedule. Generally, it is necessary to make decisions in a short period of time and close the deal quickly. In particular, Chinese listed companies also involve the process of approval by the CSRC, which has extremely high requirements for the execution process and professionalism of the team.

Many companies lack self-tests for overseas M&A capabilities, mainly in the following areas:

a. Insufficient analysis at the strategic level resulted in large differences in the company's strategy between the buyers and sellers, which undoubtedly increased the difficulty of post-merger integration.

b. Insufficient cultural understanding and failure to study the culture of the target company and the country where it is located resulted in the acquirer being unable to achieve full integration with the acquired party. As a result, it is difficult for the acquired company to have a sense of identity.

c. The financial level is not well prepared, and so the company is unable to analyze and prepare for its own investment ability, financing ability, and risk control ability. It is difficult to plan ahead and be ready when problems arise.

d. In the actual operation, companies pay too much attention to the transaction price and pay less attention to the transaction structure, design, and tax planning. They spend a lot of money and constantly adjust the organizational structure even after the completion of the M&A.

e. Affirmation of financial due diligence, lack of understanding of the importance of business due diligence, often through limited field visits by senior executives, lack of sensible estimation of market size and general pattern of target markets, lack of professional judgment, insufficient understanding of potential risks and assessment, lack of effective risk aversion programs and response measures.

f. Paying no attention to the investigation of intellectual property rights, resulting in high brand fees after the M&A, facing the risk of infringement and litigation, ignoring the differences between Chinese and foreign management concepts and practices and the differences in culture and values, resistance of the acquired management team.

g. The "first-in-command" has insufficient authorization for the M&A team and the internal decision-making system of the company is difficult to adapt to the rapid response requirements of each stage of overseas M&A.

h. Chinese companies have not realized that the main bottleneck lied in the lack of talent, rather than team's absence of overseas M&A experience.

Building a company's internal M&A team is not a one-step process. It is necessary to continuously polish the team in the actual process, so that finally it can become a combative internal M&A team. Chinese state-owned enterprises such as PetroChina and China National Chemical Corporation (here in after referred to as China Chemical Industry) attach great importance to personnel training before overseas M&A. They select those employees who are good with English from very early on and send them to Europe and the United States to study enterprise management. Through the process of study and work, they gain direct understanding of overseas thinking and business culture. When operating specific overseas M&A projects, it is possible to adjust the negotiation ideas in a targeted manner, bypass various financial and legal M&A traps, and effectively integrate overseas M&A companies. At present, the heads of overseas M&A in the three major oil companies in China (PetroChina, Sinopec, and CNOOC) all have the experience of studying and doing internships abroad. Through endogenous and exogenous development, the upstream flagship companies under the three major oil companies have entered or are close to the ranks of international super-large oil companies.

Based on author's many years of M&A experience in listed companies, in order to build a mature overseas M&A team team members need to have the following six capabilities.

1. Strong Learning Ability

The author worked for Neusoft Group Co., Ltd. (referred to as Neusoft Group) for many years and experienced rapid update of technology in the field of TMT. People in the industry often joke that the computer industry has been a "dog year", that is, 1 year in the computer industry is equivalent to 7 years in other traditional industries, and only few companies like Neusoft can live over 20 years. Members of the Neusoft M&A team need to keep an eye on the latest technological developments and keep themselves sensitive to advanced technologies such as B (Blockchain), A (AI, Artificial Intelligence), S (Security, Security Technology), I (IoT, Internet of Things), C (Cloud Computing), and explore potential M&A opportunities while paying close attention to changes in the capital market. For example, a large number of Chinese internet companies such as Sina have adopted the VIE framework (variable interest entities) to list on overseas capital markets because they cannot meet the requirements of the A-share capital market for the profitability of listed companies. At the same time, many Chinese companies listed overseas valued the high market valuation of the A-share market and chose to "restructuring red-chip" to return to the A-share market. The state has continuously introduced new policies and regulations for the Belt and Road M&A. Neusoft's overseas M&A involves a large number of such issues, hence learning and updating the knowledge of relevant industry and capital market are compulsory courses for the M&A team.

2. Understanding of Culture and Humanity

In M&A, just like everywhere else, all problems are related to people. During his tenure at the Neusoft Group, the author was fortunate enough to participate in many M&A with Dr. Liu Jiren – Chairman and CEO of Neusoft Group. As a benchmark for the Chinese software industry, Dr. Liu Jiren's attention to detail is surprising. For many overseas M&A transactions, Dr. Liu Jiren will pay close attention to the progress of each negotiation and the differences between the two sides and respond in a timely manner. Many details that we don't pay much attention to often become the key to the success of an M&A. This is why many investors say that "investment is the last job in life". The core members of the team with more life experience are the mainstay of the company's internal M&A team, which will help the team avoid many undetectable risks.

3. The International Thinking Mode

Only an international vision, an international way of thinking and an operation that conforms to market rules are enough to enable the M&A team to have equal opportunities to participate in the games under the Western rules. The mode of thinking is not on the same channel and it is easy to see the situation of "chicken and duck talk", which makes the M&A deadlocked. English is the main working language in overseas M&A. The M&A team needs to have good English communication skills and communicate freely with negotiating opponents and overseas third-party intermediaries. Many Chinese companies' M&A leaders have poor English proficiency and need to use translation to complete negotiations, which undoubtedly greatly reduces the efficiency of the negotiations. Neusoft Group has a group of employees with overseas M&A experience, who can use English to communicate with negotiating opponents during business negotiations. The opponents are often surprised by the degree of internationalization of Neusoft Group. While improving the efficiency of negotiation, they have also won the respect of the negotiating opponents.

4. Solid Professional Knowledge and Industry Knowledge

The investment, finance, legal, human resources and business professional teams can only fully play their role in the M&A team unless they have relevant professional knowledge. Otherwise, they will become the short board of the M&A team and lead the failure of M&A transaction. It is very important that the members of professional teams had good knowledge of the industry and could provide professional opinions on industry characteristics and key issues. The author deeply felt the professionalism of the Philips intellectual property team and Philips' emphasis on intellectual property in participating in the equity transaction of Neusoft Group's acquisition of Neusoft Medical. Throughout the negotiation process, we also learned a lot from the negotiating opponents that we wouldn't be able to learn from books, and improved the overall capacity of the M&A team.

5. Rich Project Experience

It is necessary to establish a professional M&A team considering the complexity and high degree of uncertainty of overseas M&A. Since overseas M&A is a difficult practical work, it is essential for M&A team to have enough project experience. According to the situation of overseas M&A at Neusoft Group, hundreds of projects can be accessed every year. Out of these hundred projects, about 20% will be promoted, about 5% will enter the stage of the due diligence, and finally only 1% will be completed. Only when the M&A team participates in a sufficient number of projects can the team have a clearer understanding of the transaction process and potential risk points of the overseas M&A, ensure the attention for each key process and complete the work in an orderly manner. After finishing hundreds or even thousands of projects, the M&A team can have a pair of "sharp eyes" to finish the transition from "quantitative change" to "qualitative change". In this regard, there are no shortcuts, and there will be completely different performances for inexperienced teams and experienced teams. We can say that "enough project experience" is the guarantee for the ultimate success of the M&A project.

6. Good Communication and Coordination Skills

Overseas M&A transactions often have a clear timetable and many buyers chase good M&A targets at the same time. Sellers often ask buyers to pay high transaction margins, submit quotations, and close the deal as soon as possible. The pressure on the buyer side is very large. The M&A team is required to effectively communicate with the seller, to gain a deeper understanding of the acquired company through various channels, to identify potential risk points, and understand the situation of competitors throughout the transaction. All of these set high requirements for M&A team's coordination skills. It is necessary for the in-house M&A team to clearly define the division of labor and actively cooperate with third-party intermediaries including investment banks, law firms, taxation consultants, and auditing consultants, human resources consultants, and public relations consultants. Many Belt and Road investment and M&A projects may involve multiple countries and multiple teams, which undoubtedly increases the difficulty of coordination. Thus, effective communication and coordination skills are very important soft powers for overseas M&A teams.

Section 3
The External Team for the "Belt and Road" Countries' Investment and M&A Projects (Third-party Intermediaries)

Trading, fiscal, and legal affairs are the three main risk points for the Belt and Road M&A project, which may include other risks such as business strategy, M&A

target credit, financing, profit margin, market, foreign exchange, inflation, tax, government approval and labor. Since the laws, culture, and finances in the country where the M&A targeted company is located are very different from those in China, it is not enough to rely solely on the internal team of the company. Generally, the company will hire third-party intermediaries to participate in the M&A projects. Belt and Road Investment and M&A is just like multi-armed regiment battle. As the saying goes "no battle without preparation", only by doing all kinds of risk prevention and management in advance can the entire transaction be smoothly completed as scheduled. How to use third-party intermediaries in the Belt and Road Investment and M&A is a big issue that all Chinese companies going overseas must consider. Below we discuss the main functions and matters of the financial advisory team, the financial and tax expert team, and the legal expert team in the M&A transaction along the Belt and Road.

1. Financial Advisory Team

The financial advisory team plays a very important role in M&A transactions. In overseas M&A, sellers generally employ investment banks as financial advisers to take the charge of the entire M&A transaction. Frankly speaking, financial advisers do not have a good reputation in the Chinese capital industry. The natural mission of this group of investors and companies should be to eliminate information asymmetry between the buyers and sellers. Many financial consultants do not provide effective services for Chinese companies, but companies still have to pay high consultant fees.

What role can the experienced financial advisers play in the Belt and Road M&A?

a. Helping companies find the target of M&A based on the strategic goals of the company. A good financial adviser needs to really go deep into the real business of the company and understand its growth logic.

b. Building the financial model of the transaction. Financial advisors need to accurately measure all the changes in assets and liabilities and expense items brought about by the growth of the target business. They will relatively accurately measure the performance growth and measure the financial costs and final returns through the MBO and LBO valuation models.

c. Designing the transaction structure and refining and confirming the core elements of M&A including time schedule, leverage ratio, transaction entities, acquisition share ratio, payment methods, financing plan, etc.

d. Helping companies review various transaction documents and assisting in communication with government and regulatory authorities. Overseas M&A involves a large number of government approvals, including the domestic National Development and Reform Commission, the Ministry of Commerce, the State Administration of Foreign Exchange, other approval departments, along with the approval of the country where the target company is located. If the buyer or seller is a listed company, it also involves the approval of the China Securities Regulatory Commission and the regulatory department. It is necessary to communicate with the approval department in advance to understand the specific approval requirements of the government.

e. Organize and coordinate with other third-party intermediaries and be responsible for communicating with the seller's financial advisory team to formulate an overall promotion schedule for M&A.

In overseas M&A more and more Chinese companies hire a team of leading financial advisers to communicate with the seller's financial advisers. The financial advisers from both parties serve as a channel of communication, a buffer zone for sellers and buyers, and play a very important role in the achievement of the entire transaction. Good financial advisers have a wealth of overseas M&A experience. They are frigates that companies go global for M&A to help companies avoid potential risks in the M&A process.

Case 4 – 3 The M&A team building of Legend Group acquisition of IBM's global PC business transaction

Transaction Amount: USD 1. 25 billion
Target Country: United States
Industry: Personal Consumer Electronics

Case Background: Lenovo Group was founded in 1984 and listed on the Hong Kong Exchanges and Clearing Limited in 1994. In 2002, Lenovo computer market share reached 27. 3%, and its market share ranked first in China. With the intensified competition and lower profits in the domestic computer market, M&A has become the preferred method for Lenovo Group's internationalization. IBM's PC business includes the production and sales of notebooks, desktops and servers, ranking third in the world after Dell and HP. IBM's PC business has unique core technologies, brands, intellectual property and sales channels. In 2004, IBM's personal computer business continued to lose money. IBM intended to transform into high-tech, high value-added areas such as IT services and was ready to sell its personal computer business. Lenovo Group hoped to gain synergy in terms of brand, technology, management, products and sales channels through the acquisition of IBM's personal computer business and enhance the company's competitiveness. After 13 months of negotiations, Lenovo Group acquired IBM's global PC business for USD 1. 25 billion and rank among the top 500 in the world.

Case Study: Lenovo Group formed a strong internal and external team to participate in the acquisition of IBM's personal computer business. Chief Financial Officer Ma Xuezheng and Senior Vice President Qiao Song of Lenovo group served as core members while the internal finance, research and development, supply chain, human resources, IT, patent, administrative, and other departments sent special personnel to participate in the negotiation process. The number of internal M&A teams was close to 100.

The entire M&A process involved all aspects of knowledge and it would be impossible to complete only by the internal team of Lenovo Group. Therefore, Lenovo Group also established a strong external M&A team. The company hired McKinsey as the consultant to fully understand the feasibility of M&A, and hired the internationally renowned Goldman Sachs Group as the financial advisers. Goldman Sachs not only gave advice to Lenovo Group, but also helped Lenovo obtain USD 600 million in financing to assist Lenovo to introduce three strategic investment partners of TPG, General

Atlantic, and Newbridge Capital Investment Group. While providing strategic support to Lenovo Group, three strategic investors also made full use of their rich experience and capabilities to help Lenovo Group successfully complete acquisitions, smooth transition, and post-merger integration. Lenovo Group hired Ernst & Young and Price Waterhouse Coopers as financial advisers and Ogilvy & Mather as the public relations consultant.

The external M&A team played a very important role in completing the entire transaction.

2. Auditing and tax expert team

The finance, auditing, and tax teams are important members of the Belt and Road investment and M&A team. The finance team mainly studies the income and profit, cost structure, financial status, assets and liabilities, receivables and payables, related party transactions, accounting systems, cash flow, and the future income of the company based on the company's past financial status. They will assess the value of the target company based on the assumptions. The audit team will also assess the authenticity of the company's financial data. The tax team assesses the company's tax situation, usually including tax types, tax rates, tax incentives, tax policies for related transactions, tax settlements, etc. , and plans a reasonable transaction structure to help save the tax costs and improve the certainty and flexibility of the transaction. Reasonable protection and compensation mechanisms will be realized through the terms of the transaction agreements. The results of financial due diligence help the company assess the financial risks and target company value, determine transaction prices and conditions, and design a reasonable transaction structure to reduce corporate acquisition costs and future post-merger integration plans.

Compared to the financial due diligence of domestic M&A transactions, that of countries along the Belt and Road has the following characteristics:

a. Generally, the target companies in countries along the Belt and Road adopt different accounting standards from those in China. Financial due diligence professional teams need compare the financial data of income, profit, and assets and liabilities of each enterprise under the unified standards, in order to facilitate the buyer's decision of transaction pricing. Because most of the countries along the Belt and Road are developing countries, their developments are relatively backward, their accounting systems are imperfect, their accounting information of enterprises is not comprehensive and their supervision is not strict enough.

b. The target enterprises of Belt and Road may sometimes conceal many one-time costs and expenses, conceal and weaken potential losses, off-balance sheet liabilities, and other unfavorable news, exaggerating intangible assets, so that the acquirer makes a wrong estimate in the valuation of the sellers.

The buyer also needs to focus on the working capital and cash flow status of the target company. In many cases, the seller has working capital pressure and cash shortages. After the completion of the acquisition, the buyer needs to invest a large amount of funds to make up for the potential funding gap. Therefore, the acquirer needs to evaluate not only financial status of the target company, but also its own cash flows. When the buyer is considering the future cash needs, it is also necessary to consider the issues of employee pension and factory closing costs involved in future enterprise integration. If the future cash demand of the target company exceeds the cash flow tolerance of the acquirer, it is necessary to make a careful decision on the acquisition.

c. Belt and Road investment and M&A are often based on zero cash and zero liabilities when pricing, and require other price adjustment mechanisms such as operating fund, net asset, Locked Box, etc. These mechanisms are rare in domestic M&A transactions. Belt and Road investment and M&As are concentrated in capital-intensive areas. The invested companies may have a large amount of debt and external guarantees. The buyer needs to thoroughly investigate the debt situation of the target company and understand whether the company has overdue fines and interest, stipulate the relevant costs that the seller needs to bear in the transaction agreement, or deduct the part of the expenses from the transaction consideration.

d. The tax planning in cross-border M&A involves a tax amount of several hundred million yuan. This is related not only to the success or failure of the transaction, but also to the survival of the enterprise. It needs to be systematically and rigorously planned. Many countries along the Belt and Road will give certain tax incentives to certain aspects of investment. Enterprises must carefully study the premise, conditions and procedures of the preferential application before starting the transaction. They need to fully enjoy the preferential policies of the target country. Different legal entities in the countries along the Belt and Road may use different tax incentives and foreign exchange control policies. When designing the transaction structure, we may consider the use of lower-cost of tax and less risky schemes. Proper tax planning in the transaction structure can help buyers save a lot of transaction costs, such as using Luxembourg or Dutch companies as intermediate holding companies to acquire European companies. With the bilateral tax agreement between China and Luxembourg and China and the Netherlands, the withholding income tax on future repatriation of profits will be saved, which will bring tax convenience for the possible disposal of company equity in the future.

3. Legal Expert Team

The legal risk of the Belt and Road investment and M&A runs through the preparation stage, the transaction stage and the post-merger integration stage of the transaction. The Belt and Road M&A involves a large number of legal related work. The team of legal experts needs to participate in the drafting and reviewing of documents including confidentiality agreement, bidding documents, letters of quotation and intent, terms and conditions list, equity/asset purchase agreement, account custody agreement, etc. from the beginning of the transaction, and to guide the company to make the transaction go smoothly through corresponding arrangements. M&A activity is the process of constant game and negotiation between buyers and sellers. M&A

transaction documents are the final result of negotiation between the two parties, the ultimate carrier of rights and obligations, and the main basis for both parties to safeguard their own interests in the event of a dispute. The author believes that hiring a team of experienced lawyers in cross-border M&A can effectively improve the efficiency of communication and negotiation in the Belt and Road M&A and avoid potential risks.

The following should be noted when building an overseas M&A legal team.

(1) Choosing the Right Law Firm

The Belt and Road M&A generally requires the application of foreign laws. The lack of understanding of foreign laws can easily lead to the failures or trigger a major legal dispute. If the M&A target is an overseas listed company, you should be familiar with the securities regulations and related trading rules of the country in which it is located. It is difficult to meet the requirements of overseas M&A by solely relying on the legal services provided by domestic lawyers. Thus, choosing a suitable foreign law firm has become the key to successfully acquiring the target company.

Neusoft Group, where the author is working, must invite several law firms to participate in the bidding before the start of the project. After comparing the professional experience, communication efficiency, response speed, service quotation and service scope of each law firm, the company will determine the legal expert team. If the M&A target has business in multiple countries and may involve legal issues in different countries, the company will need to hire a suitable local law firm to obtain legal support. The selection of a law firm, on the one hand, depends on the visibility and industry experience of the firm; on the other hand, it depends on the professional ability, time, and energy of the partners who are responsible for the project. To some extent, partners are more important than law firms. The selection criteria of the partners include multiple dimensions of metrics such as professionalism, communication ability, response speed, price, and project concentration.

(2) Conducting in-depth legal due diligence

Legal due diligence is a key part of M&A transactions, which will provide a basis for trading decisions, transaction structure design, transaction price determination and transaction negotiation. The scope of legal due diligence includes the target company's business, assets, historical evolution, legal establishment, asset ownership, license, labor and social security, environment, taxation, legal proceedings, and equity structure. Chinese companies should try to avoid taking unreasonable risks. Overseas M&A generally has a strict timetable, and the legal team needs to match the regulatory approval process with the acquisition timetable. This is one of the key factors in ensuring the ultimate success of the transaction.

(3) Risk-preventing in the Transaction Agreement

The legal risks associated with the transaction agreement may exist in all major parts of the agreement, including whether the conditions for the entry into force of the acquisition agreement and settlement meeting the requirements for transaction security, the design of the terms of the agreement violating the legal requirements of the jurisdiction or region, the applicable law and dispute resolution methods. For Chinese companies, applicable laws to the acquisition of overseas companies are often laws of places that target companies are registered in, or laws of the place where the main assets are located. If the Chinese enterprise does not understand these laws, it is easy to be passive in the negotiation of the agreement. Even if a clause that is beneficial to the Chinese company is added to the agreement through negotiation, the goal sometimes is difficult to achieve because the clause is difficult to implement under the applicable law. In addition, it may lead to legal disputes in the future if the Chinese buyers ignore some clauses that may have a significant impact on the transaction. Taking Sinochem International (Holdings) Co., Ltd. (abbreviated as Sinochem) for its failure to acquire South Korea's Incheon Refinery, for example, when signing the exclusive memorandum of understanding, Sinochem did not add additional terms to restrict Incheon Refinery's price increase. As a result, Incheon Refinery suddenly changed its mind and demanded that the original purchase price be raised. Eventually, the price exceeded Sinochem's affordability, which led to the failure of the acquisition.

(4) Being familiar with laws and regulations and foreign investment access policies of different countries

Chinese companies need to have a deep understanding of some specific legal concepts in the country where the target company is located. Here we take the "controlling right" usually as the acquisition target as an example. In the securities laws and regulations of different countries and regions, the definition of "controlling right" is different. For example, in the Code of listed companies in Singapore, holding 5% of the company's equity may form a control over the company, and holding more than 15% of the company's equity can be recognized as a "controlling shareholder". This is inconsistent with what we usually understand by holding a 51% stake in order to gain control.

In the process of overseas M&A, the host country usually proposes a national security review for the M&A activities of Chinese corporations. For example, the United States established the Committee on Foreign Investment in the United States (CFIUS) to specifically evaluate M&A activities for US-based companies. Driven by Germany, France, Italy and other countries, the European Commission began to consider emulating the United States and establishing the Committee on Foreign Investment in the Europe (CFIEU). Russia promulgated the "*Procedural Law of the Russian Federation concerning the entry of foreign capital into a strategically important operating company for safeguarding Russian national defense and national security*" (*the* "*National Security Review Procedures Act*") clearly lists 42 industries as Russian strategic industries. In addition to complying with the relevant provisions of the National Security Review Procedures Act, foreign investment is also subject to relevant industry laws and regulations. In Australia, large foreign investments usually require approval from the Australian Foreign Investment Review Board (FIRB). On January 23, 2017, the Australian Government announced the formation of a new agency called the "Key Infrastructure Center", which is responsible for registering the assets that make up the critical infrastructure. National security review risks are mainly manifested in the identification of access to special areas such as minerals, energy, national defense, finance, and the identity of China's state-owned enterprises. State-owned enterprises' overseas M&A is more likely to generate national security review risks. For example, in the case of CNOOC's failure to acquire US Unocal, the identification of corporate identity has affected the review of acquisition behavior to a certain extent. In the sensational "Sany Group v. Obama Case", the Committee on Foreign Investment in the United States issued a ban on the suspension of related projects by the Sany Group, which is a typical example of the government's restrictions on foreign investment in certain special areas. Chinese companies need to assess the possibility of passing these reviews before acquiring overseas companies.

China's Belt and Road M&A adopts a horizontal M&A model, which is relatively subject to strict supervision and is generally subject to anti-monopoly review. Antitrust review usually takes the entire group as the subject of censorship, not just the target company itself. The anti-monopoly review involves three levels of approval risk, including anti-monopoly risk of the host country, anti-monopoly risk of other countries in non-host countries, and China's anti-monopoly risk. Before investing in countries along the Belt and Road, Chinese companies need to carefully study the anti-monopoly laws of the host country, the countries involved in the anti-monopoly declaration, and the application materials and procedures that need to be prepared to avoid fines caused by illegal anti-monopoly review. M&A transactions in countries along the "Belt and Road" may involve antitrust review in multiple countries. In this case, companies should prepare early and think about countermeasures to reduce the adverse effects of antitrust review on transactions.

(5) Prevention of Other Risks

The legal risks of the Belt and Road M&A also include intellectual property risks, environmental protection risks, labor security risks, management control, and incentive risks. Due to the lack of core technology, Chinese companies need to pay high patent fees to foreign companies. At the same time, the host country has set various obstacles to restrict the transfer of intellectual property rights of products to China, and the acquisition of the core technology of foreign companies. Before the M&A, Chinese companies need to judge whether the target company really has valuable intellectual property rights, whether ownership is flawed, whether there are regional and time risks, and whether there are transfer restrictions and the value of intellectual property rights. Many Chinese companies are not aware of environmental protection and have not included environmental risks into their risk assessment systems. Considering many overseas M&As of Chinese companies that are distributed in resource industries such as minerals and energy, it is very important for them to fully demonstrate the feasibility of the acquisition from the perspective of environmental protection in advance, so as to avoid the trade protection trap under the tendency of environmental protection.

In terms of labor protection, Chinese companies should carefully study the laws and regulations of the host country's trade union, labor contract, employment and compensation, and welfare law in M&A. Shanghai Automotive Industry (Group) Corporation's acquisition of South Korea's Ssangyong Motor Corporation and TCL Group's European M&A have paid high price for neglecting local labor laws. Different labor protection standards, labor disputes, high cost of dismissal workers, and trade unions hindering M&A are several common labor risks in the process of M&A. In particular, the trade unions in some countries are too strong. As a result, the contradictions between the two sides have escalated after the acquisition. Chinese companies should avoid falling into the "mire" of local labor laws in order to successfully complete M&A. Neusoft Group took a long time to deal with local trade unions when it acquired the Harman navigation team in Germany, and gradually learned about local labor laws and related policies. After the acquisition, Chinese companies' control and incentives for the foreign management are also a new challenge.

(6) Explicitly stipulate the terms of the break fee or reverse break-up fee

The break fee usually refers to a certain amount of compensation that the target company should pay to the buyer when certain conditions are triggered. These triggering conditions include an agreement with the higher bidder of the acquirer to terminate the transaction currently in progress, the target company's shareholders refusing to approve the transaction, and the target company or seller violating the statements and warranties in the M&A transaction documents. The reverse break fee usually requires the buyer to pay a certain amount of compensation to the seller or the target company if it is unable to obtain sufficient acquisition funds or government approval. The proportion of reverse break fees is often higher than the break fee, and the break fee that sellers demand from Chinese buyers is often higher than that obtained from buyers in other countries. Chinese companies should try to avoid paying the reverse break fee. Even if they have to pay, they must make a detailed agreement on the trigger conditions.

Section 4
How to Deal with the Relationship between the Internal M&A Team and the External Third-party Agencies

The relationship between the company's internal M&A team and the external agencies can be generally divided into three categories:

a. Fully dependent. The team does not have any M&A experience and does not have independent work capacity. Any matters in the M&A from project valuation to English translation, and even internally reported PPT, require assistance from external consultants. Such a team has a very high risk of overseas M&A and transaction costs are also very high.

b. Partially dependent. The team has a certain M&A experience, but can not control the risks in the M&A. Such internal teams have a certain degree of reliance on external consultants, and many documents require external teams to assist in preparation. Such a team has a certain ability to control risks and needs more projects to hone and improve the team's ability of transaction.

c. Fully independent. The team with rich overseas M&A experience is familiar with the process and risk control points of various types of overseas M&A projects and is good at using and managing external consultants. It can reasonably borrow the help of external consultants in M&A projects; it does not rely entirely on external consultants. From the company's point of view, such a mature M&A team has a good control over the risks of M&A projects and can operate complex, large-scale Belt and Road M&A projects.

According to the author, in order to correctly use intermediary companies and control risks in overseas M&A, you need to pay attention to the following matters.

1. Define the service scope and charge standards of the intermediary

The Belt and Road investment and M&A is usually carried out by international teams, and the fees are generally calculated in US dollars per hour. The agency fee is the sunk cost for the company, that is, regardless of whether the transaction is ultimately completed, the intermediary fees must be paid. It's not uncommon for a M&A project to cost millions or even tens of millions of dollars for service fee. When many intermediary service agencies quote, the company might think that the expenses are still within the budget. However, as the project proceeds, the company will find many new service items and charges have come up, resulting in the final service cost far exceeding the original offer. In the initial stage of M&A, Chinese companies should clarify the specific scope of intermediary services and charging standards by means of agreement, so as to avoid future disputes and have effective cost control. The company can't just emphasize cost control. The charging standard of a good intermediary is much higher than that of the second-rate one. It is necessary to reasonably configure the resources of the third-party external M&A team according to the difficulty of the M&A project and the ability of the internal team.

2. Check terms for Dispute Resolution, Governing Law, Arbitration Place

It is recommended that Chinese companies try to adopt the laws of neutral countries and resolve disputes through international arbitration institutions. It is obviously not a good idea to use the local laws of the acquired company or to resolve disputes through its local courts and arbitration institutions. Even if you agree to use local laws, don't put the arbitration on the ground, otherwise it is difficult to control the risk.

3. Don't easily promise "exclusive cooperation" or "exclusive employment" to the intermediaries

Some local intermediaries often boast their ability to make unreliable guarantees. If you give a project to a local intermediary "exclusive cooperation", it will often create obstacles to business development. Business flexibility is always one of the things that is worthy of attention to the Belt and Road buyers.

4. Hold arbitrary cancellation rights

The right to terminate the contract allows the company to cancel the contract at any time when the compliance risk or potential compliance risk occurs, at least when there is evidence that the intermediary has non-compliance, the company can cancel the contract at will. In many projects, the author found that the response speed and professionalism of different law firms vary greatly. Especially in the Belt and Road M&A, some law firms or partners have not dealt with before. If there is a problem with the cooperation between the two parties, it is necessary to promptly "stop loss" and re-elect the intermediary to avoid affecting the entire M&A transaction.

5. Establish accountability and guarantee system

Professional third-party agencies are responsible for all investigations and legal documents and are subject to statements and warranties or commitments. For example, when a listed company participates in the Belt and Road M&A, because the third-party financial due diligence agency did not find the target company's external guarantee problem. After the transaction ended, the original shareholder sold their share. However, the sponsored company had problems, and the target company had to bear joint and several liabilities, resulting in the listed company losing millions of dollars. Similar problems have occurred in other Belt and Road M&A projects. Therefore, the inclusion of responsibility and guarantee mechanism in the employment agreement requires third-party companies to commit to the accuracy, comprehensiveness, and authenticity of the work done. They are responsible for damages caused by negligence of work to the buyer.

CHAPTER 5

DEAL STRUCTURE, INVESTMENT VALUATION AND THE "BELT AND ROAD" COUNTRIES' INVESTMENT AND M&A

In the modern business world, cross-border M&A transactions are driven by the globalization of regulations and business standards, showing a rapid growth trend. In cross-border M&A transactions, financial reporting standards or issues of international law are relatively easy to resolve, but company valuations and trade-offs are more challenging to enterprises.

Determining the right trading structure and valuation is a complex process that requires consideration of a range of criteria. Choosing the best trading structure is a key part of investing success and maximizing profitability. Since the application of traditional trading structures and valuation methods to the Belt and Road investment and M&A transaction will make it more complicated, investors should be familiar with important information such as international rules, local taxation systems, policies and regulations, accounting standards, and the relationship between China and the country being invested when conducting Belt and Road investment and M&A.

In choosing the right trading structure, investors need to focus on China's foreign investment policy and local policies of the host country. China's overseas investment is often considered to have a negative impact on China's foreign exchange reserves, which concerns the government about the uncertainty of Chinese investors. Although most of the control occur in specific industries, China still believes that irrational foreign investment will have many adverse effects. The government encourages companies to seek M&A opportunities in their investment decisions. Chinese companies need to acquire new expertise as a growth point to move from the global manufacturing and heavy industry center to the economic center dominated by high-end economic activities. Investment and M&A are viable means to achieve this goal.

Many countries may set limitations on the inbound investment. For example, Germany has introduced new restrictions for national security considerations: allowing ministers to investigate mergers and acquisitions that take control and acquisitions that are suspected of jeopardizing the key industries such as infrastructure and technology. Currently, some EU countries have formal systems to assess foreign investment and the risks they may pose to national security. In general, countries are increasingly aware of the threat of foreign investment and may have restrictions on specific trading structures. Investors need to ensure that business activities are not affected by regulatory changes and strategically choose a trading structure.

Important criteria for selecting the best trading structure and valuation method include local and international tax systems for different transaction types, and tax classification for them. From a valuation point of view, the buyer's key financial indicators need to be evaluated before trading decisions, and can be used as a tool to check whether the market price of the target company provided by the seller is reasonable. In predicting the financial indicators of the target company, investors should confirm the impact of the tax on the given assumptions. For example, whether the target country uses progressive tax, cumulative tax or proportional tax policy will affect the buyer's estimated return. In addition, tax exemptions have a direct and indirect impact on the key profitability of the project. In this regard, it is significant to use correct tax assumptions in the financing model. An in-depth understanding of the local tax environment of the investing country and bilateral tax treaties between them and China or other countries can ensure that the potential tax benefits of the transaction structure are maximized. From a structural point of view, buyers often achieve a tax-efficient trading structure by minimizing the tax costs. "Belt and Road" investors should focus on optimizing taxation, transfer pricing methods, target deferred income tax assets, loss carry-overs, and saving taxes in future exits when designing their trading structure. These issues will be discussed in this chapter.

Besides the international relations and tax system, other factors will also affect the nature of the "Belt and Road" investment and M&A transaction structure. This chapter will address the main factors that need to be considered for overseas investment decisions. Legal due diligence and other legal requirements will also be analyzed.

In M&A transactions, the choice of different transaction architectures depends primarily on the value of each solution, so choosing the right valuation method and considering all the limitations and assumptions of a given technology is a process that takes a long time and effort. Due diligence can take several months. M&A valuation usually requires two steps: evaluating the target company and assessing the synergy of the combined businesses. There are two models of valuation, namely the absolute valuation model and relative valuation model. The absolute value model relies primarily on mathematical and quantitative analysis, including a discounted cash flow model. Investment valuation is not only a science, but also an art. Although there are several broad formulas for assessing the value of an investment, none of them provides specific valuation values. Therefore, the professionals need to use a variety of methods to roughly estimate the value of the investment. Sometimes investors need to conduct fundamental analysis to find the exact value of the transaction, but in the real business world, most investors need to trust their intuition in the transaction process, not just depend on the valuation data provided by the valuation model.

Considering the global nature of the Belt and Road investment and M&A, its trading structure and valuation may be complicated. Some countries participating in the Belt and Road initiative may not follow international accounting standards or not have a properly functioning business system, making it impossible to use financial analysis and quantitative assessment tools. In addition, even if the investor country becomes more international in making valuation assumptions, there are still a lot of nuances to be aware of. These nuances exist in the use of financial forecasts, depreciation, and growth rates, as well as the authenticity of the data.

The art of valuation lies in understanding the pros and cons of different approaches, and in choosing the most appropriate valuation method, or combining them in the most effective way to make the most accurate assumptions about the value of investment. The chapter will discuss in details the limitations of various valuation quantification tools for the Belt and Road investment and provide guidelines on how to choose the best valuation method in each case.

Section 1
Overseas Trading Structure: Taxes, Convenience and Fees

1. Tax in Transaction

Since the launch of the Belt and Road Initiative, China has initiated major tax reforms to encourage investors. China has always been committed to establishing a fair, just, inclusive and orderly new international tax relationship with the countries along the Belt and Road.

On May 14, 2018, the Belt and Road tax cooperation conference was held in Astana, the capital of Kazakhstan. This was the first international conference on the theme of Belt and Road tax cooperation. As of 2018, the Chinese taxation department has established cooperative relations with 25 international organizations and regional taxation organizations, established bilateral tax cooperation mechanisms with 117 countries and regions, signed tax treaties with 54 countries along the Belt and Road and issued 75 country investment tax guides. In April 2015, the International Taxation Department of the State Taxation Administration announced 10 service measures related to the interests of the Belt and Road investors. These measures have generally ensured the implementation of the "Belt and Road Initiative", promoted the consistency of law enforcement in different regions, reduced the occurrence of tax-related disputes, and provided a comfortable tax environment for cross-border taxpayers. Another issue mentioned by these measures is the improvement of tax-related services. Tax authorities at provincial level are obliged to collect, analyze and research the tax information of the counterpart countries to form a docking mechanism for each province; the Belt and Road tax service websites publish national tax guides along the Belt and Road countries. They are also responsible for conducting the phased and batch training for China's "going global" enterprises, so that enterprises can use tax treaties to protect their rights and interests and prevent tax risks; provincial tax authorities should prepare annual reports on taxation analysis of "going global" enterprises in the region, submit them to the State Administration of Taxation and further discuss cross-border tax risk management mechanism, gradually establish tax prevention measures, promote "going global" enterprises to reduce tax risks, and accumulate taxation risk management methods and experience for the outbound transactions.

Before considering the tax impact on the type of transaction structure, investors should assess the overall tax environment and taxation relationship between China and the target country. They should check whether there is a diplomatic and economic relations between China and the target countries, and whether the two countries have signed *The Agreement on Economic and Trade Cooperation*, *The Memorandum of Understanding* and tax agreements. While the number of foreign investments are increasing, the Chinese companies are also faced with more tax problems and challenges. From this perspective, international tax treaties are an important tool for guiding international businesses and assessing tax planning. The State Administration of Taxation issued the "Revenue Ordinance" (Section 60) in April 2015 in order to actively interprete and promote tax treaties, and support Chinese companies' going abroad. Tax treaties are not only for the rational use of tax regulations, but also for avoiding taxation risks arising from the abuse of treaties.

(1) Free Trade Agreement (FTA)

Free trade agreements provide arrangements for an unrestricted exchange of goods and services between trading countries and define tariff policies for imports and exports. Free trade agreements enable commercial operations by managing rules of origin of goods, customs procedures, sanitary and phytosanitary measures, technical barriers to trade (such as ensuring the standards and technical requirements of Parties, avoiding unnecessary technical barriers to trade) and trade remedy measures to make business operations more dynamic and stimulate economic growth. In terms of services, this agreement governs market access, domestic regulations, payments, transfers, and transparency.

The free trade agreement is a new platform for China to further open up to the outside world and accelerate domestic reform. It is an effective way for China to integrate into the global economy and strengthen economic cooperation with other economies. It is also an important supplement to the multilateral trading system.

The free trade agreement also provides rules for logistics cooperation, environmental protection, competition (anti-monopoly), intellectual property rights and dispute resolution.

(2) The Avoidance of Double Taxation Agreements

The Avoidance of Double Taxation Agreements between trading countries is an important document that foreign investors should check. The Avoidance of Double Taxation Agreements is to ensure that individuals or business entities do not double tax on the same income. It specifies which individuals are eligible for the benefit, which taxes are covered and in which countries they should be tax-free. This agreement stems from the diversity of tax systems in each country, and each double taxation agreement is different. The terms of the agreement include resident, permanent establishment, real estate and affiliated companies. In general, The Avoidance of Double Taxation Agreements covers the income tax withholding, interest, dividends or royalties, inheritance taxes, value added tax (VAT), employment income and other taxes. In addition to taxes, the agreement also provides tax exemptions, dispute resolution mechanisms, restrictions and other related matters.

At present, China has signed The Avoidance of Double Taxation Agreements with more than 100 countries. In order to design a reasonable transaction structure, investors should check the treaty with a particular country and confirm whether the transaction is covered by the agreement and whether other rights can be exercised.

The Avoidance of Double Taxation Agreements is not only to regulate taxes, but also to encourage cross-border trade, support tax information exchange, and ensure that parties comply with tax regulations.

(3) Bilateral Investment Treaty (BIT)

Since the 1980s, China has signed the Bilateral Investment Treaty with more than 100 countries. Although many have been replaced by more complex and cumbersome trade agreements, such as the Avoidance of Double Taxation Agreements and other bilateral treaties, BITs remain important, especially for investors in emerging countries where tax laws and regulatory environments are relatively immature. These agreements also help to consolidate bilateral investment conditions between China and other developed countries.

Bilateral Investment Treaty can guarantee fair treatment, investment protection, damages and free flow of funds; they can assist in dispute resolution through diplomatic channels and provide useful information about the legal and tax environment in which the parties are located. If the investor's rights are violated, the BIT provides the right to resort to international arbitration.

Bilateral Investment Treaty is an effective tool for breaking trade barriers, such as tariffs, quotas, subsidies and other non-tariff measures, including security requirements or anti-dumping measures. These barriers may also not be directly resolved by bilateral investment agreements, but by other agreements.

(4) 59 tax guides from the State Administration of Taxation

After a comprehensive review of the international treaty and economic relations between the People's Republic of China and the target country, investors should check the internal tax system of both parties. In May 2017, in order to speed up the implementation of the "going global" strategy, promote the Belt and Road Initiative, and let Chinese investors be familiar with the taxation system of the investing countries, the State Taxation Administration issued "Tax Guides for overseas investment of Chinese Residents" (referred to as Tax Guides) for the Belt and Road Initiative. These guidelines cover countries and regins in Asia, Europe, Africa, and Oceania (see table 5-1), including the major Maritime Silk Roads and countries along the Silk Road. This list will be updated regularly as China and other countries further negotiate the terms of the "Belt and Road Initiative" and tax information continuously collected from overseas investment destinations.

Table 5-1 List of countries and regions that have been covered by China's Tax Guides

Continent	Countries and Regions
Asia	UAE, Oman, Pakistan, Bahrain, Bhutan, the Philippiness, Georgia, Kazakhstan, South Korea, Kyrgyzstan, Cambodia, Qatar, Kuwait, Laos, Lebanon, Malaysia, Mongolia, Bangladesh, Myanmar, Nepal, Saudi Arabia, Sri Lanka, Tajikistan, Thailand, Turkey, Brunei, Uzbekistan, Singapore, Armenia, Yemen, Iran, Israel, India, Indonesia, Vietnam, Hong Kong China
Europe	Albania, Estonia, Austria, White Rose, Bulgaria, Poland, Russia, Montenegro, Czech Republic, Croatia, Latvia, Lithuania, Romania, Macedonia, Moldova, Serbia, Slovenia, Ukraine, Hungary
Africa	Ethiopia, South Africa
Oceania	New Zealand

These guides help investors understand and adapt to the geography, politics, economy, and taxation of specific countries and regions. The Tax Guide also shares the experience of Chinese companies in managing tax matters, as well as tax payers' tax practices and tax-related laws and regulations.

Due to the diversity of tax systems in target countries and regions, the above guides are different, but the overall structures are generally consistent. The first chapter of the Tax Guide introduces the country profile, including politics, geography, economy and society. The investment environment overview includes economic development in recent years, resource reserves and infrastructure, key/characteristic industries, investment policies, economic and trade cooperation, and investment considerations, etc. The second chapter introduces the taxation system and taxation management methods, briefly introduces the main taxes of the country or region, and explains the transfer pricing, cost deduction rules and anti-avoidance rules. As the taxes around the investment field are diverse, this part is crucial. Although some countries have simple and investor-friendly tax systems, other systems require complex operations such as repurchase taxes, social security taxes, and bank insurance transaction taxes, etc.

In the Tax Guide, the most useful and important chapters for investors cover international tax issues and China's relationship with target countries and regions, including key tax considerations. These factors include tax credits, transfer pricing methods and requirements, potential tax risks, cross-border transactions, and indirect tax calculations. The final section of the Tax Guide includes dispute resolution mechanisms for tax jurisdiction, the main causes of disputes, arbitration procedures, preventive measures, advance rulings, and tax audit procedures. These issues are discussed in detail in the next section.

Together with the Tax Guide, China's Belt and Road Portal has published a description of the relationship between China and the countries along the Belt and Road, current or completed Chinese investment projects, plans for the Belt and Road partners and a memo of future strategies.

2. Right Trading Structure Choice in the Context of Tax Due Diligence

After obtaining specific information about the country concerned, investors are ready to make real investment decisions to choose the right trading structure. Tax due diligence requires companies to grasp the overall tax environment of the relevant country and the internal taxation attributes of the target company. From a tax perspective, companies need to do tax due diligence in two ways.

(1) Evaluation

Companies need to assess how taxation affects each transaction structure and evaluate how transactions are taxed. When considering the proposed trading structure, the more classic models are equity and asset acquisitions. Although the decision will be based on the specific circumstances of the transaction, under normal circumstances, the seller tends to buy equity, and the buyer tends to acquire assets.

(2) Reviewing the tax related to the target company

For evaluation and forecasting purposes, companies need to consider relevant tax information. First of all, it is necessary to understand the business model of the target company and the company's shareholding structure. Second, the buyer should collect tax-related information by consulting with the professionals (the company's tax experts) or by reading tax returns. This helps investors assess and quantify the company's historical tax status and develop future tax plans. It also helps companies become familiar with the level of taxation of the target company's various taxes. Then, simulate possible transaction structures and assess the impact of taxes on different transaction structures. Finally, combine tax-related information with other considerations to make decisions that best serve business interests.

The sale of the shares takes place between the buyer and the target company's shareholders. During the equity transaction, company does not recognize any gains and losses. Instead, shareholders will recognize gains or losses based on the difference between the final prices and the original prices.

Stock acquisitions are favored by seller shareholders as this model only generates corporate income tax, avoiding the double taxation (enterprise income tax and share capital gains tax) that occurs when assets are acquired. In addition, some countries encourage long-term investments and impose lower capital gains tax on shares held for more than one year. They may also prefer equity sales when the buyer can take advantage of tax attributes such as tax losses. On the other hand, due to the bad tax base of the assets, the buyer may not choose the equity acquisition. If the company's assets are taxed at historical value and cannot be depreciated to fair value, the property tax may be higher than the asset sale. When considering the impact of taxation, "Belt and Road" investors should check the property tax rate and corporate income tax rate of the country being invested (how much is the tax rate and whether low-rate is used to encourage long-term investment).

In addition, the buyer should be careful when starting the equity acquisition as the company may be held accountable by the State Taxation Administration for misconduct. Such issue can be identified and resolved by reviewing the SAT's report on the target company's liabilities.

Asset purchases usually occur after the parties have agreed on the transfer of a particular asset or liability. For this type of trading structure, the target company will recognize the profit and loss as the difference between the selling price and tax base of the asset. This strategy helps the buyer to eliminate undisclosed tax risks and choose only the assets and liabilities they want to bear (rather than all assets and liabilities). From the seller's point of view, asset sales have tax traps, such as double taxation or depreciation.

In addition to the two transaction architectures discussed above, there are many other trading models. The combination of equity purchases and asset purchases is a hybrid transaction. In the simplest hybrid transaction structure the seller sells the equity to the buyer to request exemption from capital gains and then sells the assets to the buyer to redeem the equity. In order to achieve a win-win situation, other trading models can be integrated under the consideration of specific commercial negotiations, assumptions and taxes.

Case 5 – 1   Zoomlion acquired Italian concrete machinery manufacturer CIFA

Transaction Amount: 376 million euros
Target Country: Italy
Industry: Machinery Manufacturing
Case Background: Zoomlion Heavy Industry Science & Technology Co., Ltd. (referred to as Zoomlion) was established in 1992. It is mainly engaged in R&D and manufacturing of high-tech equipment such as construction and agricultural machinery. The company was successively listed in Shenzhen and Hong Kong and became the first A + H listed company in the industry. The company achieved sales of 15 billion yuan in 2008, with an annual growth rate of more than 60%. Since its establishment, Zoomlion has acquired British PowerMole, Hunan Machine Tool Works, reorganized Puyuan Group, and acquired Zhongbiao Industrial and Huanggong Mechinary Group. The company believes that the acquisition is more effective than directly establishing the factory, and the M&A is the core strategy of the company's development.

Founded in 1928, CIFA is a long-established Italian family-owned company and a leading manufacturer of concrete equipment in Europe. Ranked third in the world's concrete machinery market after Germany's Putzmeister and Schwing, CIFA has 7 production bases in Italy and a marketing network in more than 70 countries around the world. Its products have a high market share in Western Europe, Eastern Europe. One of the CIFA's core competitive advantage is cost-effectiveness. In October 2007, CIFA's controlling shareholder decided to sell CIFA's equity because it needed to repay part of its debt in cash.

In January 2008, after China Union received CIFA's formal invitation of bid process, Zhan Chunxin, Chairman of Zoomlion and Zhao Linghuan, President of Hony Capital Investment, immediately flew to Italy to meet CIFA shareholders and quickly completed the construction of a joint acquisition team with Hony Capital, Goldman Sachs Group and the Mandolin Fund. On June 20, 2008, Zoomlion finally reached an acquisition intention with CIFA to complete the wholly-owned acquisition of CIFA in cash. After the acquisition, Zoomlion holds 60% of the shares, and Goldman Sachs, Hony and Mandalin hold 40% of the shares. The total transaction amount was 375.5 million euros, corresponding to 9.6 times the EV/EBITDA. Zoomlion paid 160 million euros, of which 200 million US dollars were borrowed, and the company's own funds paid 50 million US dollars.

Zoomlion's acquisition of CIFA is a classic case of Chinese companies' overseas mergers and acquisitions. The following aspects of experience can be borrowed by Chinese companies:

Case Study: a. Communicate actively and cooperate closely with the third-party organizations. In the process of investment and M&A, Hony Capital Investment, as a financial consultant of Zoomlion, successfully assisted Zoomlion to form a joint M&A team of Hony Capital, Goldman Sachs Group and Mandolin Fund. As a domestic professional investment institution, Hony Capital understands the domestic capital market and Zoomlion's M&A strategy; Goldman Sachs Group, as a veteran international first-class investment bank, has network and resources in various countries and is familiar with the rules of international M&A; while Mandolin Fund, which is an Italian local investment institution, is more aware of Italy's domestic capital market and target companies. The external third-party team provided strong support to Zoomlion in transaction structure, transaction process, business negotiation, valuation and other aspects, ensuring the success of Zoomlion's M&A.

b. Design a reasonable transaction structure. In order to complete the acquisition, the investor established two Special Purpose Vehicles (SPVs) in Hong Kong, China, two SPVs in Luxembourg and one SPV in Italy. The purpose of this transactional structure design is to make full use of the bilateral tax treaties, reduce tax costs, and provide liquidity and financing convenience. According to the tax agreement between China and Italy, capital or profit-seeking income from Italy is subject to a withholding tax of up to 30%, and by setting an appropriate SPV, the amount of withholding income tax can be circumvented or reduced. In this acquisition, Italy and Luxembourg are EU countries, which exempts each other of withholding income tax not flow back to the China mainland, there will be no income tax.

c. Make full use of various financial instruments to reduce the cash cost of enterprises. Cash flow is the lifeline of an enterprise. In the process of M&A, enterprises need to reduce their cash expenditures as much as possible, and reduce the capital cost of enterprises by issuing bonds, borrowing, and introducing strategic investors. The total amount of the transaction was 375.5 million euros, and Zoomlion completed the acquisition only by paying 50 million US dollars of its own funds. Hony Capital, Goldman Sachs Group and Mandolin Fund participated in the acquisition as strategic investors and held a 40% stake. As a community of interests, the three agencies will fully assist Zoomlion to complete M&A transactions and play an active role in the integration after the M&A. Zoomlion's bond issuance and borrowing are completed through SPV in Hong Kong, China. The company borrowed 200 million US dollars to provide low-cost funds for enterprises and reduce the pressure on corporate cash flow.

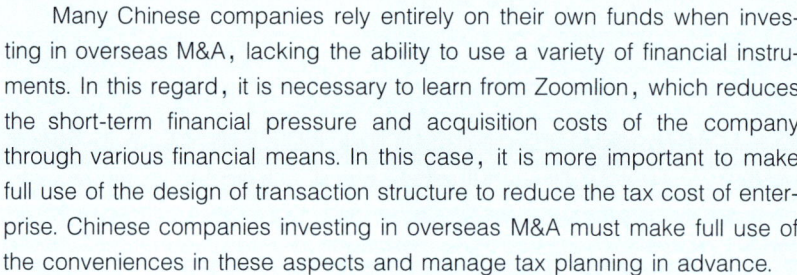

Many Chinese companies rely entirely on their own funds when investing in overseas M&A, lacking the ability to use a variety of financial instruments. In this regard, it is necessary to learn from Zoomlion, which reduces the short-term financial pressure and acquisition costs of the company through various financial means. In this case, it is more important to make full use of the design of transaction structure to reduce the tax cost of enterprise. Chinese companies investing in overseas M&A must make full use of the conveniences in these aspects and manage tax planning in advance.

Section 2
Convenience Evaluation and Cost Evaluation in M&A Transactions

In addition to the tax implications, there are two factors that must be considered when conducting M&A transaction due diligence and valuation: convenience and cost. Every investor who wants to sign a major contract through the "Belt and Road Initiative" or plans to acquire other companies hopes that after the transaction, the future profitability of the company and the security of the transaction will be guaranteed, and each possible detail which may affect the transaction structure will be considered. In assessing the convenience of transaction and associated costs (both explicit and implicit costs), investors should examine two issues: at what operating cost and convenience level does the company operate in a particular country or industry, and what associated cost and convenience of trading could be brought about by possible transaction architecture.

The potential costs associated with business and general information about national government agencies can be obtained from national briefings published by the country for investors to assess the characteristics of different countries, including political, economic and industry-specific information and regulatory levels.

Some countries have strict rules for industry access and for specific transactions. The transnational transactions involve corporate law, market regulations, and company regulations. These briefings provide guidance for understanding the procedures established by the company and the regulations that may affect the transaction. In some cases, investments that exceed relevant government regulations or industry restrictions of the target country must be reported to the Ministry of Finance. For some countries, if the proportion of M&A exceeds the regulations on foreign equity and creditor transfer in their industries, it needs to obtain the approval of the National Reserve Bank of the target country. Some countries restrict domestic foreign capital flows and have established regulations and procedures for reporting. Filing will result in an extension of trading hours. The legal system of some countries is complex and may lead to opaque decision-making processes. In this case, in order to reduce uncertainty and maximize the benefits, companies need to consult local tax, legal or industry experts, which will lead to an increase in the total cost of the transaction.

In order to assess the efficiency of government operations and the ease of business operations in the country or region where the target company is located, Chinese investors can view the Ease of Doing Business Index. The index is compiled by the World Bank based on annual corporate data, assessing the difficulty of business operations around the world and the convenience of entrepreneurial activities.

The "Ease of Doing Business Index" ranking shows the quality and simplicity of commercial regulations around the world, as well as the quality of intellectual property protection. The goal of the index is to provide research data on the impact of government on economic growth. Since the establishment of the Doing Business Group by the World Bank in November 2001, the group has published more than 800 research results, and the results show that there is a close relationship between improving business rules and economic growth.

Unlike other similar studies, Ease of Doing Business Index only studies and quantifies business-related laws, regulations, and rules, regardless of basic conditions, such as infrastructure, inflation, crime, and commercial profitability.

Investors in the Belt and Road should evaluate the politics and culture of the target country before evaluating the transaction structure. Integrating resources, breaking cultural barriers, and adjusting personnel will create "hidden costs," and companies should take these into account when making effective decisions.

In general, complex financial valuation techniques incorporate national or industry-specific systemic risks. As a matter of fact, some "Belt and Road" countries do not have financial markets, and the markets are still underdeveloped even though some other countries have such markets. The risk cannot be quantified. In this case, investors should rely on their intuition and theoretically consider the costs that may arise in the event of political or cultural deterioration.

Market expectations are unconventional factors that many companies failed to consider. Due to the uncertainty and the large average transaction size, the market is expected to affect the value of M&A transactions, which is the most important reference factor for cross-border M&A transactions. After the transaction, the increase in the market value of the buyer indicates that the market is more optimistic than the buyer. Conversely, negative market reactions indicate that the buyer may need to reassess the financial position of the company after the M&A transaction. In both cases, the buyer's market value will change when the M&A announcement is issued, which is the indirect benefit or cost of the M&A transaction.

After assessing the overall business environment and government efficiency of the target country, Chinese companies should make a practical assessment of the convenience and cost of each transaction structure. In practice, depending on the nature of the transaction and many other factors, the transaction can be conducted in a variety of ways, but for research purposes, the chapter only considers the following three general transaction structures. Other models can be created with reference to these three main structures.

1. Asset acquisition

Asset purchases are the best way for investors to eliminate hidden and unknown costs. At the same time, the purchase agreement can clearly stipulate the debt that the buyer bears when the asset is sold, which can prevent the buyer from accidental or unknown liabilities. However, some laws, including environmental laws or tax laws, may have requirement for the buyers.

This structure is typically used when the buyer wants to get only a specific business unit or a single factory for the entire company. However, this process can have significant time costs and inconvenience due to the extra effort required to identify and purchase each of the important asset associated with the business project. While certain assets (such as equipment) can be easily transferred through sales lists or other similar documents, other assets (such as intellectual property or real estate) require special transfer mechanisms and procedures. Some assets, including many licenses, are not transferable at all.

In order to transfer certain assets from the seller to the buyer, third-party consent may be required, as many contracts often expressly state that the seller cannot sell without the consent of a third party. In order to avoid delays in the transaction due to the time spent identifying and obtaining consent, the parties should identify all required third party consents in advance and obtain them in advance.

The most important advantage of asset acquisition is that it requires only a majority shareholders' confirmation, usually only more than 50% of them.

2. Equity acquisition

Equity acquisitions are faster and easier because equity acquisitions do not require third-party consent or other legal documents related to asset acquisitions. The buyer's consideration is that unless all shareholders are willing to sell their shares, the buyer will not have full control. Excessive shareholder increases the risk of delays, long-term negotiations and other complexities.

In the equity acquisition process, the target company's assets and business processes remain unchanged, avoiding the adverse effects of the third-party consent process. In some cases, however, some asset ownership contracts may involve a "change of control" clause that requires the previous owner of the company's agreement to transfer ownership to the new shareholder before trading.

3. Merger

In the traditional type of merger, it is common for two existing companies to form a single business entity. For this type of transaction structure, the target company's shareholders may receive cash, the buyer's equity, or both. In terms of ownership transfer, a merged M&A transaction is similar to an equity acquisition that transfers all assets and liabilities to the buyer. From the seller's point of view, the advantage of the merger is that it only requires the consent of the majority of the target shareholders. The merger allows the buyer to obtain the trade secrets, technology, customers, market shares and suppliers of the target company.

For companies who go out and invest in a completely unknown business environment, buyers can get help from local professionals through a combined trading model to ensure the success and continuity of business processes. On the other hand, there may be cultural differences between the parties, and all parties need to communicate in order to achieve a cultural and business integration.

Section 3
Valuation: Science or Art

If you ask yourself: "What is valuation: art or science?" The most authentic answer is: "It is a combination of both."

Models of modern financial theory are often closely related to precise science such as mathematics and statistics. But if we look at it from another aspect, there is an undeniable human factor: psychology, sociology, and psychoanalysis also play an important role in the financial world. People's irrational behavior and lack of clear rules and axioms make valuation and investment similar to art.

Let us review the Long-term Asset Valuation Model (CAPM), the method of calculating moving averages or other coverage maps and indicators and many other factors. Obviously, such financial models have a clear scientific basis based on undeniable mathematical and statistical laws. In addition, in the financial sector, a variety of models, indicators and techniques based on precise science are used.

Art is another expression of the reality. Let's think about the various market collapses caused by humans. Are they rational results? Never.

After listening to the opinions of stakeholders, individuals behave exactly the same way as those predicted by the concerned people. In this case, only instinct and pure emotions work. From the perspective of all irrational business strategies, economic collapse or leap, finance is an art (Interestingly, the creators of this art are big investors, market makers, authoritative analysts, not private investors).

Imagine what happens if the scientific financial market is affected by holidays, news, and even weather. If finance is an art, how to treat it seriously?

A mature investor understands that rules do not always operate in financial markets. Even if all the rules indicate that the economy should grow, we must also remember that people are very irrational. Human factors must be taken into account in financial analysis, and valuation is both an art and science.

"If there is only one formula, one way, we are all billionaires."

Science is linked to sustainability, impartiality, consistency and eternal results. It can be thought in a textbook, tested in experiments, and predicted. If valuation and investment are purely science, then we will be able to achieve guaranteed success and return and eliminate all the risks of failure. However, valuations are more like an art than science, and there are no formulas or textbooks which could guarantee absolute success.

Although there are many investment valuation techniques, some of the widely recognized ones are used more frequently and may be more effective in investing in the "Belt and Road Initiative" framework. They are:

a. Public Comps: Public Comps shows that companies in the same industry and with the similar size have similar valuation multiples, so that the business indicators from other companies could be used in evaluation process.

b. Discounted Cashflow Model (DCF): This method estimates the company's future cashflow by discounting the company using the required discount rate to obtain the company's net present value (NPV). Estimation of financial benefits involves calculating the net discounted income indicator of the project, defined as the future inflows and outflows converted to the present value based on the present value of each period of the estimated discount rate, and then the net present value is determined (considering currency Swell). If the net present value is more than 0, it is recommended to invest in the project. If the indicator is less than 0, it is better to reject it. Because of the evaluation of investment efficiency, companies can understand the return on investment, that is, understand the proportion of funds and profits that have been invested. When assessing the attractiveness of an investment, it not only calculates the net present value indicator, but also calculates the payback period, the return index, and the internal rate of return. A comprehensive assessment of the value of all indicators can be used to understand the effectiveness of the project. In other words, the return on investment will be assessed.

c. M&A Comps: M&A Comps shows that prices previously paid for similar companies can be used to estimate the price of a given company.

Successful investments require not just an Excel spreadsheet, but also deliberation, intuition and creativity. Theories based on the long-term investment success stories, which most business schools focus on, are considered useless.

Case 5 – 2   Shanghai Meilin's Investment of New Zealand Silver Fern Farms Beef Limited

Transaction Amount: 311 million New Zealand dollars
Target Country: New Zealand
Industry: Animal Husbandry

Case Background: Shanghai Meilin Zhengguanghe Co., Ltd. (hereinafter referred to as "Shanghai Meilin Company") is a subsidiary of Bright Food Group. The company was listed in A-shares in 1997. It owns many well-known brands such as Meilin, Guanshengyuan, Zhengguanghe, Silver Fern Farms Beef Limited (SFF), Su Shi, Aisen, White Rabbit, Bergamot, Hua Tuo, and 96858. The company is principally engaged in the manufacturing of meat products and food distribution.

Founded in 1948, SFF is New Zealand's largest meat processing company, the second largest exporter of agricultural products only second to Fonterra's. The beef and venison business accounted for the first place in the New Zealand market. SFF has the customers all over the world. SFF's processing capacity is excessive andraw materials are insufficient, requiring cash flow to pay off debts and replenish liquidity. After obtaining funds from Shanghai Meilin, SFF further optimized production facilities and production capacity. Shanghai Meilin successfully completed this overseas acquisition, and quickly became China's largest integrated beef and mutton industry group to meet China's growing demand for high quality meat.

Case Study: On September 15, 2015, Shanghai Meilin (Hong Kong) Co., Ltd., a wholly-owned subsidiary of Shanghai Meilin Company, as the main body of acquisition, increased the capital of 311 million New Zealand dollars to SFF. After the capital increase, Shanghai Meilin Company will hold 50% of the shares. Shanghai Merlin Company consolidated financial statements. The acquisition is funded by Merlin's own funds and bank loans. The transaction needs to be approved by the Overseas Investment Office (OIO). The proposed purchase assets of this transaction are all operating assets of SFF and its subsidiaries and 50% of the business interests. The transaction pricing is based on the valuation results of the SFF Group's asset valuation report confirmed by the authorized organization of the Shanghai SASAC. The

> two parties negotiated according to the principle of marketization and finalized according to the price adjustment mechanism agreed in the transaction agreement. The assessment report shows that SFF's shareholders' equity is USD 620 million, and the company's corporate value after deducting debt is USD 350 million. Considering the company's poor performance in 2013 and 2014, Shanghai Merlin's bid is 88% the company's corporate value.
>
> The entire acquisition process was full of twists and turns, and on September 20, 2016, the New Zealand OIO approved the transaction.

Why do we need to evaluate the effectiveness of an investment project and how is it implemented? In actual cases, problems in the project investment may be difficult to resolve. Research on foreign investment decision-making practices shows that in most Western companies, investment assessment methods can be used as the decision information.

The effective evaluation of an investment project consists of several phases.

Phase 1: Determine the goals and objectives of the project investment. In general, the purpose of project investment is to determine the total investment and cost, determine the attractiveness of the project from the perspective of investors, determine the investment feasibility of the company, assess the investment risk and prove the suitability of investors and partners for the project.

Phase 2: Cost analysis. This phase consists of two sets of activities designed to analyze investment costs and production costs, including their calculations and budgets, fund allocation during the project phase, and comparative analysis of profitability.

Phase 3: Evaluate investment returns. The first part of the phase calculates the overall performance indicators of the project, and the second part analyzes the effectiveness of the participating projects, including the determination of the participants and the selection of the project financing plan. The first part of the assessment reflects the social impact of the project and financial impact on regional budgets.

Phase 4: Form financing strategies. It is divided into sub-phases, including determining the source of financing, the composition of potential investors, the terms of participation, designing the investment schedule, determining the consequences of its implementation, and calculating the combined cash flow to cover all project costs.

Case 5 – 3 Midea Group acquired KUKA, Germany

Transaction Amount: RMB 29. 2 billion
Target Country: Germany
Industry: Robot

Case Background: Midea Group (000333) was founded in 1968 and entered the home appliance industry in 1980. After the establishment of Midea Group, it has completed more than a dozen acquisitions, accumulating capital quickly, expanding its scale, and developing into a leader in the industry. Midea Group achieved sales revenue of RMB 259. 7 billion and net profit of RMB 20. 2 billion in 2018. Despite the continuous decline in the profit margin of the home appliance industry in recent years, Midea Group continues to maintain steady growth due to the Midea's smart manufacturing and machine substitution measures. Midea put forward the "double intelligence" strategy of "smart manufacturing + industrial robots", starting from 2012 to improve labor productivity and automation through layout robots.

Founded in 1898, KUKA Group is the world's leading manufacturer of industrial robots with a 100-year history and a model of German manufacturing. In 1996, KUKA in Germany was independent from the KUKA Group. Together with ABB, FANUC and Yaskawa, it was called the "Four Big Family" of the robot industry. The "Four Big Family" accounted for more than 60% of the global industrial robot market share. Germany's KUKA is centered on automation. Its main customers come from the fields of automobile, logistics, plastics, medical equipment, etc. It is also the first company in the world to provide automatic welding for washing machines and refrigerators. The company has core technology advantages, and 80% of its revenue comes from Europe and the United States.

Midea Group hopes to accelerate its intelligent strategic transformation through the acquisition of KUKA, acquire the core technology of KUKA, complement its own "short board", fully exert synergy effect and further expand market share. At the same time, KUKA can use Midea's brand influence and sales resources in China to help its expansion in the Chinese market and increase its proportion in China.

Case Study: In January 2017, MECCA, a wholly-owned subsidiary of Midea Group, acquired KUKA at a price of 115 Euros per share. The purchase price was 3.7 billion Euros, equivalent to RMB 29.2 billion. Midea Group issues offer to acquire KUKA implementation report. "The offer price is not based on the assessment report or the valuation report. The acquisition has not been evaluated and valued". In fact, according to KUKA's net profit of 743 million yuan in 2015, Midea Group's acquisition of P/E is nearly 40 times. Compared to the domestic market valuation of 40 ~80 times, it is basically the lower limit of the interval.

If the common valuation method EV/EBITDA acquired overseas is applied, the multiple of the enterprise value/sales is calculated as the multiple of EV/EBITDA and is 18.2 times, while the enterprise value/sales multiple is 1.6 times. We also compare the purchase price of two comparable transactions between Omron's acquisition of Adept Technology and Teradyne's acquisition of Uniro Robot in 2015. The latter's EV/EBITDA is as high as 23.5 (Adept Technology's EBITDA is negative, cannot be compared), corporate value / sales are 3.6x and 8.9x respectively. The price of Midea's acquisition of KUKA is not high.

The acquisition premium data of the iconic strategic investors' acquisition of German listed companies since 2007 shows that the acquisition premium rate is between 30% and 69%, with an average of 46%. On the previous day of Midea's board's making the announcement of the offer decision, the premium of the closing price was 36.24%; compared to which, the premium of Midea's acquisition price is within a reasonable range.

However, from the financial data of KUKA in 2018, KUKA's net profit fell 81.2%, and revenue fell 6% to 8%, which was not satisfactory. In the short term, the situation is not optimistic. Whether the acquisition is successful or not, it is still too early to draw conclusions as it still depends on the performance of KUKA in the next few years. This case also suggests that the acquisition is only a beginning. It is the post-acquisition integration that is more important. The authors will further discuss the post-investment integration in the following sections.

For investors involved in the "Belt and Road Initiative", valuation is an integral part of M&A transactions. Which trading structure to choose depends largely on the value of each transaction to the buyer and seller. Although the seller attempts to obtain the highest and most desirable price, the buyer needs to conduct thorough due diligence and evaluate every detail of each case. In general, the three main criteria play a crucial role in decision making: the future of the business, the risks associated with a particular business, industry or country, and the capital cost.

The numerical assumptions based on the future prospects of the company have a significant impact on the net present value of the company's future cash flows, and small changes in certain important parameters can also cause large fluctuations in the net present value. For the discounted cash flow analysis, multiple sensitive factors such as income, labor costs, interest expenses, and taxes should be considered. Therefore, when making assumptions, the volatility and certainty of each factor of the model cannot be fully considered. For example, a country with a strong labor union may lead to an increase in labor costs, an unstable banking environment or an economic situation that causes interest rates to rise and the government to increase taxes. On the other hand, Chinese investors should also consider how their earnings are handled in their countries. And if the tax cannot be credited, it needs to be included in the calculation.

Another assumption that cannot be fully quantified is the risk associated with a particular business, industry or country. While some methods, such as the asset pricing model, provide a method for risk management and assessment, it is a generic model and is not always applicable to practice, especially in underdeveloped, unstable markets, with no risk discount rates or the systemic risk cannot be measured accurately. Some "Belt and Road" countries do not have their own stock market or competitive industry, and it is impractical to evaluate the risks mathematically.

For the above reasons, "Belt and Road" investors will continue to work hard to form quantitative valuation models and need to rely on their intuition. They must apply theoretical knowledge to practice and make decisions based on the quantitative and speculative data. In order to make a successful decision, investors should understand the political and economic relationship between China and the target country, the bilateral agreement between the two, China's tax regulations on overseas investment, the economic and political conditions of the country being invested and their future forecast, industry-specific characteristics and the most important information related to business. Only by combining quantitative analysis with the above theoretical knowledge, combining science with art, the investors can achieve the successful evaluation and completion of M&A transactions.

CHAPTER 6

THE "BELT AND ROAD" COUNTRIES' TRANS-ACTION DOCUMENTS

Section 1
High Costs of Transaction Documents

Assets and wealth were ultimately presented in legal documents, so this chapter will briefly introduce the main legal documents that the buyer needs to sign in the whole process of overseas M&A transaction, taking the process of M&A transaction as the timeline. When Chinese companies invest abroad, they spend the most money in transaction documents. As the author's experience, lawyers argue fiercely about key terms and definitions, even just some words. The attorney's hour fee is very expensive. Normally, a night attorney's fee can cost tens of thousands RMB. In any case, the transaction risk control mechanism of a multinational company essentially relies on the legal advisory team of the deal, which is usually the combination of 1 ~ 2 partners plus 1 ~ 2 senior lawyers and N paralegals. The risk control advice of a financial adviser is ultimately included in the transaction documents. Especially, the buyer must be aware of the risks of M&A, and must take every measure to lower the risks and control the process.

M&A transactions are usually important, and it is worthwhile to tailor a contract at a high cost, as the contract will involve a large amount of investment from the buyer, changes of control power, ownership of the company, and significant changes to the seller's assets. It includes not only the collection of assets, but also the control of business. The various assets usually involved in M&A transactions are intellectual property, real estate and regulatory licensing. Such transfers of tangible and intangible portfolios are usually accompanied by changes or transfers of contractual and non-contractual relationships with various individuals, from shareholders, directors, managers to employees and agents, from customers and suppliers to lenders and regulators. The deal usually greatly effects the operation and reputation of buyers and their management.

A typical M&A transaction involves not a contract, but a set of contracts.

The successful completion of the transaction requires signing a series of legal documents. The legal documents that need to be signed by the parties involved in the transaction can be divided into two categories: pre-transaction documents and post-transaction documents. It can also be divided into main transaction documents and auxiliary transaction documents by their importance. The main transaction documents define the conditions, transaction value and closing methods of the main transaction while the auxiliary transaction documents are a series of documents signed for the purpose of cooperating with the main transaction documents. The so-called "main transaction documents" and "auxiliary transaction documents" above should specifically include these files, the determination of which depends on the purpose, nature, object and model of dealing. The negotiation stage ends with the Share Purchase Agreement (SPA). After signature, preparation for closing usually involves collecting the necessary statutory and transaction-specific approvals.

The main transaction documents and auxiliary transaction documents are closely intertwined around the purpose, logic, process and key nodes of the main transaction, forming a seamless and interlocked legal ring. Common linkage arrangements include the following.

1. Set conditions precedent to become effective or closing

See the signature, proper effect-taking (e. g. take effect for a period and continue to take effect, etc.) or proper performance (e. g. the seller performs certain creditor's rights agreements within a certain period, etc.) of certain legal documents as the precedent condition of main transaction documents' coming into effect, payment under main transaction documents or closing.

2. Set cross-default clause or termination clause

Set cross-default or cross termination clauses between the relevant legal documents. When one party defaults under a legal document or agreement, the party also defaults under the relevant linkage agreement and thus default relief provisions under the linkage agreement should be triggered. The mechanism of cross termination clause is similar to the cross-default clause.

3. Keep the consistency of the relevant legal provisions

The consistency of key legal terms shall be kept between the main and auxiliary transaction documents. For example, unless it is necessary, in the agreement of applicable law, dispute resolution and other matters, the main and auxiliary transaction documents should be consistent and conflicts or inconsistencies should be avoided. If some inconsistencies exist, remedy for one party to claim damages may be unavailable.

Section 2
Transaction Documents Depend on Legal and Financial Due Diligence

Essentially, the target of M&A is a "used car", which is thousands of miles away. Therefore, it is necessary to investigate the target.

The purpose of due diligence is to find, quantify and control risks. Risk detection is the priority of due diligence. The buyer shall analyze the risks revealed in the due diligence report and decide to terminate or continue the transaction. If the transaction continues, the risk can be controlled by setting conditions precedent, adjusting transaction price, setting escrow account, setting up reasonable risk allocation or damage compensation mechanism in transaction documents, and strengthening Representation and Warranty clauses. Take a look at how the Chinese central state-owned enterprise China Communications Construction Company Limited (hereinafter referred to as China Communications Construction) buys "second-hand cars".

Case 6 – 1   Acquisition of Brazil Concremat

Transaction Amount: Not disclosed
Target Country: Brazil
Industry: Construction

Case Background: In January 2017, China Communications Construction successfully purchased 80% of Brazil "Concremat" company. Concremat is the largest engineering design consulting enterprise in Brazil and even in South America.

In the process of acquiring Concremat, China Communications Construction hired Luis Berger as a technical consultant, KPMG as a tax consultant, and Stocche Forbes as a legal consultant to sort out the risks in terms of technology, finance and tax as well as law to judge whether there is a deal breaker (major risk for blocking transactions). If the deal breaker is not found in due diligence, the next step is to quantify the existing technical, financial and tax as well as legal risks, and use specific amounts to show it. After quantifying risk, China Communications Construction needs to control risks in the transaction documents.

Case Study: The buyer's due diligence process is comprehensive and prudent. From team setting up, process determination, due diligence to reporting, intermediaries play a professional role.

1. Set up the due diligence team: in-house first

The buyer shall first organize his own team before carrying out the due diligence. In addition to in-house staff, the buyer will usually employ professional external consultants to assist in conducting the due diligence. Since Brazil is a Portuguese-speaking country, language barriers are obvious: laws and regulations are unique, tax is various, and taxation methods are particularly complicated. Therefore, based on the principle of "localization", China Communications Construction employs the Brazilian law firm that knows the local situation best. KPMG's Brazilian team and Luis Berger's South American team, as external consultants ensure efficient and thorough due diligence.

2. The process of due diligence: focusing targets

Usually the seller will open the virtual data room to the buyer. In addition, the buyer can draw up a list of information requirements, clarifying the information needed to the seller, so as to make the due diligence more targeted. If necessary, the buyer will also conduct on-site due diligence, including senior executive interviews and on-site project investigations. Due diligence of Concremat also follows the above procedures.

3. Content of due diligence: covering three sectors

(1) Technical due diligence

The technical due diligence includes industry, human resources, technology and operation.

(2) Financial and tax due diligence

The financial and tax due diligence includes financing, tax and labor.

The financial section includes the financial statements (including the balance sheet, income statement, cash flow statement, all after stripping) and various indicators (liquidity ratio, debt-to-equity ratio, return on equity, etc.) that reflect the operating conditions.

(3) Legal due diligence

The legal due diligence focuses on the shareholding structure, contract conditions (design consulting contract, investment agreement, insurance contract), litigation case (civil, environment, tax and labor lawsuit), all the ownership and equity (real estate and intellectual property), and antitrust approval.

1. Legal due diligence

The profession should be done by professionals, including legal due diligence. The term "due diligence" means "proper diligence" in common sense. In any case the lawyers should diligently conduct comprehensive and detailed due diligence. The scope of due diligence depends on several factors, such as the size of the transaction, the confidentiality of the transaction, the industry of the business, and the level of friendliness of the clients. The due diligence process is usually driven by external lawyers. For example, in an acquisition, the attorney will prepare the transaction documents, and the terms and conditions, representations, warranties, and disclaimers may have to be adjusted based on the results of the due diligence.

In a standard legal due diligence, a lawyer will draft and submit a preliminary list of investigations for each transaction. In the hands of an experienced and knowledgeable lawyer, the response to the investigation has been proved to be priceless on potential critical issues that might require a thorough review. A comprehensive list of due diligence can also help bring together the attention of those who provide documents or information and reduce the likelihood of supervision. Specifically, the purpose of due diligence differs from the seller's, buyer's, and lawyer's perspective. For Chinese buyers, it is the buyer who generally conducts the due diligence.

In the face of complex and diligence information, any professional will be challenged.

The client must work with the due diligence team to identify risks, and at the same time, to discover value, such as a. whether there are significant legal risks that affect the transaction; b. whether there are significant legal risks that have a significant impact on the valuation of the transaction or other trading conditions. Therefore, legal due diligence is an important part of the transaction process, which provides an important basis for the buyer's business decisions and negotiation of closing conditions.

(1) The barriers to legal due diligence

Legal due diligence is not omnipotent. Legal due diligence is restricted by four factors:

1) Awareness

The purpose of legal due diligence is to find "significant" past and present risks. However, some risks that do meet the "significance" criteria cannot be identified during investigation. In 2004 SAIC Motor Corporation Limited acquired South Korea's Ssang Yong Motor and finally lost an enormous sum of money. The due diligence was not clear about the major obstacles to the post-merger integration from South Korean Trade Unions.

2) Time

In practice, the time for conducting legal due diligence is often tight. Whether internal or government approval, the time for preparing a report is limited. How to grasp the key points in a short period of time has become a challenge for buyers. Legal due diligence relies more on experienced intermediaries. In 2016, Everbright Capital Investment Co., Ltd. and Storm group Limited by Share Ltd bought 65% share of Italian MP & Silva (hereinafter referred to as MPS) with RMB 4.388 billion, then the major risk emerged in 2019 is an important example.

3) Cost

The largest expense of overseas M&A is the legal fee. Many Chinese private enterprises are reluctant to pay the high cost of due diligence. After all, the budget of an enterprise is limited. Moreover, in the Chinese state-owned enterprises, the budget approval process is standardized. If cost increases, it is necessary to control the workload of the due diligence.

4) Method

Legal due diligence is based on reviewing the documents provided by the seller. Due to the time and space distance of cross-border M&A, or because of the large number of documents, it is common for the seller to open the database (data room) in practice for lawyers to review the scanned documents. In the face of huge file data processing, it seems inevitable that some omissions will occur.

(2) The general focus on legal due diligence

Since the overseas due diligence is always limited, according to its difficulties and characteristics, the general focus lies on: equity structure and shareholders; major contracts; pledge; labor conditions; intellectual property and proprietary technology; taxation.

1) Equity structure and shareholders

The equity structure of the target company and the status of shareholders are the most basic contents of the due diligence. In 2016, the author led a due diligence team on D-round investment of an overseas FINTECH company. After the company provides the shareholder with documents (shareholder roster, etc.), the author is most concerned about the situation of the first three rounds of investors. The logic behind this is that if the first three rounds of investors are focused on the top funds focusing on FINTECHs, subsequent investments will be more concerned about valuation. By consulting the minutes of the board meeting, the author finds that the board of directors is required to approve the equity incentive for the team. Unlike Chinese companies, the shareholder rights of European and American companies are more complicated, especially for companies with financial investors. They often issue a series of preferred shares, convertible bonds, share options and share warrants. When the company sells the options, the preferred stockholders often have strong power, including the veto rights as well as various priorities in the distribution of benefits. If the management or founders of the target company are the ones having the M&A negotiation, they often do not hold preferred shares. Under this circumstance, the buyer should review the articles of association, shareholder agreement, voting agreement and other documents to learn the rights and obligations of each shareholder, in order to avoid any shareholders challenging the legal fairness of the transaction, making the transaction impossible or increasing the cost of acquisition.

2) Major Contracts

Major contracts are what the target company will or are performing. The due diligence should be focused on whether the contracts that the target company has fulfilled have a potential dispute. For example, the author has seen that the purchase contract stipulates that "the buyer's satisfaction is the condition to pay the balance", which will bring the risk of accounts receivable. Except for investment and financing contracts, major contracts in procurement, sales and technology are also the focus the due diligence. The buyer needs to analyze the consequences of such restrictions and, if necessary, communicate with the parties of the contract in a timely manner.

3) Pledge

It includes mortgage and real estate. European and American countries have matured, comprehensive and authoritative enquiry systems, which make it possible for third-party professional institutions to complete basic inquiry work according to the requirements of the buyer with less expense. However, some "belt and road" countries do not have authoritative inquiry system, and buyers must pay attention to relevant due diligence. For real estate, if it involves sensitive areas, it is sometimes necessary to conduct the field visits. For example, as the location of real estate acquired by a foreign company is close to the Australian military base, the Foreign Investments Review Board of Australia (FIRB) requires break-up of the part of the assets on national security grounds or even the rejection of the deal. An early field trip might have prevented this result.

4) Labor Conditions

The labor laws of many countries are complicated. It is necessary to make detailed assessments of trade unions, collective contracts, pensions, and employee benefits to fully estimate the operating costs and risks after the acquisition. For example, M&As of French companies impose strict restrictions on the dismissal of employees. During the author's internship at Belgium Loyens & Loeff International Law Firm, the author found that many EU countries had legal provisions to pay wages to employees during the strike. In addition, the senior executives of the target company often hold the company's equity in various forms. In the event of an acquisition, these options or equity may increase the cost of the acquisition.

5) Intellectual Property

Chinese enterprises value their intellectual property in many overseas M&As. Everbright Capital Investment Co., Ltd. and Storm Group Limited by Share Ltd 's overseas M&A failed. According to media disclosure, the main copyright resources of MPS expire from 2018 to 2021: the copyright of core assets of Italian Series A League expires in 2018, the copyright of the UK Premier League expires in 2019, and there are lots of unpaid copyright fees in existing copyright contracts. These facts have a significant impact on the operation of MPS, which directly lead to the bankruptcy of MPS by creditors. These problems should be detected and negotiated in the due diligence stage. At present, it is impossible to know whether the professional intermediaries employed have found the above problems and whether the buyer have made risk judgments and decision-making processes on these problems.

The above case shows that, due to the regionalism of intellectual property, the buyer needs considering the purpose of the acquisition and the nature of the technology involved to decide whether the key markets (such as Europe and America areas) are only searching areas. Sometimes a team of patent lawyers, agents, appraisal agencies, and in-house technicians will be deployed.

6) Taxation

Tax due diligence usually focuses on whether the tax is compliant, and whether there are pending matters and potential risk factors in tax treatment. Tax due diligence can identify potential fatal tax deficiencies and determine whether to continue the transaction process. Tax compliance in many "Belt and road" countries is not as good as expected. Some of the South American countries from the author's experience have been alert with the risk of tax compliance for most of targets. If Chinese enterprises do not follow the rules behind the target company, the profits will be greatly reduced. Through tax due diligence, we can find out the tax environment and tax burden level, analyze the real profitability and cash flow, and reveal the existing tax risks and potential problems.

In sum, according to the problems and risks appearing in the due diligence, the buyer can take various measures including requiring the counter party to make corrections before signing the contract, making representations and warranties in the transaction documents, or the prerequisites for closing. For the uncertain risks, a legal opinion letter from a reputable local law firm may be considered. As for payment terms, risks can also be controlled by means of installment payments, deferred payments (holdback), account supervision and even by Valuation Adjustment Mechanism (VAM). The design of the risk control clause should be adjusted according to the due diligence and the relevant circumstances of the transaction.

Case 6-2 Sanpower Group issuing shares to purchase Israel housekeeping company

Transaction Amount: Not disclosed
Target Country: Israel
Industry: Health

Case Background: Since 2014, Sanpower Group and its subsidiaries have launched a series of projects. Overseas M&As include: Sanpower Group's department store Nanjing Xinjiekou Department Store co., Ltd (hereinafter referred to as Nanjing xinbai) bought House of Fraser, the oldest department store in the United Kingdom, acquired the largest pension service company Natali in Israel, bought the US listed companies, and bought a new specialty chain Brookstone with nearly 300 stores in the United States. In 2015, Hongtu Technologies, which is controlled by Sanpower Group, acquired Wanwei International, the listed company on the main board of the Hong Kong Stock Exchange and a professional female novelty product provider with worldwide marketing network. Recently, Sanpower Group acquired A. S. Nursing Company, the largest domestic care company in Israel. So far, Sanpower Group has become more and more globalized.

Case Study: This case involved two risks.

a. Litigation risk of Sanpower Group. During the reporting period, Sanpower Group and its subsidiaries were involved in several pending litigations. The plaintiffs included individuals, enterprises and trade unions, and the claims included compensation claims and personal injury compensation claims. Among them, the amount of compensation of some litigation cases involving Sanpower Group and its subsidiaries is relatively large. The Israeli labor organization Yadid Association brought a class action lawsuit against 20 Israel nursing companies, including A. S. Nursing Company. The process of Israeli class actions is time-consuming and litigation usually lasts for months or years. Although the relevant litigation information has been disclosed in details in the report, taking the continuing influence of legal proceedings into consideration, if the relevant issues cannot be handled reasonably and effectively, it will pose certain risks to the management of the Sanpower Group.

> b. The risk of Sanpower Group leased property in Israel being unable to renew it. During the reporting period, all the major business premises of Sanpower Group were leased office, warehousing, training and other needs. As of September 30th, 2016, Sanpower Group and its subsidiaries have several lease contracts that are about to expire. According to Israel's local laws and regulations on housing leasing, after the lease of the property expires, the renter and the tenant can automatically renew the lease until either party no longer agrees with the lease relationship. Considering the experience of subsidiaries of Sanpower GroupI, Natali and A. S. Nursing Company, the property lease does not have a major impact on company's operation. However, if a large number of properties Sanpower Group rented cannot be renewed, it would likely effect the operation of Sanpower Group.

2. Financial due diligence

Financial due diligence can help buyers to be familiar with the financial situation of the foreign target companies quickly, reasonably estimate the value of the target that can make adequate preparations for bidding and negotiation, and anticipate the financial and business integration matters after the completion of the transaction. By knowing the concerns of the financial due diligence, investors can understand the financial risks of the transaction and take appropriate strategies based on the degree and nature of risks. Every case has different risk level, it could be understood by deep study.

If the target of overseas M&A is assets, such as buying farmland from Australian farmers, financial due diligence is not important. However, in "second-hand car" style equity investment, financial risk must be clarified through financial due diligence, and appropriate strategies should be adopted according to the degree and nature of risk.

The author is deeply impressed with a financial due diligence in 2017. The company invested in the "Belt and Road" country, and the financial due diligence involved data on sales and sales forecasts for other overseas markets. The historical data shows that the company's sales have increased. However, when the author asked for a review of all overseas contracts and their terms, the historical growth did not confirm the assumption that sales revenue from overseas markets accounted for half of total sales revenue in 2018. Moreover, the biggest challenge is that the gross profit of overseas business is only about half that of domestic business, which means that the more products sold abroad, the slower the profit growth. In 2019, its public prospectus confirmed the author's judgment two years ago. The summary is as follows: from the point of view of the location of customers, the main business income of the company during the reporting period mainly comes from the domestic customers. Overseas customers' sales revenue accounted for ××, ×× and ×× of the main business income in the past three years, and the proportion of overseas customers' sales revenue declined year by year.

Case 6 – 3 Sanpower Group's exchange rate risks

> Foreign exchange risks. After the completion of the transaction, the daily operations of the underlying company will involve foreign currencies such as US dollars and Israeli new shekels, and the company's bookkeeping base currency of consolidated statement is RMB. If there is a major change in China's exchange rate policy or a large fluctuation in the exchange rate of RMB against foreign currencies in the future, Sanpower Group of Nanjing may face certain exchange rate fluctuation risks.

Systematic financial due diligence processes help to ensure that buyers are not kept in the dark. The basic considerations of due diligence are as follows.

Income, profit and profit trends: Is there a recent trend in the data? Up, down, stable?

Competitive rivals and industries: Study and compare the profits of competitors and understand what the target company is like.

Management and ownership: the operator of a research company. Who is operating?

Balance sheet analysis: Analysis of debt-to-equity ratios. Does the company have too much debt?

Risk: Know the industry and the company's specific risks. Are there any outstanding risks?

Expectations: How much is the future profit?

Financial due diligence can help buyers to find risks and value, familiarize themselves with the financial situation of overseas target companies as soon as possible, and reasonably estimate the value of the target company, so as to fully prepare for bidding and negotiation. It helps them to predict the finance and business integration in the post investment after the transaction is closed.

The following are five key factors for financial due diligence:

(1) Factors that terminate the transaction

For example, the actual business case of the Target Corp is quite different from that of the original negotiation basis; the financial indicators such as income and profit margin are quite different from those expected. The author was involved in a project and asked for all contracts involving the international market. The author detected that there was no basis for predicting future growth and there was a risk that the balance of payment would not be recovered.

(2) Major valuation adjustment

Even if the quality of basic financial information of overseas targets in Europe and the United States is better, serious accounting errors will occur. The failure of Everbright Capital Investment Co., Ltd. in the M&A case of Storm Group Limited is a common case. In fact, 65% of MPS's equity is not worth RMB 4.7 billion. In some "Belt and Road" countries, significant financial risks are hidden in the target. Therefore, it is necessary to determine a sustainable profitability level through careful financial due diligence as the basis of valuation calculation.

(3) The protective umbrella of M&A

During the due diligence process, some potential risks such as contingent liabilities and commitments may be detected. It is not easy for buyers and sellers to directly adjust the price. However, the purchaser needs to avoid risks by setting up protective mechanisms and agree terms in the SPA. For example, in order to avoid potential tax risks, an exemption clause should be stipulated in the transaction document. Any cost of tax recourse prior to closing of the target company in the agreed period is borne by the seller. However, if the risk occurs after the transaction has been fully paid, the right can only be claimed by legal means.

(4) Purchase price adjustments in M&A deals

The clause of Earn-out is relatively rare in overseas M&A. At the same time, overseas sellers usually require other price adjustment mechanisms, such as working capital adjustment, net asset adjustment, Locked Box and so on. Regarding price adjustment between the valuation date and the closing date, detailed analysis and measurement are required in the financial due diligence. Buyers can also reduce the price and risk by installment payment mechanism.

(5) Integration after M&A

This is the most inadequate ability of Chinese buyers. In the process of financial due diligence, intermediaries should assist buyers in analyzing post-transaction integration issues. However, some aspects, such as transitional IT systems, are not professional for intermediaries, and buyers' in-house team need to pay full attention to them.

For target companies in financial distress, due diligence will also focus on issues related to corporate restructuring (such as employee pensions, factory closure costs, etc.), and the capital needs of target companies in the next few years after debt restructuring and trading, so as to determine whether follow-up investment is necessary.

Section 3
Preliminary Transaction Documents

Due to the human, material and financial resources invested by the buyer, and the huge risks assumed, the seller is worried about the confidentiality of information. In order to obtain legally binding protection for both parties, the most commonly-used documents include confidentiality agreements, terms sheet, etc.

1. Confidentiality agreement

In the initial stage of the transaction, the owner of the underlying asset, equity or business, or the shareholder of the target company (hereinafter referred to as the "seller") is required to disclose the relevant information to the buyer. Therefore, in accordance with the established practice, the seller will require the potential buyer to sign a "Confidentiality Agreement" before the seller discloses relevant information. The obligation to disclose confidentiality of information involves restricting the use of confidential information to specific purposes, stipulating terms and responsibilities for disclosure to third parties, and other disclosure required by co-investors, banks and other financial institutions, consultants and boards of directors, regulatory bodies, courts and stock exchanges.

Case 6 – 4   Confidentiality Agreement

Confidentiality Agreement

Disclosing Party:	Recipient:
Registration address:	Registration address:
Legal representative/	Legal representative/
Authorized representative:	Authorized representative:

Disclosing Party and Recipient are entering into discussions concerning the Specified Purpose, which may involve the disclosure of Confidential Information.

Definitions and Interpretation

The following definitions apply unless the context requires otherwise.

a. Disclosing party: Refers to the party that discloses confidential information, and the Party A in this agreement. The Affiliated Companies of Party A are also involved. Affiliate means, with respect to any person, any other person that directly, or indirectly through one or more intermediaries, controls, is controlled by, or is under common control with such person; the term "control" (including the terms "controlling," "controlled by" and "under common control with") means the possession, direct or indirect, of the power to direct or cause the direction of the management and policies of a person, whether through the ownership of voting securities, by contract, or otherwise.

A reference to a person includes a corporation, trust, partnership, unincorporated body or other entity, whether or not it comprises a separate legal entity.

b. Confidential Information: Information relating to the business of the discloser and that is disclosed to the Recipient by or on behalf of the Discloser, whether the information is in oral, visual or written form or is recorded in any other medium. Such information should include, but not limited to the following marketing plans, commercial or financial information, trade information, contracts, technical knowledge, legal documents, product demonstrations, product prototypes, models, samples, methods, specifications, proprietary data, software procedures, software source documents and formulas, and all other information related to the disclosing party. In addition, the facts, statements and information of the parties involved in the discussion and negotiation of the disclosing party and the Recipient, as well as the information of the parties to the negotiators, and the summary, analysis and summary of the conference according to this Agreement are also classified as confidential information.

c. Recipient: The party that accepts confidential information under the permission of the disclosing party and refers to Party B in this agreement. It also includes the related members and employees of Party B, that is, all directors, consultants, officials, employees, employees, legal counsel, financial consultants or all other relevant personnel related to Party B and Party B.

d. Special purpose: the pointer shall reach a binding agreement on the mutual discussion, communication and negotiation between the disclosing party and the recipient on the matters, until the business or transaction covered by this agreement.

Any materials containing confidential information provided or disclosed by the Disclosing Party, including but not limited to documents, manuals, flowcharts, project listings and electronic versions of data files, printed copies, photocopies, backup documents, etc. (hereinafter referred to as Material) shall be and will remain the property of the Disclosing Party and the Disclosing Party shall have sole ownership. This Agreement does not constitute any exclusive right of the Disclosing Party to the recipient. The disclosure of confidential information by the Disclosing Party does not imply any right in the Distributing Information, nor does it form any offer or promise of the Disclosing Party to the Recipient. The Recipient shall not use the Confidential Information for registration or registration of any rights.

Recipient shall keep all Confidential Information confidential; establish and maintain the effective security measures to protect the Confidential Information against disclosure; only use the Confidential Information in accordance with the stated objectives agreed in this Agreement without the prior written consent of the Disclosing Party; do not use, disclose or exchange all or part of the confidential information for any other purpose; and may not disclose any aspect of the Confidential information to any third party in any way.

Establish and maintain the effective security measures to protect the Confidential Information in a manner no less strict lower than that it affords to its own information regarded as secret and confidential. Keep strictly confidential any information or data disclosed by the disclosing party to the receiving party containing confidential information.

Notify Disclosing Party promptly in writing if the recipient becomes aware of any suspected or actual breach of this agreement, and agree to assist the disclosing party in handling the above situations as required by the Disclosing Party.

For special purpose, the recipient can disclose the confidential information to the relevant personnel of the recipient by the prior written consent of the disclosing party, but the information must be strictly limited to the principle of "the necessary knowledge". Before the disclosure of confidential information, the recipient shall provide the disclosure party with the list of persons who intend to obtain confidential information in writing and shall sign a confidentiality agreement with all the above persons, and the confidentiality obligations of such personnel shall not be lower than the recipient. Relevant persons who have been notified by the recipient of the confidential information may not disclose the confidential information to any other person.

If the recipient has a proprietary information exchange agreement with the third party, and the terms and conditions of the agreement are not less stringent than this agreement, the recipient shall submit the agreement to the Disclosing party and only disclose the confidential information to the preceding third parties after obtaining the prior written consent of the Disclosing Party.

All ownership and other rights in the Confidential Information (including all Intellectual Property) are vested in, and shall remain the property of, Disclosing Party. For the avoidance of doubt, there is no assignment of any rights in Confidential Information or any Intellectual Property to Recipient. Nothing in this Agreement shall be deemed to confer or license the recipient any right to confidential information, nor shall it be deemed that the disclosing party has the obligation to authorize or license the recipient or any other entity to use confidential information for any purpose for which the target specified in the agreement is unexpected.

No party shall declare or disclose any intention or any other cooperative information on the contract between the parties and the recipient before the agreement is reached on the special purpose (including but not limited to the project information, the mode of cooperation, the amount of the investment, the disclosure of information, etc.) .

The Disclosing Party has no obligation to guarantee the accuracy and completeness of the disclosed confidential information, nor does it have the obligation to update the confidential information in time, if the recipient uses the confidential information disclosed by the disclosing party to conduct business or any other act, causing loss to the disclosing party, the receiving party or any third party or causing any third party to claim the right, the recipient shall bear its own responsibility. After the completion of the defined objectives agreed in this agreement or the termination of this Agreement the Recipient shall either destroy or return to the Discloser immediately upon its request all copies of the Confidential Information and all documents and any and all materials (in any medium), Including but not limited to any original, photocopy, reprint, replica, backup (including automatic backup of computer system), derivative materials (including but not limited to the hot, report, PPT, meeting minutes and other materials based on confidential information) or records and notes (including any analysis of confidential information) of confidential information stored in any medium. And within five days after the termination of this Agreement, the responsible person of the recipient shall confirm the compliance with the Terms in writing to the Disclosing Party. If the recipient fails to destroy or completely destroys and thereby causes damage to the disclosing Party, the recipient shall bear the responsibility arising therefrom.

If the special purpose as agreed in this Agreement are completed, the Recipient retains confidential information or materials containing confidential information to the extent permitted by the Disclosing Party in writing, ensuring that it is not disclosed to any third party.

The Recipient agrees that the obligations of the Recipient under this Agreement are necessary and reasonable to protect the Disclosing Party and its business. The Recipient expressly agrees that if the recipient violates any term of this Agreement or the Confidential Information under this Agreement is known to any third party due to the Recipient's reasons, the Recipient shall compensate the Disclosing Party all losses suffered by the Disclosing Party including but not limited to any direct or/and indirect, tangible or/and intangible property or/and non-property losses, and reasonable loss of attorney's fees paid by the disclosing party for investigating the recipient's breach of contract. The Recipient is responsible for any disclosure of confidential information caused by its staff, consultants, banks, etc.

This agreement shall be governed and construed in accordance with the laws and regulations of the People's Republic of China. In the event that a dispute arises from or in connection with this Agreement, the Parties hereto shall attempt in the first instance to resolve such dispute amicably through friendly consultation between the Parties. If no settlement can be reached through such consultation, any Party is entitled to submit the dispute to the China International Economic and Trade Arbitration Commission ("CIETAC") for arbitration by an arbitration tribunal of three (3) members in accordance with the Arbitration Rules of CIETAC (the "CIETAC Rules"). The arbitration shall be final and binding upon both Parties.

If any term or provision of this Agreement shall be held to be invalid or unenforceable in whole or in part under any applicable law, it shall be excluded from this Agreement (to the extent of such invalidity or unenforceability only), and all other terms and provisions of this Agreement shall continue to be in full force and effect.

The Disclosing Party reserves the right to terminate this Agreement if the Disclosing Party believes that the Recipient has disclosed confidential information to any third party or may otherwise threaten the security of the Confidential Information.

This agreement shall be effective immediately after the signature and seal of both parties and shall be valid for three years.

This agreement is in duplicate, and each party holds a copy.

Disclosing Party: Recipient:
Legal representative / agent: Legal representative / agent:
Signature: Signature:
Date: Date:

2. Bidding documents / letter of intent

In many M&A transactions, the seller is inclined to choose the buyer through tendering or competitive negotiation to obtain the best price. Many well-known transactions in the international market, as well as many transactions handled by lawyers, are carried out in the same way. Under this type of transaction, the buyer is required to submit bidding documents (for more formal tendering procedures) or Letter of Intent (for general competitive negotiations, etc.) to the seller. The commonality of the above documents is that, in terms of their legal nature, they are all the offers made by the buyer, and they are legally binding on the buyer itself during the validity period of the document, such as a price. Of course, the buyer will also stipulate a series of conventional preconditions in this letter to reduce its own transaction risk.

3. Deposit agreement

Sometimes, the seller will open an exclusive negotiation period for a certain period of time (such as 1 ~ 3 months) to the relevant bidders on the condition that the purchaser/quoter submits a certain amount of deposit. At this point, it is necessary for both parties to sign a "Deposit Agreement." In the Agreement, there are clauses such as the nature of the deposit, the conditions for the return of the deposit, the duration of the exclusive negotiation period and the closing conditions must be clearly defined. When Chinese state-owned enterprises without overseas M&A experience have to sign such an agreement, they face the challenge of decision-making process. After all, they have to pay a fee when the transaction possibility is not clear.

4. Term sheet

Often both parties spend day and night negotiating the term sheet. Once the parties enter a relatively substantive negotiation stage, they negotiate the specific business conditions of the transaction, such as transaction price, payment arrangement, closing conditions and so on. The consensus reached by the business personnel of the two parties is stipulated in terms of the "term sheet" in order to formalize it in the contract. Because of its importance, lawyers from both sides are deeply involved in the negotiation and drafting of the term sheet, which is a key document in the transaction. However, in general, the term sheet is informal and there are no formal contracts, so the term sheet is not legally binding.

Compared with the memo that is also not legally binding, the main difference between the two is that the clauses of the memorandum are generally vague, and the description of the term sheet is usually very clear and specific, and the prototype of the main transaction document is beginning to take shape. The term sheet is a more formal document provided by the buyer after the completion of the preliminary due diligence. The term sheet usually outlines the main points of the proposed offer, including specific terms, transaction structure and proposed timing. They indicate that the buyer wishes to enter an exclusive period to close the transaction with additional due diligence and certain conditions met.

Case 6 – 5 Term Sheet

Term Sheet

The purpose of this term sheet is to set out the intended terms and conditions of the acquisition between (buyer) and (seller).

This Term Sheet represents the current understanding of the parties with respect to certain of the major issues relating to the proposed private offering.

This Term Sheet is intended solely as a basis for further discussion and is not intended to be and does not constitute a legally binding obligation except as provided under "Deposit", "Failure to Perform", "Confidentiality", "Dispute Resolution", "Exclusivity", "Expenses", "Governing Law and jurisdiction" and "Failure to Perform" below. No other legally binding obligations will be created, implied, or in inferred until the Definitive Purchase Agreement are executed and delivered by all parties.

1. Proposed transaction

The purchaser will designate an entity _____ to acquire the Assets as mentioned in Article 2 and business from the seller in accordance with the terms and conditions of the final agreement.

After signing the list of these terms, the parties intend to continue to negotiate with the best efforts and in good faith, with a view to reaching a final agreement that is consistent with the contents of the list of clauses as soon as possible.

2. Assets and business

The sale of assets will include the ownership, rights and benefits of the following assets: ⋯

3. Consideration

The aggregate consideration to be paid by the Buyer will be U. S. $_____ .

Confirmed by the buyer and the seller according to the results of the due diligence after the completion of the due diligence…

4. Conditions precedent

In addition to customary conditions precedent for transactions of this type, the Acquisition will be conditional on the following:

a. Due diligence being completed to the satisfaction of the Buyer

b. Receipt of any other required governmental or regulatory approvals

c. The purchaser shall have obtained all Chinese government approvals and internal approvals for the transaction

d. There are no material adverse changes in the assets and the representations and warranties made by the seller under the final agreement are true, accurate and complete at the time of signing and transaction.

5. Representations and Warranties

The Transaction Documents will contain representations and warranties that are customary for transactions of this size and nature. Such representations and warranties shall be made and effective upon the execution of a binding final agreement and shall remain true and accurate at the closing. The final agreement shall include the seller's and buyer's customary liability for compensation.

6. Due Diligence

The Seller shall allow the buyer's representatives (including legal counsel, financial personnel, technical team and environmental consultant) to enter the property and provide all documents and information reasonably required in time for the buyer to complete the necessary research, including but not limited to the due diligence on the property.

7. Costs

The parties will meet their own costs relating to the negotiation, documentation and implementation of the Acquisition.

8. Confidentiality

The terms of this Transaction and the existence of this Term Sheet shall be kept strictly confidential by all parties unless any party is obligated by law, or applicable stock exchange rules to disclose such information; provided that each party may disclose all information relating to this Term Sheet and the Transaction to their respective employees, agents, representatives, investors, partners, shareholders, legal and financial advisors on a need-to-know basis.

9. Exclusivity

None of the Company, its shareholders, its directors, or its officers, will conduct or solicit any discussions or negotiations with any third party regarding any sale of a material number of shares in the Company or any sale of a material part of the business and assets of the Company, unless approved in advance by the Buyer in writing.

10. Expiration date

These terms are effective upon signature until, and will expire on the end of exclusivity period.

11. Severability

The term sheet shall be deemed to be separable if any provision is deemed invalid or unenforceable. Without prejudice to the respective validity and enforceability of Articles 8 to 12.

12. Governing law and jurisdiction

This Term Sheet and the formal legal documentation will be governed by the laws of…

The parties are subject to the non-exclusive jurisdiction of the courts in the region.

It is hereby certified that the representatives of the parties have signed the term sheet on the first page.

Section 4

Share Purchase Agreement (SPA)

Case 6 – 6 Jiangsu Yuyue medical equipment & supply Co., Ltd. purchasing shares of Amsino Medical Group Company Limited and related party transaction

Main Content of Investment Agreement

1. Transaction subject

Investor: Yuyue Technology Co., Ltd. (hereinafter referred to as the "Yuyue Technology"), Jiangsu Yuyue medical equipment & supply Co., Ltd. (hereinafter referred to as the "Yuyue Medical")

Other signatories: Amsino Medical Group Company Limited (Amsino Medical), Richwell Assets Limited, Richard Ya Lee

2. Investment method and framework

a. Yuyue Technology and Yuyue Medical (hereinafter referred to as Yuyue party) signed an agreement with underlying company and the founding shareholders of underlying company, as the price of USD 1.5382 per share; the underlying company received respectively USD 13 273 682 in cash from Yuyue party, adding up to USD 26 547 364.

b. After this investment, Yuyue Technology holds 8 629 255 ordinary shares of the underlying company, accounting for 19.33% of all issued ordinary shares of the company. Meanwhile, Yuyue Medical holds 8 629 256 ordinary shares of the underlying company, accounting for 19.33% of all issued ordinary shares.

c. After this investment, Yuyue party will hold the company's ordinary shares. And the company's share structure is as follows:

No.	Name of shareholders	Type of shares	Number of shares	Percent
1	Richwell Assets Limited	Ordinary	15 824 912	35.45%
2	Richard Ya Lee	Ordinary	9 681 156	21.69%
3	Yuyue Medical	Ordinary	8 629 256	19.33%
4	Yuyue Technology	Ordinary	8 629 255	19.33%
5	Other shareholders	Ordinary	1 873 780	4.20%
	Total		44 638 359	100.00%

Note: According to relevant agreements, the underlying company shall repurchase preferred stock within 30 days after the payment of shares by Yuyue party, and the underlying company will have no preferred stock after this transaction.

3. Conditions and closing

(1) Conditions of investment

Only if each of the following closing conditions is met (or remitted by Yuyue party in writing), Yuyue Technology and Yuyue Medical are obligated to pay the company total amount that promised:

a. The company has obtained and completed all necessary internal consent, approval, authorization and other actions for signing and executing this Agreement and other transaction documents on the signature date.

b. All statements and warranties, made by the company and founding shareholders in this Agreement and agreement on ordinary shares purchase by Yuyue party, shall be true, accurate and not misleading in all respects.

c. The Supplement Agreement for Preferred Share Repurchase shall be formally signed by the company and preferred shareholders on signature date, and be validated since then.

d. The founding shareholders and the company have reached an agreement with Yuyue party on the terms of Articles of Association that have been revised and restated after purchase by Yuyue.

e. As of the date that Yuyue paid for the purchase, there were no major events that caused the company to fail to operate, and no any applicable laws, court decisions and government orders that prohibited this investment or made this investment illegal or invalid.

f. To avoid doubt, if the closing conditions of Purchase Document are more detailed than these investment conditions above, the other closing conditions listed in Purchase Document (except the investment conditions above) shall be based on Purchase Document.

(2) Closing of investment

a. After the Investment Agreement is signed and all the conditions precedent set by Agreement are met, Yuyue party will pay the company full amount of this purchase no later than May 30, 2017.

b. The company shall repurchase preferred shares within 30 days after the payment of shares by Yuyue party, and shall complete the closing of shares and corresponding alterations of business registration (including without limitation the alterations of registration on company shares, shareholders and members of board of directors) within 5 days, after the repurchase of preferred shares. The parties hereby agree that the shares closing depends on the satisfaction of each of the following conditions (unless Yuyue party agrees to remit it in writing):

(a) Yuyue party sends a notice on shares closing to the company.

(b) Shares held by preferred shareholders are repurchased completely.

(c) All statements and warranties (about closing date) made by the company and founding shareholders in this Agreement are true, accurate and not misleading in all respects.

(d) The company and founding shareholders have no default in transaction documents.

(e) The company, founding shareholders and other shareholders approve the Articles of Association that have been revised and restated on shares closing, as well as other relevant rights documents.

(f) Onle all the conditions of these closing terms are met, the company will immediately issue a certain number of ordinary shares that are allocated in this Agreement to Yuyue party, and update the company's shareholder register accordingly.

4. Corporate governance

After the closing of this investment, the board of directors shall have five directors. Among them, founding shareholders have the right to appoint three directors, and Yuyue Technology and Yuyue Medical respectively have right to appoint one director. Richard Ya Lee will be appointed as the company's Chairman and CEO.

1. Main Transaction Agreements

The main transaction documents may be share purchase agreement, asset transfer agreement, business transfer agreement, capital increase agreement, etc. The main transaction document is the most critical legal document in the entire transaction. In general, the most important clauses in the main transaction document are "the seller's Representations and Warranties" "Conditions precedent to the closing" "Restriction of seller's liabilities", etc.

At the signing stage of the main transaction document, there are also some measures taken immediately after signing the main transaction document, which are usually prepared long before signing the main transaction document. These measures include not only efforts to obtain sufficient funds to pay the seller, but also necessary steps for actual transfer and preparation of statutory/regulatory documents.

(1) The seller's Representations and Warranties

The seller's Representations and Warranties mean that the Seller guarantees that the object of sale is not defective. Seller's Representations and Warranties refer to the seller's ownership of the target company, company records, finances, taxes, major contracts, real estate, major equipment, intellectual property rights, compliance, litigation (including non-litigation disputes), and confidentiality of information on the date of signing of the equity transaction documents. Unless otherwise stated, the seller will usually repeat the same Representations and Warranties on the closing date. The seller's breach of the Representations and Warranties usually results in the buyer's right to claim damages from the seller.

Seller's Representations and Warranties mostly supplement the risks that due diligence cannot solve. Due diligence generally cannot cover every aspect, such as intellectual property rights, compliance issues, data protection, anti-corruption (FCPA), etc.

(2) Conditions precedent to the closing

Risks learned through due diligence cannot be solved by Representations and Warranties, but by setting up the seller's obligations before closing. After the signing of the share purchase agreement, whether the closing of the deal (share purchase and payment of the price) is subject to the satisfaction or exemption of certain conditions is precedent.

Closing is generally subject to certain conditions that may be specific to the transaction and / or required by law. Common Conditions precedent include: government approval (including Chinese government's overseas investment approval and approval by the target government); the consent of the opposite party of the major contract to the transaction (such as the energy project, the consent of the purchaser under the power purchase agreement), significant adverse effects, etc.

Examples are statutory/regulatory conditions, especially the approval of merger and acquisition control, and regulatory approval, especially the approval of transaction regulatory authorities, etc. For example, the acquisition of 25% of German companies by non-EU/EFTA buyers is also subject to the approval by the German Ministry of Economy and Technology.

The specific conditions of the transaction may be that the third party waives the right to terminate the major contract due to the change of control right (equity transaction), the third party agrees to transfer the major contract or assets (asset transaction), and the seller completes the major preparatory action, etc. If these conditions have not been met or exempted within the agreed time limit, either party may terminate the agreement and both parties shall not be liable (except for the case of agreed breakup fee or reverse breakup fee). On the contrary, if the conditions are met as scheduled, both parties are obliged to deliver according to the contract.

(3) Restriction of seller's liabilities

The compensation clause is related to the buyer's knowledge. The buyer's knowledge is usually exempted from the seller's responsibility. Therefore, the seller's best preparation is to disclose properly before signing. In due diligence, the exclusion of liability for "knowing" due to disclosure depends on the agreement.

The minimum claim limit: It means the loss can be claimed only if the buyer's claim amount reaches a certain minimum amount, and the losses that can be claimed need to be superimposed over a certain minimum amount before the buyer can request the claim. The maximum amount of indemnification: It means that the seller's total liability does not exceed a certain limit. Generally speaking, a certain proportion is set according to the purchase consideration.

Term limitation: It means that the seller has a certain period of time, otherwise the claim cannot be made. The buyer is usually required to notify the seller in writing of compensation without undue delay.

2. *Escrow account agreement*

In order to ensure the security and normal operation of the relevant payment under the SPA, usually the parties to the transaction will arrange the payment by setting up an escrow account. As a result, the parties will need to sign the appropriate *Escrow Account Agreement* with the account custodian selected by the parties. In the *Escrow Account Agreement*, there should be conditions for the establishment of the escrow account, specific conditions and nodes for the custodian bank (or other custodians) to pay the corresponding amount to the seller.

3. Trademark / technology licensing agreement, trademark / technology transfer agreement, etc.

If the nature of the main transaction is business transfer, it usually involves trademark and/or technology licensing agreement, trademark and/or technology transfer agreement, etc. By signing such agreements, the buyer may acquire the right to use or other rights necessary for the operation of the target business with respect to the trademark or technology concerned.

4. Supplementary agreement of the original shareholder agreement

If the nature of the main transaction is to share purchase or capital increase, the buyer will become the new shareholder of the target company after the transaction is completed. Therefore, the two parties need to sign the corresponding agreement documents, that is, to identify the new shareholder status of the purchaser and define the relationship between the new shareholders and the original shareholders according to the supplementary agreement of the original shareholders' agreement of the target company. Of course, if the purchaser becomes the sole shareholder of the target company by acquiring all the shares held by the original shareholders of the company, the above-mentioned agreement documents are not neccessary. In this case, the buyer is only required to register the shareholders in the relevant business registration institution in accordance with the corresponding requirements of the corresponding laws and regulations of the target company.

CHAPTER 7

THE "BELT AND ROAD" COUNTRIES' DOMESTIC AND OVERSEAS SUPERVISION AND COMPLIANCE

Section 1
Changes of Supervision Environment

On August 18th, 2017, Article of the State Council, [2017], No. 74 were issued. It consists of six chapters. The document clarifies the current guiding ideology and basic principles in respect to guiding and regulating the cross-border investment of Chinese enterprises; it also clarifies the overseas investment that are encouraged, restricted, and prohibited and outlines some safeguarding measures. In terms of guiding ideology, it emphasizes that with the construction of the "Belt and Road" as the commander, the reform of overseas investment system and mechanism shall be deepened, enterprises' overseas investment directions shall be further guided and regulated, and enterprises shall be urged to rationally and orderly carry out overseas investment activities. Overseas investment risks shall be prevented and managed; the sustainable and sound development of the overseas investments shall be promoted; and mutual benefits and win-win results, and joint development with the investment target countries shall be achieved.

In terms of the basic principles, four principles shall be insisted on. Firstly, it insists on the principle that the enterprise is the main body. Overseas investments shall be made under the commercial principles and international practices, enterprises shall make decisions at their own discretion, assume sole responsibilities for their profits or losses, and assume risks on their own under the direction of the governments. Secondly, it insists on deepening reform. The overseas investment management method dominated by the registration system shall be insisted on, a managed market-oriented operating mechanism shall be implemented under the capital items, and the directions of enterprises' overseas investments shall be directed and regulated according to the model of "encouraging development + negative list". Thirdly, it insists on mutual benefits and win-win results. Enterprises shall be directed to consider the national conditions and actual needs of the investment target countries, and focus on carrying out mutually beneficial cooperation with local governments and enterprises. Fourthly, it insists on the principle that risk prevention is a must. The focus and rhythm of overseas investments shall be rationally grasped, the ex-ante, interim and ex-post supervision of the overseas investments shall be actively and effectively conducted, and various risks shall be effectively prevented.

On December 26th, 2017, the National Development and Reform Commission (hereinafter referred to as NDRC) issued the "Order of the NDRC, [2017], No. 11", which took effect on March 1, 2018. Compared with the current "Order of the NDRC, [2014], No. 9", "Order of the NDRC, [2017], No. 11" simplifies the ex-ante management process, further covering the interim and ex-post supervision. The most notable point is the elimination of the "trail bar" system. As "Order of the NDRC, [2014], No. 9" the so-called "trail bar" system means that for an overseas acquisition or bidding project with the amount of Chinese investment of USD 300 million or above, the investor shall, before carrying out substantive work with a foreign party, submit a project information report to NDRC. The NDRC shall, upon receipt of the project information report, issue a confirmation letter within seven working days if the project conforms to the national overseas investment policies. Indeed, "Order of the NDRC, [2017], No. 11" has become stricter for Chinese domestic investment entities. The following two points deserve special attention:

Section 2: "Overseas investment" means the investment activities that an enterprise in the territory of the People's Republic of China (hereinafter referred to as the "investor"), directly or through an overseas enterprise controlled by it, acquires overseas any ownership, right of control, right of business management, or other relevant rights and interests, by contributing assets or rights and interests, providing financing or guarantee, or any other means.

Section 63: These Measures shall apply, mutatis mutandis, to domestic enterprises and natural persons investing through enterprises controlled by them overseas or in regions such as Hong Kong, Macao and Taiwan.

These Measures shall not apply to overseas investment directly made by a domestic natural person. These Measures shall not apply to investment in Hong Kong, Macao or Taiwan region directly made by a domestic natural person.

It is worth noting that the "Order of the NDRC, [2017], No. 11" expanded the scope of application. As stipulated in the Section 62 of the Order of the NDRC, [2017], No. 11, investment in Hong Kong, Macao and Taiwan regions carried out by domestic enterprises through enterprises controlled by them applies to "Order of the NDRC, [2017], No. 11". If a natural person in the territory conducts investment abroad, through enterprises controlled by them in regions such as Hong Kong, Macao and Taiwan, the order is also applicable. For overseas investment, the "Order of the NDRC, [2017], No. 11" contains almost everything.

During the two sessions in 2017, Mr. Ding Shizhong, deputy of the National People's Congress and Chairman of the Board of Anta Group, submitted the *Proposal on Further Improving Laws and Regulations to Support Cross-border M&As of Private Enterprises*. He proposed to formulate a national unified and specialized *Law of Enterprise Cross-border M&A* or come up with a *Regulation of Private Enterprise Cross-border M&A*. The law and regulation should regulate corporate M&As, clearly stipulate the functions, procedures and rights and obligations of government administrative in M&A and clarify the asset evaluation, property ownership and tax management in M&A. It should also stipulate the treatment of creditor's right and debt, as well as the status and arrangement of employees. Mr. Ding Shizhong made this statement from the perspective of the necessary support for cross-border M&As by private enterprises. Obviously, this statement is caused by the specific needs of his own company. It is of a great practical significance for the global expansion of domestic private enterprises.

Section 2

Domestic Supervision: Development and Reform Departments, Commerce and State Administration of Foreign Exchange Departments

Under the current legal system in China, domestic enterprises are mainly supervised by the three kinds of parties for overseas investment. They are the national development and reform departments, commercial departments and state administration of foreign exchange departments. From 2016 up to the present, some new policies on overseas investment supervision have been introduced.

Section 2 of Order of the NDRC, 〔2017〕, No. 11 not only clarifies the definition of overseas investment but also enumerates investment activities, which helps investment entities to estimate whether their overseas activities are within the scope of overseas investment.

According to the Order of the NDRC, 〔2017〕, No. 11, "overseas investment activities" mainly include without limitation the following circumstances:

- Acquiring the ownership of, the right to use, and other rights and interests in land overseas.
- Acquiring a concession to prospect or exploit and other rights and interests in overseas natural resources.
- Acquiring the ownership of, the right of business management of, and other rights and interests in overseas infrastructure.
- Acquiring the ownership of, the right of business management of, and other rights and interests in any overseas enterprise or asset.

- New construction, reconstruction, or expansion of overseas fixed assets.
- Forming a new overseas enterprise or increasing investment in an existing overseas enterprise.
- Forming a new or acquiring a non-controlling stake in an overseas equity investment fund.
- Controlling an overseas enterprise or asset by an agreement, a trust, or any other means.

By Section 25 of Order of the NDRC, [2014], No. 9, "Where an investor launches an overseas investment project subject to confirmation by or registration with the NDRC, it shall, before concluding with a foreign party a legally binding final document, secure a confirmation document or registration notice issued by the NDRC; or may specify in the document that the condition for enforcement of the document is to secure the confirmation document or registration notice issued by the NDRC according to the law." In the international market, governmental confirmation is usually not a condition for the agreement to be effective, but it is treated as a closing condition. In fact, the reality is not completely consistent with regulations to a certain extent. For example, many cross-border M&A still used governmental confirmation as a closing condition rather than an effective condition. Section 32 of Order of the NDRC, [2017], No. 11 changes the confirmation and registration from conditions making agreements effective to conditions making projects implemented. This article stipulates that "for a project subject to confirmation or recordation management, the investor shall obtain a project confirmation document or registration notice before implementing the project." According to this article, "before implementing the project" means obtaining the same documentation before the investor or an overseas enterprise controlled by it invests assets or rights and interests [except front-end costs of the project that are already undergoing confirmation or recordation in accordance with Section 17 of Order of the NDRC, [2017], No. 11] or provides financing or guarantee for the project.

1. Encouraging development plus a negative list

The statement "encouraged overseas direct investments" was first proposed as a system in the Article, [2017], No. 74 of the State Council The wording of the Overseas Direct Investment (ODI) is opposite of Foreign Direct Investment (FDI). Negative list was announced in FDI, which corresponds to ODI. And the negative list system was also introduced in ODI. Now, the main negative list contains some restricted, encouraged and prohibited items by the Article of the State Council, [2017], No. 74. In addition, the State-owned Assets Supervision and Administration Commission of the State Council (hereinafter referred to as SASAC) has proposed a negative list of the overseas investment by central state-owned enterprises, including some prohibited items of certain industries. Therefore, the supervision of overseas investment is mainly based on the encouraging development and negative list.

(1) Large adjustments in sensitive industries

Based on Order of the NDRC, [2014], No. 9, the Order of the NDRC, [2017], No. 11 adjusted the scope of "sensitive countries and regions" and "sensitive industries", and clearly defined overseas investment involving sensitive countries, regions and industries as "sensitive items". For sensitive industries in addition to simply listing, Order of the NDRC, [2017], No. 11 also authorizes NDRC to publish a catalogue of sensitive industries. On January 31st, 2018, NDRC issued the *Catalogue of Overseas Investment Sensitive Industries* (2018). For the first time, sensitive industries for overseas investment in the form of separate sensitive industry catalogues is published; the catalogue lists down the research, production or maintenance of arms, exploitation or utilization of cross-border water resources and news media as sensitive industries for overseas investment. According to Article of the State Council, [2017], No. 74, the industries whose cross-border investment needs to be restricted (including Real estate, Hotel, Movie, Entertainment, Sports club and PE fund or investment platform setting no specific industry project overseas) are also in the catalogue, as form7-1.

Form 7-1　Changes in Sensitive Industries

Order No. 9 (2014) of NDRC	Content	Changes
➤ Basic telecommunication operation; ➤ Exploitation or utilization of cross-border water resources; ➤ Large-scale development of land; ➤ Electric Transmission mains; ➤ Power grid; ➤ News media.	➤ Research, production or maintenance of arms; ➤ Exploitation or utilization of cross-border water resources; ➤ News media; ➤ Industries of which cross-border investment needs to be restricted according to Article of the State Council, [2017], No. 74: 1) Real estate; 2) Hotel; 3) Movie; 4) Entertainment; 5) Sports club; 6) PE fund or investment platform setting no specific industry project overseas.	➤ Deleted: Basic telecommunication operation, Large-scale development of land, Transmission mains, Power grid; ➤ Added: Research, production or maintenance of arms, industries whose cross-border investment needs to be restricted (including Real estate, Hotel, Movie, Entertainment, Sports club and PE fund or investment platform setting no specific industry project overseas); ➤ Reserved: Exploitation or utilization of cross-border water resources, News media.

(2) Clear guidance for overseas investment

By Article of the State Council [2017], No. 74, the regulation of overseas investment introduces a "negative list" model similar to the foreign direct investment, and divides overseas investment into three types: encouraged, restricted and prohibited.

1) Encouraged overseas investment

The list includes: overseas investments on the infrastructures conducive to the construction of the "Road and Belt Initiative"; overseas investments advancing the output of superior production capacity, high-quality equipment, and applicable technology; investment cooperation with overseas high-tech and advanced manufacturing enterprises to establish research and development centers abroad; Investments on exploration and development of the overseas oil and gas, minerals and other energy resources ; investment cooperation in the agriculture, forestry, animal husbandry, fishery and other areas; overseas investments in the business, culture, logistics and other service fields. In addition, it supports qualified financial institutions to establish branches and service networks overseas to conduct business in compliance with the laws and regulations.

2) Restricted overseas investment

Restricted overseas investment includes five cases. They are:

a. overseas investments made in the sensitive countries and regions that have not established diplomatic relations with China, that are in chaos caused by war, or that need to be restricted as prescribed by the bilateral and multilateral treaties or agreements concluded with China;

b. overseas investments in real estate, hotels, movie, entertainment, and sports clubs, among others;

c. PE fund or investment platform setting no specific industry project overseas;

d. overseas investments made with backward production equipment failing to satisfy the technical standards or requirements of the investment target countries;

e. overseas investments that do not meet the standards of the investment target countries in terms of environmental protection, energy consumption or safety standards. As Article of the State Council, [2017], No. 74 stipulates, the first three categories of overseas investments shall be approved by the competent departments of the overseas investments.

3) Prohibited overseas investment

Article of the State Council, [2017], No. 74 prohibits domestic enterprises from participating in overseas investments that endanger or may endanger national interests and national security; it lists five cases, including:

a. overseas investments involving the output of the core technologies and products of the military industry without the approval of the state;

b. overseas investments using the technologies, techniques and products prohibited to be exported by China;

c. overseas investments in the gambling industry, the pornography industry, etc.

d. overseas investments prohibited as prescribed by the international treaties concluded by China or taken part in by China;

e. other overseas investments that endanger or may endanger national interests and national security.

2. Registration is the mainstream with the confirmation as a supplement

Registration is the main mechanism with the confirmation being a supplement. This mechanism is not novel. The NDRC and Ministry of Commerce have kept pace. In general, it is a guiding ideology of administrative decentralization.

(1) Division of registration and confirmation & division of authority by NDRC

Overseas investment consists of two parts; one is overseas direct investment (ODI), and the other is domestic enterprises and natural persons investing through enterprise controlled by them overseas or in regions such as Hong Kong, Macao, and Taiwan. Now, overseas direct investments are divided into sensitive and non-sensitive. Sensitive direct investments involves sensitive countries, regions and industries. If your potential investment project is sort out as sensitive one, the investment must get the confirmation of NDRC. If it is non-sensitive items, it depends on the investor. If the investor is a central state-owned enterprise (a state-owned enterprise that SASAC directly as the investor), it needs to go directly to NDRC for registration. For local enterprises, if it is a large-amount & non-sensitive project, it is directed to NDRC for registration; if it is less than USD 300 million, then it is directed to the local development and reform department for registration.

Overseas indirect investments are also divided into sensitive and non-sensitive parts; the former need to get recorded by NDRC, while a large number of the latter need to submit a pre-report to NDRC; it's a new system and no longer the registration. In the online reporting system of the NDRC, it is required to just input relevant project information and the report is concluded. For the amount that is less than USD 300 million, there is no need to comply with the regulatory procedures under Order of the NDRC, [2017], No. 11.

The beforehand regulatory procedures that all overseas investment projects shall implement under Order of the NDRC, [2017], No. 11, as form 7-2.

Form 7-2 The beforehand regulatory procedures that all overseas investment projects shall implement under Order of the NDRC, [2017], No. 11

Project Type	Domestic Investor's Investment	Overseas investment projects directly undertaken by the investment entity (involving the direct investment of domestic investment entities in assets, interests or providing financing and guarantees)	An overseas investment project undertaken by an investment entity through an enterprise controlled by it overseas or in regions such as Hong Kong, Macao, and Taiwan (not involving domestic investment entities directly investing in assets, rights or providing financing or guarantee)
Sensitive Project	Regardless of size	Confirmed by NDRC	Confirmed by NDRC
Non-sensitive Project	USD 300 million and above	Recorded by NDRC	Report large non-sensitive project to NDRC
	Less than USD 300 million	Central state-owned enterprise: recorded by NDRC Local enterprise: recorded by Provincial Development and Reform Department	No need to perform confirmation, recordation and prereport

(2) Division of registration and confirmation & division of authority by commercial department

Next is the division of system filling approval and authority division of the commercial department. If it is both a central state-owned enterprise and a "double sensitive" project, you need to get confirmation from the Ministry of Commerce, while if it is a central state-owned enterprise but not a sensitive project, only approaching the Ministry of Commerce for registration is necessary. For local enterprises, if it is a "double sensitive" project, it shall be initially reviewed by the provincial commerce department, then it needs to receive the final confirmation by the Ministry of Commerce. If it is a non-sensitive project, it only needs registration of the provincial commerce department. The specific confirmation and registration authority of the commerce department is mainly divided into the central or local enterprises and by whether sensitive countries, regions and industries are involved. The specific classification standards are as form 7-3.

Form 7-3 The specific classification standards of sensitive countries

Company Type	Project Type	Approving Authority		Remarks
		Ministry of Commerce	Provincial Commercial Department	
Central state-owned enterprises	Involving sensitive countries and regions, sensitive industries	Confirmed		
	Other projects	Recorded		
Local enterprises	Involving sensitive countries and regions, sensitive industries	Confirmed	Preliminary examination	For overseas investment, which corresponds to the confirmed process, local enterprises should apply to the Ministry of Commerce through provincial commercial department.
	Other projects		Recorded	

(3) Registration procedure of Administration of Foreign Exchange Department

The State Administration of Foreign Exchange (hereinafter referred to as "SAFE") is a foreign exchange registration department, although it cannot be regarded as an investment supervision department in a strict sense. But overseas investment should be examine and confirmed by SAFE during the critical process of overseas investment remitting money overseas. In fact, it is as important as the NDRC and the Ministry of Commerce mentioned earlier. According to the "*Operating Guidelines for Foreign Exchange Business in Direct Investment, the Annex of Notice of the*

State Administration of Foreign Exchange on Further Simplifying and Improving Policies for the Foreign Exchange Administration of Direct Investment (*No.* 13 〔2015〕 *of the SAFE*)" issued by SAFE in 2015, the main procedures for the registration of upfront expenses and foreign exchange for overseas direct investments by domestic institutions are listed in form 7-4.

Form 7-4 The main procedures for the registration of upfront expenses and foreign exchange for overseas direct investments by domestic institutions

Bank handling business	Audit material	Work principle	Remarks
Registration of upfront expenses for overseas direct investment by domestic institutions	(1) For the business remitting overseas and directly investing upfront fees, the following materials should be submitted: 1) *Overseas direct investment of Foreign Exchange Registration Application Form.* 2) Business license and Organization code certificate. (2) For the domestic institutions purchasing overseas property for its overseas branches, representative agencies or other non-independent accounting institutions, the following materials should be submitted: 1) *Overseas direct investment of Foreign Exchange Registration Application Form.* 2) Confirmation/recordation documents or registration certificates of non-independent accounting institutions such as branches or representatives established abroad. 3) Overseas housing purchase contract or agreement. 4) Other authenticity documents.	1) Domestic institutions (including domestic enterprises, banks and non-bank financial institutions, the same below) remit overseas upfront expenses, the total remittances shall not exceed USD 3 million in principle and shall not exceed 15% of the total amount of Chinese investment. 2) The upfront expenses of domestic institutions remitted abroad may be included in the total amount of their overseas direct investment. 3) After the bank processes the pre-payment procedures for the domestic institutions through the capital project information system of the foreign exchange bureau, the domestic institutions will go to the bank for the payment of the subsequent funds. 4) If a domestic investor has not established an overseas investment project or purchased an overseas property within 6 months from	Not on the premise of obtaining *The Certificate of Overseas investment*

Form 7-4 continued

Bank handling business	Audit material	Work principle	Remarks
Registration of foreign exchange for overseas direct investment by domestic institutions	1) *Overseas direct investment of Foreign Exchange Registration Application Form.* 2) Business License or Registration Certificate with Organization Code Certificate (If multiple domestic institutions jointly implement an oversea direct investment, they should submit Business License or Registration Certificate with Organization Code Certificate from each institutions). 3) The overseas investment of a non-financial enterprise should offer *The Certificate of Overseas investment*; The overseas investment of a financial institution shall provide the confirmation document or no-objection letter of the relevant financial authorities for the investment. 4) Domestic Company or its shareholders must offer charging foreign-invested enterprise confirmation certificate and filling of the foreign investment enterprise business license if they get the overseas equities when the foreign investors acquire the domestic company.	the date of remittance of the upfront expenses, it shall report the use of the previous fee to the foreign exchange bureau of the place of registration and return the remaining funds. If there is an objective reason, the account opening entity may submit an explanation letter to the original registered bank to apply for an extension, with the consent of the bank, the 6-month period may be extended appropriately, but the maximum period may not exceed 12 months. 5) If there is an objective reason for which the early stage of the cost of the total amount remitted in excess of USD 3 million or more than 15% of total Chinese investment, domestic investors need to submit an application to the registered foreign exchange bureau (the foreign exchange bureau shall operate the case-by-case business review system).	Need to obtain *the Certificate of Overseas Investment and Recordation Notice*

3. Importance of interim and ex-post supervision

Originally, the Order of the NDRC, [2014], No. 9 and the Order of the

Ministry of Commerce, [2014], No. 13 more focused on ex-ante supervision, which are the confirmation, recordation and reporting. After the issuance of Order of the NDRC, [2017], No. 11, these links became more detailed. Meanwhile, Order of the NDRC, [2017], No. 11 and the Order No. 24 [2018] (Shang He Fa [2018] No. 24), Circular of the state-owned Assets Supervision Commission of the people's Bank of China, China Securities Regulatory Commission, China Insurance Regulatory Commission, and foreign exchange bureau of the Ministry of Commerce on printing and distributing the Interim Measures for foreign investment record (APPROVAL) report, led by the Ministry of Commerce and joined by many ministries, will focus on the reporting system to achieve overseas interim investment and ex post investment supervision. "Mandatory reporting for each registration (or confirmation)", the following progresses of projects need to submit corresponding reports to the National Development and Reform Commission (NDRC), and then submit annual reports to the Ministry of Commerce. These reports are routine reports, containing periodic information such as the progress achieved, the money invested, and the project implementation content. Besides, some sudden, major and adverse situations also need to be reported to the Ministry of Commerce. For example, if there are major accidents in the projects or diplomatic disputes with the host country, reports need to be submitted. If these interim and ex post reports are not submitted and the competent departments detect it, the punishment is at place. The most typical punishment is the entry of the violation information into the national credit information sharing platform. In more serious cases, the confirmation and registration of the overseas investments would be suspended, including new projects and taking corresponding measures.

(1) Supervision by development and reform department

Section No. 43, 44, 45 of Order of the NDRC, [2017], No. 11 separately added the system of reporting materially adverse circumstances, reporting the completion of the project and inquiring as well as reporting the major matters. The supervision by development and reform department is not only the part of ex-ante process, but also of the interim and ex-post processes. As Article No. 44 of Order of the NDRC, [2017], No. 11 referred, "For a project subject to confirmation or registration management, the investor shall, within 20 working days of the completion of the project, submit a project completion reporting form through the network system. It refers to the completion of the construction project, the delivery of the equity or assets of the investment object, the completion of the investment amount of the Chinese side, etc."

Overseas investments carried out by the domestic enterprises shall get confirmation or registration of its projects, report related information and cooperate in the inspection. According to the Order of the NDRC, [2017], No. 11, the main legal basis, the supervision object concludes non-financial or financial enterprise, public institutions, social groups, and other non-enterprise organizations and domestic enterprises and natural persons investing through enterprises controlled by them overseas or in regions such as Hong Kong, Macao and Taiwan. Compared to Order of the NDRC, [2014], No. 9, Order of the NDRC, [2017], No. 11 enlarges its scope of supervision objects and proposes to supervise indirectly the overseas investments. and for the first time, the main body of domestic enterprises located abroad and the overseas enterprises controlled by domestic natural persons or enterprises from Hong Kong, Macao and Taiwan regions are included in the scope of supervision.

(2) Supervision by commercial or financial departments

Financial and non-financial enterprises shall get confirmed or recorded by the commerce department or financial department when carrying out overseas investments. The commerce departments make management of confirmation and registration for the non-financial enterprises by Order of the Ministry of Commerce, [2014], No. 3, and issue *the Overseas Investment Certificate for Enterprises* to enterprises that are granted registration or confirmation. Meanwhile, competent financial departments (China Security Regulatory Commission, China Banking and Insurance Regulatory

Commission) shall respectively make management of confirmation and registration for the financial enterprises by regulations.

It's reminded that overseas investments carried out by the central state-owned enterprises are supervised and managed by Order No. 35 of the SASAC.

(3) Management by administration of foreign exchange department

After the development and reform department as well as commerce or financial departments grant the confirmation or registration, investors shall register for the direct overseas investments in the light of the requirements of foreign exchange department. Notice of the No. 13 [2015] of the SAFE, published on February 28, 2015 canceled confirmation system of direct overseas investments, changing it into the model of bank handling and SAFE supervising. Banks handle registration of direct overseas investments directly and SAFE supervises that through banks indirectly.

According to the current law and regulation, the investments by domestic natural persons that are directly investing in enterprises overseas or in regions such as Hong Kong, Macao, and Taiwan are not under the supervision of Order of the NDRC, [2017], No. 11. The management of this is led by SAFE, while the development and reform department and commerce department are not responsible for it. No. 37 [2014] of the SAFE, hereinafter referred to as "Article No. 37" is the main legal base for the direct overseas investment by the domestic natural persons. In accordance with Article No. 37, SAFE shall manage the companies with the special purpose established by the domestic individuals and related registration matters, before the domestic residents contribute capital to the company with special purpose through domestic legal assets or interests; they shall apply to SAFE for foreign exchange registration. After the overseas investment is registered, the following business can be handled. However, it should be noted that Article No. 37 only applies to the overseas investment and financing activities of domestic natural individuals for the purpose of inbound investment, and does not apply to the overseas industrial investment by the domestic natural individuals.

(4) Main content of *interim measures for the registration (or confirmation) and reporting of overseas investment*

After Order of the NDRC, [2017], No. 11, the Ministry of Commerce, the People's Bank of China, the SASAC, the former China Banking Regulatory Commission, the former China Securities Regulatory Commission, the China Insurance Regulatory Commission and the State Administration of Foreign Exchange jointly issued Order of the Ministry of Commerce, [2018], No. 24, taking effect from the date of publication. The Interim Measures adopt an administrative mode of multilevel administration by categorization, unified information management, and joint punishment of violations of regulations.

According to the Interim Measures, the commerce and financial regulatory departments shall, according to their respective duties, be responsible for administering the registration or confirmation processes of outbound investment made by domestic investors. SASAC shall be responsible for the supervision and administration of outbound investment made by central state-owned enterprises in which it performs duties as a capital contributor. Furthermore, the Interim Measures clarified the division of responsibilities of confirmation and registration for different overseas investors. The Measures stipulate that the Ministry of Commerce shall collect the information on the confirmation, registration and reporting of overseas investment; each department shall regularly notify the Ministry of Commerce of this information; the Ministry of Commerce shall regularly provide the aforesaid departments and institutions with feedback on the information collected for sharing; this can initially establish the collecting and sharing mechanism of internal information between departments, which helps each department to carry out monitoring reports, analysis and early warning, and effective intervention based on the aggregated information.

At the same time, the Interim Measures also clarified the corresponding disciplinary measures for violations by the domestic investors. For example, "Where a domestic investor fails to undergo the registration (or confirmation) formalities or performs the information reporting obligations as required by these Measures, the Ministry of Commerce shall, in conjunction with the relevant departments, take reminding, interview, notification, and other measures according to the circumstances, input the violation of regulations case in the national credit information sharing platform when necessary, and if any administrative punishment is imposed on the enterprise, record and publish it under the enterprise's name through the national enterprise information publication system. " Besides, "where, in the course of regulation, a relevant department discovers any conduct such as tax evasion or avoidance or foreign exchange fraud of a domestic investor, it shall notify the taxation, public security, industry and commerce, foreign exchange administration, and other departments for handling the matter according to the law. "

Section 3
Overseas Supervision: Anti-monopoly Review and Governmental Approval

1. Anti-monopoly review

The legislative basis of anti-monopoly law is M&As, which deduces that enterprises monopolize. It is following the subsequent reasoning: the industry leader consumes the secondary leader – the industry leader becomes a dominant one – and there is no competition in the industry from then on. Therefore, M&As only benefit for capital, enterprises.

Anti-monopoly law is a law to supervise the distribution of economic power in business. It is an important law to ensure healthy competition, prosperity and economic growth of enterprises. The Anti-monopoly law applies to almost all industries and sectors, covering all levels of business, including manufacturing, transportation, distribution and marketing. Anti-monopoly law prohibits many business activities that restrict trade, such as price manipulation, mergers of enterprises that may weaken the enthusiasm of certain market competition, and predatory acts aimed at acquiring or holding monopoly rights. The purpose of anti-monopoly law is to prevent excessive concentration of economic power on large enterprises or groups. Because these enterprises or groups may take advantage of the dominant position or economic advantage of monopoly, which will adversely affect free competition and ultimately damage the interests of consumers.

The following two highly concerning Chinese central state-owned enterprises' overseas investment M&As involve overseas antitrust review:

On March 11th, 2016, the spokesperson of Ministry of Foreign Affairs announced: China welcomes the EU's approval of Sino-French enterprises to cooperate in the construction of the Hinckley Point nuclear power plant in the UK and looks forward to continuous progress. According to reports, the EU recently approved the cooperation between EDF and China General Nuclear Power Corporation to build the Hinkley Point nuclear power plant. According to the findings of the EU anti-monopoly regulator, the cooperation will not hinder the competition of the UK electricity market. The spokesperson said that China welcomes the EU's decision.

In April 4th, 2017, the US Federal Trade Commission (FTC) approved the acquisition of Syngenta by ChemChina. The FTC approved the transaction on the condition that ChemChina would peel off herbicide paraquat, insecticide avermectin and fungicide chlorothalonil three products in the United States business. According to the FTC, Syngenta owns these three products and has an important market share in the United States. At the same time, Adama, the subsidiary of ChemChina is the most popular pesticide supplier in the United States. Without divestiture, mergers are likely to create monopolies in the United States, forcing customers to pay the high prices for these products.

After evaluating the M&A, the anti-monopoly law enforcement agency may give three possible feedbacks: prohibition, approval with conditions or approval. In case of the following two examples of listed companies, the necessity of obtaining anti-monopoly review for M&A transactions becomes clear.

Case 7 – 1 *Announcement of Hebei Xuanhua Construction Machinery Co., Ltd. on passing the South African anti-monopoly review*

Stock code: 000923   Stock short name: Hebei Xuangong   No. 2017-36

Hebei Xuanhua Construction Machinery Co., Ltd.

Announcement on the restructuring of material assets passing

South African anti-monopoly review

The company and all members of the board of directors guarantee the truthfulness, accuracy and completeness of the information disclosure, and there are no false records, misleading statements or major omissions. Hebei Xuanhua Construction Machinery Co., Ltd. (hereinafter referred to as the "Company") recently received approval without conditions from the Competition Tribunal of South Africa. The company's material asset restructuring has passed the anti-monopoly of South Africa. The company's material asset restructuring still requires China's anti-monopoly review, the confirmation/recordation by the China's ministry of commerce, development and reform department and China Securities Regulatory Commission's approval of issuing shares to purchase assets, collecting matching funds and making related transactions; it can be implemented only after approval by the relevant departments. The company will timely disclose information based on the progress of this material asset restructuring, and ask investors to pay attention to investment risks.

Notice is hereby given.

Hebei Xuanhua Construction Machinery Co., Ltd. Board of Directors

May 26, 2017

Case 7 – 2   Announcement of China Molybdenum Co. , Ltd. on obtaining Turkish competition authority's approval without conditions

China Molybdenum Co. , Ltd. Announcement on acquisition of Tenke Fungurume Mine subordinated to the Freeport-McMoRan Inc. obtaining Turkish competition authority's approval without conditions

China Molybdenum Co. , Ltd. (hereinafter referred to as the "Company") has published the "China Molybdenum Co. , Ltd. Material Asset Purchase Report (Acquisition of Overseas Copper and Cobalt) (Draft)" on the Shanghai Stock Exchange website and company website, and disclosed that CMOC, Ltd. , wholly-owned subsidiary, purchased the Tenke Project subordinated to the Freeport-McMoRan Inc. (hereinafter referred to as "this acquisition").

On August 19, 2016, the company received a notice from the Turkish competition authority. The Turkish Competition Management Committee unconditionally approved the company's acquisition of Tenke project subordinated to the Freeport-McMoRan Inc. in accordance with relevant laws and regulations.

The approval of Turkish competition authority is the procedure required for the implementation of this acquisition project. See the report on major asset purchase of Luoyang Luanchuan Molybdenum Group Co. , Ltd. (acquisition of overseas copper and cobalt business) (Draft) disclosed by the company for other relevant approvals needed to be obtained for the acquisition project.

The company will pay close attention to the progress of the matter, actively promote the relevant work, and perform the obligation of information disclosure in a timely manner in strict accordance with the provisions and requirements of relevant laws and regulations.

Notice hereby

Board of directors of China Molybdenum Group Co. , Ltd
August 22, 2016

2. Host governmental approval

(1) Australia

1) Australian Foreign Investment Review Board

Cross-border M&A leads to foreign investors entering markets, therefore many of the host governments make the approval mandatory. In 2016, Dakang Pasture Farming Co., Ltd. failed to purchase an Australian target, because of the veto by Australian Foreign Investment Review Board (hereinafter referred to as "FIRB"). FIRB claimed the total area of the target Anna Creek is over 100 000 square kilometers. The FIRB system is derived from the *"Foreign Acquisition and Takeover Act in 1975"* (also known as FATA) and investment policy. FIRB is responsible for implementing FATA, so the approval system is called FIRB approval.

Case 7 - 3 Announcement of Dakang Pasture Farming Co., Ltd. on the progress of tender offer of the equity of S. Kidman & Co., Ltd.

Announcement on the progress of tender offer of the equity of S. Kidman & Co Ltd

1. Progress overview

Dakang Australia Holdings Pty Ltd (hereinafter referred to as "Dakang Australia") applied to FIRB for the acquisition of 80% equity of S. Kidman & Co Ltd (hereinafter referred to as "Kidman"), on April 29, 2016; the Australian Finance Minister vetoed the application on the grounds of national interest and asked the buyer to respond before May 3, 2016, Australia time. On May 3, 2016, Hunan Dakang Pasture Farming Co., Ltd. (hereinafter referred to as "the company") signed "Termination Deed" (hereinafter referred to as "The Deed") with Kidman, Dakang Australia, Australia Rural Capital Ltd (a public company listed on the Australian Stock Exchange (ASX) that wanted to acquire 20% stake of Kidman, hereinafter referred to as "ARC") and Anna Creek Pty Ltd. (hereinafter referred to as "Anna Creek"). The agreement terminated the valid conditional "Bid Implementation Agreement" (hereinafter referred to as "BIA") signed by the parties on April 29, 2016.

2. Main content of the agreement

The contracting parties unanimously agree to terminate the BIA Agreement (except for the obligation of confidentiality and other general obligations) and other related agreements, including: the bidder agrees to withdraw the offer; Dakang Australia agrees to withdraw the FIRB application; Kidman refunds the deposit; And Dakang Australia, ARC and Kidman will continue to negotiate on the acquisition in the next three months and seek together to obtain a feasible proposal accepted by Kidman's board of directors, shareholders and Australian Finance Minister.

3. Other instructions and risk tips

a. In the next three months, the company will actively consult with counterparties to form an accepted acquisition plan; the total amount of the offer that the company or subsidiary company and Kidman's BIA promised will not change, but the following negotiation is non-exclusive, that is, the tender offer sent by Kidman this time will not exclude other competitive negotiating opponents.

b. In view of the fact that the company has submitted the "Proposal on Signing the Valid Conditional Bid Implementation Agreement" and the "Feasibility Study Report on the Equity Acquisition of S. Kidman & Co Ltd" to 2015 Annual Shareholder Meeting on April 30, 2016, the company will not give up purchasing and continue to form a practical offer that could get the Australia's FIRB approval; at the same time, all investors need to be cautious about the vote on the proposal, without changing the amount of the offer to purchase the BIA agreement.

c. Since there is still a lot of uncertainty in this tender offer, the investors should pay special attention to the risks.

4. Documents for reference

"Termination Deed" signed by the company with Kidman, Dukang Australia, ARC and Anna Creek.

Hunan Dakang Pasture Farming Co., Ltd. Board of Directors
May 4, 2016

2) The rules of Australian agricultural land investment

Foreign Investment Review Board in Australia (FIRB) Guidance Notes 17 Agricultural land investment

a. Agricultural land investment.

Proposed investments in the agricultural land by foreign individuals (excluding the foreign government investors) generally require approval where the cumulative value of a foreign individual's agricultural land holdings exceeds 15 million, with exceptions applying to the investors from Australia's trade agreement partners (as specified below). All acquisitions of agricultural land by foreign government investors requires approval.

All acquisitions of interests in agricultural land by foreign individuals regardless of whether they require approval and regardless of value must be notified to the Australian Taxation Office Register of Foreign Ownership.

This Guidance Note provides information for foreign investors proposing to invest in Australian agricultural land, including when an acquisition of agricultural land is a notifiable action, it's approval processes and compliance.

b. Significant and notifiable actions.

The acquisition of an interest in Australian agricultural land by a foreign individual is a significant and notifiable action if the threshold test is met in relation to the land. The threshold test is met if the total value of all interests in agricultural land held by the foreign person (and their associates) and the consideration for the acquisition of the interest in the agricultural land is more than USD 15 million. A foreign person who proposes to enter an agreement to take a notifiable action must notify the Treasurer before entering the agreement.

An investment in agricultural land that is a notifiable action will also be a significant action. This means the Treasurer may:

- decide not to object to the action and give the person a no objection notification not imposing conditions;
- decide not to object to the action provided that one or more conditions that ensure the action are met and would not be contrary to the national interest and the person has no objection regarding the notification imposing conditions; or
- decide that the action would be contrary to the national interest and make an order prohibiting the proposed significant action.

If a significant action has already been taken which is contrary to the national interest, the Treasurer may make an order, known as a disposal order, which is directed at unwinding the action. Alternatively, the Treasurer may impose conditions.

c. Thresholds for agricultural land investments.

The applicable threshold value depends on the nationality of the foreign individual and whether the foreign individual is a foreign government investor.

- For *foreign government investors*, a USD 0 (nil) threshold applies.
- For *non-foreign government investors* (*except those from Chile, New Zealand, Thailand and the United States*), a cumulative USD 15 million threshold applies.

To meet the cumulative threshold, the total value of all interests in agricultural land in Australia held by the foreign individual (and their associates) and the consideration for the acquisition of the interest in the agricultural land together must exceed USD 15 million.

d. Australian opportunity—an open and transparent sale process.

As part of the national interest test, the decision maker will consider whether there was an opportunity for Australians to acquire a given parcel of agricultural land. The decision maker will have regard to the openness and transparency of the sale process.

Generally, approval will not be granted for any acquisition of agricultural land that was not offered for sale publicly and "marketed widely" for a minimum of 30 days. The purpose of this requirement is to ensure Australians have had sufficient opportunity to bid in any sale process of agricultural land.

An open and transparent sale process means:

- public marketing/advertising was undertaken for the sale of the property, using channels that Australian bidders could reasonably access (e. g. advertised on a widely used real estate listing site or large regional/national newspaper);
- the property was marketed/advertised for at least 30 days; and
- there was an equal opportunity for bids or offers to be made for the property while still available for sale.
- The responsibility is on the applicant to demonstrate how they became aware

that the property was advertised for sale and whether the acquisition was subject to an open and transparent sale process. Applicants may be requested to provide evidence of the sale process.

Exceptions to this requirement include acquisitions where the applicant:

- is acquiring a property via a private sale that was marketed/advertised in the above manner in the last six months but were not sold or where the sale fell through;
- has a substantial Australian ownership share (i. e. 50 per cent or more), as this constitutes an opportunity for Australian bidders, despite a foreign ownership share; or
- is required to make the acquisition to comply with the state or commonwealth law e. g. mining buffer zones.

Case 7-4 Two examples of agricultural land investment

Example 1 When the Advertisement is In Progress

Michele is a foreign person and wishes to acquire Joe's farm. She first saw Joe's farm advertised in a local newspaper and spoke to the realtor who has had the property listed for the last two months.

Michele confirms with the realtor that the property has been advertised through multiple channels for a period of at least 30 days, including online, through rural real estate brokers, and via advertisements in local and national media. If Michele applies to the Foreign Investment Review Board to acquire Joe's farm, the sale process is unlikely to raise the national interest issue.

Example 2 Five Months Ago Advertised

Susan has been directly approached by a foreign investor seeking to buy her farm. Susan's farm is not on the market for sale. However, it was advertised for sale five months ago but was taken off the market as it was not sold (either no offers were received or the offers received were not accepted).

The foreign investor, Green Forestry Co, approached Susan because they have significant holdings of land near Susan's farm for their forestry business and now have the capital available to expand their business.

Green Forestry Co applies to the Foreign Investment Review Board to acquire the property. This acquisition would satisfy the requirement for an open sale process as the property was advertised in the last 6 months.

e. Development conditions—residential development.

Standard development conditions will apply to all agricultural land acquisitions that are for residential development. That is, the acquisition would be conditional for the development commencing within the five years' period.

f. Exemptions for certain investors.

The thresholds for agricultural land and the agricultural land significant and notifiable action framework do not apply to non-foreign government investors from Chile, New Zealand, Thailand and the United States.

- In such cases, the framework applying to other types of Australian land such as commercial land and residential land still applies where the land in which the interest is to be acquired is both agricultural land and another type of Australian land.

- If a target entity is a land entity, investors from these countries may disregard interests in land that are used wholly and exclusively for a primary production business. If the action is another type of significant action or notifiable action under Australia's Foreign Investment Framework this will still apply (for example, acquiring a substantial interest in an Australian entity above the applicable threshold).

- For *Thai investors* who propose to acquire land, which is being used wholly and exclusively for a primary production business, it is a notifiable and significant action if the land is valued at more than USD 50 million.

g. Exemptions for owners or operators of wind or solar power stations.

The thresholds for agricultural land do not apply to certain acquisitions of agricultural land by owners or operators of wind or solar power stations. A "wind or solar power station" is defined in section 5 of *the Foreign Acquisitions and Takeovers Regulation* 2015 to mean a wind power station or solar electricity generation system that is an accredited power station as defined in the *Renewable Energy (Electricity) Act* 2000.

Owners and operators of solar and wind power stations that acquire an interest in agricultural land that contains a wind or solar power station, and their acquisition is for the sole purpose of operating the wind or solar power station on the land can disregard the fact that the land is agricultural land for the Act.

In such circumstances, even if the land still meets the usual test for agricultural land it is treated as if it is not agricultural land for the purposes of screening and specified thresholds for the other type of land will apply. For example, if it is considered non-vacant commercial land then the applicable threshold for such land will apply. See Guidance Note 14 for more information. For more information on wind or solar power stations, see Guidance Note 50.

h. Definition of agricultural land.

Agricultural land is a land in Australia that is used, or that could reasonably be used, for a primary production business. This includes land, which is partially used for a primary production business, or land where only part of the land could reasonably be used for a primary production business.

Agricultural land also includes land which may, from time to time, be covered by water (for example, a farm dam or stream). However, agricultural land does not include land where the only primary production business that the land is or could reasonably be used for is a primary production business relating to submerged plants and animals. For example, fish farming or oyster beds in estuaries and bays, the estuaries and bays would not be agricultural land.

Land includes a building or a part of a building. However, a building or a part of buildings that do not have any direct connection with land that is used or that could reasonably be used for a primary production business is not included within the meaning of the agricultural land. For example, an administrative office for a primary production business that is on a strata title in an office block in a city centre is not included within the definition of agricultural land.

i. Primary production business.

The definition of a primary production business is the same as the definition in subsection 995-1 (1) of the *Income Tax Assessment Act* 1997 (ITAA 1997). The definition includes cultivating or propagating plants; maintaining animals for the purpose of selling them or their bodily produce; conducting operations relating directly to taking or catching fish and certain other marine animals; planting or tending trees in a plantation or forest that are intended to be felled; or felling trees in a plantation or forest.

A person is undertaking a primary production business if the person carries on a business of:

• Cultivating or propagating plants, fungi or their products or parts (including seeds, spores, bulbs and similar things), in any physical environment;

• Maintaining animals for the purpose of selling them or their bodily produce (including natural increase);

• Manufacturing dairy produce from raw material that you produced;

• Conducting operations relating directly to taking or catching fish, turtles, dugong, bêche-de-mer, crustaceans or aquatic molluscs;

• Conducting operations relating directly to taking or culturing pearls or pearl shell;

• Planting or tending trees in a plantation or forest that are intended to be felled;

• Felling trees in a plantation or forest; or

• Transporting trees, or parts of trees, that you felled in a plantation or forest to the place:

——Where they are first to be milled or processed; or

——from which they are to be transported to the place where they are first to be milled or processed.

Various indicators should be considered to decide if an activity is a business of primary production, including whether:

- the activity has a significant commercial purpose or character;
- the person is undertaking the activity to make a profit and have a prospect of profit from the activity;
- there is repetition and regularity of the activity;
- the person carries out the activity in a similar manner to that of the ordinary trade in that line of business; and
- the person plans, organizes and carries on the activity in a business-like manner with the purpose of making a profit.

For more information see Tax ruling TR 97/11: *Income tax: am I carrying on a business of primary production?*

For information on the implications of agistment, see Taxation Ruling No. IT 225: *Primary production agistment income.*

j. Concept of "could reasonably be used for".

Whether land could reasonably be used for a primary production business depends on the facts and circumstances of the land. Factors that may provide a reasonable indicator that the land could (or could not) reasonably be used, either alone or together with other factors, may include the following:

You are not carrying on a business if the activity is better described as a hobby, a form of recreation, or a sporting activity.

- The primary uses allowed on the land under its zoning: These are likely to provide a reasonable indicator of whether the land could reasonably be used for a primary production business. For example, if zoning allowed for primary production activities are to be undertaken without the further approval of the local regulatory body, this would likely indicate that the land could reasonably be used for a primary production business. However, the land within a rural residential zone, where zoning requirements either explicitly do not allow for primary production activities, or would only be approved in special circumstances, is not land that could reasonably be used for a primary production business.

- Land use history: If the land has been used in a primary production business in recent years, this is likely to indicate that the land again could reasonably be used for a primary production business, unless there have been one or more significant changes in the land in the meantime (for example, significant permanent environmental degradation, water depletion or pollution, or removal or loss of the earlier primary production business infrastructure). However, even if the land has not been used in a primary production business in recent years it does not necessarily mean that it could not reasonably be used for a primary production business in the future. Examples of this is if the land is not being used in a primary production business due to:

——an extended extreme climatic event, such as a long-term drought;

——a recent natural disaster, such as bushfire or floods; or

——other activities, such as mineral exploration and development on the land after which expected, or legally required, land remediation works would mean that the land in whole or part again could reasonably be used for a primary production business.

- Land characteristics (for example, climate, crop yield, land size, remoteness, soil quality, stock holding capacity, topography, vegetation and water availability): Land must be of a sufficient size to allow for the operation of a stand-alone primary production business in some or all cases within the site, with land of one hectare or less not considered agricultural land. Remoteness of the land from goods transport and other infrastructure, as well as key agricultural service providers, may mean that the land could not reasonably be used for a primary production business, until such infrastructure and/or services become available.

- Lease or licence conditions or limitations: Where there is a right to occupy agricultural land under a lease or licence whose term (including any extension or renewal) is reasonably likely to exceed five years, there may be a land use conditions or restrictions attached to the lease or licence.

——Where these explicitly allow for primary production activities to be undertaken, the land could reasonably be used for a primary production business, irrespective of whether the lessee or licence holder's intention during the lease or licence term.

——Where these do not permit use for a primary production business by the lessee or licence holder, this in isolation should not be considered as the land that could not reasonably be used for a primary production business. Other factors, such as those outlined above, and the rationale for such a restriction on the lease or licence would be relevant to an assessment. For example, if a lessor has retained adjacent land on which he is operating a primary production business and has restricted the uses of the lessee so that he can incorporate the land back into his operations he should decide to do so at the end of the lease term (after the land has been left fallow to raise productivity), then the land could reasonably be used for a primary production business.

It is also not generally expected that dwellings within city limits would be considered to be on the land that could reasonably be used for a primary production business, although it may be feasible or legal for small scale intensive primary production activities, or administrative activities related to a primary production business to occur on such land in some cases (where the land in question is larger than one hectare – see Exclusions below). However, such land is agricultural land if non-ancillary activities of a primary production business are carried out on the land. For example, market gardens or propagating plants as part of a plant nursery.
Agricultural Land Investments

k. Exclusions.

The *Foreign Acquisitions and Takeovers Regulation* 2015 (Regulation) at section 44 explicitly excludes land that is not being used wholly or predominantly for a primary production business and meets one or more of the following conditions.

• Land for which zoning requires the government approval for primary production businesses;

——If zoning allows the land to be used for one kind of primary production without approval, it is deemed agricultural land irrespective of whether approval is required for another kind of primary production business the prospective investor intends to use the land for.

• Land for which zoning allows use for a primary production business and an application has been made to, and is awaiting a final determination from, a relevant government authority for:

——the land to be rezoned as land for which zoning does not allow use for a primary production business; or

——approval for a mine, oil or gas well, quarry, or other similar operation under a mining or production tenement, (a mining operation) to be established on the land; or

——approval to locate infrastructure relating to a mining operation on the land (such as infrastructure for processing the material extracted by the operation and accommodation for miners); or

——approval for waste from a mining operation to be stored on the land.

——an approval (including accreditation) for establishing or operating a wind or solar power station to be located on the land (whether on or beneath the surface);

• Land used wholly and predominantly for a mining operation, to locate infrastructure relating to a mining operation, or to store waste from a mining operation;

• An approval of a government authority (that is not a mining or production tenement) is in force allowing a mining operation to be established or operated on the land, infrastructure relating to a mining operation to be located on the land; or waste from a mining operation to be stored on the land;

——The land was acquired solely, or is used wholly or predominantly to meet a condition of such an approval than relates to other land.

• Land used for the wind or solar power stations, including when an approval is in place to allow the wind or solar farm to be established or operated on the land, or the land was acquired solely for the purpose of meeting a requirement of government approval for the solar or wind farm.

——In the examples above, the land is to be treated as either vacant or non-vacant commercial land. If a wind or solar power station is located on the surface of the land the land will be considered non-vacant. See Guidance Notes 14 and 50 of FIRB-for more information.

• Land used, under a law of the Commonwealth, a State or a Territory or a legally binding agreement, wholly or predominantly for the purposes of the protection or conservation of the environment;

• Land used wholly or predominantly for the purposes of a wildlife sanctuary or for rehabilitating animals;

• Land located within an area that has been approved by a government authority as an industrial estate;

• The area of the land is one hectare or less;

• The use of the land has been approved by a government authority for providing facilities for tourism, outdoor education or outdoor recreation to the public.

The Regulation also excludes land where the only primary production business that the land is or could reasonably be used for is conducting operations relating directly to taking or catching fish or culturing pearls or other aquatic life, including plant and animal products.

l. Exemption certificates for agricultural land.

Foreign individuals (including the foreign government investors) are able to apply for an exemption certificate to cover a program of acquisitions of interests in agricultural land.

Exemption certificates for agricultural land would generally be considered where:

- the total proposed value of acquisitions over a three-year period does not exceed USD 100 million;
- the regions or localities where the agricultural land in which interests are to be acquired are defined clearly.

Exemption certificates would generally be granted subject to a condition that limits the maximum value for a single transaction (i. e. value of the property, not the value of individual titles) to USD 10 million and a periodic reporting condition on acquisitions made during the period.

The above limits are to be used as a guideline only. The actual limit granted may be lower than these limits depending on factors, including but not limited to:

- the location restrictions on the exemption certificate;
- the track record of the acquiring party;
- the future usage of the land including any capital investment plans;
- the total value of recent FIRB approvals, either individually or via an exemption certificate.

Standard development conditions will be applied to all agricultural land exemption certificates that are for residential development. The exemption certificate would be conditional on development commencing within a five-year period.

Foreign individuals acquiring interests that require notification for the Register of Foreign Ownership Administered by the Australian Taxation Office should comply separately with their notification requirements under the *Register of Foreign Owner-*

ship of Water or Agricultural Land Act 2015, for any applicable acquisitions and disposals made while an exemption certificate is in place.

For more information on the guidelines for exemption certificates, see Guidance Note 21.

m. Fees.

The fee is payable at the time of application. Processing commences when the correct fee is paid.

For more information on the fees applying to foreign investment applications, see Guidance Note 30 of FIRB.

n. Penalties.

Strict penalties (including civil and criminal penalties) may apply to breaches of Australia's foreign investment rules.

o. Further information.

Further information is available on the FIRB website at www. firb. gov. au.

(2) America

The Committee on Foreign Investment in the United States (CFIUS) is the most famous in terms of the national security review. Since 1988, the President or CFIUS has only officially rejected a few transactions in more than 2 000 cases. However, since the Trump administration took office, it has become common practice for CFIUS to veto Chinese investor's projects.

Case 7 – 5 Announcement of Shenzhen Selen Science & Technology Co., Ltd. on terminating the Acquisition of Equity of Akron Polymer Systems, Inc.

Announcement of Shenzhen Selen Science & Technology Co., Ltd. on terminating the Acquisition of Equity of Akron Polymer Systems, Inc

Shenzhen Selen Science & Technology Co., Ltd. (hereinafter referred to as "the company") held the "Twenty-Ninth Meeting of the Fourth Board of Directors" on May 10, 2018, passing the *Proposal on Terminating*

Acquisition of Equity of Akron Polymer Systems, Inc. This deal, in view of the restrictions on the company's acquisition of 45% equity of AkronPolymer Systems, Inc. by CFIUS, could not be implemented as planned, the company's board of directors agreed to terminate the acquisition of the equity of Akron Polymer Systems, Inc, and the details are as follows:

1. Purchase overview

In order to further enhance the company's R&D and innovation capabilities in the photoelectric display industry chain and layout the next generation market of flexible display material through resource integration, the board of directors reviewed and approved this acquisition. The company plans to purchase 45% equity of AkronPolymer Systems, Inc. (hereinafter referred to as "target company") through a wholly-owned subsidiary Selen Science & Technology (Hong Kong) Co., Ltd. (hereinafter referred to as "Hong Kong Xinlun"). For details, please refer to the "*Announcement on the Acquisition of 45% Equity of Akron Polymer Systems, Inc.*" released by the company on December 12, 2017 (No. 2017-132).

2. Reason for termination

Since the target company has participated in projects involving US military materials, the transaction requires revision and approval by CFIUS before closing. According to *the Equity Purchase Agreement* signed by Hong Kong Xinlun and the target company, if CFIUS has notified the purchaser or the target company in writing or verbally, it means that CFIUS intends to send or has sent a report to the President, and the report will recommend president to suspend or prohibit the transaction under this Agreement, or to restrict it. Besides, if either the target company or the purchaser can't accept this restriction, it may be terminated by either of them. This Agreement can be seen in the Announcement No. 2017-132.

By May 2018, CFIUS still claims to impose restrictions on this transaction after repeated communication; this transaction cannot be carried out smoothly as planned. Therefore, in order to protect the interests of the listed company and shareholders, the company decided to terminate this equity acquisition after consultation with shareholders of the target company.

3. Impacts of termination

a. The parties to the transaction have promised that this termination will not lead to claim and litigation. The audit, evaluation, and legal fees incurred in the transaction shall be borne by the two parties themselves.

b. The termination of this transaction will not affect the company's continued cooperation with Akron; the company will continue to expand its

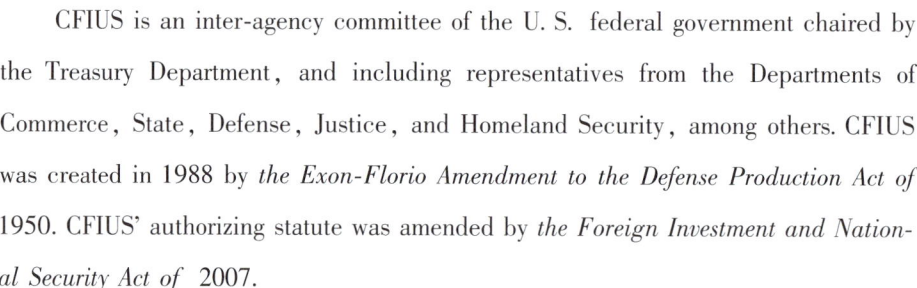

business in the field of photoelectric display relying on the joint venture Polytren Material Technology and Science Co. Ltd. established by Akron in Shenzhen.

 c. As the equity acquisition has not been completed and is expected to bring certain obstacles to the introduction of related technologies, investors are advised to pay attention to investment risks. please investors pay attention to the risk. The company will actively communicate with the overseas partners to avoid adverse impact on the company's business.

 Notice is hereby given.
  Shenzhen Selen Science & Technology Co. , Ltd. Board of Directors
   May 11, 2018

CFIUS is an inter-agency committee of the U. S. federal government chaired by the Treasury Department, and including representatives from the Departments of Commerce, State, Defense, Justice, and Homeland Security, among others. CFIUS was created in 1988 by *the Exon-Florio Amendment to the Defense Production Act of 1950.* CFIUS' authorizing statute was amended by *the Foreign Investment and National Security Act of* 2007.

1) What authority does CFIUS have

CFIUS may assert its authority over covered transactions:

a. Any merger, acquisition, or takeover resulting in control of a U. S. business.

U. S. business includes the U. S. operations of a foreign company.

b. As a result of the transaction, control will rest in a foreign person.

Questions focusing on the ultimate parent and use of acquisition vehicles or holding companies do not affect this analysis.

c. Control.

Not simply a question of shareholding percentages-fact-intensive inquiry that looks at governance and other factors.

Submissions to CFIUS are voluntary, but a pre-closing clearance provides a safe harbor as the un-notified transactions may be reviewed by CFIUS post-closing, which can lead to the U. S. government forcing the parties to unwind the transaction or foreign parties to divest their interests in U. S. business.

2) Among CFIUS's priorities

a. Securing U. S. defense industrial base.

b. Protecting critical technologies.

c. Protecting critical infrastructure.

d. Protecting U. S. technological leadership.

e. Assuring the government and defense supply chain.

f. Compliance with important U. S. national security policies (e. g. , counter-terrorism, non-proliferation and export controls) .

g. Energy security.

h. Government ownership.

In practice, CFIUS is likely to consider a number of other factors, including the nationality of the acquiring individuals or entities.

3) Areas of CFIUS's potential concern

CFIUS' interest in transactions has steadily evolved from the core national secu-

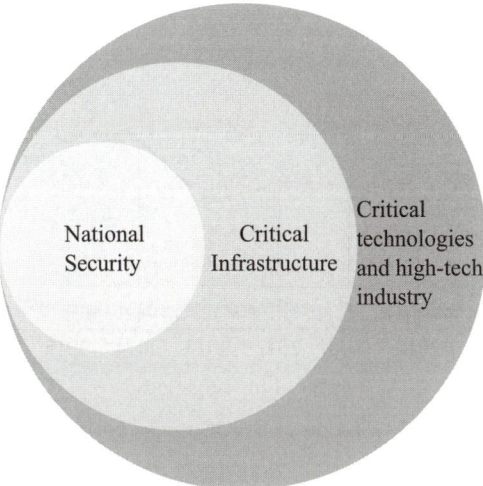

Figure 7-1　Areas of CFIUS's potential concern

rity matters and issues of critical infrastructure, to a broader interest in critical technologies and high-tech industry in general, as shown in Figure 7-1.

4) Recent CFIUS statistics

CFIUS regularly releases statistics on reviewed transactions (the details of individual transactions usually remain confidential). CFIUS also issues annual reports to Congress, as shown in the Form 7-5, Figure 7-2.

Form 7 – 5 Statistics on CFIUS reviewed transactions of 2014 – 2016

Unit: PCS

Year	Number of Resulting Notices	Number of Investigations	Percentage of Notices Resulting in Investigations	Presidential Decisions	Notices Rejected	Total Notices Withdrawn	Notices Withdrawn and Refiled	Notices Withdrawn and Transactions Abandoned in Light of the CFIUS – Related National Security Concerns	Notices Withdrawn and no Explanation
2014	147	51	35%	0	1	12	7	2	3
2015	143	66	46%	0	1	13	9	3	1
2016	172	79	46%	1	0	27	15	5	7

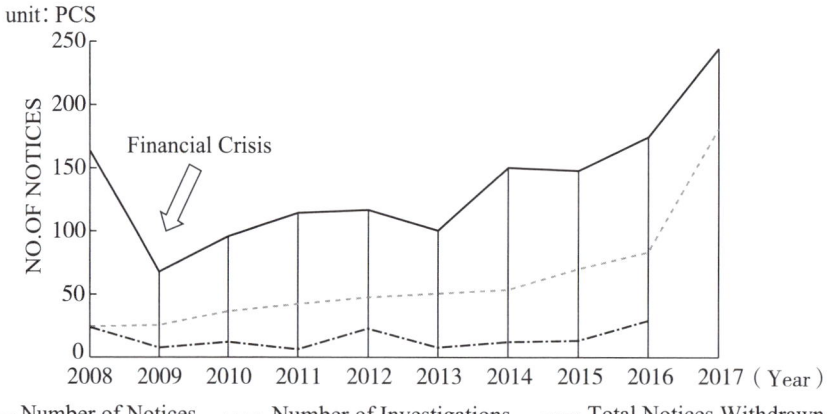

Figure 7-2 Trends of CFIUS reviewed transaction

5) Spotlight on China

a. Acquisition of Global Communication Semiconductors, LLC (GCS) Holdings

(2016).

Following CFIUS concern regarding San'an Optoeletronics Co's acquisition of GCS Holdings, Inc., the parties entered into a joint venture to avoid further national security scrutiny.

b. Acquisition of Lumileds (2016).

After failing to mitigate national security concerns, the USD 2.9 billion sale of a majority stake in Philips Lumileds business by Chinese investors was terminated.

c. Acquisition of Fairchild Semiconductor (2016).

Fairchild rejected a potential acquisition by China Resources Microelectronics Ltd. and Hua Capital Management Co. Ltd. because of a potential CFIUS risk.

d. Acquisition of Aixtron (2016).

Chinese investor Fujian Grand Chip Investment Fund LP attempted to acquire German semiconductor company Aixtron SE, which had a U.S. subsidiary.

CFIUS allegedly recommended that the President block the transaction on the basis that "the military applications of the overall technical body of knowledge and experience of Aixtron".

German national security authorities were also reviewing the transaction and were raising their own questions.

e. Acquisition of Lattice (2017).

Canyon Bridge Capital Partners, a PE firm allegedly funded by the Chinesegovernment, attempted to acquire the American semi-conductor company Lattice Semiconductor Corporation.

Canyon Bridge and Lattice engaged in an 8-month campaign to close the deal with several rounds of withdrawal and refile after a full CFIUS investigation.

Lattice set forth a series of mitigation proposals intended to satisfy any national security concerns, but ultimately was unsuccessful in persuading either the Committee or the President.

f. Acquisition of Qualcomm (2018).

Singaporean company Broadcom Limited sought to acquire semi-conductor manufacturer Qualcomm Incorporated via hostile takeover, deal valued between USD 117billion ~ 142 billion.

Qualcomm submitted a unliteral voluntary notice to CFIUS on January 29, 2018, "voluntarily invited CFIUS to review of Broadcom Limited's [...] solicitation of proxies for the purposes of selecting a majority of the directors of Qualcomm".

After communicating with both Qualcomm and Broadcom, CFIUS issued an Interim Order on March 4, 2018, which among other things required Qualcomm to delay its annual shareholders meeting (scheduled for March 6th), where Broadcom was expected to obtain seats on Qualcomm's board. The purpose of the interim order was to preserve the status quo between the parties.

On March 11, 2018, CFIUS notified the SEC that it determined that Broadcom's actions violated the Interim Order. The following day, on March 12, 2018, President Trump issued an Executive Order blocking the transaction.

g. Acquisition of MoneyGram (2018).

Despite multiple attempts to gain the CFIUS approval, Chinese Ant Financials' attempts to acquire MoneyGram International, a money transfer company, officially collapsed in early January 2018 when CFIUS rejected the proposed mitigation.

h. Acquisition of Xcerra Corporation (2018).

CFIUS refused to approve Hubei Xinyan's USD 580 million acquisition of Xcerra Corp, a producer of equipment used in the semi-conductor manufacturing process. But in January 2018, U. S. authorities approved the USD 15 million acquisition of Akrion Systems LLC, a manufacturer of semi-conductor equipment, by China-based Naura Microelectronics Equipment Co., Ltd in January 2018.

For coping with overseas review, firstly, enterprises should fully understand the regulatory requirements of the foreign M&As in relevant countries and regions. Secondly, they should evaluate the possible impact of such approval on transactions, such as national security review, anti-monopoly review and special restrictions on the state-owned enterprises. Finally, informal communication will be helpful for regulatory authority's understanding of transactions and recognition of M&A case.

Case 7 – 6 Spinning off Long Beach Container Terminal (LBCT), COSCO Shipping Holdings Co. , Ltd. purchasing Orient Overseas (International) Ltd (OOIL) .

Transaction Value: USD 6. 3 Billion
Target Country: America
Industry: Port

Case Background: In March 2012, OOIL and the US Long Beach Port signed a long-term lease worth USD 4. 6 billion for a period of 40 years. OOIL will invest USD 1. 2 billion in cooperation with the Long Beach Port to merge the two old terminals into a new modern terminal, which is expected to be completed in June 2019. The new terminal will effectively enhance the throughput capacity, it is expected to double to 3. 3 million TEU a year, using the world's most advanced cargo handling technology. In addition, by adding more rail lines in the terminal, using electrified cargo handling equipment and shore power systems, air pollution will be halved, by then, the terminal will become the most competitive, efficient and environmentally friendly container terminal in North America.

Previously on June 29 2018, the COSCO received "*Anti-monopoly Review No Prohibit Decision*" made by Anti-Monopoly Bureau of the State Administration for Market Regulation, the decision decided not to prohibit its acquisition of OOIL and all the conditions precedent are met. Later, the joint offeror issued a comprehensive offer document to all shareholders of OOIL on July 6 2018. As the document noted, Faulkner Global and ShanghaiPort Group (BVI) made an offer to all OOIL's shareholders at a price of HKD 78. 67 per share, the final date for accepting the offer was July 27, 2018.

On July 6 2018, COSCO announced that in order to ensure OOIL's listing status maintained after the completion of tender offer, Faulkner Global reached an equity transfer agreement with PSD Investco, Crest Apex and Rongshi International. According to the agreement, if OOIL's public shareholding is less than 25% after the completion offender offer, Faulkner Global will transfer up to15. 1% total shares issued to the investors above, and PSD Investco, Crest Apex and Rongshi International will respectively subscribe for up to 7. 73% , 4. 99% and 2. 38% of the total shares issued.

Case Study: Faulknerm Global, a wholly-owned subsidiary of COSCO Shipping Holdings Co. , Ltd. (601919. SH; 01919. HK), joining hands with Shanghai Port Group (BVI) Holding Co. , Ltd. , issued an tender offer to all shareholders about the acquisition of Orient Overseas (International) Co. , Ltd. (OOIL, 00316. HK) on July 9, 2017, one year after that, the case was released by CFIUS, meaning that the acquisition was near to completion.

Then, how did the transaction pass the CFIUS approval? The essence behind it is following:

Faulkner Global and OOIL have signed a National Security Agreement with the U. S. Department of Homeland Security and Department of Justice, promising to sell LBCT (in USA, operated and owned by OOIL) to unrelated third parties and handing over LBCT to the US Trust in favor of OOIL before the sale. Based on the signatures of *National Security Agreement* above, the parties have received a letter sent from CFIUS on July 6, in the letter the CFIUS has ensured that there was no unresolved national security risk in the tender offer.

Section 4
Information Disclosure and Compliance of Domestically-listed Companies

In addition to meeting the regulations of the NDRC, MOFCOM, SAFE and SASAC, the overseas M&A of listed companies must also comply with the special regulations of the CSRC and the stock exchange regarding the listed companies governing, material asset restructuring and information disclosure.

The overseas M&As of listed companies are subject to the approval of multiple regulatory authorities. Therefore, it is particularly important to confirm the order of approval by relevant regulatory authorities. To improve the efficiency of approval and further optimize the market environment for M&A, the Ministry of Industry and Information Technology of the People's Republic of China (hereinafter referred to as MIIT), China Security Regulatory Commission (hereinafter referred to as CSRC), NDRC and MOFCOM jointly formulated *the Work Plan for the Parallel Approvals in the Administrative Licensing of Mergers, Acquisitions and Restructuring of Listed Com-*

panies in October 2014; it clearly regulated the order of approval that domestic enterprises need to get. Specifically, three administrative approval items, including confirmation and registration of the overseas investment projects by NDRC, confirmation of foreign investors' strategic investment in listed companies by the Ministry of Commerce, and review of concentration of undertakings by the Ministry of Commerce, are changed into parallel approvals. The parallel approvals, led by MIIT and carried out by multi sector, greatly shortened the approval time and improved the efficiency of overseas M&A of listed companies.

The CSRC has formulated a series of rules to regulate the transactions of listed companies, including *Measures for the Administration of the Material Asset Restructurings of Listed Companies* (2016 Revision), *Measures for the Administration of the Takeover of Listed Companies* (2014 Revision), *Administrative Measures for the Issuance of Securities by Listed Companies*, and *Detailed Implementation Rules for the Non-Public Offering of Stocks of Listed Companies* (2017 Revision), etc. According to *the Implementation Plan for Separation Review System of M&A*, the separation review system of M&A for listed companies has been officially implemented on October 8, 2013. For the listed companies that can be free of review or can be reviewed quickly, if they acquire companies in cash, the CSRC shall exempt the review and directly approve it; and if they acquire assets in issuing shares, the CSRC shall cancel the pre-review and directly submit it to M&A Committee for review.

Any transaction of a listed company needs to disclose information as required, therefore, listed companies need to pay special attention to the information disclosure when conducting overseas M&As. In the process of purchasing overseas assets, the listed company shall perform obligations of information disclosure in accordance with the relevant regulations, such as *Administrative Measures for the Disclosure of Information of Listed Companies*, *Measures for the Administration of the Material Asset Restructurings of Listed Companies*, *Measures for the Administration of the Takeover of Listed Companies* and stock listing rules of Shanghai and Shenzhen Stock Exchanges. Meanwhile, the information disclosure guidelines of Shanghai

Stock Exchange and information disclosure memorandum of Shenzhen Stock Exchange clearly stipulate the content and format of the specific matters disclosed, as well as the suspension of resumption of stock.

Nanjing Xinbai acquired approximately 89% equity of the UK's established department store House of Fraser affiliated with "Highland Group Holdings Limited" in full cash, making it the largest overseas direct acquisition in the history of A-share retailers. With over 160 years of history, House of Fraser is the oldest royal authorized department store chain in the UK with more than 60 stores in the UK and Ireland. After the acquisition, Nanjing Xinbai introduced House of Fraser to the Chinese market and created the "Oriental Fraser (House of Fraser)" department store.

Case 7 -7 Nanjing Xinbai Department Store Co., Ltd. Announcement on Equity Acquisition of Highland Group Holdings Limited

Announcement on Equity Acquisition and Overseas Investment of Highland Group Holdings Limited

1. Overview of overseas investment

a. Basic information of overseas investment: according to *the Equity Purchase Agreement* signed by Nanjing Xinbai and Highland Group Holding Limited (hereinafter referred to as "Highland Group"), Nanjing Xinbai plans to acquire approximately 89% equity of Highland Group in cash (hereinafter referred to as "the underlying asset").

b. Highland Group is a UK-based department store group established on June 14, 2006 and headquartered in London, UK. House of Fraser Ltd (hereinafter referred to as "House of Fraser"), a business owned by Highland Group, is a department store that sells goods in multi-channels of offline store, website and mobile phone in the United Kingdom and Ireland; it's House of Fraser brand has more than 160 years of history and the products sold include men, women, kid &baby, beauty, accessories and home & garden. As a package deal, Nanjing Xinbai signed *the Agreement on Purchasing Class A Common Stock and Preferred Stock*, *Agreement on Purchasing Class B Common Stock* and *Agreement on Purchasing Preferred Stock* (hereinafter referred to as "Equity Purchase Agreement") respectively with stockholders of class A and preferred stock, stockholders of class B and stockholders of preferred stock. Since preferred common stock, preferred stock, class A common stock and class B common stock have differences in voting rights and benefit order; the consideration is different. For details, please refer to Basic Information of Counterparty. After this transaction, Nanjing Xinbai obtained 88.89% of the voting rights of the target company and obtained 88.96% of the total number of shares.

c. The company plans to set up a wholly-owned subsidiary in the UK as the main purchaser, and it will pay GBP 155 330 878 of cash in the form of its own funds and debt financing to acquire 600 500 shares of the preferred common stock (hereinafter referred to as "PO shares"), 8 888 890 shares of Class A common stock (hereinafter referred to as "A shares"), 151 111 110 shares of preferred stock and 526 316 shares of Class B common shares (hereinafter referred to as "B shares"). After this transaction, the company will hold approximately 89% equity of the underlying company. The price of this transaction is determined by the parties after negotiation, referring to the pre-assessment results issued by the evaluation agency with securities qualifications. According to *the Equity Purchase Agreement*, the consideration for the underlying asset is approximately 15.33 million. Based on January 25 2014 as a valuation date, the pre-assessment value of the underlying company's whole equity was 201.67 million pounds, and the 89% equity was approximately 179.49 million pounds. The consideration of the underlying asset has no premium over the pre-assessment value.

d. This acquisition was reviewed and approved by the sixth meeting of the seventh board of directors of the company. The meeting reviewed and approved *the Proposal on Signing the Equity Purchase Agreement* with 9 votes in favor, 0 votes against, and 0 abstentions. According to *the Stock Listing Rules* by Shanghai Stock Exchange and *Articles of Association of Nanjing Xinjiekou Department Store Co., Ltd.*, this acquisition and overseas investment matters need to be submitted to shareholders meeting for deliberation.

e. There is no relationship between each counterparty and the company, controlling shareholders and actual controllers in this transaction. This transaction is not a related party transaction.

f. The amount of this transaction accounted for more than 100% of the final net assets recorded in the audited consolidated financial accounting report of Nanjing Xinbai in 2013. According to *the Measures for the Administration of Material Asset Restructurings of Listed Companies*, this transaction is a material asset restructuring and needs to be confirmed by CSRC.

g. Up to the date of this announcement, the due diligence, auditing, and evaluation of this transaction are underway. The company will hold the board of directors meeting as soon as possible to deliberate this purchase matters of the material assets and to disclose *Plan of Material Asset Purchase*.

2. Basic information of related parties

(1) Basic information of counter parties

The counter parties to this transaction include PO shareholders, preferred and A shareholders and B shareholders in the Highland Group Holdings Limited. Details are as follows:

1) About PO shareholders

The PO shares enjoy the priority claim in the profit distribution and settlement of the remaining property after bankruptcy liquidation, and do not enjoy voting rights. Up to now, there are 600 500 PO shares totally, and Bank of Scotland plc holds 100% PO shares. The Bank of Scotland plc, founded by the Scottish law, is the oldest bank in Scotland founded in 1695 and headquartered in Edinburgh. The Bank of Scotland plc provides a range of financial services, including retail banking, corporate banking, asset management, and private banking, both inside and outside the UK. Now it is part of Lloyds Banking Group, one of the UK's largest financial institutions.

Shareholder name	Shareholding number shares	Shareholding ratio in PO shares
Bank of Scotland plc	600 500	100%
Total	600 500	100%

2) About preferred and A shareholders

Preferred stocks do not participate in a profit distribution of the underlying company, take second place in the settlement of the remaining property after bankruptcy liquidation, and do not enjoy voting rights. The A-shares take a second place in the profit distribution and third place in the settlement of the remaining property after bankruptcy liquidation, only A-shares enjoy voting rights. Each A-share represents one voting right.

Under *the terms of Equity Purchase Agreement*, both BG Holding ehf and Kevin Stanford are obligated to transfer the equity of the underlying company that is not subject to any pledge or mortgage to Nanjing Xinbai on closing date.

3) About B shareholders

The shareholders of B-shares are management of the underlying company.

They are in the second place with A-shares in the profit distribution and the fourth place in the settlement of the remaining property after bankrupt liquidation, they do not enjoy voting rights and cannot be publicly transferred.

(2) Basic information of underlying company

The underlying company is an internationally renowned department store group whose operator, House of Fraser, has a history of more than 164 years and is the oldest royal authorized department store chain in the UK. House of Fraser was listed on the main board of the London Stock Exchange for a long time before being privatized and was selected as FTSE100constituent stock. The underlying company has its own brands, sourcing brands and special brands, the goods categories mainly cover men's wear, women's wear, children's wear, beauty, accessories and home & garden. House of Fraser's suppliers cover a wide range of international brands including PRADA, HUGO BOSS, DIESEL, Ralph Lauren and more. Among its special brands, the top 15 companies are business partners who have cooperated for more than ten years. In addition, House of Fraser's own private brands, such as Howick, Dickins & Jones, Linea, have also won widespread market influence with stylish design and affordable prices. House of Fraser opened 59 stores in the UK, a store in Ireland, and a franchise store in the Middle East city of Abu Dhabi with a total sales area of over 4.9 million square feet. Because of the long history of House of Fraser, most of the company's stores are located in the core business districts of the city, mainly for middle-class consumers pursuing high-end brands, such as London's Oxford Street, Glasgow's Commercial Street, Manchester's King Street, etc.

In addition, House of Fraser has established a unified online sales platform for global consumer, HouseofFraser.com, to enhance the customer's shopping experience through online orders, mail orders, online order&offline delivery, etc. In 2014, the company's total turnover was GBP 1,191.6 million (unaudited), and its market share ranked among the top of the UK department store.

Highland Group is the holding company of House of Fraser and the party purchased in this transaction. This transaction is a market-based acquisition, the price of this transaction is determined by the parties after negotiation, referring to the pre-assessment results issued by the evaluation agency with securities qualifications. Based on January 25, 2014 as a valuation date, the pre-assessment value of the underlying company's whole equity was GBP 205.67 million, which was 89.90% higher than the latest book net assets (unaudited). The reasons for the increase are: a. House of Fraser has a long history, with rich brand assets, business circle resources and supplier partnerships; b. After the privatization of House of Fraser, the financial indicators have gradually improved, and there is a large room for growth in the future; c. The European whole retail market is recovering, market valuation of department store retail industry is being repaired. However, the final assessment results are still subject to confirmation by the asset appraiser and will be disclosed in *the Material Asset Purchase Report*.

(3) Changes in shareholding structure

Before and after this transaction, for the sales of special brand of the target company, the operating income in the financial statements is the net sales commission income, while the total turnover is the sales commodity income of special brand. There are differences between the two calculation standards.

(4) Explanation of incidence relation

There is no incidence relation between each counterparty and the company, controlling shareholder or actual controller in this transaction. Therefore, this tran-saction is not a related transaction.

3. Main contents of *the Equity Purchase Agreement*

(1) Consideration

The number of shares is the total amount of PO shares, preferred shares, A shares and B shares held by each counterparty. After this transaction, the shareholding ratio of Nanjing Xinbai is 88.96%. The parties agreed that, under*the Equity Purchase Agreement*, the transferee intends to pay GBP 155 330 878 of cash (this is the base consideration) to acquire approximately 89% shares of the Highland Group held by transferor, including 600 500 PO shares, 8 888 890 A shares, 151 111 110 preferred stocks and 526 316 B shares. Among them, the deposit is 10 000 000 pounds, the transferee must transfer the deposit into the designated account within 10 working days after signing this agreement; There are adjustment clauses in the above basic consideration, and the final consideration paid depends on a series adjustment factors, including additional remuneration, deduction of the part that EBITDA did not meet expectations in 2014, idle funds interest, etc.

(2) Conditions precedent for closing

The parties' obligation to complete the transaction has condition on, if these conditions were achieved at or before the time of closing, purchaser gives up or these conditions can be achieved once closing, parties must fulfill the obligation:

1) Supervision condition

a. The Jiangsu DRC accepted the recordation of this transaction;
b. The Ministry of Commerce confirmed the transaction;
c. The SAFE Jiangsu branch registered the transaction;
d. The CSRC approved the transaction ("Supervision conditions").

2) Condition for shareholder approval

The shareholders of Nanjing Xinbai, which holds not less than two-thirds of the voting rights, approves this transaction at the official shareholder's meeting (in person or through a proxy) ("Condition for shareholder approval"). Ps. Referring to the exchange rate of April 14, 2014 (1 : 10.2911), it is approximately RMB 1 598 525 599.

(3) Trusteeship

After signing *The Equity Purchase Agreement*, the parties agree to appoint an escrow agent as soon as possible and take necessary or reasonable measures to sign an escrow agreement with the agent to stipulate the relevant terms of the transaction. Subject to the relevant terms, if the escrow trigger event has not occurred at the time of closing, a termination fee of GBP 6 000 000 will be credited to the escrow account.

(4) Effectiveness of the agreement

The Equity Purchase Agreement takes effect upon being signed by parties.

(5) Termination of the agreement

The termination conditions of *The Equity Purchase Agreement* include: a. Termination by written contract between parties; b. Spontaneous termination: closing conditions are not met or CP gives up at or before 23:59 on the deadline, unless agreeing otherwise in accordance with other relevant terms. c. The transferee has the right to terminate the transaction on or before closing date, if these situations occur: a) Deloitte & Touche has issued an audit report with a qualified opinion on the company's 2014 consolidated financial report (or failed to deliver any audit report); b) Any one of John King, Mark Gifford and Nigel Oddy resigned or received a dismissal notice from the underlying company or its subsidiaries.

(6) Breach of the agreement

The defaulting party shall compensate the non-defaulting party for the loss, and the observant party may also apply for specific performance.

Limit of claim time. The transferor shall not be liable for violation of any transferor's warranty (except for any claim related to basic warranty), unless the transferee sends a notice of claim to the transferor within 18 months after closing.

Minimum claim amount. If the amount of the claim, a series claims or similar claims (no matter what terms may be) are not over GBP 100 000, the transferor shall not be liable for violation of any transferor's warranty (except for any claim related to basic warranty) for any individual claim (or claims of the same nature). If the amount of the claim, a series claims or similar claims is over GBP 100 000, subject to other regulations, the relevant transferor shall be liable for the claim or the claim amount specified by agreement, not only for the excess.

Total minimum claim amount. The transferor shall not be liable for the violation of any transferor's warranty (except for any claim related to basic warranty) for any claim, unless the amount of all claims (including previous claims) that transferor shall to bear surpasses GBP 2 000 000. If the amount of claim that transferor should bear by agreement is over GBP 2 000 000, subject to related terms, the relevant transferor shall be liable for the claim or the claim amount specified by agreement, not only for the excess.

Maximum liability. Subject to related terms, all the claims for violation of transferor's warranty (except for any claim related to basic warranty) and the total liability amount of the claims related to UK's Office of Fair Trading or the Competition Commission shall not exceed GBP 6 000 000, and each transferor shall be liable for no more than certain corresponding proportion of GBP 6 000 000. As to responsibility for the above claims, all claim amounts need to be paid out of the balance of credit account in the escrow account. The total liability amount that each transferor shall be liable for claims shall not exceed certain proportion of consideration.

(7) The applicable law and dispute settlement of the agreement

This Agreement, the documents to be signed by this Agreement, and any non-contractual obligations arising from this Agreement or such documents will apply English law. The parties irrevocably agree that the English court will have exclusive jurisdiction to resolve any dispute arising from this Agreement or the documents to be signed by this Agreement. Accordingly, any legal proceedings arising from this Agreement or documents to be signed by this Agreement shall be submitted to such courts. The parties irrevocably accept the jurisdiction of the courts and cannot raise any objection to procedure on the grounds of location or legal process at an inconvenient location.

CHAPTER 8

POST-MERGER INTEGRATION OF INVESTMENT AND M &A ALONG THE "BELT AND ROAD" COUNTRIES

CHAPTER 8
Post-merger Integration of Investment and M&A along the "Belt and Road" Countries

"Post-merger integration is the biggest shortcoming of China's overseas investments. We don't pay much attention to post-merger integration, and we lack the ability, level of knowledge, experience and talents of post-merger integration." Tu Guangshao, general manager of CIC, spoke at the 2017 Bund International Financial Summit on November 20, "Overseas investments are not just about finding a good project to put money in. Moreover, buyers need to conduct effective post-merger integration after they invested, which is even more important than the investment decision. Investors with practical experience in this area have these common understandings."

More and more global cases have shown that post-merger integration is an important part of the success of mergers and acquisitions. In many cases, although Chinese companies have spent a lot of time in developing strategies that are in line with the company's future development needs, chosen a suitable target and paid a reasonable price, but if the target company is not successfully integrated, then the transactions are not beneficial. KPMG Global CFO survey 2013 results were surprising with more than 70% of M&A transactions below expected value. More than half of the respondents indicated that the company's failed to achieve expected synergies, because of the difficulties in the integration phase. The main failure of integration is: the loss of key talents, insufficient customer attention, organizational confusion and differentiation, cultural conflicts, and weak competitive response.

Many Chinese companies planning to conduct overseas M&A did not even have merger and acquisition teams. Pre-decision making process for many Chinese companies did not include an appropriate patent due diligence, environmental assessment, and commercial due diligence. The failure of mergers and acquisitions is inevitable, if the lack of in-depth research and analysis on M&A targets remain unchanged.

Section 1
Challenges after Post-merger Integration

If post-investment management and integration is neglected, Chinese companies will have poor investment behavior overseas, undermining the goodwill and trust of overseas people in Chinese enterprises, directly affecting the income of overseas investment projects and national interests. Corporate M&A failures can often be attributed to "three Not two Excessive": not complying with host country laws and regulations, not paying attention to corporate social responsibility, not respecting local religious culture and social customs; excessive pursuit of short-term interests, excessive competition and neglect of cooperation.

On the whole, Chinese companies face the following four challenges during the process of post-merger integration.

1. Corporate culture integration risk

In the "Belt and Road" countries' mergers and acquisitions, cultural integration risk is the top risk. The integration of culture involves all aspects of the enterprise and has an inestimable influence on the development of the enterprise. Corporate culture includes values orientation, codes of conduct and traditional habits. When the inherent culture of an enterprise is impacted and destroyed by foreign companies, it will produce an instinctive rejection. Chinese companies should actively communicate with the acquired companies, in order to strengthen understanding, follow the principle of seeking common ground while reserving differences, understand and respect the cultural differences between enterprises. The culture of both sides should be infiltrated and integrated, rather than simply and rudely replacing one culture with another. There is a big difference between Chinese culture and the cultures of the "Belt and Road" countries. The corporate cultures are also very different. If there is no cultural integration between the two sides, it will eventually lead to the failure of the entire merger and acquisition.

2. Strategic level integration risk

The external environment and internal resources faced by the enterprise have changed after the completion of the mergers and acquisitions. It is necessary to formulate a new strategic plan based on the new internal and external environment, involving the reconstruction of the company's development strategy, product strategy, market strategy, and capital strategy. Chinese companies need to redeploy resources from the market, operations, capital, technology, etc. , and continue to track and evaluate sales, costs and profits, in order to give full play to synergy effect. For example, after TCL acquired Thomson, the emergence of LCD TVs led to a significant drop in traditional TV sales. TCL did not adjust the company strategy according to market changes, brought great losses to the company.

3. Operation risks

After the merger and acquisition, the original suppliers and customers of the target company may have doubts and distrust of the capabilities of the new company, resulting in a decline in market acceptance and a sharp decline in sales. Due to the lack of international management experience and international management talents, unfamiliarity with the target countries and target markets, the enterprises are easy to make mistakes in decision-making, leading the enterprises TO FAILURE after mergers and acquisitions.

4. Personnel integration risks

Chinese enterprises may make changes to the target enterprise's human resources system, which will lead to the loss of the company's core employees, especially senior employees. The loss of talents can lead to the decline in productivity and customer loss, resulting in business shrinking. For companies with light assets, the purpose of the mergers and acquisitions is to acquire core employees and market share. The loss of the core employees and market share, to some extent, means the failure of the transaction. Sometimes, Chinese companies will LAY OFF some employees to reduce costs. In some countries, the trade unions are very strong. The layoffs will lead to employee resistance, and the union will even resist the layoff plan, and make some behaviors that are not conducive to the companies.

Section 2
M&A Integration Content and Methodology

Mergers and acquisitions can be classified into four levels: the first level is the right to obtain the target company's property rights (including equity, assets, etc.) and the right to passively obtain income; the second level is the right to obtain the control of the target company and right to actively obtain income; the third level is the integration of strategy, operation and finance; and the fourth level is the integration of management and culture.

The value creation of mergers and acquisitions comes from the capability of management during the process of mergers and acquisitions. To achieve the effect of "1 + 1 > 2", we must pay attention to three fundamentals, the protection of capabilities, the transfer and diffusion of capabilities, and the development of capabilities during the integration of enterprise strategy, culture, human resources and business processes.

1. The content of M&A integration

Post-merger integration includes the following aspects: strategy integration, human resources integration, financial resource integration, goodwill and other intangible resources integration, and culture integration. Among them, culture integration is the biggest challenge faced by Chinese private enterprises in the process of overseas M&A integration. As a "soft indicator" in M&A activities, cultural factors, to a certain extent, are even more important than the factors of financial and technical markets.

(1) Strategy integration

Strategy integration management includes the integration of corporate mission and objectives, overall corporate strategy, business strategy and functional strategy. The success of post-merger integration depends on the transfer of strategic capabilities between the two companies, and the transfer of strategic capabilities depends on the interdependence of the strategic capabilities of the two parties. The strategy of the target company should be compatible with and integrated with the strategy of the buyer. Otherwise it will be difficult to exert positive synergy effect. However, the target company should also formulate appropriate strategies according to its own situation. For example, the comprehensive cost reduction strategy of the target company or the company-Wide personnel policy adjustment may not be conducive to the target enterprise characterized by research and development to establish a competitive advantage in product innovation.

(2) Human resources integration

The integration of human resources after mergers and acquisitions is the key to the success of the transaction. Neusoft Group, which the author works for, is a software company. Its main purpose of oversea mergers and acquisitions is to acquire talents and markets. A considerable number of oversea mergers and acquisitions of Chinese companies are to obtain the "soft assets" of the target companies. The so-called "soft assets" refer to the knowledge value of the employees of the acquired companies, the relationship with the customers, and the new products or services that are being developed with technological advantages and potential market opportunities. Therefore, it is an important and urgent task to retain key talents in the acquired companies. The acquisition companies need to develop and implement a comprehensive and thorough re-employment plan. During the integration transition period, due to the large number of personnel flow and the staff overlap, it is necessary to adjust the personnel structure of the new organization and re-establish the authority of managers at different levels. The acquirers can retain the management team of the target enterprises, timely grasp the operation of the organization through various financial reports, and implement indirect control. The acquirers need to provide employees with a clear and timely understanding of the overall situation of M&A, the strategic significance of M&A for the new company, the development prospects and direction of the company, the work plan, and the supervisor and responsible person in some aspects. By analyzing the appeals of employees of the target companies, the acquirers can propose attractive goals and commitments to enhance the employees' trust and dependence of the target companies on the acquirers.

(3) Financial resource integration

In the process of mergers and acquisitions, financial personnel can use purchase method and equity method to combine financial statements. The purchase method only incorporates the profits realized by the acquired enterprise after the combination date into the income statement, and the equity method incorporates the profits of the acquired enterprise for the whole year into the income statement. If the business activities of the acquired company are expected to be acquired, the inventory of the acquired company needs to be adjusted according to the inventory valuation standard of the buyer.

(4) Goodwill and other intangible resources integration

In the M&A activity, the company has four naming methods: adopting the name of the acquiring company, retaining the name of the acquired company, using a combination of names of the two companies, and using a brand new name. When the acquired company owns a famous trademark, the acquired company usually retains its trademark. In general, consumers only care about the name of a brand rather than the change in ownership.

(5) Culture integration

In the process of mergers and acquisitions, the culture integration has the central position. The difference between management style and corporate culture is the main reason for the success or failure of mergers and acquisitions. Many companies that seem to be able to bring synergies may have a culture that seriously jeopardizes the coexistence of both parties. The culture integration of Chinese companies after completing overseas mergers and acquisitions is crucial and plays a decisive role in the success of M&A activities. 80% of M&A integration failures are due to the cultural factors. According to the relationship between the two sides of mergers and acquisitions, the culture integration model of M&A can be classified into four categories: cultural injection, cultural fusion, cultural immersion and cultural promotion. The corporate culture strategy is the key to determining the effect of corporate culture integration. We should consider the strength of relationship between the two parties' cultures and choose the appropriate culture integration strategy.

The culture integration of the "Belt and Road" countries mergers and acquisitions faces the challenges due to the dual differences between national and corporate culture. At the same time, the risk of these two cultural differences for overseas mergers and acquisitions is also affected by the cultural recognition of two sides in mergers and acquisitions and the degree of integration of mergers and acquisitions. Many problems of M&A activities stem from the human factors, as either the employees of different companies are not sure how the M&A will affect their work, or due to the cultural incompatibility, a decline in security and lack of trust. These factors have caused employees to be hostile to mergers and acquisitions. Another result of mergers and acquisitions is the loss of employees' recognition of the organization, resulting in a decline in job satisfaction and employee turnover. The greater the difference in organizational culture between the acquiring company and the target company, the greater risk of culture integration of overseas mergers and acquisitions are. With the continuous implementation of mergers and acquisitions integration, the risks of overseas M&A culture integration may decrease as the synergy effect is realized, and may increase as the contradictions intensify. In addition, the study also found that positive cooperation experiences before mergers and acquisitions help to reduce the risk of cultural integration between the two parties, and positive cooperation experiences will eventually lead to a better performance after M&A.

2. The methodology of M&A integration

Companies should initiate post-merger integration at the same time as the transaction is announced, select the leaders of the integration team, and set the integration schedule and stop loss points. The target company shall carry out process transformation and grafting according to the resources and management system of the buyer, and strive to achieve "seamless docking" with the buyer, and maximize the synergy effect of operation and management. At the same time, the acquirer also needs to maintain the normal operation of the acquired company's business by setting clear goals and developing incentives.

The project management approach is an appropriate way to manage the transition phase of integration. For the post-merger integration management organization, an effective and practical structure should include the following three levels: the Steering Committee, management team, and various types of functional groups. The Steering Committee is composed of the senior managers of two companies, providing strategic and policy guidance for the integration, ensuring that the objectives of integration are consistent with the purpose of the mergers and acquisitions; management team consists of 3 to 5 full-time staff to promote the integration work, maintaining the integrity and continuity of management, focusing on solving and coordinating problems and contradictions from all aspects of the organization; functional groups solve specific problems of mergers and acquisitions in finance, manpower, information technology and other aspects. Throughout the PMI implementation process, continuous discussion and communication is necessary to reduce misunderstandings and conflicts, integrate culture, and build future communication goals.

According to the successful M&A experience of Chinese companies along the "Belt and Road" countries, we conclude that successful post-investment management cases usually include the following six aspects.

(1) Clarifying the M&A vision, formulating the integration strategy and roadmap

Formulating a clear integration strategy is the basis for the successful integration of M&A projects. The company should set clear development goals for the acquired objects according to different trading drivers and the company's actual circumstances, that is, what kind of enterprise will the acquired company become in the future. Companies with a rich experience in mergers and acquisitions along the "Belt and Road" countries often consider this issue at the stage of screening targets, for example, what is the position of acquired assets in the company's overall strategy? What role should it play? In the management and control mode, should the original management system of the acquired company be retained, or should the acquired company be transformed into its own management system? The answers to these questions will determine the general direction of the integration. ON THIS FOUNDATION, the enterprises can formulate the objectives of the integration and form a clear integration strategy.

When Neusoft Group makes mergers and acquisitions, it usually considers what its advantages are and whether it can effectively integrate the target after the completion of the mergers and acquisitions. Neusoft Group's mergers and acquisitions are mainly in the field of healthcare, and have acquired a number of companies in the fields of medical IT, social security software, and health management. As these three areas are the advantageous business areas of Neusoft Group, the integration can be realized soon after the completion of the mergers and acquisitions, helping the target enterprises to improve their performance and achieve synergy effect.

(2) Establishing a full-time integration team to participate in the whole process of the M&A project

In many overseas M&A projects of Chinese companies, it's two completely different teams that be responsible before and after the transaction. Often it is the case that the information is missing after handing over the work. Because the two groups have different ways of dealing with the problems, it is easy to give the acquired party the impression that the attitudes and practices of the Chinese enterprises are inconsistent before and after the closing. In addition, the staffing requirements of the transaction and the integration team are different. The transaction team is mainly composed of strategy, finance, legal affairs and external consultants. The post-merger integration requires a large number of experts in organization, operations and production management, human resources management, technology research and development. Some Chinese companies have set up a full-time integration teams responsible for developing integration methodology, designing integration processes, finishing integrating work, accumulating and disseminating integration experience.

In the actual project, the responsibilities of the integration team mainly include:

a. Assess integration risks and determine integration goals;

b. Finding integration risk points to provide support for transaction negotiations;

c. Managing and guiding the actual integration work, coordinating the work of various integration teams, and serving as the communication bridge between the two parties.

M&A transactions are closely linked to the integration process, but there are significant differences in work content and objectives. Companies with extensive experience in M&A projects often set up full-time transaction and integration teams, which coordinate with each other, but work in parallel. The integration team will intervene in the whole process to ensure that the mergers and integrations are not out of touch. This will help the acquired company to establish and strengthen the trust of the acquirer and minimize the conflicts of the organizational structure, business, personnel management and culture that may occur during the integration process.

Neusoft Group's business team will participate in M&A transactions from the very beginning, and even many M&A projects are recommended by the business team to the headquarter. The business team has a very clear understanding of the strengths and risks of the target company, so the company's executives also attach great importance to the business team's opinion on M&A transactions. In the process of mergers and acquisitions, the business team will fully assess the integration risks and communicate with the target company in advance to lay a good foundation for future post-investment integration. Once the acquisition is completed, the business team will fully integrate the target company immediately.

(3) Establish a reasonable and efficient management and control system

Overseas business management and control has always been a weak point for the Chinese companies' overseas projects. When choosing a business management model, companies need to consider factors such as business strategy, shareholding structure, synergies and potential risks. According to the degree of group participation and business collaboration, the four basic management and control modes that enterprises can choose are: direct operation, strategic operation, strategic design, and financial control. For each type of management and control model, enterprises need to define specific management principles in five aspects: corporate governance structure, vertical functional system construction, core personnel management, performance tracking, service and operational improvement.

After Neusoft Group acquired the Harman navigation team in Germany, it showed respect to the original company's history, culture and employees. After the completion of the acquisition, Neusoft Group did not replace any management team members, only sent a financial controller to participate in the management of the company, and incorporated the group's Romanian business into the company. The executives of the target company also frequently visit China, communicate frequently with the business team in the headquarters and feel the culture of the parent company. After the completion of the mergers and acquisitions, the management team and employees of the target company were very stable, the business continued to develop, and the number of teams doubled in five years.

(4) Integrating the superior resources of both parties to achieve synergy effect

When an enterprise launches an M&A project, it usually expects the transaction to achieve synergy effect. The two sides complement each other by developing cooperation and sharing business resources, so that the overall benefit of the company after the mergers and acquisitions is greater than the sum of the benefits of two enterprises before, that is, "1 + 1 > 2". When conducting project feasibility analysis, screening investment targets and conducting due diligence, companies need to analyze in depth whether the purchased assets can meet the company's strategical needs, identify sources of synergy effect, and set targets for synergy effect. The post-merger integration phase is a crucial period for implementing synergies. Enterprises need to rationally design the management and control mode, management principles, operating mode, and financial management systems of acquired assets after the transaction and integrate the superior resources of both parties for synergy effects. In general, the synergy effect includes operational and financial synergies. Operational synergy also includes revenue and cost synergy. Revenue synergy can be achieved by integrating the two markets and customer resources. Cost synergy can be achieved through procurement cost savings, sales and management cost savings. Financial synergy can be achieved through capital market and listing financing, unified management and distribution of funds. Sources of synergies include economies of scale, integration of sales channels and customer resources, mutual support of upstream and downstream businesses in the industry chain, and new skills or joint forces of R&D teams.

After formulating the synergy implementation plan, the company also needs to track and monitor the implementation of the plan, and periodically and irregularly adjust the synergy implementation plan according to the market changes, implementation effects, and accumulated experience and lessons learned in actual operations.

Successful mergers and acquisitions along the "Belt and Road" countries will result in the growth in performance, especially in the Chinese market. For example, after Geely acquired Volvo, Volvo's sales in China achieved rapid growth, and many advanced technologies and management methods of Volvo have also driven the rapid growth of Geely's China business and achieved synergy effect of "$1 + 1 > 2$". In comparison, TCL's acquisition of Thomson's color TV business did not only fail to achieve growth in China business, but the business in Europe and North America has also been faltering, dragging TCL into the quagmire.

(5) Coping with the challenges of corporate culture integration and smoothly implementing employee integration

The mergers and acquisitions along the "Belt and Road" countries involve the integration of Chinese and foreign corporate cultures. When Chinese companies acquire foreign companies, there are big differences in working methods, values, leadership styles and behavioral norms. If not handled properly, these differences can easily lead to conflicts and opposition between Chinese and foreign parties, which affect all aspects of business operations. One of the key areas of the M&A project along the "Belt and Road" countries culture integration is employee integration, and the key point of employee integration is to communicate with the acquired employees on the integration strategy, goals and plans, understand and fully consider the premise of employees' concerns. The acquirers should conduct all-round communication to dispel the acquired employees' concerns, win their support, so that they have a sense of identity and belonging.

In the long run, culture integration needs to strengthen work in the areas of executive integration, concept integration, human resources system, and daily management, and fundamentally establish a new corporate culture of "tolerance and integration of the cultural differences".

Considering the diversity of the "Belt and Road" national culture, successful mergers and acquisitions must require the sufficient integration of culture. Chinese enterprises must do their homework before conducting the mergers and acquisitions along the "Belt and Road" countries, fully study the country culture where the target is located and company culture, and fully respect the dual differences of the country and company culture in the process of integration. For example, when Geely acquired Volvo, it adopted the strategy of "Volvo's executive team would manage it", fully respecting the cultural traditions of Volvo executives, employees and the company, instead of transplanting the management culture of Geely's headquarters. Similarly, Neusoft Group's acquisition of the German Haman navigation team also adopted the same strategy and achieved success.

(6) Establish an efficient communication mechanism and win the recognition of stakeholders

During the process of mergers and acquisitions, Chinese companies often ignore the importance of communication with various stakeholders, disclose less information, have little communication with stakeholders, and lack public relations management experience. In the M&A projects along the "Belt and Road" countries, companies should recognize that there may be differences in the interests of various stakeholders. For example, customers hope that the new company will still maintain the quality of products, services, and customer experience. The partners want to understand the company's future business direction, such as business strategy, business model, supplier management, etc., to consider whether it is necessary to adjust the way of cooperation with the new company. Employees are concerned about the position setting, job responsibilities, salary and benefits, business reporting line during the process of transferring ownership of the enterprise. Other stakeholders, such as government agencies, analysts and the media, may be more concerned with corporate social responsibility, earnings expectations, and future investment plans.

Poor communication will bring about barriers, which will lead to opposite emotions. However, it is not difficult to break such barriers. Companies must first identify that various stakeholders involved in local investments, have to determine public relations strategies, brand image and provide information flow between the corporation and these stakeholders. Companies may set up public relation department with professional staffs or seek professional guidance from public relations service providers. When communicating with all parties, companies should pay attention to the information of the transaction itself, including the investment strategy of the enterprise, the positioning and future planning of the acquired target, the source of synergy effect, and the employment and economic development opportunities that will be brought to the host country. This will help community to understand the business purpose of corporate mergers and acquisitions, rather than focusing on non-commercial factors.

Section 3
Assessment and Management of M&A Integration

Integration refers to the process of adjusting the components of a company and integrating them. Post-merger integration is an art of theoretical and practical significance that combines two or more companies and is owned by a common owner. PMI (Post-merger integration) is the integration after the M&A, and the content is extremely rich. Among them the strategic integration, financial integration, human resources integration and culture integration are the most researched areas because of their importance. Transaction Gap and Transition Gap are two reasons for M&A failure. The former can be compensated by M&A negotiation and bargaining, while the latter needs to be compensated through post-merger integration activities such as business process, information system and production integration. Bruce Wasserstein clearly pointed out: "The success of mergers and acquisitions is not based solely on the ability of acquired companies to create value, but rather on the integration after mergers and acquisitions." Improper mergers and acquisitions will lead to the destruction of wealth.

There are two theories in the academia on the post-merger integration: synergy effect, successful integration will bring more than expected performance; friction effect, the deep integration of mergers and acquisitions having a negative impact on the success of mergers and acquisitions, will destroy the target resources that originally attracted the acquirers. The risks of enterprise integration include internal resource risks, that is, the risks brought by the internal producers due to organization, management, and strategic capabilities; the external resource risks are mainly the risks brought by the external consumers of the enterprise affected by the market segmentation and product positioning.

The risks in post-merger integration have been focus of the attention. In 2003, Michael E. Porter conducted research on Fortune 500 companies, arguing that more than 70% of companies could not achieve successful integration of unrelated resources. In the five years after the acquisition, they chose to strip out the acquired companies. Only when the technical differences between the two parties are moderate, which means that certain differences exist and are within the acceptance ability of the acquirer, the technical integration after the mergers and acquisitions may be efficient. However, we should highly guard the decline in the motivation of exploratory learning caused by the similarity, which leads to the uncertainty of technology integration and new technology output levels. For example, in 2009, Sichuan Tengzhong acquired the US Hummer, the subsequent technology integration, technical support and development model faced great challenges. In February 2010, Tengzhong had to announce the acquisition failure. Geely also expressed its intention to acquire

Hummer, but Geely believes that Hummer does not fit its own strategic direction, and subsequently chose to buy Australian DSI. The acquisition of DSI has greatly enhanced Geely's automatic transmission technology development and production capacity. After the post-merger integration, Geely's technical capabilities significantly improved. In 2010, Geely acquired Volvo to improve the company's environmental protection, safety and energy saving capabilities.

During the integration of the mergers and acquisitions, the acquirer must make a correct judgment on the differences between two parties and make rational use of the complementary mechanism. If the acquirers choose the wrong strategy, they adopt the centralized strategy for the resources with distinctive differences, and the diversification strategy for the resources with little difference, this will result in increased internal conflicts and a waste of resources, which will lead to a decline in the overall performance of the company. If the difference between the two parties is small, the target company is very likely to accept the new resource allocation; on the contrary, the employees will be more inclined to maintain the original social identity, so that the new resources are not so easy to integrate. In this case, only focusing on the speed of integration will be detrimental to the performance after the mergers and acquisitions, which may cause internal conflicts and instability.

Before the post-merger integration, Chinese companies need to first objectively evaluate the difficulty of integration of the underlying assets, access and evaluate their own ability to digest and integrate, so that they must know themselves and the target company. They can develop the targeted strategies and tactics of the post-merger integration. Many Chinese companies focus on hard factors, while ignoring soft factors, which ultimately leads to integration failure. For the hard factors, it can be solved by hiring various consultants and setting up a branch in the local market. However, the integration risk caused by soft factors is difficult to understand through the short-term due diligence. These factors are hidden in daily communication, and the contradictions often end up over time, such as strikes caused by labor relations, community relations, religious and cultural differences, and even conflicts caused by misunderstandings. This requires the buyer to be patient in the future integration management, and to have an open mindset for the target companies, employees, communities, customers, willing to truly understand and respect the local culture, rather than bring dominant attitude of "take all-in", or the tycoon-like way of "whoever pays is a grandfather".

As shown in Figure 8-1 and Figure 8-2, Chinese companies need to assess themselves from the two dimensions prior to mergers and acquisitions. Meanwhile, they also need to evaluate the target companies.

Figure 8 – 1   Self – assessment of mergers and acquisitions of the acquirer

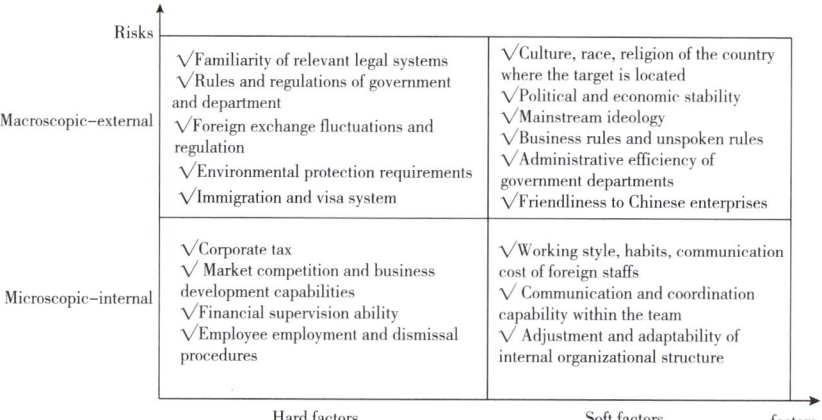

Figure 8 – 2   Evaluation of integration difficulty of target company

After assessing themselves and the target, the companies need to develop post-investment management models. Different management models have their own advantages and disadvantages. There are both successful and failed cases for the model of actively managing board of directors who are fully involved in the management; there are also successful cases for the model of not actively managing board of directors, or inadequate intervention in the management. It seems from person to person variance and adaptation to local conditions is the essence of post-investment management art.

In the mergers and acquisitions along the "Belt and Road" countries, Chinese companies can learn from the experience of Japanese companies. Japanese companies tend to let overseas companies operate for a period of time, such as 2-3 years. Japanese companies spend more energy on governance structure design, long-term incentive programs, decision-making authority definition, different committee responsibilities and conference schedule design. They reduce the transaction risk through reasonable governance structure and effective performance management.

Japanese companies usually adopt the bonus-type retention schemes to retain the management team and key employees of the target companies. Retention bonuses are usually cashed at a constant rate, i. e. 50% in the first year and 50% in the second year. For performance indicators, Japanese companies usually adjust their assessment indicators after they have a certain understanding of the target companies in 3-4 months after closing the transaction. In the case of limited understanding of the target companies' business, Japanese companies usually follow the performance indicators of the previous 1-2 years, and decide whether to adjust the performance indicators or not and how to link the acquired company with the headquarters after gradually understanding the target companies.

Japanese companies are also paying attention to "balance of decentralization and control" to achieve effective management through scientific design of corporate governance structures. They also pay attention to the strategic direction and effective use of resources, and seek a balance between "full decentralization" and "excessive interference". For the difference between the two corporate cultures, Japanese companies gradually identify the differences by working together, and gradually strengthen mutual understanding during their work.

Case 8 – 1 Kyocera Acquires AVX

Transaction Amount: unknown
Target Country: United States
Industry: Electronics
Case Background: AVX was a world leader in the field of capacitors. In order to develop Kyocera into a comprehensive electronic parts company, Inamori Kazuo made an acquisition request to the chairman of AVX, and the AVX chairman agreed with the request. The acquisition took the form of "stock exchange", which putted a 50 percent premium on the stock AVX shares on the New York Stock Exchange, exchanged the shares of AVX with the Kyocera stock with a price of USD 82 for USD 30. The chairman of AVX Company considered that the price of USD 30 was too low and he hoped to trade at USD 32. At that time, the presidents and lawyers of the Kyocera American Company strongly opposed it. They thought that they would easily agree to such requests and AVX would be insatiable. Inamori Kazuo believed that the chairman was responsible to shareholders of AVX and agreed to the chairman's request.

However, when the stocks of both parties were to be exchanged, the Dow Jones index fell sharply, and Kyocera's stock price also fell by USD 10 to USD 72. The chairman of AVX Company proposed to change the original USD 82 to USD 32 exchange conditions to USD 72 to USD 32. The Kyocera side was unanimous to advocate rejecting request of AVX. However, Inamori Kazuo accepted unfavorable changes as the acquisition is the combination of two completely different enterprises. It is like a "marriage" between enterprises, and needs to consider the interest of the partner to the maximum extent.

After the acquisition, Kyocera's stocks rose all the way, AVX's shareholders made a profit, and their joy infected the company's employees. In general, the employees of the acquired company always have conflicts and dissatisfaction with the acquiring company, but the AVX employees have a friendly attitude from the beginning because of Kyocera's high-profile attitude, and naturally accepted the operation philosophy of Kyocera.

Case Study: Kyocera, founded by Inamori Kazuo, is a representative of Japanese-style operations and a pioneer in Japanese companies' overseas mergers and acquisitions. Since the 1970s, Kyocera has conducted more than 40 overseas mergers and acquisitions. Many Japanese companies acquired American companies, but they had to retreat or sell the acquired company because of losses.

In comparison, Kyocera received a generous return. This is in line with the philosophy of Inamori Kazuo not only considering their own interests but also thinking about the partner's interests.

Kyocera has a common point in selecting the companies to be acquired. The company is temporarily in trouble due to some special reasons. The acquisition of such a company, on the one hand, will have the advantage of low transaction costs, but on the other hand, it will face greater challenges in the subsequent operational improvement, especially in the case of cross-cultural and cross-regional situations. However, from the actual effect of Kyocera's overseas mergers and acquisitions, it can successfully rebuild the acquired enterprises in almost every transaction, the key is Kyocera's unique post-merger integration and management model and skills. The secret of success is to successfully transform the corporate culture by injecting Kyocera's Eastern-style management philosophy into the troubled Western companies, thus achieving a breakthrough transformation.

An important part of these methods is also the foundation of Kyocera's management culture: to expand the scope of communication within the company, to optimize communication effects, to enhance employees' sense of participation, and to introduce the concept of "daily improvement". In the 1970s, Kyocera bought a San Diego factory from the American Fairchild Company. Due to a long-term mismanagement, the factory had been in a state of losing money for years. The situation was very chaotic: the management was far away from the front line of business, in order to cope with the increasingly difficult business situation, the management team only took measures on various cost-cutting details; the staff also had no work enthusiasm. After Kyocera bought the company, Kyocera first taught the employees about the practice and experience of on-site improvement. Meanwhile, Kyocera focused on shortening the distance between management and employees and increasing the frequency of communication. In addition, in order to improve the overall communication effect, Kyocera aimed to transform the office area into an open office environment to enhance the communication effect and resolve the gap between management and employees.

Similarly, Kyocera also showed respect for AVX's original history, culture and employees during the acquisition of AVX. After the completion of the acquisition, Kyocera not only retained the AVX company name and management team, but also integrated the Kyocera North American Electronic Components Division with outstanding performance and the newly formed Kyocera North American plant with AVX. This confidence and sincerity for the development of AVX has been greatly recognized and supported by AVX employees. It has laid a good foundation for subsequent improvements in AVX. After the acquisition, AVX's business continued to grow and got re-listed on the New York Stock Exchange in less than five years. In the process of re-listing, Kyocera received a generous return by selling AVX stocks.

Section 4
Classic Cases of Post-merger Integration

Based on years of overseas M&A experience and the successful M&A cases, the author finds that Chinese companies that can achieve effective integration and good synergy effect have some common features, including: a. Recognizing the importance of overseas M&A integration, it is difficult to achieve synergy and transaction objectives without post-merger integration; b. Fully consider the business model and integration strategy before signing the contract; c. Start the integration work as soon as possible, so that the teams of both parties can work together and lay the foundation for business docking; d. Formulate the "management and control model" from how to achieve business development goals more effectively, and ultimately finish the design of corporate governance, organizational structure and decision-making authorization system; e. Recognize the existence of cultural differences to meet the challenge with an open mind, and establish an effective communication mechanism to win the sense of identity and belonging of the other side; f. Take the opportunity of mergers and acquisitions along the "Belt and Road" countries to enhance the company's international operation and management capabilities, establish a training mechanism for international talents, and develop a long-term financial goals based on the M&A strategy.

Geely Automobile and Guangming Group are two successful companies in China's overseas mergers and acquisitions. Chinese companies can learn from their successful experiences. TCL's acquisition of Thomson is a negative case served as an alarm in the mergers and acquisitions along the "Belt and Road" countries of Chinese companies.

Case 8 – 2 Geely Acquires Volvo

Transaction Amount: USD 1.8 billion
Target Country: Sweden
Industry: Automotive
Case Background: In 2010, Volvo was at the forefront of corporate survival. Although Volvo was famous brand and was known as "the safest car in the world", the customers were unwilling to purchase it. The company has been losing money for years. From the moment of Volvo's birth, Volvo's car-making technology has been recognized by the whole industry. Volvo has never lacked the praise from its peers. Therefore, the car giant Ford generously acquired Volvo's 100% share when its European market was initially squeezed out. However, Ford did not expect that after the completion of the acquisition, Volvo could not regain its vitality and continuously lose money, and decide to sell Volvo to take out the "hot potato".

On August 2, 2010, Geely held the final closing ceremony for the acquisition of the entire equity of Volvo in London. This acquisition is a classic case of overseas mergers and acquisitions in China. From today's point of view, the acquisition decision is undoubtedly correct. Volvo's sales in 2014 exceeded its annual sales record for the first time since 2007, and China has become Volvo's largest market in the world. In 2015, Volvo's global sales exceeded 500,000 unit for the first time and its profit increased by 2 times year-on-year. It not only regained the European market, but also improved its performance in the US market. In 2017, its global sales reached a record high of 543,000 units, revenue increased by 10%, and profits rose 66%. At the same time, the acquisition also led to the economic development of Volvo's headquarters in Gothenburg, Sweden led the development of local spare parts industry. The similarity and complementarity of resources between Geely and Volvo, and the high matching of their integration behaviors, are the key to the success of Geely's acquisition of Volvo.

On December 27, 2017, Geely acquired 8.2% stake in the Volvo Group to accelerate its global presence. With 100,000 employees and build factories in 18 countries, the Volvo Group covers 190 countries and regions and have the famous brands of Volvo, Volvo Penta, UD, Terex trucks, Renault trucks, Nova buses, Pavo buses, and Mike trucks. The investment was completed seven years after Geely invested in Volvo Cars, marking Geely's completion of the integration of Volvo Cars and the deployment of a larger and broader scope with the Volvo Group's larger platform.

Case Study: After the completion of the merger and acquisition, not only Volvo's sales have increased, but Geely has also benefited a lot from this process. Geely has always been regarded as a low-end product, which is not conducive to the transformation and upgrading of enterprises and the integration with the international market. Volvo's excellent brand value can fully promote Geely's strategic transformation. Although Geely has developed rapidly in the domestic market, its automotive design, manufacturing and R&D capabilities are far from the world level. Volvo can provide Geely with advanced automotive manufacturing technology and help Geely quickly reduce the manufacturing gap with the world's top car brands. Through the acquisition of Volvo, the introduction of international advanced management team, and independently cultivate a group of teams with international management experience, Geely has obtained sales channels and networks in the European and American markets, providing a strong guarantee for its globalization strategy.

Geely's mergers and acquisitions of Volvo was not smooth. After a few years of the transaction, Volvo's performance was not satisfactory. By 2012,

Volvo's sales in China fell by 10%, which led Geely to replace Volvo's management team. From 2012 to 2014, Geely and Volvo also carried out other integration actions: 1) At the end of 2012, Geely and Volvo signed three technology transfer cooperation agreements to achieve synergy effect; 2) In 2013, they announced the establishment of a Geely-Volvo joint R&D center in Sweden to develop the middle-end market, almost at the same time, Volvo announced a layoff of 1,000 employees to avoid another loss; 3) In September 2014, Volvo launched the first new car XC90 after the acquisition.

Geely's successful integration of Volvo includes the following five aspect of experiences.

First, the independence of the target: Geely is not depriving Volvo of independent management team after the mergers and acquisitions. After the transaction was completed, Geely managed Volvo as "Volvo's executive team would manage it", allowing Volvo to maintain a separate operating system, not to interfere with Volvo's operations management, retain the executive team, and promised the union not to transfer the factory and not lay off employees. Li Shufu stated that, "Geely is Geely and Volvo is Volvo", which embodies this principle of integration. Geely did not directly use Volvo's technology. It is conceivable that if Geely uses Volvo's technology in a large amount, Volvo's high-end brand image and sales volume will be greatly reduced.

Second, cultural integration: Geely's "people-oriented" corporate culture is highly consistent with Swedish mainstream culture and Volvo's corporate culture. Geely retains the Gothenburg team elite and factory, R&D center, trade union agreement and dealer network in Sweden, which reflects the respect for Volvo's international image and supports the cultural integration of both sides.

Third, independent brand: Volvo is a luxury car brand, Geely is a low-end car brand, and lacks the talents with the experience and ability to operate in the international market. After the mergers and acquisitions, Geely respected the Volvo brand and maintained Volvo's independent brand. The principle that Geely is applying while operating Volvo is accepting and learning from Volvo's existing management experience rather than dominating it. Geely also guarantees the independence of Volvo's brand and operation after the mergers and acquisitions and gives full play to the core value of the original brand.

Fourth, deliberately slowing down the integration speed: After a long period of mergers and acquisitions, both parties continued to work together on the concept and technical direction of product development. After both parties reached a consensus, Geely began the project of the localization of Volvo engines in Zhangjiakou in 2012 and introduced a series of advanced turbine speed-increasing small displacement engines. Geely's slower integration speed was based on the fact that Volvo has little similarity in terms of culture and management concepts.

Fifth, the integration of talent and technology: Although Geely acquired a 100% stake in Volvo, it did not acquire 100% of the intellectual property of Volvo. Volvo's platform and engine were shared with Ford and Mazda, and Geely cannot directly apply Volvo's technology and production standards. That is to say, Volvo's core technology is still in the hands of Volvo, Geely can only obtain Volvo's technology and talent through various means. Geely spent RMB 20 billion to develop Volvo Car's structure. The development of the architecture was completed by both parties and Geely's R&D capability was greatly improved. Geely's Lectra and Boyue have used Volvo's technology extensively and achieved good sales. Volvo's executives and technicians joined Geely and brought Volvo's innovation, ideas and technology. Geely has set up a European R&D center in Sweden. The center has 1,600 experts from more than 20 countries and regions. Through the European R&D center, Geely can continuously extract the essence of European car-making for hundreds of years and continuously improve its product and technology level.

Case 8 – 3 Guangming Group's overseas mergers and acquisitions

Transaction Amount: unknown

Target Country: Australia, New Zealand, Israel, Spain etc.

Industry: Food

Case Background: On August 8, 2006, Guangming Food (Group) Co., Ltd. (hereinafter referred to as Guangming Group) was established, consisting of the relevant assets of Shanghai Yimin Food First Factory (Group) Co., Ltd., Shanghai Agriculture and Industry (Group) Co., Ltd., Shanghai Sugar Industry Alcohol (Group) Co., Ltd., and Jinjiang International (Group) Co., Ltd.

At the beginning of its establishment, Guangming Group's annual revenue was RMB 41.4 billion. In 2009, before the opening of overseas mergers and acquisitions, the annual revenue reached RMB 50.8 billion. In 2010, the acquisition of New Zealand's New Wright Dairy opened the curtain of Overseas M&A of Guangming Group. Since then, Guangming Group has completed 8 overseas M&A projects within 5 years. Guangming Group has acquired majority stake in Salov Group, has acquired Filippo Berio, New Zealand dairy giant New Wright, Australian Manason Food Group, French DIVA wine company, Israeli dairy giant Tnuva, and Spanish Miguel. Guangming Group focused on the food industry and deployed a number of fields in the world, and committed to the integration of global resources to create a global manufacturing and distribution system. Driven by overseas M&A projects, Guangming Group's revenue in 2014 exceeded RMB 120 billion, an increase of 136% compared with 2009.

Case Study: In the process of overseas mergers and acquisitions, Guangming Group concluded a set of effective overseas mergers and acquisitions methods.

First, target selection: The M&A target selection of Guangming Group follows the following five criteria. 1) Be In line with the development strategy of Guangming Group and produce "1 + 1 > 2" synergy effect after the acquisition. For example, Guangming Group acquired the internationally renowned olive oil brand, Filippo Berio, a family-owned company with a history of 100 years. It has an absolute leading position in the olive oil market in Europe and America. The company develops steadily and its business maintains steady growth every year. Guangming Group evaluated the various risk points and considered the company to be the target for the acquisition. The reason why the company chose to be acquired is also to use the Guangming Group's resources to better develop the Chinese market and achieve faster growth. Finally, the two sides reached the cooperation. After the acquisition, the company achieved a three-digit annual increase in the Chinese market. 2) The excellent management team of the target enterprise can effectively manage the enterprise and reduce the management cost. 3) Controllable risks: Guangming will carefully evaluate each risk point of the project, including financial conditions, local laws and regulations, pensions and other factors. For example, when Guangming Group was acquiring the Weetabix Food Company, the UK's second-largest breakfast cereal brand, the amount of the pension gap has been the focus of debate between the two sides. Finally, Lion Capital invested £ 30 million to make up for the Guangming Group, reducing the risks due to the pension gap. 4) Accelerate the pace of listing of overseas companies and make full use of the global capital market to serve for the Guangming Group's international strategy. 5) Establish a long-term cooperative relationship with the team.

Second, reasonable planning: Before the mergers and acquisitions, Guangming Group considered whether after the target company would increase to a certain scale, if it gets listed, integrated, or injected into its existing listed companies. The whole process diversifies the value-added means of Guangming Group's overseas acquisition and ensures that the value of the acquired assets can be maintained and increased.

Third, the hierarchical management system: Guangming Group's acquired enterprises are distributed all over the world, far from China, and it is impossible for all the matters to be reported to and handled by the headquarters. Thus, Guangming Group classifies the different affairs into various decision-makings levels. The different levels of affairs are decided by different levels of management team. Only when the level of the affairs is high enough, it will be submitted to the chairman for decision-making, which greatly shortens the decision-making chain and improves the efficiency of decision-making.

Fourth, talent training and management system: Although Guangming Group has been conducting overseas mergers and acquisitions, the lack of international management talents has always been its bottleneck. In practice, Guangming Group solves the problem through several ways: 1) Selecting senior managers who understand Western management concepts to join local management teams, accumulating experience and reserving talents; 2) Cooperating with international human resources companies, recruiting overseasexecutives; 3) Retaining the original shareholders and the management team of the acquired company. For example, in the acquisition of Weetabix Food Company, Guangming Group and the former controlling shareholder of Lion Capital jointly managed Weetabix Food Company and retained part of the management team, and Lion Capital continued to hold Weetabix Food Company as a 40% minority shareholder. Guangming Group adopted equity and cash incentives for the management team of Weetabix Food Company, enacted a reward and punishment system, and defined the goals of the company and employees.

Case 8-4 TCL's acquisition of Thomson's color TV business

Transaction Amount: USD 560 million
Target Country: France
Industry: Home Appliances

Case Background: On November 4, 2003, TCL Group and France Thomson officially signed an agreement to reorganize the color TV and DVD business of both parties. The joint venture company named TCL Thomson Electronics, referred to as TTE. TCL holds more than 60% of the shares as a controlling shareholder. Thomson holds a 33% stake in TTE and incorporates 9 000 Thomson employees into the new company. The new company has more than a dozen production bases in Europe, America and Asia, with annual sales of 18 million color TV sets. TCL became the world's largest supplier of color TV at the time.

At that time, Thomson's color TV and DVD business lost EUR 254 million, but TCL Group Chairman Li Dongsheng did not take it seriously and shouted the 18-month profit slogan. However, TCL still implanted Chinese management to France in the course of the replacement of CRT (cathode ray tube) technology and the integration of employees, In the following three years, TCL was completely passive in the European market. It did not effectively developed the new market and the ways to deal with original issues. There were also many contradictions within the enterprises, and a series of problems such as capital, talents, technology, management, brands and channels have emerged. After the completion of the merger, TTE suffered huge losses in successive years with a net loss of RMB 4 billion for three years. The stock of TCL was put on ST's hat. The huge loss of European color TV business became a black hole that swallowed the profits of TCL Group. Li Dongsheng lamented: "Our original team is too optimistic, the integration offect has not been played, the enterprise is still operating according to the original style. " TCL's acquisition of the Thomson color TV business and Lenovo's acquisition of the IBM Personal Computer Division are two landmark events for the internationalization of Chinese companies around 2003. Compared with Lenovo's acquisition of the IBM Personal Computer Division to become the world's largest computer manufacturer in 2012, TCL's acquisition of the Thomson color TV business is undoubtedly a failure.

Case Study: In the case of TCL's acquisition of Thomson, several common problems of Chinese companies' mergers and acquisitions along the "Belt and Road" countries were exposed.

a. Lack of necessary preparation and due diligence. TCL's acquisition of Thomson took only eight months, lacking meticulous preparation and full understanding of the target company. In comparison it took Lenovo 3 years from the start of the contact and 13 months for the negotiation to acquire IBM. The biggest driver of TCL's acquisition of Thomson's came from becoming the world's number one color TV manufacturer. Li Dongsheng himself, treated the acquisition of Thomson as the once-in-a-lifetime opportunity to become bigger and stronger, TCL only took four months to contact, and decided to acquire Thomson. Therefore, it is not surprising that TCL turned a blind eye to the risk warning given by the third-party agency. (At the time, Morgan Stanley had a neutral view of the acquisition, while Boston Consulting disagreed with the transaction because of the high risks.)

b. Not understanding the French policy led to the huge personnel costs. In *TCL Internationalization: Li Dongsheng's nightmare in oversea M&A*, the author mentioned: "TTE quickly fell into the embarrassing situation of 'cannot recruit and lay off the employee'. On the one hand, the color TV industry belongs to the sunset industry in Europe and America. There are very few talents to recruit in this area. On the other hand, the layoffs in Europe are very complicated. In addition to 3 months' notice in advance, it is also necessary to pay a high amount of compensation. If the number of layoffs exceeds 10, the amount of compensation must be negotiated by the shareholder and trade union. Therefore, after TCL acquired the company in Europe, due to the pressure of the trade union, the international integration was delayed. In China, this is a situation that is impossible to encounter." After the acquisition, Li Dongsheng said, what he did not expect was that it was so difficult to lay off an employee in Europe, which greatly pushed up the company's operating costs. Li Dongsheng revealed in his Weibo that dismissing personnel in Europe must prioritize to provide the position for those who are old and weak, that is, if you want to dismiss employees, you must first dismiss those capable and young people because these people can easily find a job. This is in contradiction with the original intention of dismissal. Now, according to the law, it is not self-defeating to dismiss the capable people.

c. Culture integration is difficult. TTE Vice President Tong Xuesong said in an interview with *China Business JOURNAL* in late 2005: "TCL once envisioned sharing Chinese-designed molds with Thomson to save the huge cost of mold design. Although the color TVs produced according to these molds are very popular in the United States, the French people looked down on these molds." TCL has encountered a lot of similar cases. For example, some French have a sense of language superiority and do not want to speak English. There is no one in TCL who can speak French. The communication between the two sides is very difficult. Both parties cannot reach consensus for a simple matter even after a long meeting.

d. Capital chain problems. Transaction cash and working capital in the integration process are obtained through syndicated loans and corporate listing financing. After the completion of the transaction, the operating, investment and financing cash were all negative, and the overall cash and cash equivalents showed a significant decline.

e. Incorrectly estimated the cost of overseas mergers and acquisitions and the value of the Thomson brand. M&A costs include consulting agency fees, evaluation fees, negotiation fees, payments to the acquired companies, and integration costs, exceeded TCL's expectations. TCL originally thought that the Thomson RCA brand had matured in the North American market and there was room for further improvement. However, the RCA brand's vitality was almost exhausted and there was a huge loss in the North American market. Due to the underestimation of M&A transaction costs and integration costs before the transaction, TCL's financial performance dropped sharply and the company experienced a business crisis.

f. The development trend of color TV was not expected. At that time, color TV manufacturers promoted the replacement of ear-projection color TV to flat-panel TV, and Thomson invested all research funding in the development of technology for rear-projection products. TCL's acquisition of Thomson during the period of color TV technology revolution is undoubtedly an adventure.

If adequate market research had been done before the acquisition, TCL may not have encountered such a problem. "Why did Thomson sell its color TV business? The world's first color TV is produced by it. In the anti-dumping lawsuit filed by the EU against Chinese TV companies, Thomson was one of the behind-the-scenes ambassadors. Because it enjoyed the patent dividend, Thomson was reluctant to invest in the development of flat-panel TV, but flat-panel TV was the trend of consumption in the future. Thomson sold its TV business in order to get rid of the burden. Even so, TCL did not get the 'outdated' technology when it acquired Thomson. " The former TCL Group's color TV spokesperson Liu Buchen said. At the beginning of 2012, Li Dongsheng said when he talked about the lesson of Thomson's acquisition: "When TCL acquired Thomson, TCL had a wrong judge about the direction that the TV technology would go in the future, whether it was plasma or LCD TV. At that time, more people thought It was plasma TV. Because Thomson had a strong DLP (Digital Light Processing) technology, TCL thought that Thomson's rear-projection technology was better than plasma technology, which resulted in big loss."

After the mergers and acquisitions, TCL obviously lacked the capability of post-merger integration, which is usually a common problem in Chinese companies´ overseas mergers and acquisitions. The case of TCL's acquisition of Thomson's color TV business has undoubtedly provided a strong warning and reference value for Chinese companies´ mergers and acquisitions along the "Belt and Road" countries.

APPENDIX

CASES OF INVESTMENT AND M&A ALONG THE "BELT AND ROAD" COUNTRIES

Case 1
CEFC Acquired 14.16% Stake in Rosneft Oil (Failure)

Keywords: integrated oil, integrated gas, stock, risk
Acquirer: CEFC China Energy Company Limited (CEFC China)
Target Company: Rosneft Oil Russia

【Timeline】

• CEFC China Energy Company Limited (hereinafter referred to as CEFC) agreed in 2017 to purchase 14.16% of Rosneft Oil's shares worth USD 9.1 billion from Glencore Group (hereinafter referred to as Glencore) and Qatar Investment Authority (QIA).

• After the failure to sell shares to CEFC, in April 2018, Qatar Investment Authority announced that it would replace CEFC's acquisition of a 14.16% stake in Rosneft Oil, paying USD 4.4 billion.

• On May 4, 2018, Rosneft Oil issued a notice canceling the agreement to sell 14.16% of the shares to CEFC.

• CEFC has spent about USD 400 million on this acquisition and the money will not be repaid.

【Introduction to the Transaction Subject】

With nearly 50 000 employees and annual revenues of more than USD 40 billion, CEFC has won the title of China's most influential enterprise and the top 10 most internationally competitive Chinese leading companies. CEFC has been ranked among the Fortune Global 500 for four consecutive years and ranked 222nd in 2017.

Founded on September 29 1995, Rosneft Oil is the leader of the Russian oil industry and the world's largest listed oil company. The business scope includes oil and gas exploration and production, upstream offshore drilling projects, oil and gas refining and crude oil, domestic and foreign gas and product marketing. The company has approximately 320 000 employees and ranked 158th in Fortune Global 500 in 2017.

Glencore is one of the world's largest diversified natural resource companies and a major producer and distributor of more than 90 commodities, with approximately 150 mining and metallurgical bases and a large number of oil production assets and agricultural facilities.

Glencore's industrial and marketing activities span the globe, with nearly 160,000 employees and more than 90 offices in more than 50 countries and regions. Glencore's customers are mostly in the automotive, steel, power generation, petroleum and food processing sectors, but they also provide financing, logistics and other services to producers and consumers of commodities.

Founded in 2005, QIA is the Qatar Sovereign Wealth Fund and the largest sovereign wealth fund in the Middle East. As of September 2018, the total assets were USD 320 billion. Its funding is mainly derived from Qatar oil revenues, with the aim of strengthening the country's economic strength by diversifying into new asset classes. Based on Qatar's investment more than 30 years ago, its growing long-term investment portfolio helps to complement the country's vast wealth of natural resources and provide long-term stable returns.

[Transaction Review]

Glencore and the Qatar Investment Authority bought a 19.5% stake in Rosneft Oil Russia for USD 11.3 billion in December 2016. Due to the complexity of the transaction structure, Glencore and Qatar Investment Authority actually only hold 4.5% of the shares, which is the reason for the joint sale of 14.16%.

In September 2017, CEFC announced the acquisition of the 14.16% stake held by Glencore and Qatar Investment Authority with a consideration of USD 9.1 billion. Upon the completion of the acquisition, CEFC will become the third largest shareholder of the Rosneft Oil Russia. The two sides also signed agreements on strategic cooperation agreements and long-term supply contracts for crude oil. The agreement stipulates that the two sides will carry out in-depth cooperation in the upstream and downstream oil industry chain, financial services and asset transactions. However, as Chairman of the Board of Directors of China CEFC Energy Co., Ltd. Ye Jianming was exposed to investigations by relevant departments, CEFC was caught in a serious debt crisis and dispute.

Russia's *Vedomosti* reported that according to the agreement, CEFC failed to pay the first payment for the acquisition of shares in Rosneft Oil Russia in April 2018. The first payment accounted for 20% of the total value of the transaction, about USD 1.8 billion, and the rest was originally due for payment at the end of September 2018. The media said that China CEFC Energy Co., Ltd. has spent about USD 400 million on the acquisition, and the money will not be refunded.

In April 2018, the Qatar Investment Authority announced the acquisition of the 14.16% stake in Rosneft Oil Russia. Upon completion of the transaction, the Qatar Investment Authority will own 18.93% of the shares of the Rosneft Oil Russia, becoming the third largest shareholder of the Rosneft Oil Russia, Glencore will retain a 0.57%

stake. The entire transaction is worth 3.7 billion euros (about USD 4.4 billion).

At the same time, the Rosneft Oil Russia plans to buy back USD 2 billion worth of shares from the open market between 2018 and 2020. Rosneft Oil Russia announced that it has appointed UBS as an independent agent to implement its open market share repurchase program. In August 2018, the UBS Board of Directors approved a plan to purchase up to USD 2 billion in stocks by the end of 2020. The Rosneft Oil Russia announced in a statement: "The plan approved by the board of directors aims to provide excellent shareholder returns in the face of large market volatility."

【Conclusion】

Our conclusion is that CEFC's acquisition was unsuccessful. The action, capability and ambition of the Chinese acquirer did not match. In this case, a lot of money and time was wasted.

From 2014 to 2016, CEFC's assets have almost doubled year by year, and its operating income has increased year by year, from RMB 17.406 billion to RMB 247.255 billion. Despite the rapid growth of corporate income, the absolute value of net profit has not kept up with the increase in total income. The return on assets reflecting its profitability has declined year by year, from 7.4% to 2.9%, and its net profit margin has been below 2% for a long time.

The strategy of Chinese companies' M&A along the "Belt and Road" countries needs to match with the company's own volume and capabilities. However, many private enterprises in China are too radical in their strategies, and they hope to achieve rapid growth in their business through investment and M&A. Along with a series of radical M&A, the deep-seated contradictions within the company have been exposed, leading to the deterioration of the company's cash flow, which ultimately led to the failure of the transaction, and even dragged the company into the abyss.

Case 2
PetroChina Acquired an 8% Stake in ADCO Petroleum Company

Keywords: energy, oil, strategic relationship
Acquirer: China National Petroleum Corporation (CNPC)

Target Company: United Arab Emirates Abu Dhabi Company for Onshore Oil Operations (ADCO)

[Timeline]

• On February 19, 2017, China National Petroleum Corporation (hereinafter referred to as PetroChina) and the United Arab Emirates Abu Dhabi National Oil Company (ADNOC) signed a stock purchase agreement, PetroChina obtained Abu Dhabi Company for Onshore Oil Operations (ADCO) 8% equity and 8% of ADCO onshore oilfield development projects, with a maturity of 40 years.

[Introduction to the Transaction Subject]

PetroChina is China's largest oil and gas producer and supplier, one of the world's leading oilfield service providers, and a world-renowned engineering construction contractor. Its crude oil production accounts for 52% of the country's total, and natural gas production accounts for 71% of the country's total. With offices in nearly 70 countries and regions, PetroChina owns oil and gas assets and interests in countries and regions in Africa, Russia, the Americas ⋯ and is seeking to play a greater international role.

ADNOC is one of the world's leading oil and gas companies and is wholly owned by the Abu Dhabi Emirate Government. The company was founded in 1971 and is active in all areas of the oil and gas industry. It has 17 specialized subsidiaries and joint ventures with operations in both the upstream and downstream sectors. ADNOC is active all over the world and produces about 3 million barrels of crude oil a day. In recent years, in order to meet the growing demand of industrial gas users, ADNOC has made significant achievements in expanding the development of natural gas fields and has increased gas injection requirements.

While carrying out all business activities, ADNOC is committed to sustainable development, ensuring a harmonious balance between people's needs and the earth's resources, supporting the implementation of environmental protection principles in all projects, and the performance of its HSE (Health, Safety and Environmental Management System) is not only at the Gulf first level but also at the international first level.

ADCO is the main onshore producer within the ADNOC Group, producing 1.6 million barrels of oil and 1.59 billion cubic metre of natural gas per day. ADCO is owned as to 60% by ADNOC, and other shareholders include BP (10%), France Total (10%), PetroChina (8%), Nippon Oil Development Corporation (5%), China CEFC (4%) And South Korea GS Energy (3%).

[Transaction Review]

The ADCO onshore oilfield development project is an open tender project approved by the Abu Dhabi government. ADNOC holds 60% of the shares, while the other 40% is reserved for foreign partners. PetroChina invested 6. 5 billion dirhams (USD 1. 77 billion) in registered capital to acquire an 8% stake in the ADCO onshore oilfield development project and an 8% stake in the project joint operation company ADCO.

The United Arab Emirates is China's second largest trading partner in the Middle East, and the trade between the United Arab Emirates and China is estimated to increase from USD 54. 8 billion in 2015 to USD 60 billion in 2016.

【Conclusion】

Our conclusion is that the deal is a relatively successful transaction.

As the world's second largest energy consumer, China was a major importer of crude oil in 2016. Sia Energy, a Beijing-based consulting firm, estimates that due to the need for replenishment of stocks, strong gasoline demand and booming fuel exports, China's crude oil imports in 2016 will increase by 860, 000 barrels, which increase nearly 13%.

This landmark agreement marks an important new phase in the strategic relationship between PetroChina and ADNOC. As part of the agreement, PetroChina will play an active role in the design and development of technical applications for mature fields through the establishment of a tailor-made technology center at ADNOC.

The deal strengthens and deepens the relationship between the United Arab Emirates and China. The two sides share the greatest value of economic value with the common value interests and jointly optimize energy opportunities to support the long-term development of ADNOC and PetroChina. This will be a mutually beneficial partnership that will maintain strong production levels while at the same time maximizing returns from a very attractive, long-term and sustainable opportunity.

> Follow-up: At the end of 2017, China Petroleum Engineering Construction Corporation signed a USD 1. 52 billion EPC general contract with ADCO for the Bab oilfield complex development project. In March 2018, PetroChina signed an agreement with ADNOC to acquire 10% of the shares in two oil fields of ADNOC for USD 1. 175 billion.
>
> On July 19, 2018, ADNOC and Bureau of Geophysical Prospecting INC., China Natio (BGP), a subsidiary of PetroChina, reached a cooperation agreement worth 58. 8 billion dirhams (about RMB 10. 8 billion). Through this agreement, ANDOC awarded BGP an important 3D seismic reflection survey to explore the undeveloped oil and gas resources in Abu Dhabi. The two sides also intend to continue to seek more cooperation opportunities, joint investment in the downstream investment field and internationally.

Case 3
HNA Holding Acquired CWT Singapore

Keywords: logistics, renaming
Acquirer: HNA Holding Group Co., Limited
Target Company: CWT Limited Singapore
Changed name to: CWT International Limited

【Timeline】

• In 2013, HNA Holding Group Co., Ltd. (hereinafter referred to as HNA Holding), a subsidiary of HNA Group, a large multinational company, INVESTED IN a leading integrated logistics solutions provider in Singapore, CWT Limited (CWT), and later became a controlling shareholder.

• In September 2017, HNA Holding acquired CWT through a voluntary comprehensive offer, establishing a greater advantage in integrated logistics services, international commodity trading and financial services. Since December 2017, CWT Limited has been renamed " CWT International Limited" .

【Introduction to the Transaction Subject】

HNA Holding is a listed company on the Main Board of the Hong Kong Stock Exchange. It is a high-growth investor and developer with a mission to open up a potential global investment market. Its largest shareholder, HNA Group, is a leading corporate group listed on the Fortune Global 500, with its core businesses covering aviation, holding, tourism, capital and logistics. A solid financial foundation, including strong capital and liquidity, ensures HNA Group's ability to meet its commitments.

Founded in 1970, CWT Group's main business is to provide warehousing and container shipping services for container terminals, and to support a diverse global customer base through a global network of integrated commodity service and service partners. CWT combines industry capabilities, global scale, and business in merchandising, financial services and integrated logistics to deliver comprehensive business solutions while helping customers succeed and thrive.

【Transaction Review】

HNA Holding announced that the total number of CWT shares it has owned, controlled or agreed to acquire and valid acceptance of the offer as of 5 pm (Singapore time) on November 2, 2017, amounted to 589 million shares, accounting for approximately 98.1% of the total issued CWT shares. HNA Holding changed its name to CWT International Limited after its acquisition in Singapore.

HNA Holding acquired CWT, a Singapore logistics and bulk commodities company, for USD 1 billion, CWT's merchandising, financial services and logistics operations will also become the core business of the group. The acquisition of CWT by HNA Holding is a " snake swallow" transaction. At the end of 2016, HNA Holding's revenue and gross profit were HKD 183 million and HKD 63 million, whereas CWT's revenue and profit reached HKD 50.9 billion and HKD711 million.

The acquisition of CWT by HNA Group was praised by Xinhua News as a model for the "small but beautiful" project. In late October 2017, the share price of HNA Holding Co., Ltd. soared 26% in one day. As some media sources reported company's acquisition of CWT is one of China's "Belt and Road" top ten investment and M&A cases.

The HNA Group Board of Directors believes that the company's name change after the merger will better reflect the Group's strategy and be consistent with the Group's business and development strategy. Name change of the company is assumed to be in the best interests of company itself and all the shareholders.

[Conclusion]

Our conclusion is that the deal is a relatively successful transaction. HNA Group's own brand has become a pioneer in overseas expansion, and has opened up a new market with a strong localization strategy. CWT's main profit comes from logistics services and financial services, which is a significant synergy with HNA Group's business. Through the acquisition of CWT, HNA Holding can enhance its profitability. As an international logistics hub, Singapore is more conducive to the expansion of HNA Holding's global business. HNA Holding can further expand its service capabilities in global supply chain logistics using CWT channels and networks. Prior to the acquisition of CWT, HNA Group's Tianhai Investment completed the acquisition of Ingram Micro, the world's largest supply chain service provider, for USD 6 billion. HNA Group has continuously expanded its layout in the logistics field. Although the acquisition process has been relatively successful, HNA Group is also faced with the problem of how to deeply integrate the acquisition target.

Southeast Asia has become an important investment area for Chinese companies to invest overseas. After analysis, the author believes that there are the following four reasons. First, good political and business relations: Southeast Asian countries have good relations with China, and Southeast Asian countries welcome China's local investment. Second, cultural identity is high: the proportion of Chinese in Southeast Asian countries is high, and this aspect has its influence on cultural similarities; so it is easier for Chinese companies to acquire and integrate. Third, the population of Southeast Asia is large and the economical development speed is high; the total population of Southeast Asia is over 600 million. The huge population base provides the possibility for the business expansion of Chinese enterprises. As China's labor costs increases, many European and American companies shift manufacturing to Southeast Asia, bringing rapid development of the local economy and increasing purchasing power. Many industries in China are saturated, and the Southeast Asian market is a new growth point for Chinese companies. Fourth, the investment cost is relatively low: compared to the investment costs of Europe and the United States, the investment cost in Southeast Asia is relatively low. As the most developed country in Southeast Asia, Singapore has many first-class pharmaceutical, logistics, technology, and financial companies. These companies have also become the preferred targets for Chinese companies to invest and acquire.

> Follow-up: On December 11, 2017, HNA Group has exercised its legal right to acquire all shares from the dissident shareholders of Singapore-based logistics company CWT, thus ending the USD 1 billion acquisition. On behalf of HNA Group, HNA Financial Advisors announced that the offer price for CWT shareholders who have not accepted the tender offer is 2.33 Singapore dollars (USD 1.73) per share. The price is the same as for other CWT shareholders, and the deal is valued at 1.399 billion Singapore dollars (USD 1.04 billion).

Case 4
Alibaba Doubled the Bet with a New USD 2 Billion Investment

Keywords: online shopping, mobile phone
Acquirer: Alibaba Group
Target Company: Southeast Asian e-commerce company Lazada

【Timeline】

• On March 19, 2018, Alibaba Group (hereinafter referred to as Alibaba) announced that it will invest another USD 2 billion in Lazada to accelerate the growth plan of Southeast Asia's largest e-commerce platform and deepen its integration with the Alibaba ecosystem.

[Introduction to the Transaction Subject]

Alibaba was founded by Ma Yun in 1999. His purpose is to make it easy to do business anywhere. Alibaba's goal is to build the infrastructure of the future e-commerce, let customers meet, work and live in Alibaba, and become a company that lasts at least 102 years. Alibaba operates in more than 200 countries and regions, with more than 500 million people using its shopping app every month.

Lazada, established in 2012, is the No. 1 online shopping platform in Southeast Asia, covering Indonesia, Malaysia, the Philippines, Singapore, Thailand and Vietnam. As a pioneer in the Southeast Asian e-commerce ecosystem, Lazada provides tailored marketing, data and service solutions to more than 145 000 local and international sellers and more than 3 000 brands through its market platform, and provide services ranging from consumer electronics to household items, toys, fashion products, sports equipment and daily necessities for the region's 5.6 billion consumers. Lazada is focused on delivering a superior customer experience with a variety of logistics services and payment methods through its first and last mile distribution departments, including cash on delivery, comprehensive customer service and accessible returns. At present, Alibaba holds a majority share of Lazada.

[Transaction Review]

On March 19, 2018, Alibaba announced that it will invest another USD 2 billion to accelerate the growth plan of Southeast Asia's largest e-commerce platform. Including this new plan, Alibaba would have invested USD 4 billion in Lazada. In 2016, Alibaba took control of Lazada with a USD 1 billion investment and invested another USD 1 billion in 2017 to further increase its shareholding ratio to 83%.

The investment in 2018 highlights Alibaba's confidence in the future success of Lazada's business and highlights the growth prospects of the Southeast Asian market as well, which is a key part of Alibaba's global growth strategy.

Amazon began to enter the Southeast Asian market in 2017, but only tested it in Singapore. Shopee is also a company that entered Southeast Asia earlier. It was invested by Sea, was formerly known as Garena, and raised more than USD 1 billion in IPO in the United States. Alibaba has not restricted its development in Southeast Asia to support Lazada, and has invested USD 1.1 billion in Indonesian e-commerce company Tokopedia. Indonesia is the largest economy in Southeast Asia and the fourth most populous country in the world. Competitors have invested billions of dollars in the region to build a broad logistics infrastructure. In 2017, Amazon launched a two-hour delivery service in Singapore, and JD also established its own logistics network in Indonesia, and in January 2018 announced an investment in the Vietnamese e-commerce platform tiki. vn.

The investment is expected to promote Lazada's integration into the Alibaba ecosystem and enable Lazada to leverage Alibaba's resources to further serve consumers in innovative ways and enhance the competitiveness of Southeast Asian businesses. The investment highlights Alibaba's commitment to providing a broad platform for local talents in Southeast Asia to contribute to the development of the digital economy in Southeast Asia.

With the support of huge cash and stock soaring, Alibaba has invested new funds in the loss of Lazada, in order to ensure its greater share in the rapidly growing e-commerce market, which highlights the Alibaba'sambition of globalization.

[Conclusion]

Our conclusion is that this is a relatively successful transaction.

2017 is a year of rapid expansion of Alibaba and its payment subsidiary Ant Financial in Southeast Asia. It is also a year confronted with the world's largest online retailer Amazon, and faces the challenge of JD's exploring new consumers in the region.

Southeast Asia is highly valued by Alibaba because of its young population, high mobile penetration rate and online business that currently accounts for only 3% of retail sales in the region. In fact, with 640 million consumers, a growing middle class and increasing smartphone penetration, Southeast Asia is gradually becoming the main battleground for technology giants. Consulting firm Frost & Sullivan predicts that the total value of e-commerce goods in the region will rise from USD 20.5 billion in 2016 to USD 65.5 billion in 2021.

There is already ample evidence that the relationship between Alibaba and Lazada has been strengthened. In 2018, Lazada began to offer Taobao products in Southeast Asia. Alibaba has replaced Lazada's technology team leadership with its own executives. In addition, in order to develop cloud business, Alibaba has also built a data center in the region and invested heavily in infrastructure to promote the development of e-commerce and payment services. Ant Financial also acquired equity in several other Southeast Asian payment companies. Since Alibaba's first investment, Lazada has made remarkable progress.

Case 5
KS ORKA Acquired 95% of Indonesia SGI Shares

Keywords: energy, geothermal, fundraising
Acquirer: Zhejiang Kaishan Compressor Co., Ltd.

Tool Company: KS ORKA

Target Company: PT Sokoria Geothermal Indonesia (SGI)

【Timeline】

• In August 2016, KS ORKA, a joint venture company controlled by Zhejiang Kaishan Compressor Co., Ltd., signed an agreement to acquire 95% of the shares of Indonesian Sokoria Geothermal Indonesia (SGI) from PT Bakrie Power (PTBP) and Xped Ltd. (formerly Raya group).

• On January 16, 2017, KS ORKA completed the acquisition of the SGI geothermal project, and KS ORKA intends to accelerate the development of the SGI project. The first geothermal generating set was scheduled to go live in December 2018.

【Introduction to the Transaction Subject】

SGI holds the right to develop the Sokoria Geothermal Power Project (SGPP) in Indonesia. The development of the SGI project will provide a stable, long-term power supply to Flores Island, meeting local electricity demand and promoting local economic development. Geothermal is an increasingly important renewable energy source. Indonesia is known as the "Volcano Country" and Indonesia is reported to have 40% of the world's potential geothermal energy, with an estimated total capacity of 28 000 MW.

KS ORKA is a joint venture company of Icelandic company Hugar Orkaehf and Zhejiang Kaishan Compressor Co., Ltd. KS ORKA combines the expertise of Icelandic geothermal project development with the power plant technology and manufacturing expertise of the Kaishan to form the only vertically integrated geothermal and waste energy company in Asia.

【Transaction Review】

In August 2016, KS ORKA signed an agreement to acquire a 95% stake in SGI from PTBP and Xped. SGI has the right to develop the Sokoria Geothermal Power Project in Indonesia, located on Flores Island in East Nusa Tenggara, Indonesia, for a 30 MW geothermal power project, including the installation of power plants, substations, generators and turbines, as well as laying power lines.

The transaction is a conditional M&A transaction and KS ORKA has signed a conditional equity purchase agreement with Xped and PTBP. Under the terms of the agreement, KS ORKA loaned SGI USD 1.5 million to pay for franchise fees, land use taxes and related development expenses, and Xped and PTBP guaranteed this by the 98% stake in SGI. If the preconditions for the transaction are met within three months, KS ORKA will acquire a 95% stake from Xped and PTBP for USD 1. Otherwise, Xped and PTBP need to return the loan. After the equity transfer, KS ORKA will host the SGI geothermal exploration and development project. If the exploration results meet the requirements, KS ORKA will pay USD 2 million to Xped and PTBP; if not, according to the actual situation of exploration, the payment amount will be reduced accordingly.

At present, Indonesia is the third largest geothermal energy power generation country in the world after the United States and the Philippines. In 2007, geothermal energy accounted for 1.9% of Indonesia's total energy supply and 3.7% of Indonesia's electricity. In 2011, the installed capacity of the six geothermal fields in Java, North Sumatra and North Sulawesi was close to 1 200 MW.

With the promotion of the "Belt and Road" Initiative, under the guidance of the innovation-driven development strategy, Zhejiang Kaishan Compressor Co., Ltd. successfully developed a screw expansion power generation technology with independent intellectual property rights. And a new way of geothermal power generation technology has been opened up with "one well and one station".

The first geothermal generating set was scheduled to go live in December 2018. The implementation of the project will be carried out simultaneously with the integration of the Flores grid, planned by Perusahaan Listrik Negara (PLN), and the drilling is underway.

【Conclusion】

Our conclusion is that the deal is a relatively successful transaction. At present, Zhejiang Kaishan Compressor Co., Ltd. is fully implementing the strategy of transforming to the renewable energy operator with the core technology of the independently developed geothermal wellhead power station. This foreign investment is part of its strategy to transform into a renewable energy operator, which will help improve the company's future operating income and profits. The project is ideally suited to showcase the company's screw-expansion technology for geothermal power generation and to replace the high-cost diesel-fired power generation in the Indonesian power grid. If the agreement is implemented smoothly, it is of great significance for Zhejiang Kaishan Compressor Co., Ltd. and KS ORKA to achieve the goal of developing 500 MW of geothermal power generation capacity as soon as possible and to develop the global geothermal market.

When investing in M&A along the "Belt and Road" countries, the success of transaction delivery sometimes depends on conditions such as government approval, actual exploration, and intellectual property licensing, so there is greater uncertainty. Under such circumstances, the setting of the transaction preconditions can maximize the interests of the acquirer. The entire transaction can be divided into several stages. Under certain conditions, the acquirer pays a certain fee and the transaction enters the next stage. If the transaction preconditions cannot be met, the transaction terminates on its own. The preconditions for trading depend on the comparison and game between the strengths of the two parties. Chinese buyers sometimes need to pay a deposit when investing in M&A. If the transaction cannot be carried out due to the buyer's reasons, the deposit will not be returned. In this case, the design of the terms of the transaction is very beneficial to the buyer, and the interests of KS ORKA are protected to the maximum extent and are worth learning by Chinese companies.

Case 6
YY Participates in the Singapore Video Social Platform Bigo's D Round Financing

Keywords: TMT, further investment
Acquirer: China YY Inc.
Target Company: BIGO Inc. Singapore

【Timeline】

• In 2014, YY Inc. (YY) held a 27.8% stake in BIGO Inc. (Bigo).

• On June 5, 2018, YY subscribed Bigo's D-round preferred stock for $272 million and became the largest shareholder of Bigo.

• In March 2019, YY completed a wholly-owned acquisition of Bigo with a total transaction value of approximately USD 1.45 billion, including USD 343 million in cash and the corresponding YY shares.

【Introduction to the Transaction Subject】

YY is China's leading live streaming media platform. Users on the platform contribute to a vibrant community by creating, sharing and enjoying a wide range of entertainment content and activities. YY enables users to interact in real-time via live online media and provide users with a unique immersive entertainment experience. YY was listed on NASDAQ in November 2012. In 2018, YY's total revenue for the year reached USD 15.764 billion, a year-on-year increase of 36%; and the net profit was RMB 1.642 billion, an increase of 18.4% year-on-year.

Founded in 2014, Bigo has live broadcast platform Bigo live, short video social platform Like, live game APP Cube TV and a variety of social APP products. The company's business is mainly concentrated in Southeast Asia, South Asia, Middle East and America. By the end of 2018, Bigo live had 225 million registered users, more than 40 million active users, and users spent an average of 40 minutes a day on the platform. The company officially achieved profit in October 2017, with total revenue of USD 300 million. Bigo's investors also include first-line venture capital institutions such as Ping An Insurance Overseas Holdings and Bertelsmann Asia Investment Fund.

【Transaction Review】

YY announced that it has invested USD 272 million in its D round financing of Singapore-based social media platform Bigo, becoming its largest shareholder. In addition, YY has also obtained exercisable option one year after the completion date of the investment agreement to purchase additional Bigo shares at fair market prices, and to ultimately obtain over 50.1% of the Bigo's voting rights. Other investors also participated in the D round financing with YY, including Mr. Li Xueling, Chairman and Acting CEO of YY, who used his personal funds to invest in Bigo. Bigo is a fast-growing video-based global social media platform. Headquartered in Singapore, Bigo has the world's leading live broadcast platform, Bigo live, and video editing and sharing platform Like. Bigo has created a video-based online community for younger generations around the world, building strong influence in emerging markets such as Southeast Asia, South Asia and the Middle East, paving the way for further global expansion.

Although Bigo was originally launched in Southeast Asia, it has surpassed the region and has established a total of 20 local offices. Bigo live is one of the top 10 app in the "Social Networking" category on iOS, not only in Southeast Asia, but also in Saudi Arabia, Pakistan and New Zealand.

With the latest investment, YY has become the largest shareholder of Bigo. The link between YY and Bigo can be traced back to the date of the establishment of Bigo. The Bigo live app quickly spread after its launch in March 2016.

After completing the C round financing, Bigo live has a market value of more than USD 400 million, which has surpassed the live webcast and added more apps. These include Cube TV, a streaming service app focused on mobile games, and an app named Like for editing and sharing short films. Since then, Bigo's registered users have nearly tripled in just over a year, from 70 million to 200 million.

But before Bigo officially launched, YY participated in the company's work. In 2014, YY already holds a 27.8% stake in Bigo. At the time, the CEO of Bigo was Li Xueling. In addition, Bigo's co-founder and chief technology officer Hu Jianqiang is also an employee of YY.

Bigo seems to be making a big bet on AI, starting research on the technology in Singapore and planning to equip it with 100 AI experts and engineers. Bigo has tested this technology on its own platform. With the support of YY, Bigo's revenue in 2017 reached USD 1.6 billion, putting more pressure on its competitors. Previously, Bigo's financing announcement followed the competitor M17 Entertainment initial public offering (IPO). The goal of the M17 Entertainment is to raise about USD 115 million. As a private company backed by a profitable parent company, Bigo has a financing advantage over the unprofitable M17 Entertainment. Once listed, M17 Entertainment will face pressure from profitability. And as of March 31, 2018, the M17 Entertainment's live streaming app has only 33 million registered users, which is insignificant compared to Bigo.

【Conclusion】

Our conclusion is that the deal is a relatively successful transaction. Given that the development of China's live broadcast business has stabilized, YY's global expansion with Bigo has important strategic significance. *South China Morning Post* quoted iResearch as saying that since December 2016, China's overall live broadcast ratings have been declining. Despite this, YY's financial results for the first quarter of 2018 indicate an increase in revenue, monthly active users (MAU) and monthly paying users.

The Chinese market is changing rapidly, and so is Chinese consumers' interest. We believe that the rise of short videos may have some impact on live broadcasts, and another reason may be due to changes in government policies. In fact, the Indonesian government has recently used Bigo's AI technology solutions to help them with network monitoring. With an AI monitoring system and a global team of monitors, the government is able to identify 96% of inappropriate content on the platform with limited manpower. Bigo also recently opened a research and development center in Singapore, which is also the main base for the company's future research and development.

Mr. Li Xueling, Chairman and Acting CEO of YY, said: "We are very pleased to announce the completion of the acquisition of Bigo. This is an important milestone for the YY Group and demonstrates our confidence and commitment to the globalization strategy. YY and Bigo's combination of strong business in China and overseas will help us create higher quality live content, expand international influence, and provide a world-class user experience for our global user community, making YY the world's leading video social platform company."

The rapid development of China's Internet industry has evolved from the original model of learning from American Internet companies, the so-called C2C (copy to China) model, into CFC (copy from China). Chinese Internet companies are adding successful models in China to overseas Internet products. Internet companies such as Alibaba, Tencent, Xiaomi, and YY have achieved great success in overseas markets, and more Chinese Internet companies will join the ranks.

Case 7
SAIC's Acquisition of GM's Halol Plant in India

Keywords: car, sharing
Acquirer: Shanghai Automotive Group Co., Ltd.
Target Company: Halol Plant, General Motors, India

【Timeline】
- In June 2017, Shanghai Automotive Group Co., Ltd. (SAIC) announced that it will take over GM's Halol plant in Gujarat, India, and plans to invest 20 billion rupees (about RMB 2.1 billion) in the next five years.

【Introduction to the Transaction Subject】
SAIC is the largest listed company in China's A-share market with a total share capital of 11.683 billion shares. SAIC strives to grasp the development trend of the industry and accelerate the transformation of innovation-driven industries, from traditional manufacturing companies to a full range of automotive products and travel service providers.

General Motors Halol Plant is General Motors´ Harold factory located in Harlol, Gujarat, India. It produces a variety of Chevrolet cars for the Indian market, with an annual capacity of 110,000 vehicles and a total of approximately 1,100 employees.

【Transaction Review】
GM has entered the Indian market for more than 20 years, but has never achieved profitability, with a market share of about 1.2%. So GM had to adjust its strategic layout in India and consider selling the Halol factory.

In June 2017, SAIC announced that it will take over GM's Halol plant in Gujarat, India. In the Indian market, SAIC will employ approximately 1 000 local employees with the support of the local government. The plant will be commissioned in 2019 with an annual production capacity of between 50 000 and 70 000.

SAIC pointed out that it will become the first car manufacturer in China to produce cars in India. Currently, India is the fourth largest auto market in the world. It is estimated that by 2020, India will become the world's third largest auto market. In addition, SAIC's development in India will be operated independently by its subsidiaries, which makes SAIC Group more flexible in the Indian market.

After General Motors of India completed the handover of the Halol factory, SAIC accelerated the renovation and localization of the Halol plant. In 2017, SAIC achieved a total of 170,000 vehicle exports and overseas sales, an increase of 31.8% over the same period of the previous year. The sales volume of vehicle exports continued to rank first in the country. SAIC Group has entered the Indian market in 2019. In the early stage of mergers and acquisitions, the transformation of the Halol factory was promoted in an orderly manner in 2018, and the supplier park was also accelerating construction. The first Internet car products were being developed as planned and planned to be put into production in 2019.

SAIC will sell its iconic British GM brand through its newly established local subsidiary, GM Motor India, which is the main focus of SAIC's global passenger vehicle strategy and has established assembly and distribution operations in the Asia Pacific region.

[Conclusion]

Our conclusion is that the deal is a relatively successful transaction. SAIC's own brand has become a pioneer in SAIC's expansion of overseas markets. The acquisition will lay the foundation for SAIC's development in the Indian automotive market.

India and China are the two most populous developing countries. Compared with China's population structure, India has a more advantageous population structure and a larger proportion of young people. 65% of India's population is young, with an average age of 29 years. After Modi came to power, he adopted a series of reform measures to improve the business environment in India. The Indian economy has developed rapidly and has become a hot spot for global investment. In 2018, overseas investors invested USD 39.5 billion in India, which has exceeded the number USD 32.8 billion in China. Moreover, Chinese companies are also optimistic about India's future economic development. Xiaomi, Alibaba, Huawei, Lenovo, Fosun, OPPO, vivo, etc. have all spent heavy investment in the Indian market.

Case 8
Changdian Technology Co., Ltd Acquired STATS ChipPAC

Keywords: IC packaging and testing industry, cash payment
Acquirer: Jiangsu Changdian Technology Co., Ltd

Target Company: STATS ChipPAC Ltd. (Singapore)

【Timeline】

· In early 2015, Jiangsu Changdian Technology Co., Ltd. (hereinafter referred to as Changdian Technology) announced the acquisition of STATS ChipPAC.

· On May 9, 2016, Changdian Technology announced the completion of the acquisition of STATS ChipPAC, with a total transaction amount of RMB 4.78 billion (USD 780 million).

【Introduction to the Transaction Subject】

Changdian Technology provides customers with a comprehensive product portfolio including discrete, lead, wire bonding, flip chip, MEMS and sensors, integrated passive devices (IPD), and molded interconnect systems (MIS), advanced wafer level package (WLP), through silicon via (TSV) and system in a package (SIP) solutions. Headquartered in Jiangyin, China, Changjiang Electronics Technology has an extensive global manufacturing base with operations centers in China, Singapore and South Korea, and customer support offices in Asia, the Americas and Europe.

STATS ChipPAC provides innovative packaging and test solutions for semiconductor companies in mature markets such as communications, consumer and computer, and semiconductor companies in emerging markets such as automotive electronics, Internet of Things (IoT) and wearables.

【Transaction Review】

Changdian Technology's M&A of STATS ChipPAC is a strategic move that has changed the competitive landscape of the global semiconductor industry. The project spans multiple countries and regions such as Singapore, South Korea, the United States, and China's Taiwan, and involves multiple stakeholders. The design of the transaction structure is cumbersome and rigorous. In order to meet the policies and regulations on foreign M&A in relevant regions, Changdian Technology has divided and reorganized its acquisition targets.

On May 9, 2016, JCET-SC announced the completion of the acquisition of Singapore seal manufacturer STATS ChipPAC. When the acquisition was announced, it caused a huge response in the industry. According to income data, STATS ChipPAC ranks fourth in the global sealing field, while Changdian Technology ranks sixth. This kind of acquisition and reorganization case is extremely complicated, and it takes nearly one and a half years from the proposed acquisition, to the specific operation, and to the end of the acquisition.

The acquisition is mainly divided into two parts.

Part I: Changdian Technology, together with National Integrated Circuit Industry Investment Fund Co., Ltd. (hereinafter referred to as Industry Fund) and Siltech Semiconductor (Shanghai) Co., Ltd. (hereinafter referred to as Siltech Semiconductor) sets up Changdian Xinke in Suzhou. The shareholding ratio of the three parties is 50.98%, 29.41%, 19.61%, and the total investment is USD 510 million. Changdian Xinke also established a second-tier company, Changdian Xinpeng, with the Industry Fund, with a total investment of USD 520 million. Changdian Xinke holds 98.08% of the shares of Changdian Xinpeng, and the Industry Fund holds the remaining 1.92%. Subsequently, Changdian Xinpeng established a subsidiary JCET-SC (Singapore) in Singapore as the main acquirer of the acquisition of STATS ChipPAC. Later, JCET-SC acquired a 100% stake in STATS ChipPAC at a price of 0.465 77 Singapore Dollar per share for a total investment of approximately USD 780 million. The USD 780 million includes a USD 520 million investment from Changdian Xinpeng, USD 140 million loan from the Industry Fund to Changdian Xinpeng, and a loan commitment letter from Bank of China of USD 120 million.

Part II: Changdian Technology and STATS ChipPAC reached an agreement to reorganize their Taiwan subsidiaries while making an offer. In terms of operations, STATS ChipPAC established a new independent company in Singapore, Blomeria. The assets of the two Taiwan subsidiaries were divested to Bloomeria, thereby making the assets of the two Taiwan subsidiaries not included in the acquisition case to meet policy requirements in Taiwan.

After the completion of the acquisition, STATS ChipPAC became a wholly-owned subsidiary of JCET-SC and the company was delisted from the Singapore Exchange.

[Conclusion]

This is a steady strategic acquisition. From the technical level of M&A, there are several unique aspects worth learning, such as how to choose strategic alliances, how to achieve the balance of interests between co-investors, etc., involving complex M&A processes and transaction structure design. STATS ChipPAC has operations in Singapore, South Korea, the United States and other countries and regions. This means that Changdian Technology's acquisition of STATS ChipPAC must comply with the relevant national and regional mergers and acquisitions policies and regulations, and the operational procedures are extremely complex, the most important of which is the separation and reorganization of acquisition targets.

Changdian Technology adheres to the concept of sustainable development and win-win, and advocates the harmonious development of employees, customers, shareholders and society. It has been rated as "China's key high-tech enterprise" and "China's top ten semiconductor companies". At present, the number of patents for packaging technology of Changdian Technology is the first in the industry in the US and China, and its market share ranks third in the world.

Case 9
Jingxin Pharmaceutical Invested USD 10 Million in Israel Mapi

Keywords: pharmaceutical industry, synergy
Acquirer: Zhejiang Jingxin Pharmaceutical Co., Ltd.
Target Company: Mapi Pharma Ltd. Israel

【Timeline】

• In December 2015, Zhejiang Jingxin Pharmaceutical Co., Ltd. (hereinafter referred to as Jingxin Pharmaceutical) announced the use of its own funds to subscribe for 925,900 shares of Mapi Pharma Ltd. (hereinafter referred to as Mapi) at a price of USD 10.8 per share, with a total investment of USD 10 million.

• On August 16, 2018, Jingxin Pharmaceutical announced a capital increase of USD 10 million for Mapi.

【Introduction to the Transaction Subject】

Jingxin Pharmaceutical is a listed pharmaceutical company integrating R&D, manufacturing and sales. It ranks among the top 100 chemical pharmaceutical companies in China.

Founded in 2008, Mapi is a pharmaceutical company focused on the development of clinically advanced central nervous drugs for high threshold and high value-added life-cycle management (LCM) products for large markets and non-patented drugs (APIs) and formulations that include complex active pharmaceutical ingredients. Mapi's strengths are strong chemical and pharmaceutical R&D capabilities, a deep understanding of global markets and regulatory needs, and the ability to promote collaboration in all countries and regions in which it operates. Headquartered in Israel, Mapi has research and development facilities in Israel and China and production facilities in the Neot-hovavo Eco-Industrial Park south of Beersheba, Israel. Mapi has strong intellectual property rights and has filed numerous patent applications for APIs and formulations.

【Transaction Review】

After investing USD 10 million in 2015, Jingxin Pharmaceutical added another USD 10 million to Mapi, and the company's shareholding in Mapi increased from 5.87% to

9.71%. The new funding is mainly used for Mapi's drug development and marketing for indications such as neuropathic pain and multiple sclerosis. As of August 2018, Jingxin Pharmaceutical has completed the investment of seven overseas innovative pharmaceutical companies, and through the deployment of overseas innovative companies, the company's research and development capabilities have been enhanced to promote rapid growth in performance.

Mapi, an Israeli pharmaceutical company in its development stage, has received a round of USD 10 million in financing from its Chinese counterpart, Jingxin Pharmaceutical. Mapi is transferring funds from a new round of financing to develop two new products, one for the treatment of schizophrenia and the other for the treatment of pain.

Mapi is committed to the development of high threshold, high value-added lifecycle management drugs, complex APIs and formulations. The funds raised will support the future development of Mapi and enable the company's channels to expand to more drug and sustainable innovation products.

【Conclusion】

Mapi has established a new mode of cooperation with Chinese companies to take advantage of both sides. The investment of Jingxin Pharmaceutical is part of the product development agreement, Mapi will develop products specifically for Jingxin Pharmaceutical and will support the registration, manufacturing and marketing of Jingxin Pharmaceutical in the Chinese market. But despite this, Mapi will still have global intellectual property and marketing rights.

At present, the cooperation between Chinese pharmaceutical companies and foreign companies has such characteristics: China directly purchases corresponding innovative products and technologies from abroad, thereby participating in the investment and cooperative development of new drugs; The cooperation field is mainly cancer drugs and mainly the non-core areas of large foreign companies. The cooperation model is mainly for Chinese companies to obtain exclusive transfer rights in China, and there is almost no global transfer. However, from the development path of international pharmaceutical giants such as Pfizer and Roche, investing in or acquiring early projects is a good development path. It is expected that more and more Chinese pharmaceutical companies will embark on the path of international investment and M&A in the future.

However, from the perspective of past cooperation, the foreign investment and M&A cooperation model of Chinese pharmaceutical companies needs to be explored. Some opportunities for direct acquisitions have disappeared, a more robust model is to follow the international M&A funds to participate in equity investments in order to fight for risks below earnings.

Case 10
Jingxin Pharmaceutical Acquired P2B Shares for USD 5 Million

Keywords: pharmaceutical industry, shares
Acquirer: Zhejiang Jingxin Pharmaceutical Co., Ltd.
Target Company: Pharma Two B Ltd. (P2B) Israel

【Timeline】

· On March 22, 2017, Jingxin Pharmaceutical announced that it will invest USD 5 million in Pharma Two B Ltd. (hereinafter referred to as P2B), to acquire no more than 5% of its equity.

【Introduction to the Transaction Subject】

P2B is an Israeli biopharmaceutical company dedicated to the development of compound preparation with "non-commercially available doses", "low toxicity" and "superior effect". The company's main product is P2B001, which is an innovative compound preparation with indications for Parkinson's disease and is now in clinical trials.

【Transaction Review】

On March 22, 2017, Jingxin Pharmaceutical announced that it will invest USD 5 million to acquire P2B's equity of no more than 5%, and has the right to P2B001 innovative compound preparation products in the Chinese market. P2B001 is expected to be on the market in China around 2021. Through this investment, Jingxin Pharmaceutical has become a shareholder of Israel's P2B company, which is conducive to consolidating the cooperation and retaining potential advantages for Jingxin Pharmaceutical.

【Conclusion】

Jingxin Pharmaceutical has done a lot of work in the technical investigation of target companies. At the same time, the investment field is the pharmaceutical industry and therapeutic field which it is also familiar with. Through domestic and international comparisons and research, Jingxin Pharmaceutical finally invested in optimistic about P2B technology.

Jingxin Pharmaceutical occupies a global innovation highland and promotes the rapid development of enterprises by acquiring individual champions of pharmaceutical companies from Denmark, Israel, and the United States. According to statistics, Jingxin

Pharmaceutical achieved operating income of RMB 2. 944 billion in 2018, a year-on-year increase of 32. 66%, with a net profit of RMB 370 million, an increase of 39. 97%, and deducted non-net profit of RMB 316 million, an increase of 653. 97%. In the coming period, Jingxin Pharmaceutical also plans to carry out large-scale investment and acquisition of RMB 1 billion to further improve the industrial layout.

Case 11
Geely Acquired Proton and Lotus in Malaysia

Keywords: automobile industry, equity

Acquirer: Zhejiang Geely Holding Group Co., Ltd.

Target Company: Proton Holdings Berhad (PHB), Lotus Cars, DRB-HICOM (parent company of Proton)

【Timeline】

• Since 1996, Proton Holdings Berhad (hereinafter referred to as Proton) has been the owner of Lotus Cars.

• In May 2017, Malaysian DRB-HICOM announced plans to sell its 49. 9% stake in Proton and 51% of Lotus to Geely.

• The transaction was signed in June 2017. Since then, Lotus has ceased to be a subsidiary of Proton.

• On September 29, 2017, Zhejiang Geely Holding Group Co., Ltd. (hereinafter referred to as Geely) and DRB-HICOM jointly announced the list of board members and some senior executives of Proton Holdings Berhad and Perusahaan Otomobil Nasional Sdn Bhd.

【Introduction to the Transaction Subject】

Geely is a privately held global automotive group headquartered in Hangzhou, Zhejiang Province in southeastern China. It is one of the largest independent automobile brands in China. Founded in 1986, the group was originally a refrigerator manufacturer. It began to produce motorcycles in the 1990s. In 1997, it entered the automotive industry with the Geely automobile brand. In 2002, it launched its first car and acquired Volvo from Ford in 2010. The company sells passenger cars from brands such as Geely Automobile, Lotus, Lectra, Proton and Volvo, as well as commercial vehicles under the London Electric Vehicle Company and Remote Car brands. In 2017, Geely sold more than

1.8 million vehicles worldwide, with total sales revenue of RMB 278.2 billion (up 33% year-on-year) and net profit of RMB 18.8 billion (up 61% year-on-year). The company's total assets exceed RMB 200 billion and it has been selected into Fortune Global 500 companies for seven consecutive years.

Proton is a Malaysia-based company active in automotive design, manufacturing, distribution and sales. Founded in 1983, Proton is the only national car brand company in Malaysia until Perodua appeared in 1993. "PROTON" is an abbreviation for Perusahaan Otomobil Nasional (Malay of the National Automobile Company). Proton was originally owned by DRB-HICOM and a minority stake was held by members of the Mitsubishi Group. In 2004, Mitsubishi sold all of its shares in Proton. In 2012, Proton was acquired by DRB-HICOM.

【Transaction Review】

Geely Holding, the parent company of Geely Automobile, acquired a 49.9% stake in Proton and a 51% stake in Lotus. After the completion of the acquisition, Geely Holding will own six car brands including Geely Automobile, Lectra, Volvo, London Electric Vehicle, Proton and Lotus, covering low-end and mid-end brands, luxury brands and special brands. Geely's original major markets are in China and Europe and are now expanding further into Southeast Asia.

On May 24, 2017, Geely announced that it has acquired a 49.9% stake in Malaysian automaker Proton and obtained a platform to enter the Southeast Asian market. As part of the deal, Geely acquired a 51% stake in British automaker Lotus from Proton for GBP 51 million (USD 66.2 million). However, DRB-HICOM (the parent company of Proton) has a 50.1% stake, which means that Proton is still a national brand in Malaysia.

Proton has two factories, including an underutilized plant in Tanjung Malim, Malaysia, which produces 150 000 Geely cars a year. Proton also has a ready-made sales network in Malaysia, which Geely can use to sell cars.

Tian Jianhua said that Malaysia will allow Geely to develop right-hand drive models, and it is possible to introduce Volvo cars with increasing income. He estimates that Malaysia's car ownership rate is about one-fifth that of China, 40 times lower than that of the United States, which possesses great development potential.

【Conclusion】

Our conclusion is that the deal is a relatively successful transaction. If Geely acquires Volvo for Volvo's brand and technology, then the acquisition of Proton is to enter the Southeast Asian market. For Geely, Malaysia is only a springboard. Indonesia and even Southeast Asia are the important battlefields for Geely's future. Non-Japanese brand auto companies have been struggling in Southeast Asia, and the deal has established a distribution network for Geely in Southeast Asia. At the same time, Proton has also obtained an economically strong partner and may acquire more advanced technology.

With the addition of Proton and Lotus, Geely has accelerated the pace of globalization and established a beachhead position in Southeast Asia. Geely's goal is to produce 500,000 vehicles for the Southeast Asian market by 2020. In addition to being an entry point into Southeast Asia, Proton has facilitated Geely's entry into the worldwide right-hand drive (RHD) market, including Malaysia, the UK, India and Australia.

The investment was based on a multi-billion dollar deal recently signed between China and Malaysia, but Proton is an asset wrapped in national pride and a symbol of Malaysia's post-independence industrialization and economic growth.

The industry generally believes that trade barriers and regional economic turmoil are the main reasons for the shrinking of automobile exports. In addition, China's Chery and JAC major exporters are Russia, Brazil and other countries, but due to the currency depreciation and economic recession of these countries, China's automobile export sales have gradually declined. However, the "Belt and Road" initiative has brought the gospel to the export of Chinese automobile companies. For example, India is a country along the "Belt and Road". In 2016, China's automobile exports to India increased by nearly five times year-on-year. In addition, ASEAN is China's largest trading partner. Compared with other countries and regions, China's own brand vehicles have more advantages in exporting to Southeast Asia. First, because China and ASEAN signed the China-ASEAN Free Trade Agreement, it created a good trading environment and achieved zero tariffs on 90% of commodities. Second, there are tariff preferential agreements between the ten ASEAN countries. According to the *World Journal* of Thailand in June 2014, the trade tariffs between the ten ASEAN countries are close to zero, leaving only a few sensitive commodities still not being implemented zero tariffs. And ASEAN will continue to implement zero-tariff measures. At this point, Geely's intention to acquire Malaysia Proton is very clear.

Case 12
Fosun Group Acquired the Entire Share Capital of AHAVA for 290 Million New Shekel

Keywords: beauty industry, 100%
Acquirer: Fosun Group

Target Company: AHAVA Dead Sea Laboratory Co., Ltd.

【Timeline】

• On April 10, 2016, Chinese company Fosun Group signed an agreement to acquire a 100% stake in Israel's AHAVA for 290 million new Shekel (about RMB 496 million).

【Introduction to the Transaction Subject】

Founded in 1994, Fosun Group is a leading medical group in China. Focusing on the mission of improving human health, Fosun Group covers all key areas of the healthcare industry chain, including pharmaceutical manufacturing and research and development, medical services, medical devices and medical diagnostics, as well as pharmaceutical distribution and retail. Fosun Group always regards innovation as the driving force for business growth.

AHAVA was founded in the Dead Sea region in 1988 and is recognized worldwide as the Dead Sea Clay Skin Care brand. As a company authorized by the Israeli government, AHAVA has the right to develop Dead Sea resources and make full use of the Dead Sea resources with its excellent formula and superb technology. At the same time, by cooperating with various natural plant extracts, AHAVA has grown rapidly and become a unique national high-techcompany unique to Israel.

【Transaction Review】

On April 10, 2016, an important signing ceremony was held at the David Castle Hotel in Jerusalem: Fosun Group, China's leading investment group, signed an agreement with the AHAVA shareholders represented by Gaoen Holdings to acquire a 100% stake of AHAVA with 290 million new Shekel.

Liang Xinjun, vice chairman and chief executive officer of Fosun Group, and Guy Regev, CEO of Gaoen Holdings, signed an agreement under the witness of senior Israeli government officials and representatives of both companies.

Fosun Group is full of confidence in the Israeli market and is constantly looking for suitable investment opportunities in various fields. Fosun Group believes that AHAVA is a successful brand built with credibility and strength. Fosun Group is pleased to successfully complete the transaction and achieve win-win results for all parties.

Fosun Group hopes to further deepen the cooperation between Chinese companies and Israeli companies in the future by investing in Israeli companies. Fosun Group's investment in the Israeli market began in 2013 when it acquired Alma Lasers, Israel's leading laser beauty equipment company. Since the investment of Fosun Group, Alma Lasers has achieved remarkable results in its development in China and successfully developed the Chinese market into its largest single market.

【Conclusion】

China's economic growth will be increasingly driven by consumption. The most important aspect of consumption is the protection and appreciation of family wealth, and the pursuit of healthy management and happy life. Therefore, in the future, Fosun Group will pay more attention to the B2F (business-to-family) business model of assets and invest in a rich, healthy and happy industry. Fosun Group will use its core resources both internally and externally to build products with the spirit of craftsmanship, providing a rich, healthy and happy one-stop comprehensive solution for the family, providing customers with good services and creating rich value.

AHAVA is a mineral skin care brand originally created in the Dead Sea region and enjoys a worldwide reputation. Its top facial products include Dead Sea Osmoter facial extracts, mineral extracts, and skin-activated moisturizing gels. These products are loved by consumers around the world. AHAVA means "love" in Hebrew, and Fosun has been actively practicing its "China Power Grafting Global Resources" investment model, which will provide AHAVA product representing "love from Israel" to the world.

Israel has a total population of less than 9 million, and technology contributes more than 90% of GDP. Israel's advantageous industries, including medical care, energy-saving materials, new materials, high-tech, etc., have a very high compatibility with Chinese companies, which have become the main Israeli investor second only to US companies. Many Chinese companies such as Fosun Group, Crystal Optoelectronics, Hebang Bio, Sancell Group, and Giant Network have completed multiple M&A transactions in Israel. With the transformation and upgrading of China's economy, the focus of Chinese companies' overseas M&A has shifted from the original resources and energy industries to the medical, consumer, high-tech industries. Israel has the world's leading technology and innovative talents, attracting more and more Chinese companies to go to invest in M&A in Israel.

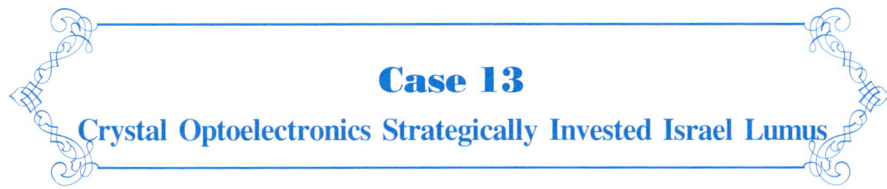

Case 13
Crystal Optoelectronics Strategically Invested Israel Lumus

Keywords: high-tech industry, convertible bonds
Acquirer: Zhejiang Crystal Optoelectronics Technology Co., Ltd.

Target Company: Lumus Limited Israel

【Timeline】

· On May 17, 2016, Zhejiang Crystal Optoelectronics Technology Co., Ltd. (hereinafter referred to as Crystal Optoelectronics) subscribed for 18 months of unsecured convertible bonds issued by Lumus Limited (hereinafte reffered to as Lumus) with its own funds of USD 3 million.

· On November 15, 2016, Crystal Optoelectronics announced that it will acquire 100,000 common shares held by Lumus shareholder Yaakov Amitai with its own capital of USD 2.2 million, and subscribe for 93 355 new C-round preferred shares for USD 5 million. The USD 3 million unsecured convertible bond held by the subsidiary was converted into 67 362 shares of C-round preferred stock.

【Introduction to the Transaction Subject】

Crystal Optoelectronics is a state-level high-tech enterprise established on August 2, 2002. It was listed on the Shenzhen Stock Exchange on September 19, 2008. Crystal Optoelectronics is a domestic company specializing in the research, development and manufacture of optical imaging, LED, microdisplay and reflective materials. The company has certain technical accumulation in the field of optical machine design, development capability and optical component processing. The company has three wholly-owned subsidiaries—Zhejiang Jingjing Photoelectric Co., Ltd., Jiangxi Crystal Optoelectronics Co., Ltd., Zhejiang Fangyuan Night Vision Reflective Material Co., Ltd., a holding subsidiary—Zhejiang Taijia Electronic Information Technology Co., Ltd. It is also a shareholder of Japan Optorun Co., Ltd., Zhejiang University Joint Innovation Investment Management Partnership (Limited Partnership), and of Ningbo Lianchuang Foundation Investment Partnership (Limited Partnership).

Lumus is a startup high-tech company with leading design capabilities in penetrating video glasses and a large number of European and American customer resources.

【Transaction Review】

In 2016, Lumus announced that it has received USD 15 million in Series B financing, led by Shanda Group and Crystal Optoelectronics. The funds raised by Lumus will be used for company R&D, production capacity enhancement and market expansion to compete with products such as Hololens and Meta. Upon completion of the transaction, Crystal Optoelectronics will hold 260 715 shares of Lumus, representing 3.06% of the total share capital after the completion of the transaction. With Lumus's advantages in penetrating video glasses and European and American customer resources, this investment will help Crystal Optoelectronics accelerate its development in virtual display.

【Conclusion】

Crystal Optoelectronics is an optical component company with thin film optical products, sapphire and reflective materials as its core technology. It has become a major supplier to Sony, Samsung and Kodak. In recent years, Crystal Optoelectronics is actively deploying smart display fields such as VR/AR. After the acquisition of Lumus, Crystal Optoelectronics tried to achieve a leapfrog transition from component suppliers to solution providers in the smart glasses business. Crystal Optoelectronics became a strategic investor of Lumus by participating in the subscription of the C-round preferred stock and the equity of the original shareholder. The acquisition will not only help strengthen the deep cooperation between the two parties in the technical field, but also help Crystal Optoelectronics to further expand the overseas market by utilizing Lumus's high-quality European and American customer resources. Unlike many Chinese companies that acquire control of the target company, Crystal Optoelectronics has become a small shareholder of Lumus by means of equity participation, which reduces the company's acquisition costs and lays the foundation for more in-depth capital cooperation in the future.

Admittedly, Israel's AR technology is indeed welcomed by domestic investors. In 2016, Alibaba invested USD 15 million in Israeli Infinity AR.

Case 14
Anta Acquired the Trademark Use Rights and Management Rights of FILA in China for RMB 332 Million

Keywords: trademark use rights and management rights, busin-ess model
Acquirer: Anta Sports Products Limited
Target Company: Belle International

【Timeline】

· In September 2005, FILA entered the Chinese market.

· In 2007, Belle International acquired all rights to the FILA brand in Mainland China, Hong Kong and Macao for USD 48 million.

· In August 2009, Belle International sold the brand concession of FILA China to Anta Sports Products Limited (hereinafter referred to as Anta) at a price of RMB 332 million.

【Introduction to the Transaction Subject】

Anta is China's leading sportswear brand and was selected as the " China Olympic Committee's 2009-2012 sportswear partner." Anta, which is sold in 6,000 retail stores nationwide, has its own design, R&D, manufacturing and marketing team. Before the acquisition, Anta was a local Chinese brand and could not really compete with international brands. Anta's market mainly covers China's second-and third-tier cities, while first-tier cities are often dominated by international brands such as Adidas and Nike.

Founded in 1991, Belle International is the largest women's shoe retailer in China, with 22% of the women's footwear market in China, producing, distributing and retailing a variety of footwear brands such as Belle, Staccato, Teenmix, Tata, Fato, Jipi Japa, Joy&Peace and Bata.

Founded in 1911, FILA is the world's top ten sports brand. It has developed golf, tennis, fitness and other products to present a classic, stylish, sexy and high-quality Italian image.

[Transaction Review]

Belle International will sell all of its 85% Full Prospect shares, who owns the trademark franchise of the FILA Group in Mainland China, Hong Kong and Macao. FILA Group reserves the remaining shareholding of Full Prospect joint venture with Belle. Belle will also sell the franchise of the retail business of FILA Group in Hong Kong and Macao at a price of HKD 50 million. The advantages of Belle International are women's shoes, but it lacks experience in the development of international high-end sports brands. Due to poor management, the influence and high-end image of FILA brand are increasingly marginalized. Anta believes that the acquisition of global sportswear brand represents an opportunity to enter the high-end sportswear market. It also has important strategic significance for FILA's brand recognition in China.

A very important decision after the acquisition of Anta is to change the brand positioning of FILA from the original high-end sports brand to "return to fashion". The target customers are young people between the ages of 25 and 35. While adding the elements of fashion, FILA's original sports brand features are retained. In the product chain, Anta designed new products for the Chinese people's body characteristics, and constantly added new innovative elements. At the same time, all the stores were taken back from the dealers and changed into a direct mode.

Anta has changed the original business model of FILA in a targeted manner and gradually showed very good results. In the five years after the acquisition, the growth rate of the FILA annual sales exceeded 50%. In 2014, it achieved a turnaround. By the end of 2017, FILA's market stores in China reached 1,086, and it is expected to maintain a growth rate of 30% in the next five years and the sales revenue accounts for 20% of the Group's revenue.

[Conclusion]

The acquisition of FILA is both an opportunity and a challenge for Anta. On the one hand, it can help Anta enter the higher end market and join the first-line brand team. In addition, the acquisition of FILA may be an opportunity for Anta to enhance its brand awareness and recognition, thus enhancing its brand equity. On the other hand, there is a huge gap between the brand image of FILA and Anta, and it may be difficult for Anta to maintain Fila's position in the global market. The acquisition gives Anta the opportunity to learn from the "giants" in its industry and maybe it will enter the international market in the next few years. However, Anta must first prove that it can run a global scale brand and maintain its success, so as to prove itself at home. Anta chooses to acquire the right to use and operate the trademark, compared with the acquisition of the whole company, the cost is lower and it is easier to integrate. China has the largest single market in the world, consumption upgrading is quietly going on, the growth space of China's sports market is huge, and it is also the battlefield for global giants to compete.

On the basis of the successful acquisition of FILA, Anta has again successfully acquired Korean outdoor brand Kolon, mountaineering brand Sprandi and winter sports brand Descente, realizing the operation and management mode of "single focus, multi brand and all channel".

Case 15
Everbright International Acquired NOVAGO for EUR 123 Million

Keywords: environmental protection
Acquirer: China Everbright International Co., Ltd.
Target Company: NOVAGO Poland

[Timeline]

• On June 23, 2016, China Everbright International Co., Ltd. (hereinafter referred to as Everbright International) signed an initial sales agreement.

• On August 31, 2016, Everbright International announced the completion of its acquisition of NOVAGO for EUR 123 million, including a share value of EUR 118 million (approximately RMB 862 million) and a land reserve of EUR 5 million.

【Introduction to the Transaction Subject】

Everbright International is a flagship company of industrial investment under the China Everbright Group. Everbright Group was jointly established by Central Huijin Investment Co., Ltd. and the Ministry of Finance. China Everbright Group ranked 322th in the 2018 Fortune Global 500.

NOVAGO is the largest solid waste treatment company in Poland. The company was named one of the most dynamic companies in Poland by Forbes in 2016 and was named the fastest growing company in Poland by Gazele Biznesu in 2015.

【Transaction Review】

The deal is China's largest investment project in Poland, and the two sides continued to negotiate for several months before and after the M&A negotiations.

Everbright International said that the overseas acquisition was the first China-Poland cooperation project actively implemented by China Everbright Group after President Xi Jinping visited Poland in June 2016. Everbright International signed the preliminary acquisition agreement on June 23 2016, and successfully completed the delivery on August 29, local time in Poland.

On the acquisition and delivery ceremony held in Poland, Deputy Minister of Development of Poland, Domakursky, said in his speech that he hopes that this investment will bring profits to both parties and believes that the cooperation will be successful. He is convinced that this investment from China is a very good investment, which can bring new employment opportunities and new technological developments to Poland. This innovative investment will be strongly supported by the Polish government.

Looking at technical cooperation and Central and Eastern European market data, NOVAGO was founded in 1992 as the largest independent solid waste treatment company in Poland. Its business includes waste treatment, landfill recycling, biogas production, refuse derived fuel (RDF) production, and biogas cogeneration.

NOVAGO has a market share of more than 30% in the two core business districts of Warsaw and Olsztyn, with six leading integrated waste treatment plants in four provinces in Poland. In 2015, NOVAGO handled 890 000 tons of solid waste. In 2015, it was selected as the most dynamic Polish company in Bitzer Bizenesu. In 2016, it was selected as one of the most dynamic Polish companies in Forbes. In 2015, the operating income exceeded PLN 135 million (about RMB 220 million).

NOVAGO Vice President Micha D browski explained that the merger negotiations lasted for several months. After a series of talks and analysis between the two parties, Everbright International decided to acquire NOVAGO. After that, NOVAGO executives also visited Everbright International's environmental projects in Shanghai and Hong Kong to gain a deeper understanding of the strength of the acquirer.

The merger and acquisition will mainly help the two sides to cooperate on the technical level, and also help Everbright International to develop the Central and Eastern European markets.

After the acquisition, NOVAGO can not only continue to develop the existing technology in Poland, but also develop new technologies designed by Everbright International in China, which is a good opportunity for NOVAGO. In the future, more advanced waste disposal equipment will be applied not only to Poland but also to Central and Eastern Europe.

Everbright International has four business units: environmental energy, environmental water, environmental protection and environmental science and technology. As of June 30, 2016, Everbright International has implemented 187 environmental protection projects with a total investment of approximately RMB 48.568 billion; the total investment of completed projects is approximately RMB 21.457 billion; the investment in construction projects is approximately RMB 10.298 billion; the investment in projects in preparation is about RMB 16.813 billion.

Everbright Group established the International Business Department in early 2017, specializing in international market development, and has obtained Polish solid waste projects and Vietnam projects. In the future, the Central Asia, West Asia, North Asia and Southeast Asia markets will become target of the Everbright Group.

【Conclusion】

Our conclusion is that this is a perfect choice and a successful example of cooperation.

The acquisition is the first time that Everbright International has acquired solid waste treatment companies in Europe. This is not only the largest investment project of China in Poland, but also the largest acquisition of China's environmental protection market in Eastern Europe and Central Europe in 2017.

The investment layout in the "Belt and Road" countries is an important strategy of Everbright International. Everbright International hopes to use NOVAGO's influence in Poland, its experience in waste incineration, and its technology in environmental protection, new energy and equipment manufacturing to actively promote its development in Central and Eastern Europe.

参考文献

[1] 桑百川. 全球价值链重构攸关中国外贸 [N]. 上海证券报, 2016 - 03 - 24 (12).

[2] 程鹏. 全球产业链重构为中国企业带来新机会 [N]. 南方日报, 2017 - 01 - 12 (03).

[3] 中国国际商会. 2018 "一带一路" 大事记 [J]. 大陆桥视野, 2019 (1).

[4] 仁敏. "一带一路" 倡议五周年 [J]. 老同志之友, 2018 (18).

[5] 德勤. 新阶段 新机遇——"一带一路" 倡议纵深发展背景下对外投资的趋势和解决方案 [EB/OL]. (2018 - 3 - 28) [2019 - 4 - 22]. https://www2.deloitte.com/cn/zh/pages/soe/articles/belt - and - road - whitepaper - issue1.html.

[6] 张守营. 2017 年中国对外直接投资步伐有望放缓 [N]. 中国经济导报, 2017 - 04 - 12 (06).

[7] 王旭. 国内多家企业海外布局锂资源 [N]. 中国有色金属报, 2018 - 05 - 26 (04).

[8] 德勤. 并购活跃, 整合滞后——中国企业海外并购及并购后整合现状调查 [EB/OL]. (2017 - 8 - 27) [2019 - 4 - 22]. https://www2.deloitte.com/cn/zh/pages/str - ategy - operations/articles/survey - on - china - outbound - activities - and - post - deal - integration.html.

[9] 吴定祥. 企业文化整合: 跨国并购中的一道难题——TCL 收购阿尔卡特失败案例分析 [J]. 对外经贸实务, 2010 (5).

[10] 孙健, 郑海航. 青岛海尔兼并案例及其产权效率分析——海尔兼并案例调查 [J]. 中国工业经济, 1997 (10).

[11] 松涛. 海尔兼并: 不吃 "死鱼" [J]. 国际融资, 2004 (7).

［12］赵奂．联想集团战略管理会计的应用研究［D］．吉林：吉林财经大学，2015．

［13］裴欣．中国企业海外并购法律问题探析［J］．科技与企业，2013（13）．

［14］李锋．俄罗斯国家安全审查制度研究［J］．国际经济合作，2012（7）．

［15］姜军，赵慧芳．交易结构化：中联重科海外并购案例的再分析［J］．财务与会计（理财版），2013（1）．

［16］胡杰武．中联重科并购 CIFA 获得了什么？——5 周年之后的回顾与反思［J］．中国软科学，2016（4）．

［17］沙海燕．海外并购法律文件盘点［J］．首席财务官，2013（11）．

［18］赵健．海外并购尽职调查浅析——以收购巴西 Concremat 公司为例［J］．国际工程与劳务，2017（4）．

［19］张华．海外并购尽职调查要义［J］．新理财，2016（5）．

［20］孙蕊．境外并购股权转让协议核心条款分析［J］．山东国资，2017（8）．

［21］马乐．安全与反垄断审查：中企海外并购两道坎［N］．第一财经日报 2016-11-14（11）．

［22］冯并．"一带一路"全球经济的互联与跃升［M］．北京：中国民主法制出版社，2016．

［23］邹统钎，梁昊光．中国"一带一路"投资与安全研究报告 2016-2017［M］．北京：社会科学文献出版社，2017．

［24］［日］稻盛和夫．经营十二条［M］．北京：中信出版社，2011．

［25］秦剑．企业并购的战略整合［J］．财经科学，2005（5）．

［26］彭晓华，沈进．试论企业并购中的人力资源整合管理［J］．江苏商论，2004（10）．

［27］黄冰清．企业文化并购整合探究［J］．会计师，2014（9）．

［28］马守旺．项目管理在企业并购的战略整合中的应用［J］．江苏科技信息，2012（3）．

[29] 干春晖. 并购经济学 [M]. 北京：清华大学出版社, 2004.

[30] 徐绍史. "一带一路" 双向投资研究与案例分析 [M]. 北京：机械工业出版社, 2016.

[31] 王开定, 黄梦婷, 汤馨然. 我国境外投资管理制度再优化 [N]. 国际商报, 2017 - 11 - 7（A2）.

[32] 宋博. 七部委重点稽查 3 亿美元以上投资 [N]. 中国联合商报, 2018 - 01 - 29（A01）.

[33] 柯贝. 大康牧业撤回拟并购澳公司申请 [N]. 上海证券报, 2016 - 5 - 4（004）.

[34] 徐剑华. 从三宗外国资本投资美国港口交易案看 CFIUS 的宽严度 [J]. 中国船检, 2018（7）.

[35] 彭晓华, 沈进. 试论企业并购中的人力资源整合管理 [J]. 江苏商论, 2004（10）.

[36] 李少林, TCL 折戟汤姆逊往事 [N]. 中国证券报, 2012 - 02 - 02（A11）.

[37] 矫春虹. 奥特佳 8.5 亿元收购空调国际 [N]. 中国汽车报, 2016 - 1 - 12.

[38] 李锋. 俄罗斯国家安全审查制度研究 [J], 国际经济合作, 2012,（7）.

[39] 陈燕青. 上海梅林拟收购新西兰公司 [N]. 深圳商报, 2015.

[40] 王珍. 为什么收购库卡的是美的 [N]. 第一财经日报, 2016 - 7 - 28.

[41] 南京新街口百货商店股份有限公司发行股份购买资产并募集配套资金暨关联交易报告书 [M]. 2017 - 01 - 14.

[42] John C. Coates TV. M&A Contracts: Purposes, Types, Regulation, and Patterns of Practice [M/OL]. https：//dash. harvard. edu/handle/1/17743076. 2015 - 4 - 11.

[43] Alexandra Reed Lajoux. The art of M&A integration [M]. New York：McGraw - Hill Press, 1998.

书目介绍

乐贸系列

书名	作者	定价	书号	出版时间

📖 **国家出版基金项目**

书名	作者	定价	书号	出版时间
1. "一带一路"国家投资并购指南	冯 斌　李洪亮　Gvantsa Dzneladze(格)　Tamar Menteshashvili(格)	98.00元	978-7-5175-0422-1	2020年3月第1版
2. "质"造全球：消费品出口质量管控指南	SGS通标标准技术服务有限公司	80.00元	978-7-5175-0289-0	2018年9月第1版

📖 **跟着老外学外贸系列**

书名	作者	定价	书号	出版时间
1. 优势成交：老外这样做销售（第二版）	Abdelhak Benkerroum（阿道）	58.00元	978-7-5175-0370-5	2019年10月第2版

📖 **外贸SOHO系列**

书名	作者	定价	书号	出版时间
1. 外贸SOHO，你会做吗？	黄见华	30.00元	978-7-5175-0141-5	2016年7月第1版

📖 **跨境电商系列**

书名	作者	定价	书号	出版时间
1. 跨境电商全产业链时代：政策红利下迎机遇期	曹 磊　张周平	55.00元	978-7-5175-0349-1	2019年5月第1版
2. 外贸社交媒体营销新思维：向无效社交说No	May（石少华）	55.00元	978-7-5175-0270-8	2018年6月第1版
3. 跨境电商多平台运营，你会做吗？	董振国　贾 卓	48.00元	978-7-5175-0255-5	2018年1月第1版
4. 跨境电商3.0时代——把握外贸转型时代风口	朱秋城（Mr. Harris）	55.00元	978-7-5175-0140-4	2016年9月第1版
5. 118问玩转速卖通——跨境电商海外淘金全攻略	红 鱼	38.00元	978-7-5175-0095-7	2016年1月第1版

📖 **外贸职场高手系列**

书名	作者	定价	书号	出版时间
1. 新人走进外贸圈　职业角色怎么选	黄 涛	45.00元	978-7-5175-0387-3	2020年1月第1版
2. Ben教你做采购：金牌外贸业务员也要学	朱子赋（Ben）	58.00元	978-7-5175-0386-6	2020年1月第1版
3. 思维对了，订单就来：颠覆外贸底层逻辑	老A	58.00元	978-7-5175-0381-1	2020年1月第1版
4. 从零开始学外贸	外贸人维尼	58.00元	978-7-5175-0382-8	2019年10月第1版
5. 小资本做大品牌：外贸企业品牌运营	黄仁华著	58.00元	978-7-5175-0372-9	2019年10月第1版
6. 金牌外贸企业给新员工的内训课	Lily主编	55.00元	978-7-5175-0337-8	2019年3月第1版
7. 逆境生存：JAC写给外贸企业的转型战略	JAC	55.00元	978-7-5175-0315-6	2018年11月第1版

书名	作者	定价	书号	出版时间
8. 外贸大牛的营与销	丹 牛	48.00 元	978-7-5175-0304-0	2018 年 10 月第 1 版
9. 向外土司学外贸 1：业务可以这样做	外土司	55.00 元	978-7-5175-0248-7	2018 年 2 月第 1 版
10. 向外土司学外贸 2：营销可以这样做	外土司	55.00 元	978-7-5175-0247-0	2018 年 2 月第 1 版
11. 阴阳鱼给外贸新人的必修课	阴阳鱼	45.00 元	978-7-5175-0230-2	2017 年 11 月第 1 版
12. JAC 写给外贸公司老板的企管书	JAC	45.00 元	978-7-5175-0225-8	2017 年 10 月第 1 版
13. 外贸大牛的术与道	丹 牛	38.00 元	978-7-5175-0163-3	2016 年 10 月第 1 版
14. JAC 外贸谈判手记——JAC 和他的外贸故事	JAC	45.00 元	978-7-5175-0136-7	2016 年 8 月第 1 版
15. Mr. Hua 创业手记——从 0 到 1 的"华式"创业思维	华 超	45.00 元	978-7-5175-0089-6	2015 年 10 月第 1 版
16. 外贸会计上班记	谭 天	38.00 元	978-7-5175-0088-9	2015 年 10 月第 1 版
17. JAC 外贸工具书——JAC 和他的外贸故事	JAC	45.00 元	978-7-5175-0053-7	2015 年 7 月第 1 版
18. 外贸菜鸟成长记(0～3岁)	何嘉美	35.00 元	978-7-5175-0070-4	2015 年 6 月第 1 版

外贸操作实务子系列

书名	作者	定价	书号	出版时间
1. 外贸高手客户成交技巧 3：差异生存法则	毅 冰	69.00 元	978-7-5175-0378-1	2019 年 9 月第 1 版
2. 外贸高手客户成交技巧 2——揭秘买手思维	毅 冰	55.00 元	978-7-5175-0232-6	2018 年 1 月第 1 版
3. 外贸业务经理人手册(第三版)	陈文培	48.00 元	978-7-5175-0200-5	2017 年 6 月第 3 版
4. 外贸全流程攻略——进出口经理跟单手记(第二版)	温伟雄（马克老温）	38.00 元	978-7-5175-0197-8	2017 年 4 月第 2 版
5. 金牌外贸业务员找客户(第三版)——跨境电商时代开发客户的 9 种方法	张劲松	40.00 元	978-7-5175-0098-8	2016 年 1 月第 3 版
6. 实用外贸技巧助你轻松拿订单(第二版)	王陶（波锅涅）	30.00 元	978-7-5175-0072-8	2015 年 7 月第 2 版
7. 出口营销实战(第三版)	黄泰山	45.00 元	978-7-80165-932-3	2013 年 1 月第 3 版
8. 外贸实务疑难解惑 220 例	张浩清	38.00 元	978-7-80165-853-1	2012 年 1 月第 1 版
9. 外贸高手客户成交技巧	毅 冰	35.00 元	978-7-80165-841-8	2012 年 1 月第 1 版
10. 报检七日通	徐荣才 朱瑾瑜	22.00 元	978-7-80165-715-2	2010 年 8 月第 1 版
11. 外贸实用工具手册	本书编委会	32.00 元	978-7-80165-558-5	2009 年 1 月第 1 版
12. 快乐外贸七讲	朱芷萱	22.00 元	978-7-80165-373-4	2009 年 1 月第 1 版
13. 外贸七日通(最新修订版)	黄海涛（深海鱿鱼）	22.00 元	978-7-80165-397-0	2008 年 8 月第 3 版

出口风险管理子系列

书名	作者	定价	书号	出版时间
1. 轻松应对出口法律风险	韩宝庆	39.80 元	978-7-80165-822-7	2011 年 9 月第 1 版
2. 出口风险管理实务(第二版)	冯 斌	48.00 元	978-7-80165-725-1	2010 年 4 月第 2 版
3. 50 种出口风险防范	王新华 陈丹凤	35.00 元	978-7-80165-647-6	2009 年 8 月第 1 版

书名	作者	定价	书号	出版时间
外贸单证操作子系列				
1. 跟单信用证一本通(第二版)	何源	48.00 元	978-7-5175-0249-4	2018 年 9 月第 2 版
2. 外贸单证经理的成长日记(第二版)	曹顺祥	40.00 元	978-7-5175-0130-5	2016 年 6 月第 2 版
3. 信用证审单有问有答 280 例	李一平 徐珺	37.00 元	978-7-80165-761-9	2010 年 8 月第 1 版
4. 外贸单证解惑 280 例	龚玉和 齐朝阳	38.00 元	978-7-80165-638-4	2009 年 7 月第 1 版
5. 信用证 6 小时教程	黄海涛(深海鱿鱼)	25.00 元	978-7-80165-624-7	2009 年 4 月第 2 版
6. 跟单高手教你做跟单	汪德	32.00 元	978-7-80165-623-0	2009 年 4 月第 1 版
福步外贸高手子系列				
1. 外贸技巧与邮件实战(第二版)	刘云	38.00 元	978-7-5175-0221-0	2017 年 8 月第 2 版
2. 外贸电邮营销实战——小小开发信 订单滚滚来(第二版)	薄如骢	45.00 元	978-7-5175-0126-8	2016 年 5 月第 2 版
3. 巧用外贸邮件拿订单	刘裕	45.00 元	978-7-80165-966-8	2013 年 8 月第 1 版
国际物流操作子系列				
1. 货代高手教你做货代——优秀货代笔记(第二版)	何银星	33.00 元	978-7-5175-0003-2	2014 年 2 月第 2 版
2. 国际物流操作风险防范——技巧·案例分析	孙家庆	32.00 元	978-7-80165-577-6	2009 年 4 月第 1 版
通关实务子系列				
1. 外贸企业轻松应对海关估价	熊斌 赖芸 王卫宁	35.00 元	978-7-80165-895-1	2012 年 9 月第 1 版
2. 报关实务一本通(第二版)	苏州工业园区海关	35.00 元	978-7-80165-889-0	2012 年 8 月第 2 版
3. 如何通过原产地证尽享关税优惠	南京出入境检验检疫局	50.00 元	978-7-80165-614-8	2009 年 4 月第 3 版
彻底搞懂子系列				
1. 彻底搞懂信用证(第三版)	王腾 曹红波	55.00 元	978-7-5175-0264-7	2018 年 5 月第 3 版
2. 彻底搞懂关税(第二版)	孙金彦	43.00 元	978-7-5175-0172-5	2017 年 1 月第 2 版
3. 彻底搞懂提单(第二版)	张敏 张鹏飞	38.00 元	978-7-5175-0164-0	2016 年 12 月第 2 版
4. 彻底搞懂中国自由贸易区优惠	刘德标 祖月	34.00 元	978-7-80165-762-6	2010 年 8 月第 1 版
5. 彻底搞懂贸易术语	陈岩	33.00 元	978-7-80165-719-0	2010 年 2 月第 1 版
6. 彻底搞懂海运航线	唐丽敏	25.00 元	978-7-80165-644-5	2009 年 7 月第 1 版
外贸英语实战子系列				
1. 十天搞定外贸函电(白金版)	毅冰	69.00 元	978-7-5175-0347-7	2019 年 4 月第 2 版
2. 让外贸邮件说话——读懂客户心理的分析术	蔡泽民(Chris)	38.00 元	978-7-5175-0167-1	2016 年 12 月第 1 版
3. 外贸高手的口语秘籍	李凤	35.00 元	978-7-80165-838-8	2012 年 2 月第 1 版

书名	作者	定价	书号	出版时间
4. 外贸英语函电实战	梁金水	25.00 元	978-7-80165-705-3	2010 年 1 月第 1 版
5. 外贸英语口语一本通	刘新法	29.00 元	978-7-80165-537-0	2008 年 8 月第 1 版

📖 外贸谈判子系列

书名	作者	定价	书号	出版时间
1. 外贸英语谈判实战（第二版）	王慧 仲颖	38.00 元	978-7-5175-0111-4	2016 年 3 月第 2 版
2. 外贸谈判策略与技巧	赵立民	26.00 元	978-7-80165-645-2	2009 年 7 月第 1 版

📖 国际商务往来子系列

书名	作者	定价	书号	出版时间
国际商务礼仪大讲堂	李嘉珊	26.00 元	978-7-80165-640-7	2009 年 12 月第 1 版

📖 贸易展会子系列

书名	作者	定价	书号	出版时间
外贸参展全攻略——如何有效参加 B2B 贸易商展（第三版）	钟景松	38.00 元	978-7-5175-0076-6	2015 年 8 月第 3 版

📖 区域市场开发子系列

书名	作者	定价	书号	出版时间
中东市场开发实战	刘军 沈一强	28.00 元	978-7-80165-650-6	2009 年 9 月第 1 版

📖 加工贸易操作子系列

书名	作者	定价	书号	出版时间
1. 加工贸易实务操作与技巧	熊斌	35.00 元	978-7-80165-809-8	2011 年 4 月第 1 版
2. 加工贸易达人速成——操作案例与技巧	陈秋霞	28.00 元	978-7-80165-891-3	2012 年 7 月第 1 版

📖 乐税子系列

书名	作者	定价	书号	出版时间
1. 外贸企业免抵退税实务——经验·技巧分享	徐玉树 罗玉芳	45.00 元	978-7-5175-0135-0	2016 年 6 月第 1 版
2. 外贸会计账务处理实务——经验·技巧分享	徐玉树	38.00 元	978-7-80165-958-3	2013 年 8 月第 1 版
3. 生产企业免抵退税实务——经验·技巧分享（第二版）	徐玉树	42.00 元	978-7-80165-936-1	2013 年 2 月第 2 版
4. 外贸企业出口退（免）税常见错误解析 100 例	周朝勇	49.80 元	978-7-80165-933-0	2013 年 2 月第 1 版
5. 生产企业出口退（免）税常见错误解析 115 例	周朝勇	49.80 元	978-7-80165-901-9	2013 年 1 月第 1 版
6. 外汇核销指南	陈文培等	22.00 元	978-7-80165-824-1	2011 年 8 月第 1 版
7. 外贸企业出口退税操作手册	中国出口退税咨询网	42.00 元	978-7-80165-818-0	2011 年 5 月第 1 版
8. 生产企业免抵退税从入门到精通	中国出口退税咨询网	98.00 元	978-7-80165-695-7	2010 年 1 月第 1 版
9. 出口涉税会计实务精要（《外贸会计实务精要》第二版）	龙博客工作室	32.00 元	978-7-80165-660-5	2009 年 9 月第 2 版

📖 专业报告子系列

书名	作者	定价	书号	出版时间
1. 国际工程风险管理	张燎	1980.00 元	978-7-80165-708-4	2010 年 1 月第 1 版

	书名	作者	定价	书号	出版时间
2.	涉外型企业海关事务风险管理报告	《涉外型企业海关事务风险管理报告》研究小组	1980.00元	978-7-80165-666-7	2009年10月第1版

外贸企业管理子系列

	书名	作者	定价	书号	出版时间
1.	外贸经理人的MBA	毅冰	55.00元	978-7-5175-0305-7	2018年10月第1版
2.	小企业做大外贸的制胜法则——职业外贸经理人带队伍手记	胡伟锋	35.00元	978-7-5175-0071-1	2015年7月第1版
3.	小企业做大外贸的四项修炼	胡伟锋	26.00元	978-7-80165-673-5	2010年1月第1版

国际贸易金融子系列

	书名	作者	定价	书号	出版时间
1.	国际结算单证热点疑义相与析	天九湾贸易金融研究汇	55.00元	978-7-5175-0292-0	2018年9月第1版
2.	国际结算与贸易融资实务（第二版）	李华根	55.00元	978-7-5175-0252-4	2018年3月第1版
3.	信用证风险防范与纠纷处理技巧	李道金	45.00元	978-7-5175-0079-7	2015年10月第1版
4.	国际贸易金融服务全程通（第二版）	郭党怀 张丽君 张贝	43.00元	978-7-80165-864-7	2012年1月第2版
5.	国际结算与贸易融资实务	李华根	42.00元	978-7-80165-847-0	2011年12月第1版

毅冰谈外贸子系列

	书名	作者	定价	书号	出版时间
毅冰私房英语书——七天秀出外贸口语		毅冰	35.00元	978-7-80165-965-1	2013年9月第1版

"创新型"跨境电商实训教材

书名	作者	定价	书号	出版时间
跨境电子商务概论与实践	冯晓宁	48.00元	978-7-5175-0313-2	2019年1月第1版

"实用型"报关与国际货运专业教材

	书名	作者	定价	书号	出版时间
1.	国际货运代理操作实务（第二版）	杨鹏强	48.00元	978-7-5175-0364-4	2019年8月第2版
2.	集装箱班轮运输与管理实务	林益松	48.00元	978-7-5175-0339-2	2019年3月第1版
3.	航空货运代理实务（第二版）	杨鹏强	55.00元	978-7-5175-0336-1	2019年1月第2版
4.	进出口商品归类实务（第三版）	林青	48.00元	978-7-5175-0251-7	2018年3月第3版
5.	e时代报关实务	王云	40.00元	978-7-5175-0142-8	2016年6月第1版
6.	供应链管理实务	张远昌	48.00元	978-7-5175-0051-3	2015年4月第1版
7.	电子口岸实务（第二版）	林青	35.00元	978-7-5175-0027-8	2014年6月第2版
8.	报检实务（第二版）	孔德民	38.00元	978-7-80165-999-6	2014年3月第2版

书名	作者	定价	书号	出版时间
9. 现代关税实务（第二版）	李 齐	35.00 元	978-7-80165-862-3	2012 年 1 月第 2 版
10. 国际贸易单证实务（第二版）	丁行政	45.00 元	978-7-80165-855-5	2012 年 1 月第 2 版
11. 报关实务（第三版）	杨鹏强	45.00 元	978-7-80165-825-8	2011 年 9 月第 3 版
12. 海关概论（第二版）	王意家	36.00 元	978-7-80165-805-0	2011 年 4 月第 2 版

"精讲型"国际贸易核心课程教材

书名	作者	定价	书号	出版时间
1. 国际贸易实务精讲（第七版）	田运银	49.50 元	978-7-5175-0260-9	2018 年 4 月第 7 版
2. 国际货运代理实务精讲（第二版）	杨占林 汤 兴 官敏发	48.00 元	978-7-5175-0147-3	2016 年 8 月第 2 版
3. 海关法教程（第三版）	刘达芳	45.00 元	978-7-5175-0113-8	2016 年 4 月第 3 版
4. 国际电子商务实务精讲（第二版）	冯晓宁	45.00 元	978-7-5175-0092-6	2016 年 3 月第 2 版
5. 国际贸易单证精讲（第四版）	田运银	45.00 元	978-7-5175-0058-2	2015 年 6 月第 4 版
6. 国际贸易操作实训精讲（第二版）	田运银 胡少甫 史 理 朱东红	48.00 元	978-7-5175-0052-0	2015 年 2 月第 2 版
7. 进出口商品归类实务精讲	倪淑如 倪 波 田运银	48.00 元	978-7-5175-0016-2	2014 年 7 月第 1 版
8. 外贸单证实训精讲	龚玉和 齐朝阳	42.00 元	978-7-80165-937-8	2013 年 4 月第 1 版
9. 外贸英语函电实务精讲	傅龙海	42.00 元	978-7-80165-935-4	2013 年 2 月第 1 版
10. 国际结算实务精讲	庄乐梅 李 菁	49.80 元	978-7-80165-929-3	2013 年 1 月第 1 版
11. 报关实务精讲	孔德民	48.00 元	978-7-80165-886-9	2012 年 6 月第 1 版
12. 国际商务谈判实务精讲	王 慧 唐力忻	26.00 元	978-7-80165-826-5	2011 年 9 月第 1 版
13. 国际会展实务精讲	王重和	38.00 元	978-7-80165-807-4	2011 年 5 月第 1 版
14. 国际贸易实务疑难解答	田运银	20.00 元	978-7-80165-718-3	2010 年 9 月第 1 版

"实用型"国际贸易课程教材

书名	作者	定价	书号	出版时间
1. 外贸跟单实务（第二版）	罗 艳	48.00 元	978-7-5175-0338-5	2019 年 1 月第 2 版
2. 海关报关实务	倪淑如 倪 波	48.00 元	978-7-5175-0150-3	2016 年 9 月第 1 版
3. 国际金融实务	李 齐 唐晓林	48.00 元	978-7-5175-0134-3	2016 年 6 月第 1 版
4. 国际贸易实务	丁行政 罗艳	48.00 元	978-7-80165-962-0	2013 年 8 月第 1 版

中小企业财会实务操作系列丛书

书名	作者	定价	书号	出版时间
1. 做顶尖成本会计应知应会 150 问（第二版）	张 胜	48.00 元	978-7-5175-0275-3	2018 年 6 月第 2 版
2. 小企业会计疑难解惑 300 例	刘华 刘方周	39.80 元	978-7-80165-845-6	2012 年 1 月第 1 版
3. 会计实务操作一本通	吴虹雁	35.00 元	978-7-80165-751-0	2010 年 8 月第 1 版

《"质"造全球：消费品出口质量管控指南》

作者：SGS通标标准技术服务有限公司

定价：80.00元

书号：978-7-5175-0289-0

出版日期：2018年9月

内容简介

本书由SGS通标标准技术服务有限公司组织的41位相关行业的全球质量管控专家撰写，是一本从产品出口角度，全面分析全球市场消费品质量管控体系的出版物，主要涉及电子电气、纺织服装、轻工三大领域。本书特色包括：

1. 除了解读欧美等发达国家（地区）的质量管控相关法规、认证内容外，引入了"一带一路"沿线国家产品的符合性评定要求；

2. 结合中国出口企业真实案例，从操作层面为企业"量身定制"应对策略，助力企业打破贸易壁垒，货销全球；

3. 开创性地探索了跨境电商存在的质量管控问题，并给出解决方案，帮助企业规避交易风险。

《外贸经理人的 MBA》

作者：毅 冰
定价：55.00 元
书号：978-7-5175-0305-7
出版日期：2018 年 10 月

内容简介

本书结合世界 500 强企业先进管理方法和作者多年从事外贸企业管理的经验进行编写，读完这本书你将收获以下技能：

1. 突破经理人的思维误区，完成从王牌业务员到优秀管理者的角色转变，做到适度参与、合理放权；

2. 了解薪酬体系与人才架构的设置技巧，让专业的人干专业的事，摆脱高薪却留不住人的烦恼；

3. 摆脱国外 MBA 课程内容难以在中国企业落地的难题，借鉴本土化的管理方法，优化效率、提升业绩。